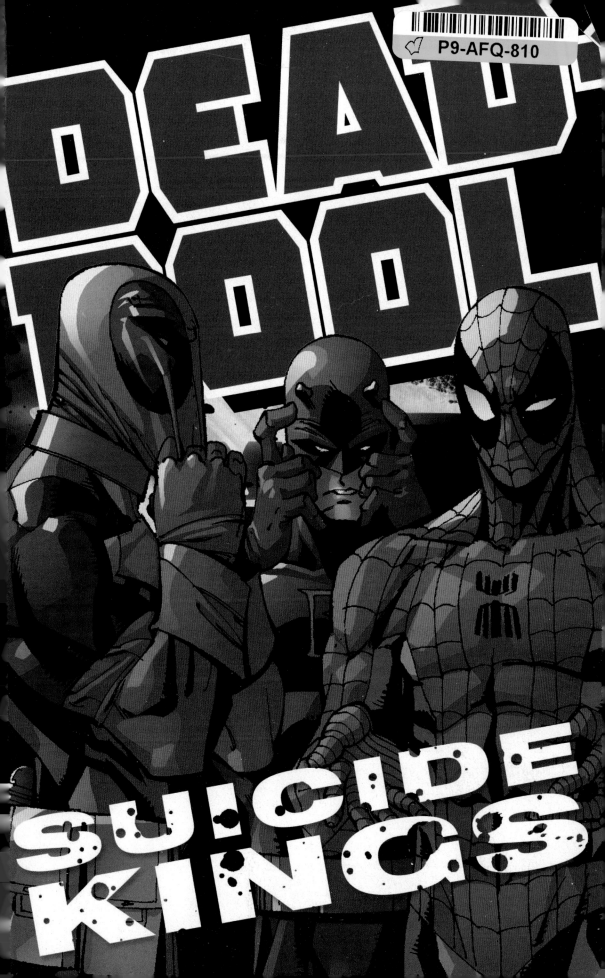

DEADPOOL

SUICIDE KINGS

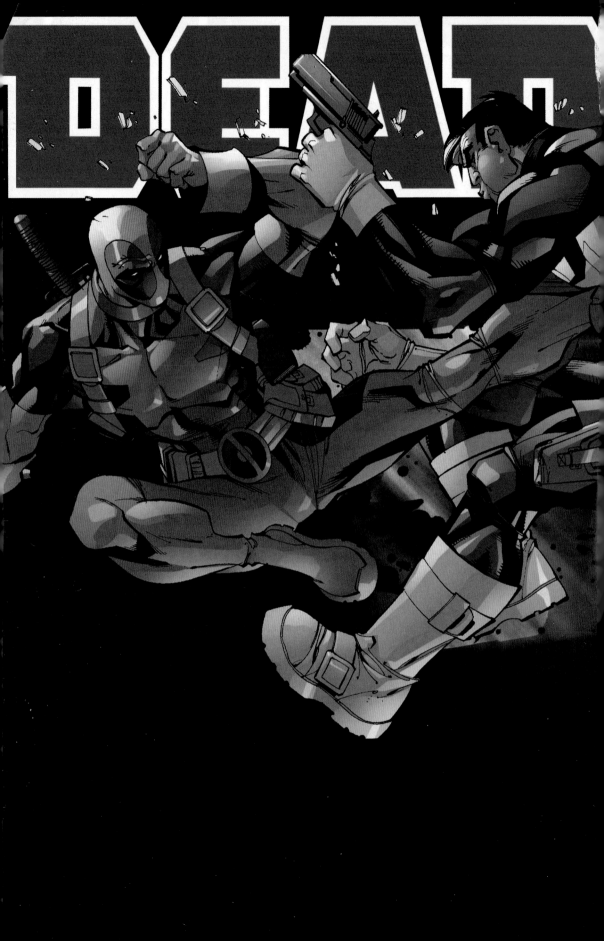

POOL SUICIDE KINGS

WRITERS: **MIKE BENSON & ADAM GLASS**
PENCILS: **CARLO BARBERI**
INKS: **SANDU FLOREA**
COLORS: **MARTE GRACIA**
LETTERS: **VIRTUAL CALLIGRAPHY'S CORY PETIT**
COVER ARTISTS: **MIKE MCKONE**
WITH ANDRES MOSSA AND MORRY HOLLOWELL

"GAME$ OF DEATH"

WRITER: **MIKE BENSON**
ART: **SHAWN CRYSTAL**
COLORS: **LEE LOUGHRIDGE**
LETTERS: **VIRTUAL CALLIGRAPHY'S CORY PETIT**
COVER ARTISTS: **GREG LAND WITH JUSTIN PONSOR**

ASSISTANT EDITOR: **JODY LEHEUP**
EDITOR: **AXEL ALONSO**

COLLECTION EDITOR: **CORY LEVINE**
ASSISTANT EDITOR: **ALEX STARBUCK**
ASSOCIATE EDITOR, SPECIAL PROJECTS: **JOHN DENNING**
EDITORS, SPECIAL PROJECTS: **JENNIFER GRÜNWALD & MARK D. BEAZLEY**
SENIOR EDITOR, SPECIAL PROJECTS: **JEFF YOUNGQUIST**
SENIOR VICE PRESIDENT OF SALES: **DAVID GABRIEL**
BOOK DESIGN: **RODOLFO MURAGUCHI**

EDITOR IN CHIEF: **JOE QUESADA**
PUBLISHER: **DAN BUCKLEY**
EXECUTIVE PRODUCER: **ALAN FINE**

1

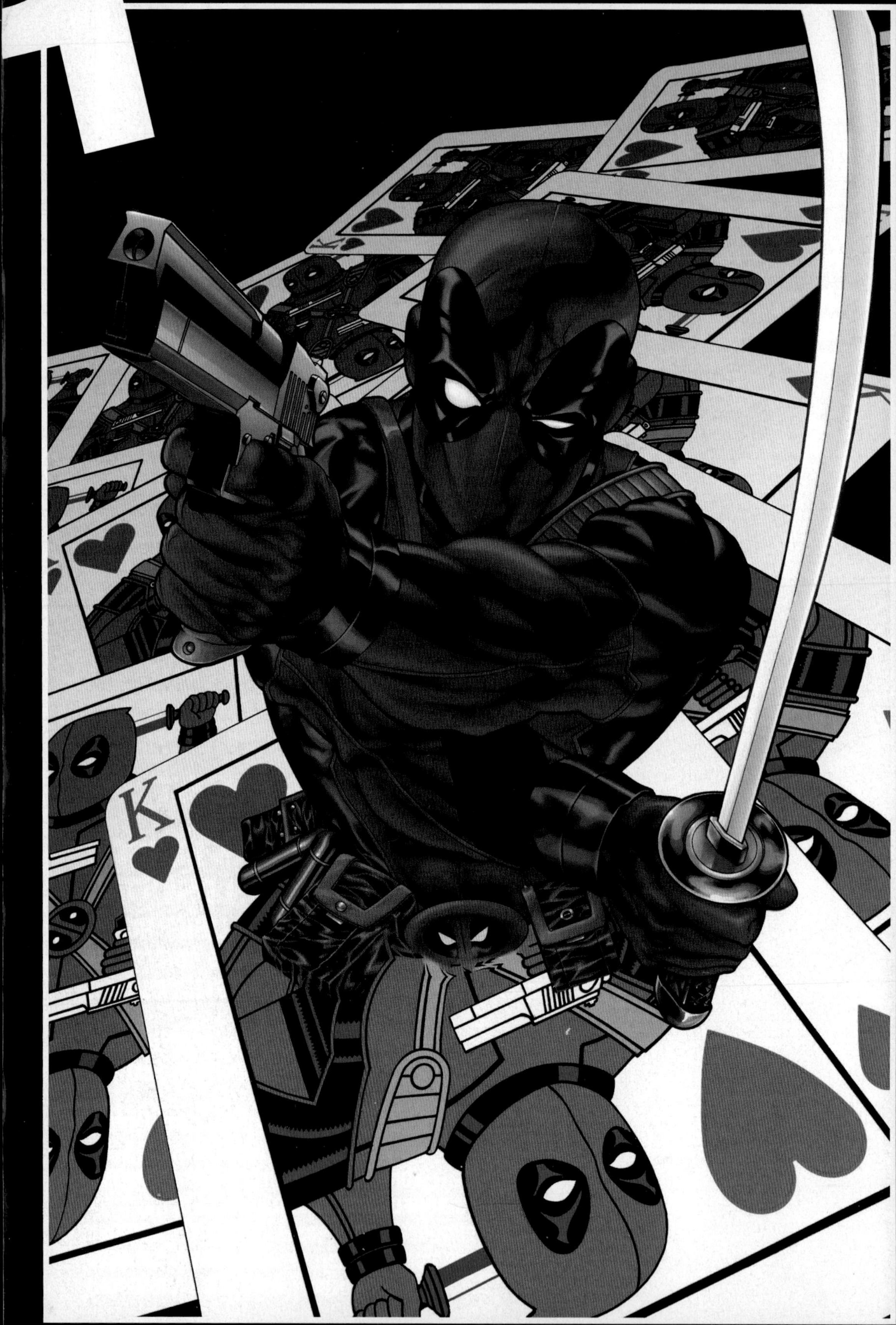

Some jobs are just too tough for your average fast talkin' hightech gun for hire. Sometimes...to get the job done right...you need someone crazier than a sack'a ferrets. You need Wade Wilson. The Crimson Comedian. The Regeneratin' Degenerate. The Merc with a Mouth...

DEADPOOL

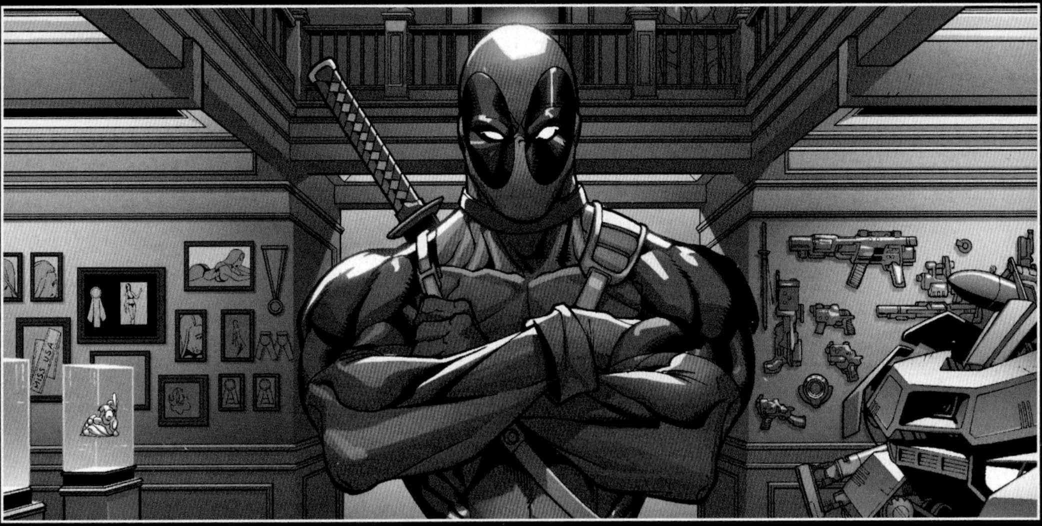

MISS USA

Deadpool is a graduate (VICTIM) of the secret super-soldier program, Weapon X. There he was trained to be a living weapon (EXPERIMENTED ON) and hailed as the greatest of the program's warriors (REJECTED AS A FAILURE). Now, he's not only one of the world's most dangerous men (THAT'S TRUE), but he's also one of the world's most intelligent (INSANE) and attractive bachelors (ACTUALLY HE'S HIDEOUS). So ladies-- (IF YOU SAW HIS FACE YOU WOULD PROBABLY--) Hey--(--PUKE ALL OVER YOUR--) Dude. (WHAT?) What are you doing? (WHADDAYA MEAN?) Tryin' to give a bio here. (WELL THEN GET YOUR FACTS STRAIGHT.) It's *OUR* bio, bro! (...OH...)

Anyway. I'm a a hero (MERCENARY) and I'm out to make (MONEY) the world safe. Story. Go.

Dude! (WHAT?!) Nothing. Shut up. (YOU SHUT UP.)

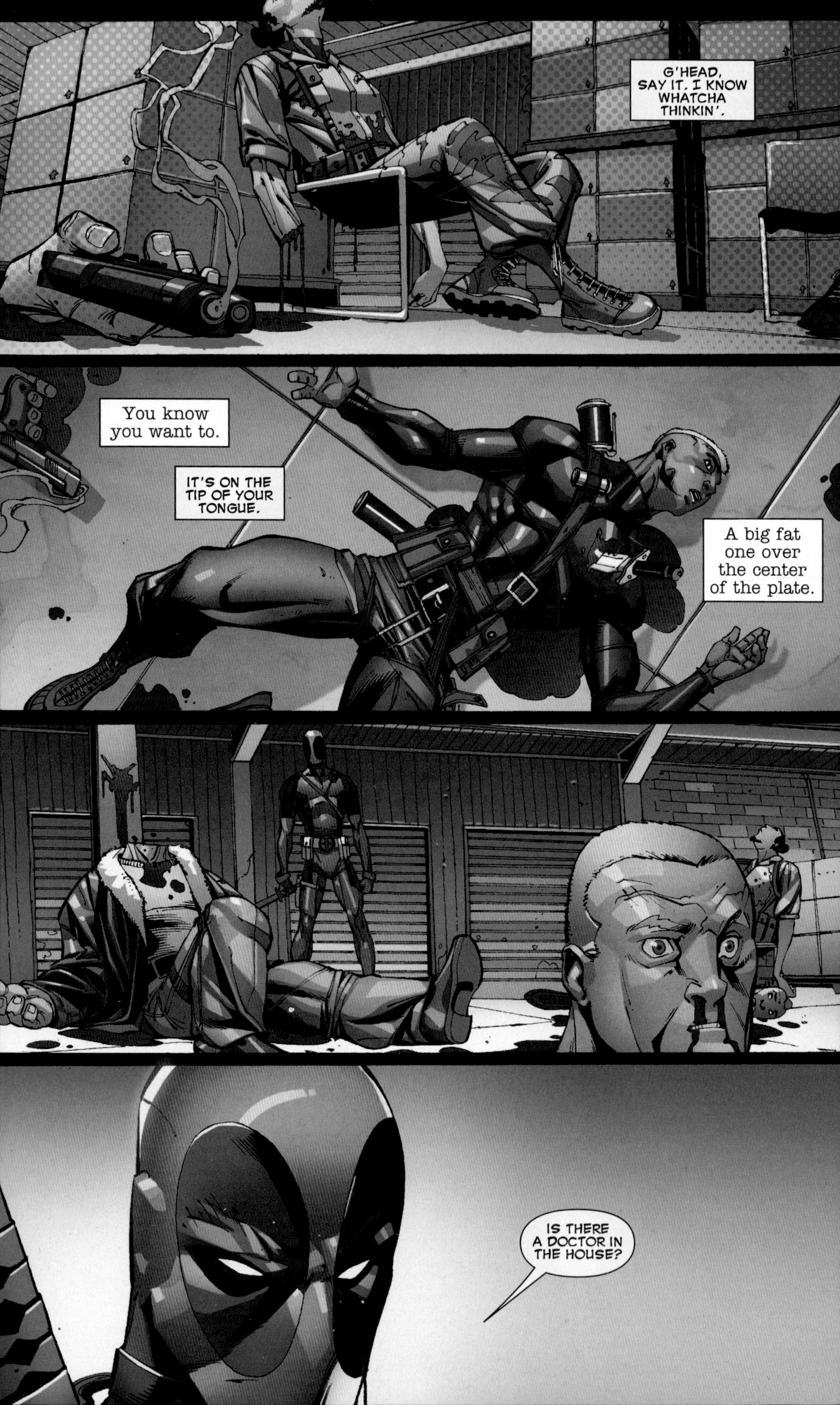
G'HEAD, SAY IT. I KNOW WHATCHA THINKIN'.
You know you want to.
IT'S ON THE TIP OF YOUR TONGUE.
A big fat one over the center of the plate.
IS THERE A DOCTOR IN THE HOUSE?

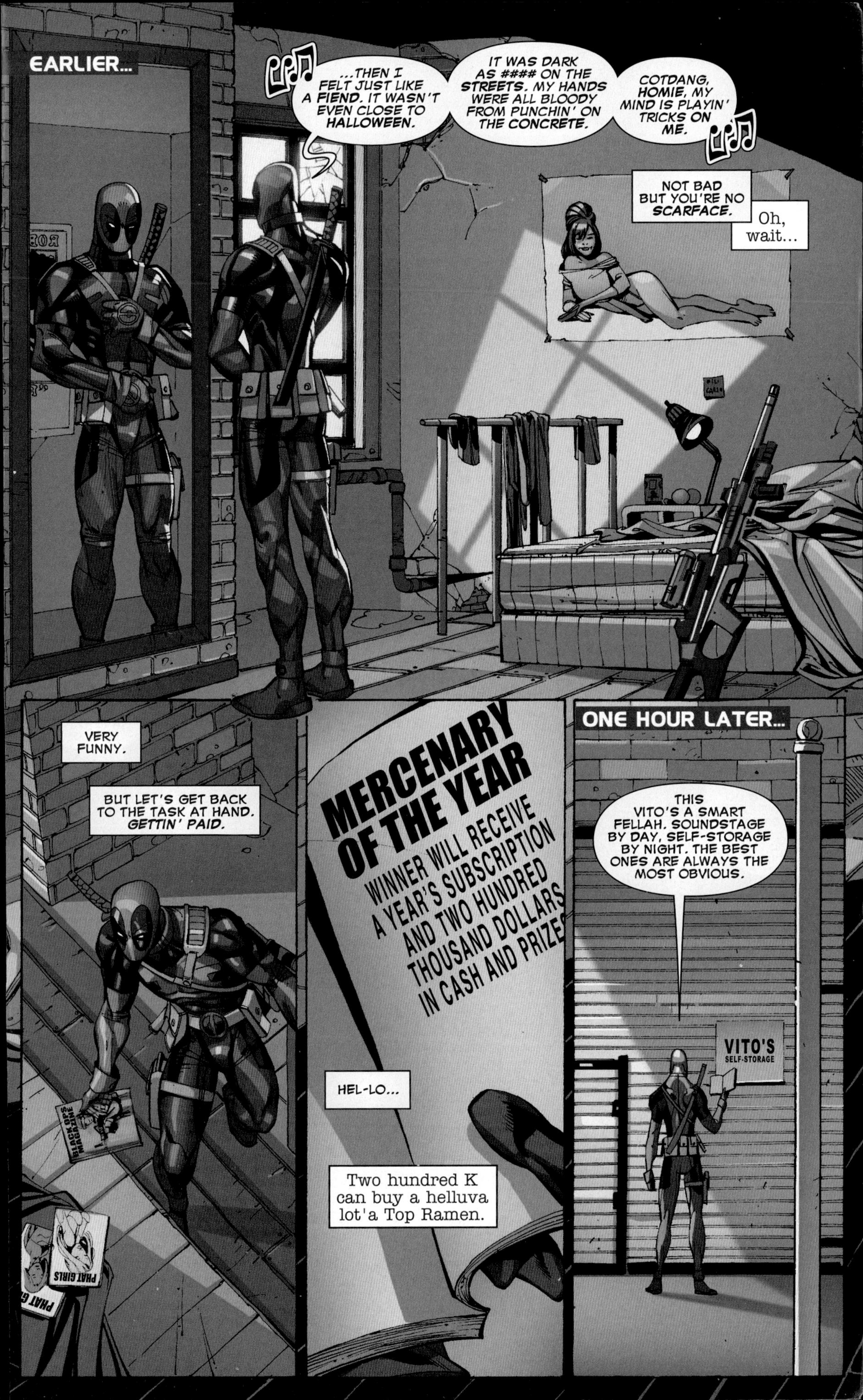
EARLIER...
...THEN I FELT JUST LIKE A FIEND. IT WASN'T EVEN CLOSE TO HALLOWEEN.
IT WAS DARK AS #### ON THE STREETS. MY HANDS WERE ALL BLOODY FROM PUNCHIN' ON THE CONCRETE.
COTDANG, HOMIE, MY MIND IS PLAYIN' TRICKS ON ME.
NOT BAD BUT YOU'RE NO SCARFACE.
Oh, wait...
VERY FUNNY.
BUT LET'S GET BACK TO THE TASK AT HAND. GETTIN' PAID.
BLACK OPS MAGAZINE
PHAT GIRLS
MERCENARY OF THE YEAR
WINNER WILL RECEIVE A YEAR'S SUBSCRIPTION AND TWO HUNDRED THOUSAND DOLLARS IN CASH AND PRIZES
HEL-LO...
Two hundred K can buy a helluva lot'a Top Ramen.
ONE HOUR LATER...
THIS VITO'S A SMART FELLAH. SOUNDSTAGE BY DAY, SELF-STORAGE BY NIGHT. THE BEST ONES ARE ALWAYS THE MOST OBVIOUS.
VITO'S SELF-STORAGE

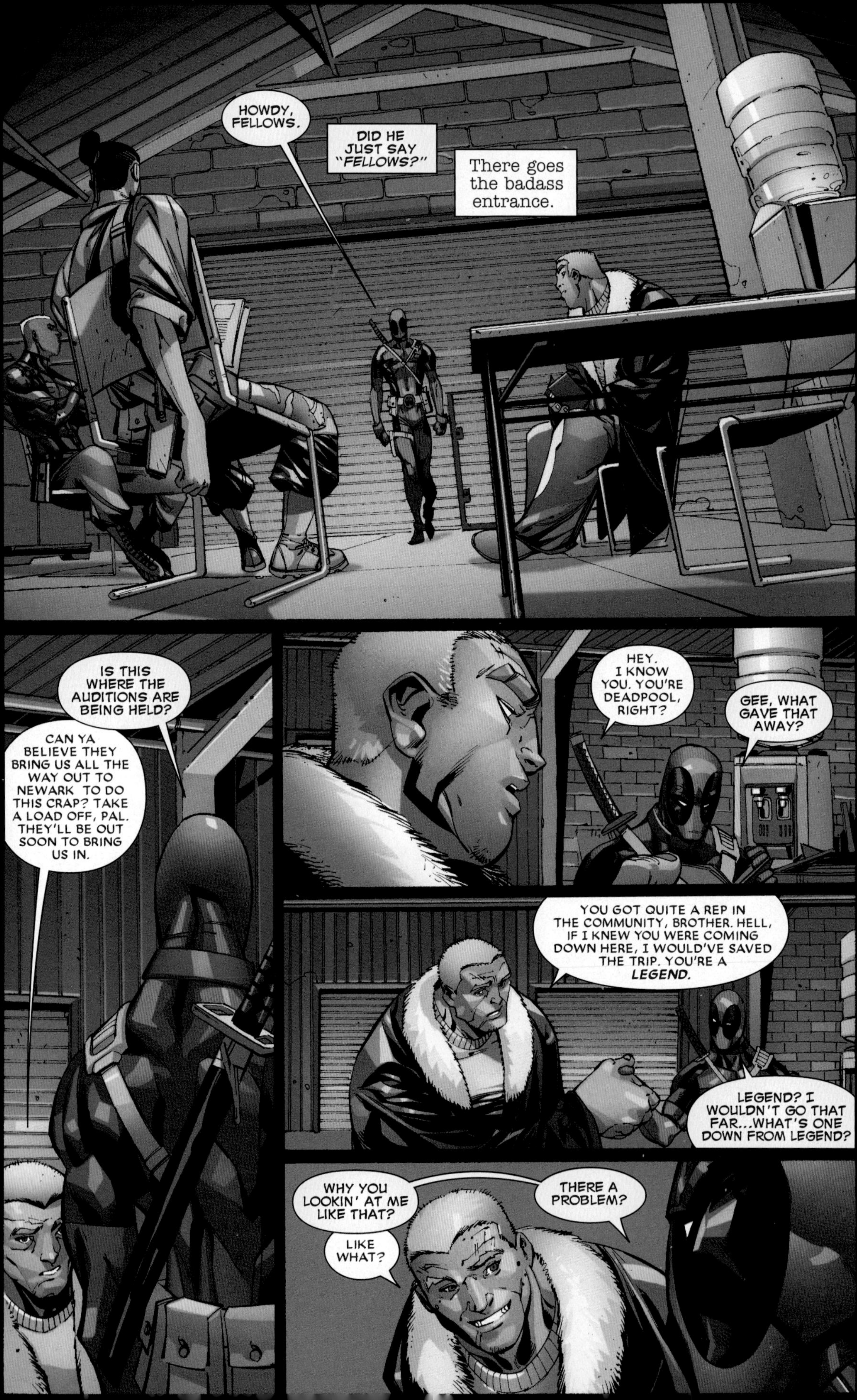
HOWDY, FELLOWS.
DID HE JUST SAY "FELLOWS?"
There goes the badass entrance.
IS THIS WHERE THE AUDITIONS ARE BEING HELD?
CAN YA BELIEVE THEY BRING US ALL THE WAY OUT TO NEWARK TO DO THIS CRAP? TAKE A LOAD OFF, PAL. THEY'LL BE OUT SOON TO BRING US IN.
HEY. I KNOW YOU. YOU'RE DEADPOOL, RIGHT?
GEE, WHAT GAVE THAT AWAY?
YOU GOT QUITE A REP IN THE COMMUNITY, BROTHER. HELL, IF I KNEW YOU WERE COMING DOWN HERE, I WOULD'VE SAVED THE TRIP. YOU'RE A LEGEND.
LEGEND? I WOULDN'T GO THAT FAR...WHAT'S ONE DOWN FROM LEGEND?
WHY YOU LOOKIN' AT ME LIKE THAT?
LIKE WHAT?
THERE A PROBLEM?

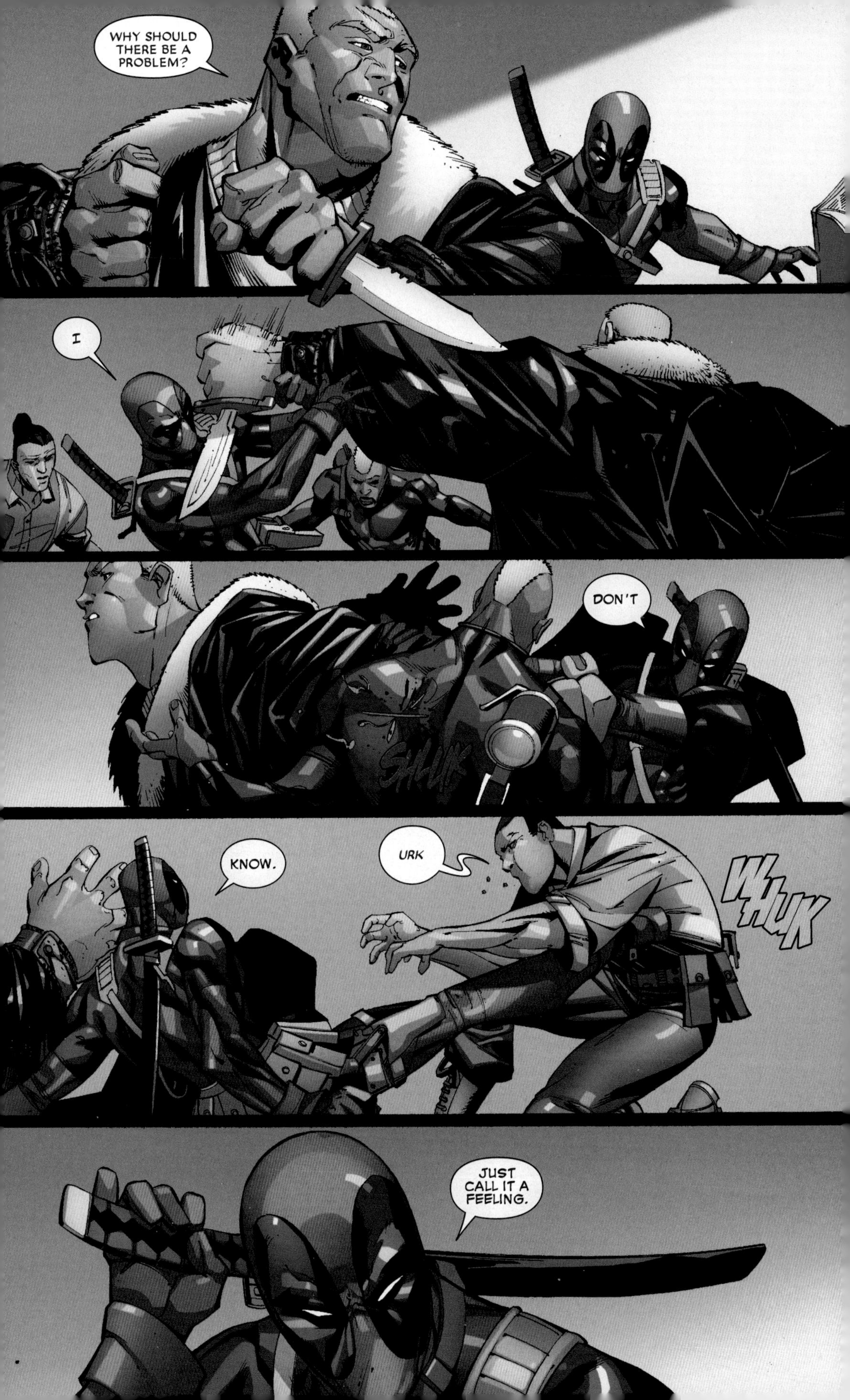
WHY SHOULD THERE BE A PROBLEM?
I
DON'T
SHUUK
KNOW.
URK
WHUK
JUST CALL IT A FEELING.

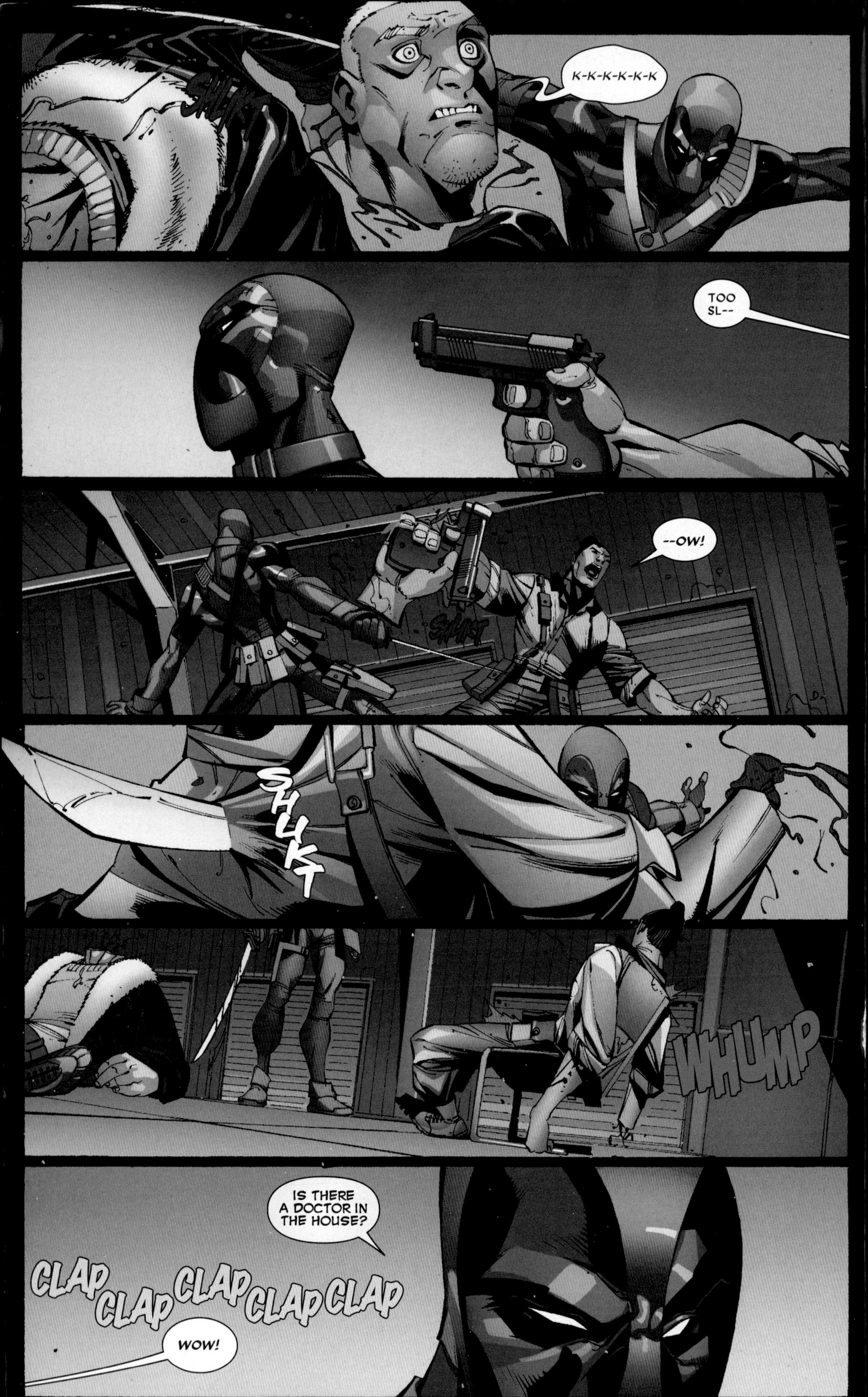

K-K-K-K-K-K-K
TOO SL--
--OW!
SHUKT
WHUMP
IS THERE A DOCTOR IN THE HOUSE?
CLAP CLAP CLAP CLAP CLAP
WOW!

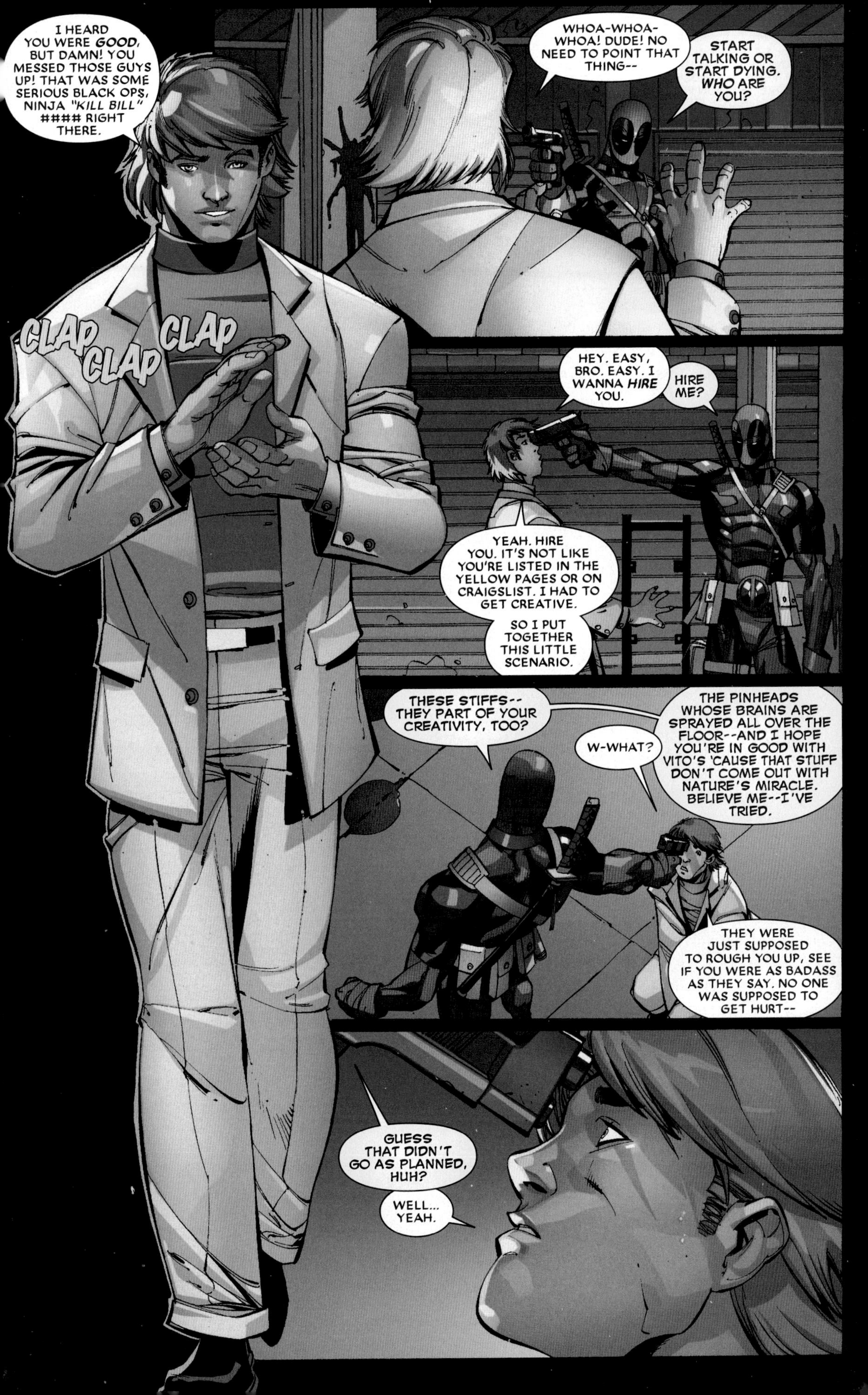
I HEARD YOU WERE GOOD, BUT DAMN! YOU MESSED THOSE GUYS UP! THAT WAS SOME SERIOUS BLACK OPS, NINJA "KILL BILL" #### RIGHT THERE.
CLAP CLAP CLAP
WHOA-WHOA-WHOA! DUDE! NO NEED TO POINT THAT THING--
START TALKING OR START DYING. WHO ARE YOU?
HEY. EASY, BRO. EASY. I WANNA HIRE YOU.
HIRE ME?
YEAH. HIRE YOU. IT'S NOT LIKE YOU'RE LISTED IN THE YELLOW PAGES OR ON CRAIGSLIST. I HAD TO GET CREATIVE.
SO I PUT TOGETHER THIS LITTLE SCENARIO.
THESE STIFFS--THEY PART OF YOUR CREATIVITY, TOO?
W-WHAT?
THE PINHEADS WHOSE BRAINS ARE SPRAYED ALL OVER THE FLOOR--AND I HOPE YOU'RE IN GOOD WITH VITO'S 'CAUSE THAT STUFF DON'T COME OUT WITH NATURE'S MIRACLE. BELIEVE ME--I'VE TRIED.
THEY WERE JUST SUPPOSED TO ROUGH YOU UP, SEE IF YOU WERE AS BADASS AS THEY SAY. NO ONE WAS SUPPOSED TO GET HURT--
GUESS THAT DIDN'T GO AS PLANNED, HUH?
WELL... YEAH.

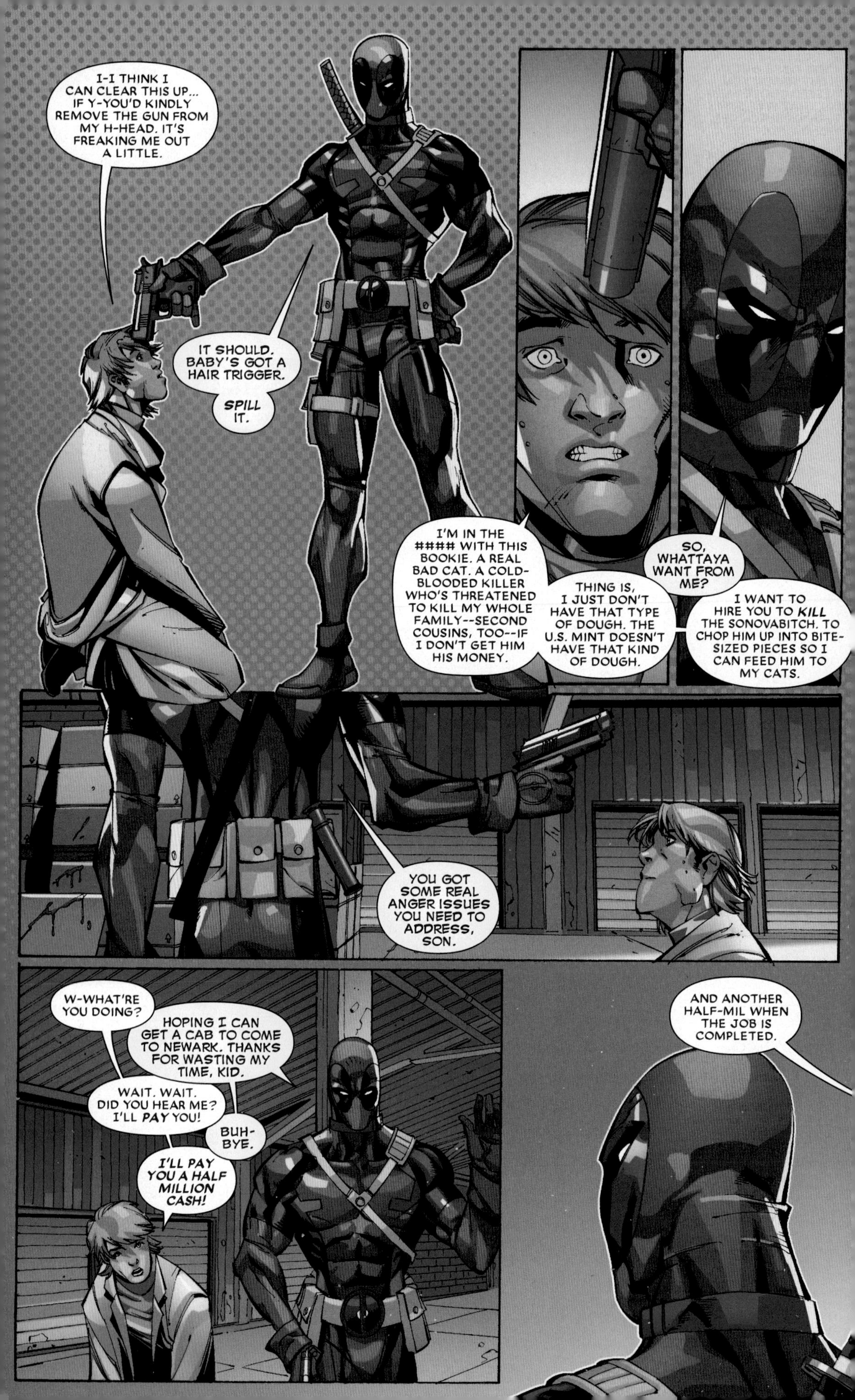

I-I THINK I CAN CLEAR THIS UP... IF Y-YOU'D KINDLY REMOVE THE GUN FROM MY H-HEAD. IT'S FREAKING ME OUT A LITTLE.
IT SHOULD. BABY'S GOT A HAIR TRIGGER.
SPILL IT.
I'M IN THE #### WITH THIS BOOKIE. A REAL BAD CAT. A COLD-BLOODED KILLER WHO'S THREATENED TO KILL MY WHOLE FAMILY--SECOND COUSINS, TOO--IF I DON'T GET HIM HIS MONEY.
THING IS, I JUST DON'T HAVE THAT TYPE OF DOUGH. THE U.S. MINT DOESN'T HAVE THAT KIND OF DOUGH.
SO, WHATTAYA WANT FROM ME?
I WANT TO HIRE YOU TO KILL THE SONOVABITCH. TO CHOP HIM UP INTO BITE-SIZED PIECES SO I CAN FEED HIM TO MY CATS.
YOU GOT SOME REAL ANGER ISSUES YOU NEED TO ADDRESS, SON.
W-WHAT'RE YOU DOING?
HOPING I CAN GET A CAB TO COME TO NEWARK. THANKS FOR WASTING MY TIME, KID.
WAIT. WAIT. DID YOU HEAR ME? I'LL PAY YOU!
BUH-BYE.
I'LL PAY YOU A HALF MILLION CASH!
AND ANOTHER HALF-MIL WHEN THE JOB IS COMPLETED.

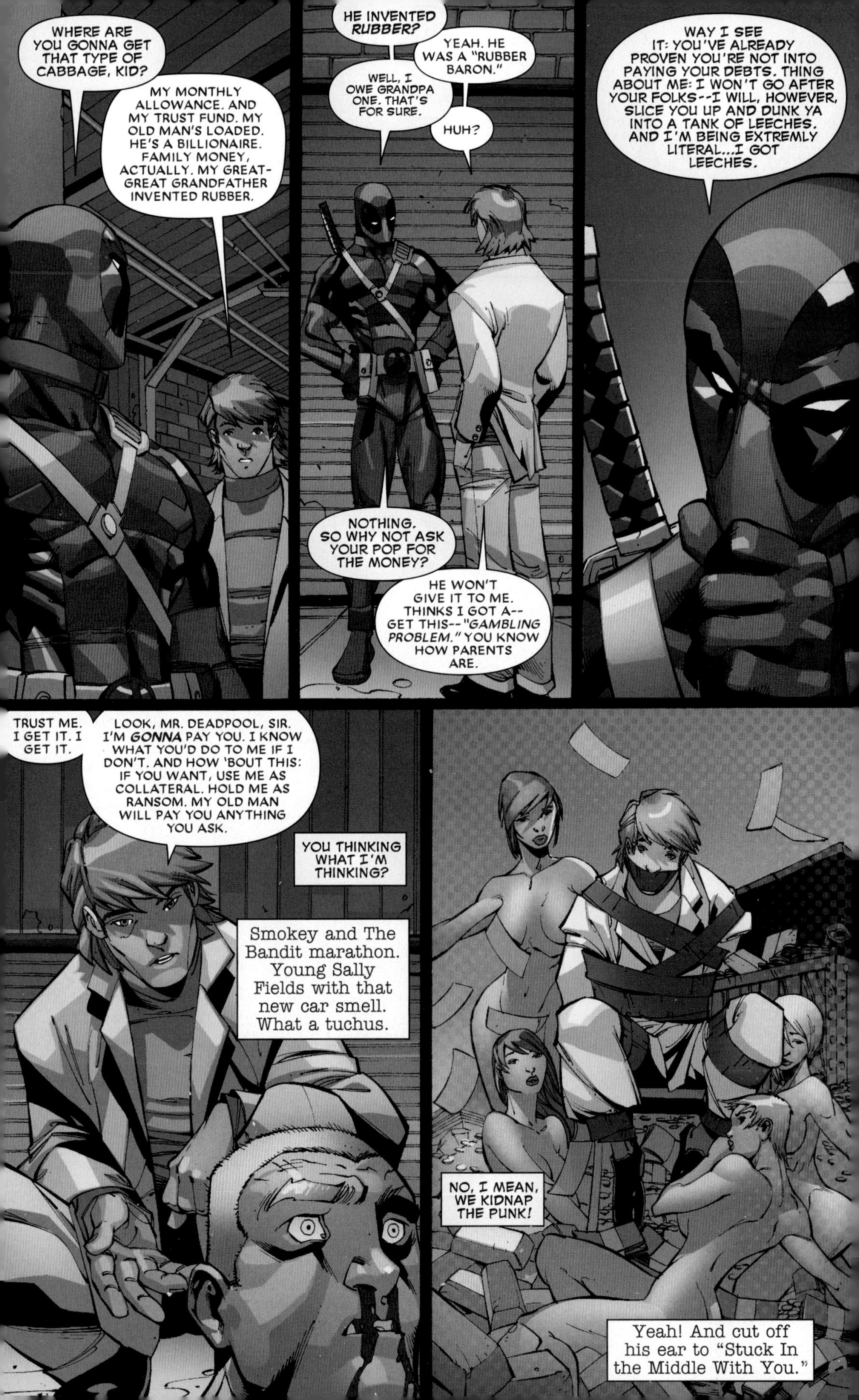
WHERE ARE YOU GONNA GET THAT TYPE OF CABBAGE, KID?
MY MONTHLY ALLOWANCE. AND MY TRUST FUND. MY OLD MAN'S LOADED. HE'S A BILLIONAIRE. FAMILY MONEY, ACTUALLY. MY GREAT-GREAT GRANDFATHER INVENTED RUBBER.
HE INVENTED *RUBBER?*
YEAH. HE WAS A "RUBBER BARON."
WELL, I OWE GRANDPA ONE. THAT'S FOR SURE.
HUH?
NOTHING. SO WHY NOT ASK YOUR POP FOR THE MONEY?
HE WON'T GIVE IT TO ME. THINKS I GOT A-- GET THIS--"*GAMBLING PROBLEM.*" YOU KNOW HOW PARENTS ARE.
WAY I SEE IT: YOU'VE ALREADY PROVEN YOU'RE NOT INTO PAYING YOUR DEBTS. THING ABOUT ME: I WON'T GO AFTER YOUR FOLKS--I WILL, HOWEVER, SLICE YOU UP AND DUNK YA INTO A TANK OF LEECHES. AND I'M BEING EXTREMLY LITERAL...I GOT LEECHES.
TRUST ME. I GET IT. I GET IT.
LOOK, MR. DEADPOOL, SIR. I'M *GONNA* PAY YOU. I KNOW WHAT YOU'D DO TO ME IF I DON'T. AND HOW 'BOUT THIS: IF YOU WANT, USE ME AS COLLATERAL. HOLD ME AS RANSOM. MY OLD MAN WILL PAY YOU ANYTHING YOU ASK.
YOU THINKING WHAT I'M THINKING?
Smokey and The Bandit marathon. Young Sally Fields with that new car smell. What a tuchus.
NO, I MEAN, WE KIDNAP THE PUNK!
Yeah! And cut off his ear to "Stuck In the Middle With You."

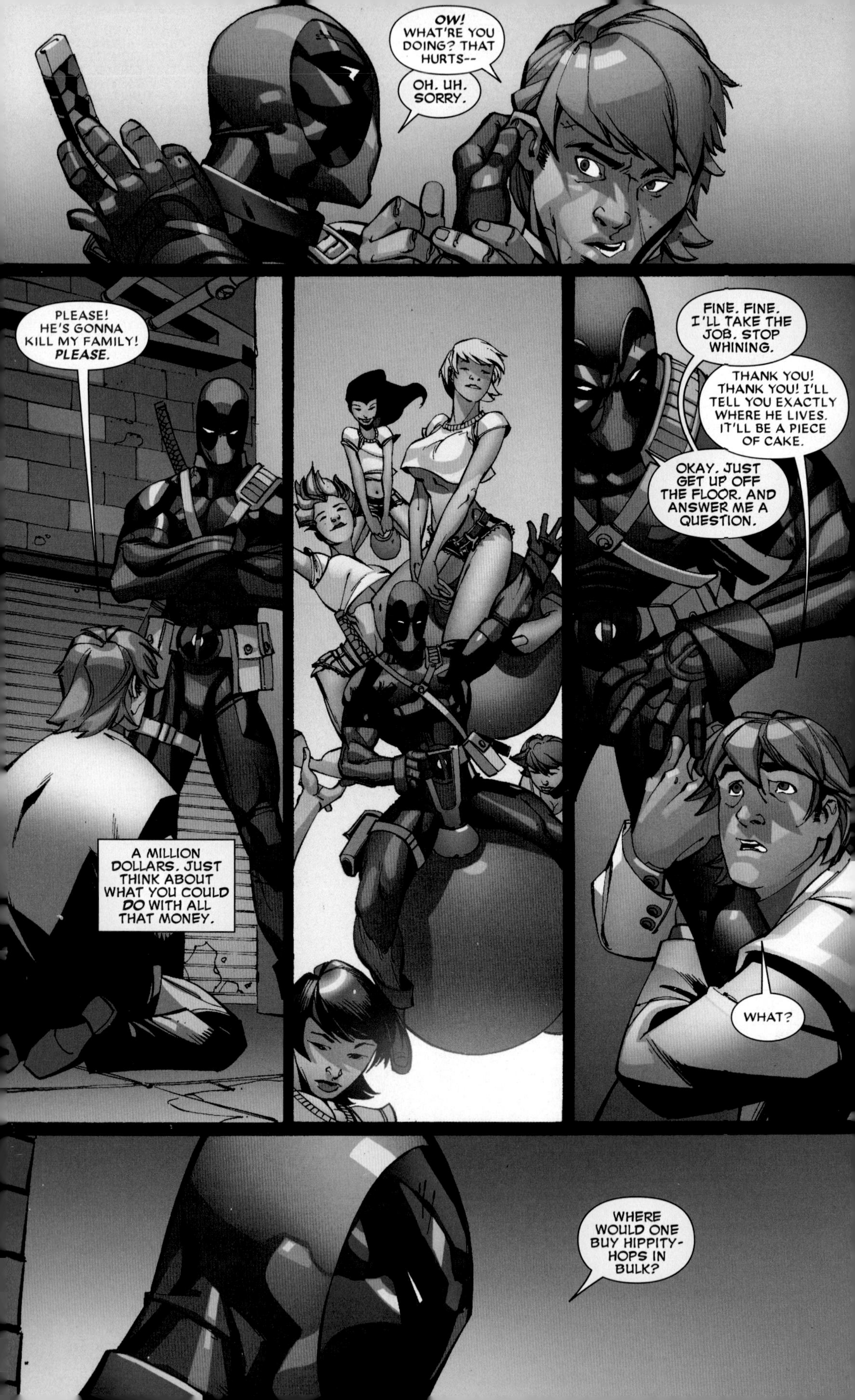
OW! WHAT'RE YOU DOING? THAT HURTS--
OH. UH. SORRY.
PLEASE! HE'S GONNA KILL MY FAMILY! PLEASE.
A MILLION DOLLARS. JUST THINK ABOUT WHAT YOU COULD DO WITH ALL THAT MONEY.
FINE. FINE. I'LL TAKE THE JOB. STOP WHINING.
THANK YOU! THANK YOU! I'LL TELL YOU EXACTLY WHERE HE LIVES. IT'LL BE A PIECE OF CAKE.
OKAY. JUST GET UP OFF THE FLOOR. AND ANSWER ME A QUESTION.
WHAT?
WHERE WOULD ONE BUY HIPPITY-HOPS IN BULK?

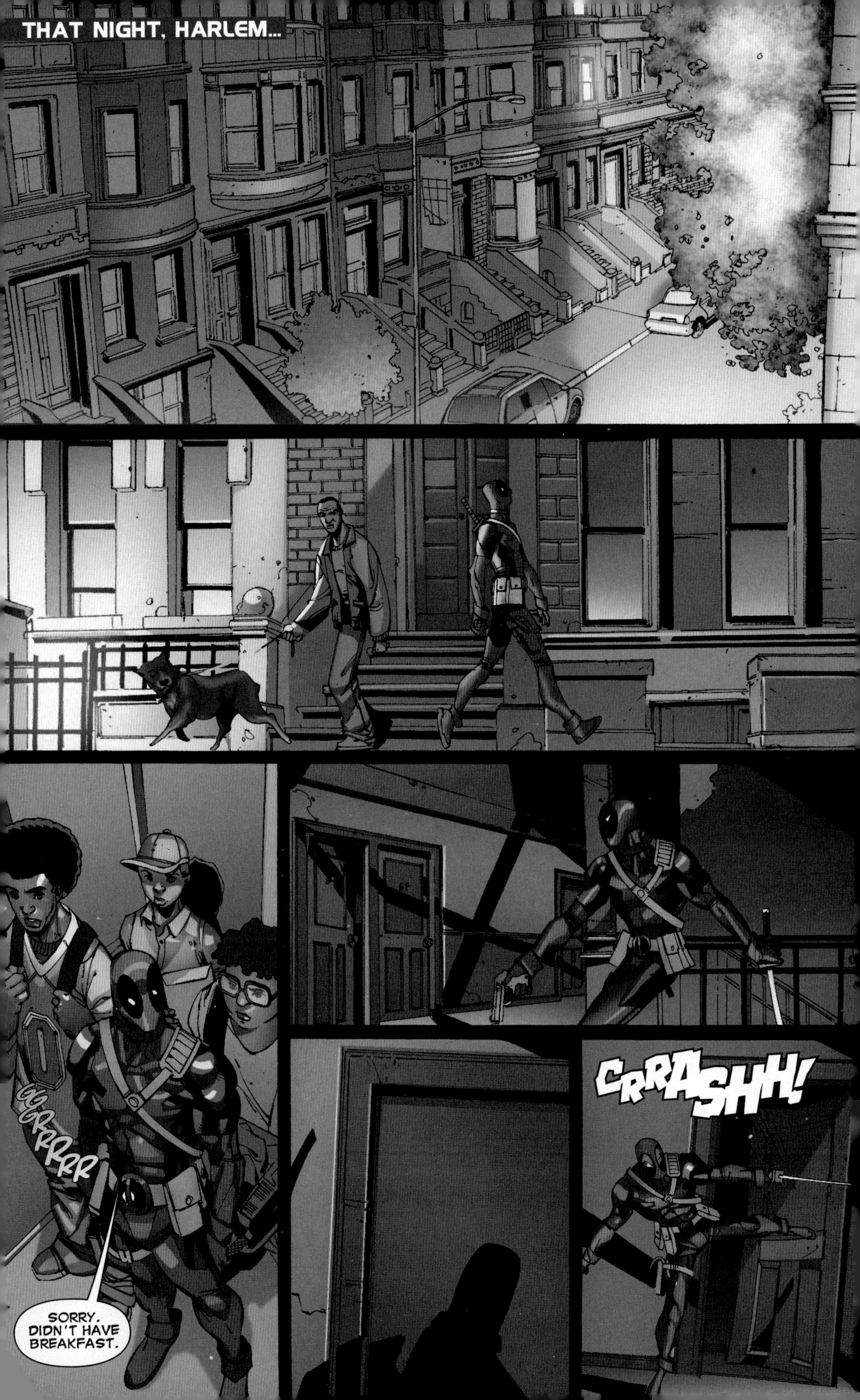
THAT NIGHT, HARLEM...
GGRRRRR
SORRY. DIDN'T HAVE BREAKFAST.
CRRASHH!

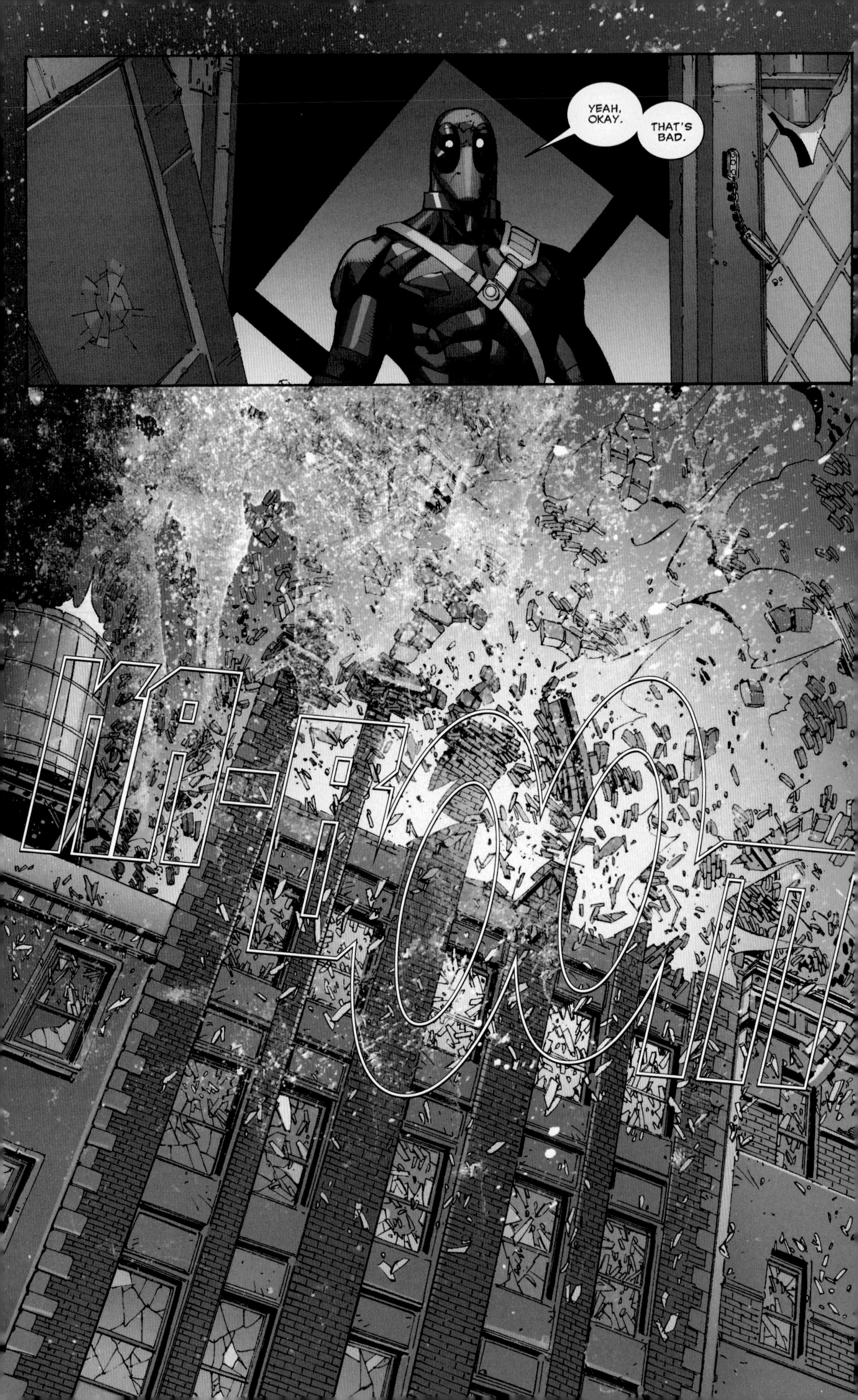
YEAH, OKAY.
THAT'S BAD.

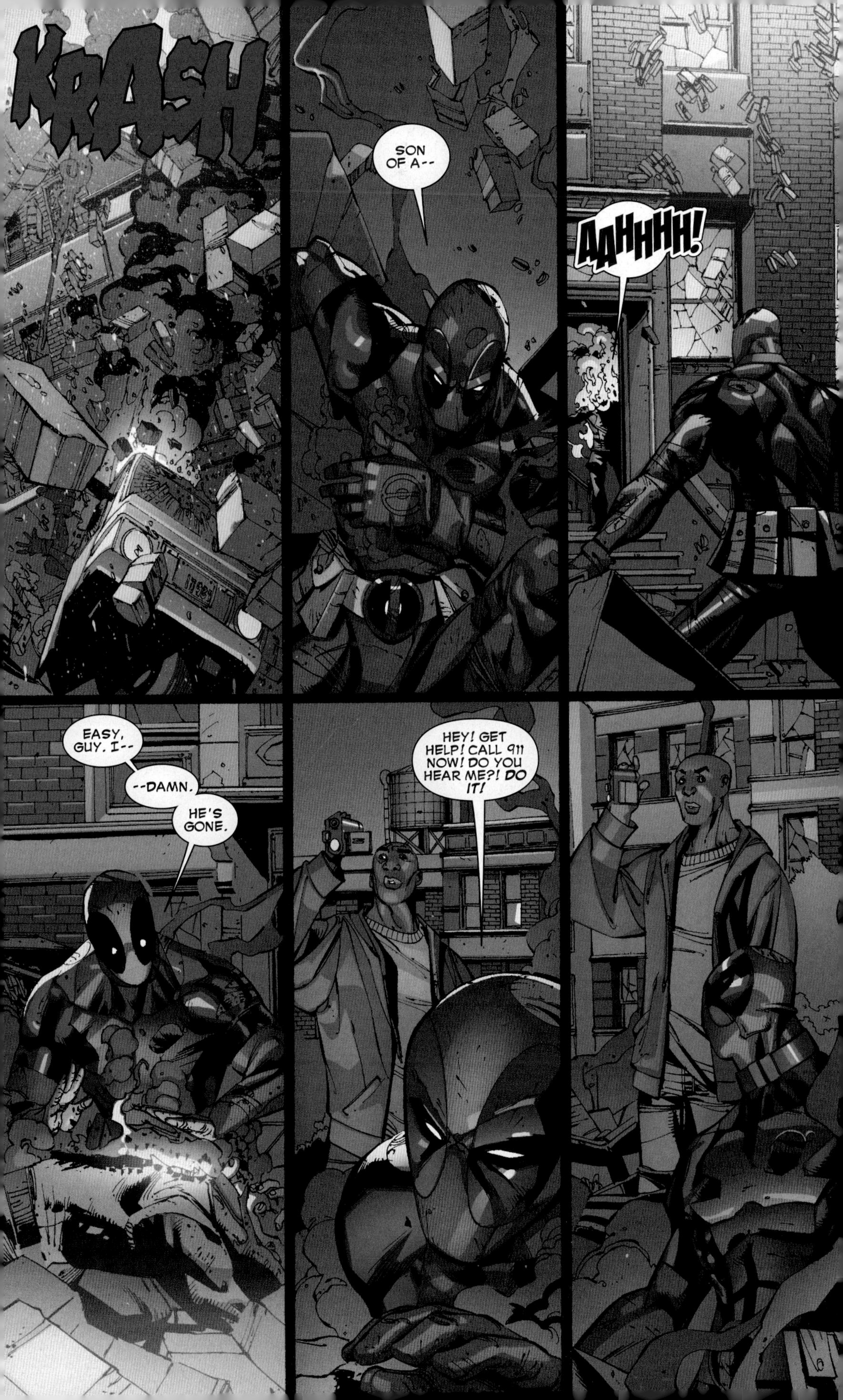
KRASH
SON OF A--
AAHHHH!
EASY, GUY. I--
--DAMN.
HE'S GONE.
HEY! GET HELP! CALL 911 NOW! DO YOU HEAR ME?! DO IT!

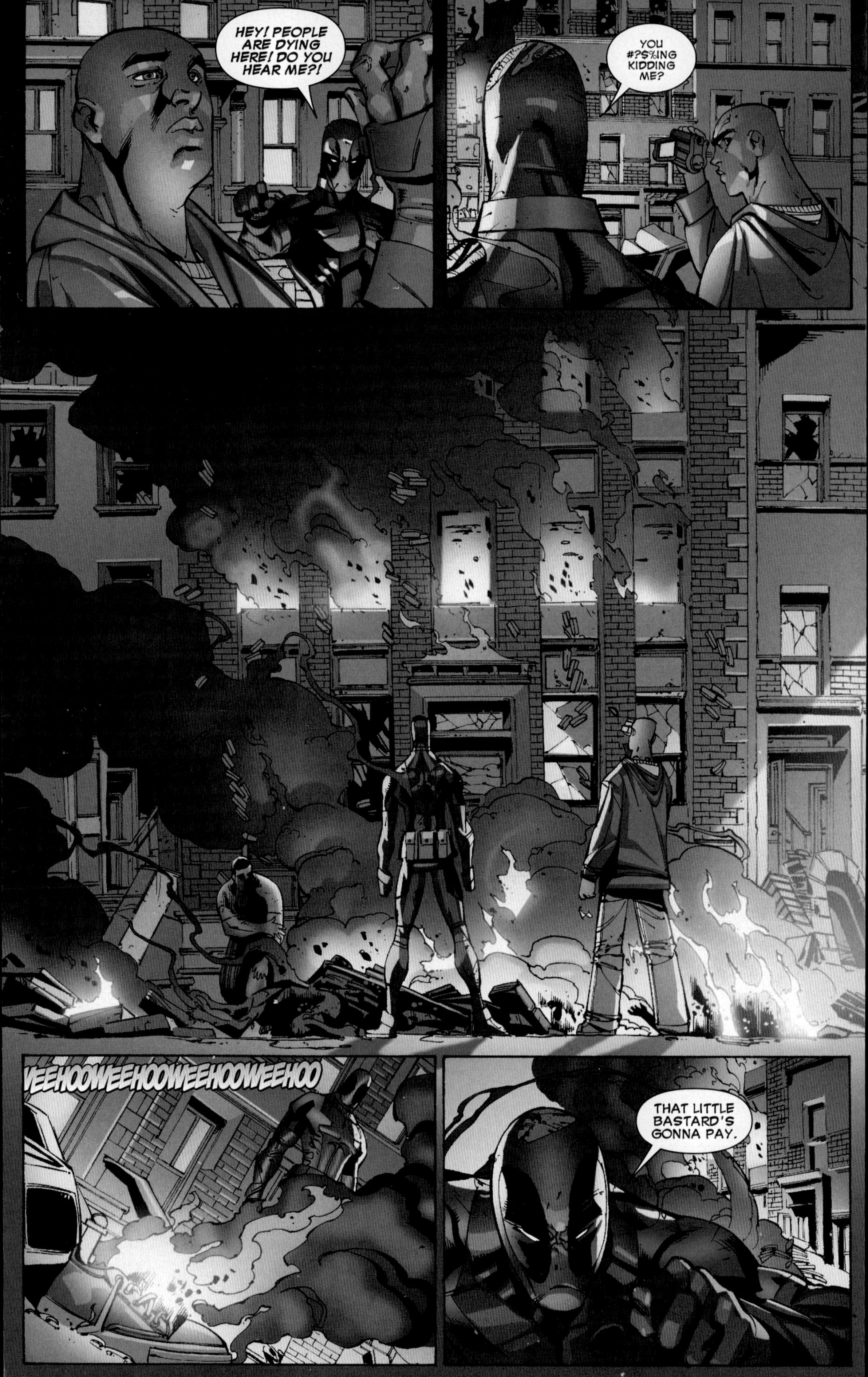
HEY! PEOPLE ARE DYING HERE! DO YOU HEAR ME?!
YOU #?$%ING KIDDING ME?
WEEHOOWEEHOOWEEHOOWEEHOO
THAT LITTLE BASTARD'S GONNA PAY.

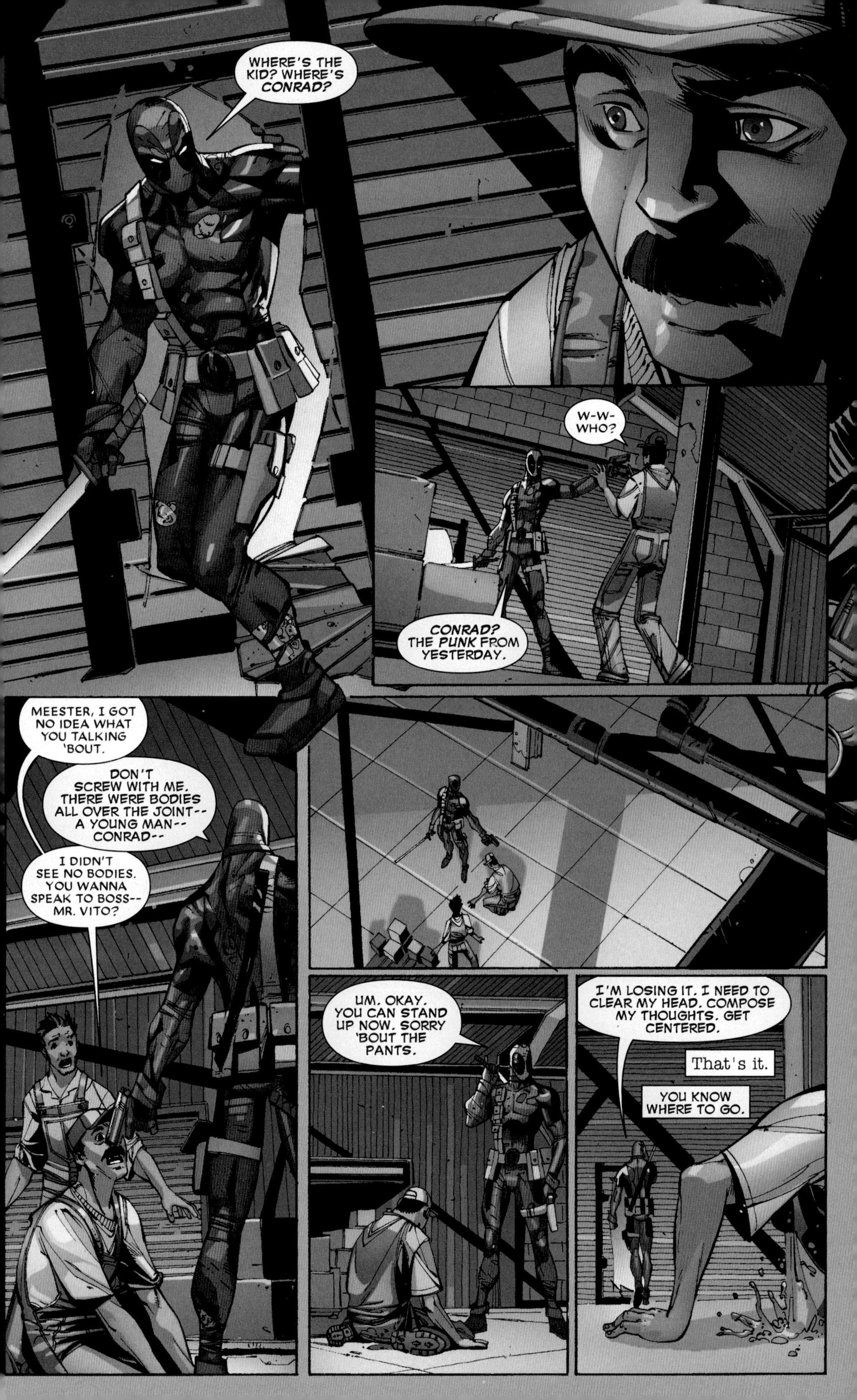
WHERE'S THE KID? WHERE'S CONRAD?
W-W-WHO?
CONRAD? THE PUNK FROM YESTERDAY.
MEESTER, I GOT NO IDEA WHAT YOU TALKING 'BOUT.
DON'T SCREW WITH ME. THERE WERE BODIES ALL OVER THE JOINT-- A YOUNG MAN-- CONRAD--
I DIDN'T SEE NO BODIES. YOU WANNA SPEAK TO BOSS-- MR. VITO?
UM. OKAY. YOU CAN STAND UP NOW. SORRY 'BOUT THE PANTS.
I'M LOSING IT. I NEED TO CLEAR MY HEAD. COMPOSE MY THOUGHTS. GET CENTERED.
That's it.
YOU KNOW WHERE TO GO.

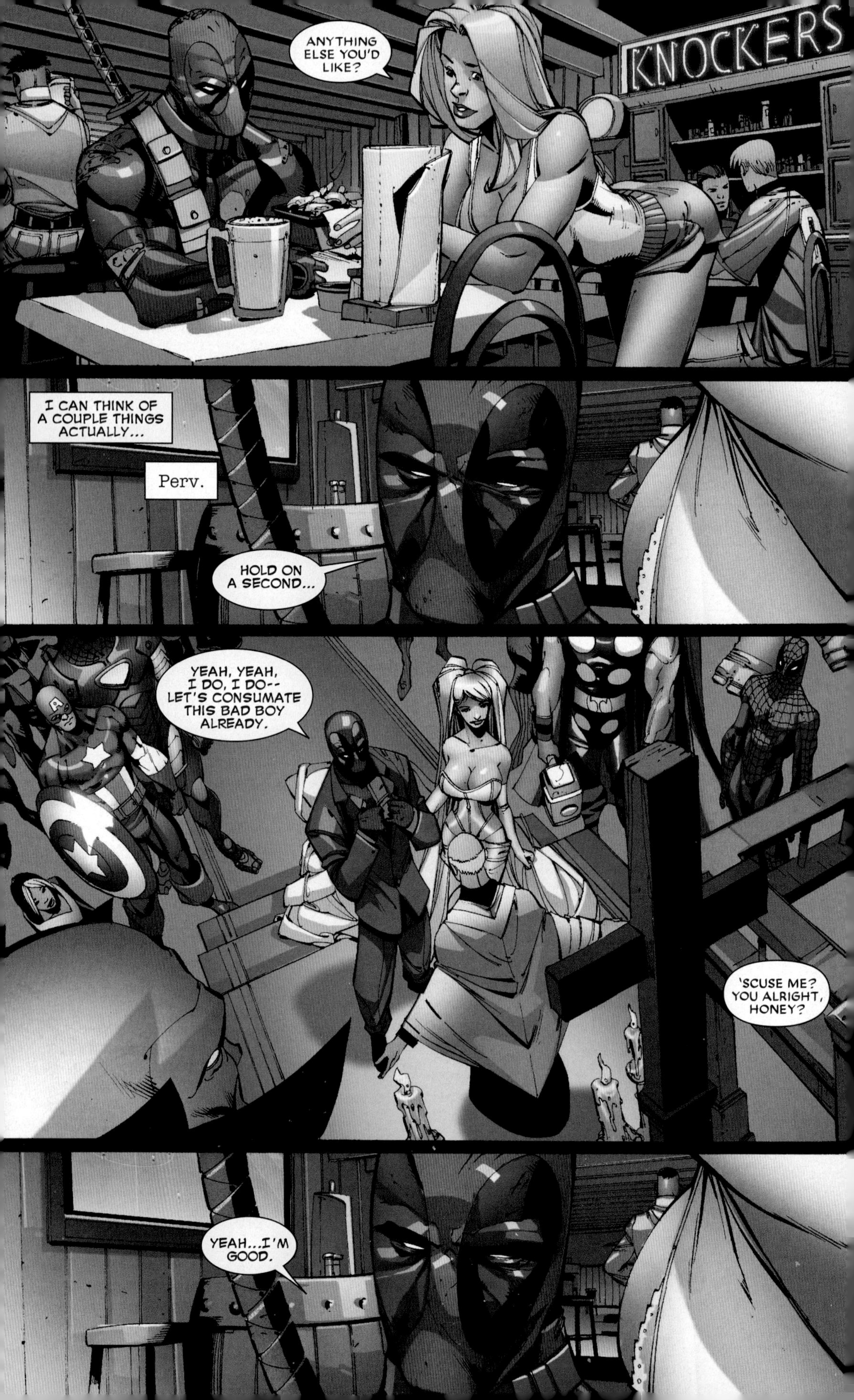
KNOCKERS
ANYTHING ELSE YOU'D LIKE?
I CAN THINK OF A COUPLE THINGS ACTUALLY...
Perv.
HOLD ON A SECOND...
YEAH, YEAH, I DO, I DO-- LET'S CONSUMATE THIS BAD BOY ALREADY.
'SCUSE ME? YOU ALRIGHT, HONEY?
YEAH...I'M GOOD.

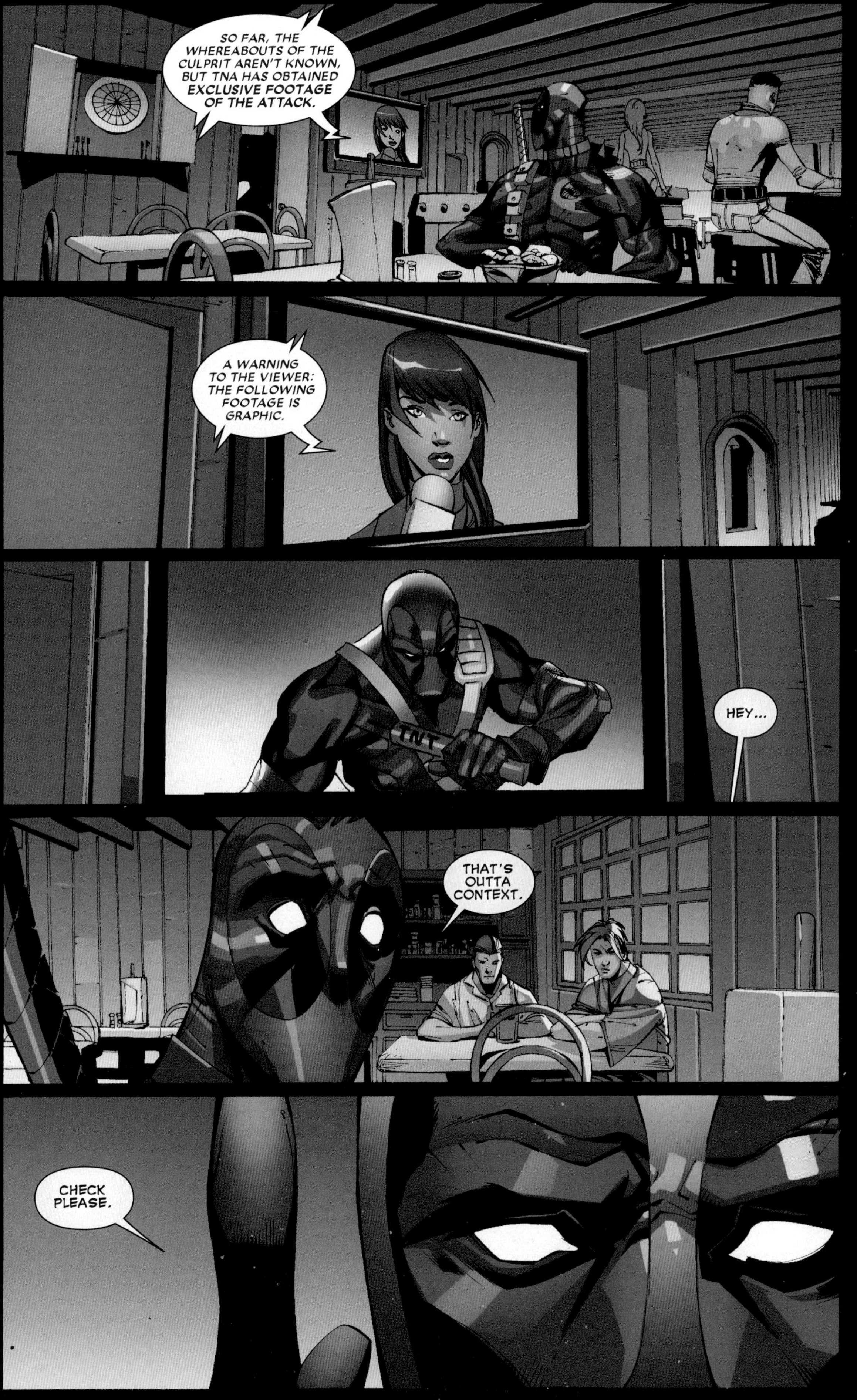
SO FAR, THE WHEREABOUTS OF THE CULPRIT AREN'T KNOWN, BUT TNA HAS OBTAINED EXCLUSIVE FOOTAGE OF THE ATTACK.
A WARNING TO THE VIEWER: THE FOLLOWING FOOTAGE IS GRAPHIC.
TNT
HEY...
THAT'S OUTTA CONTEXT.
CHECK PLEASE.

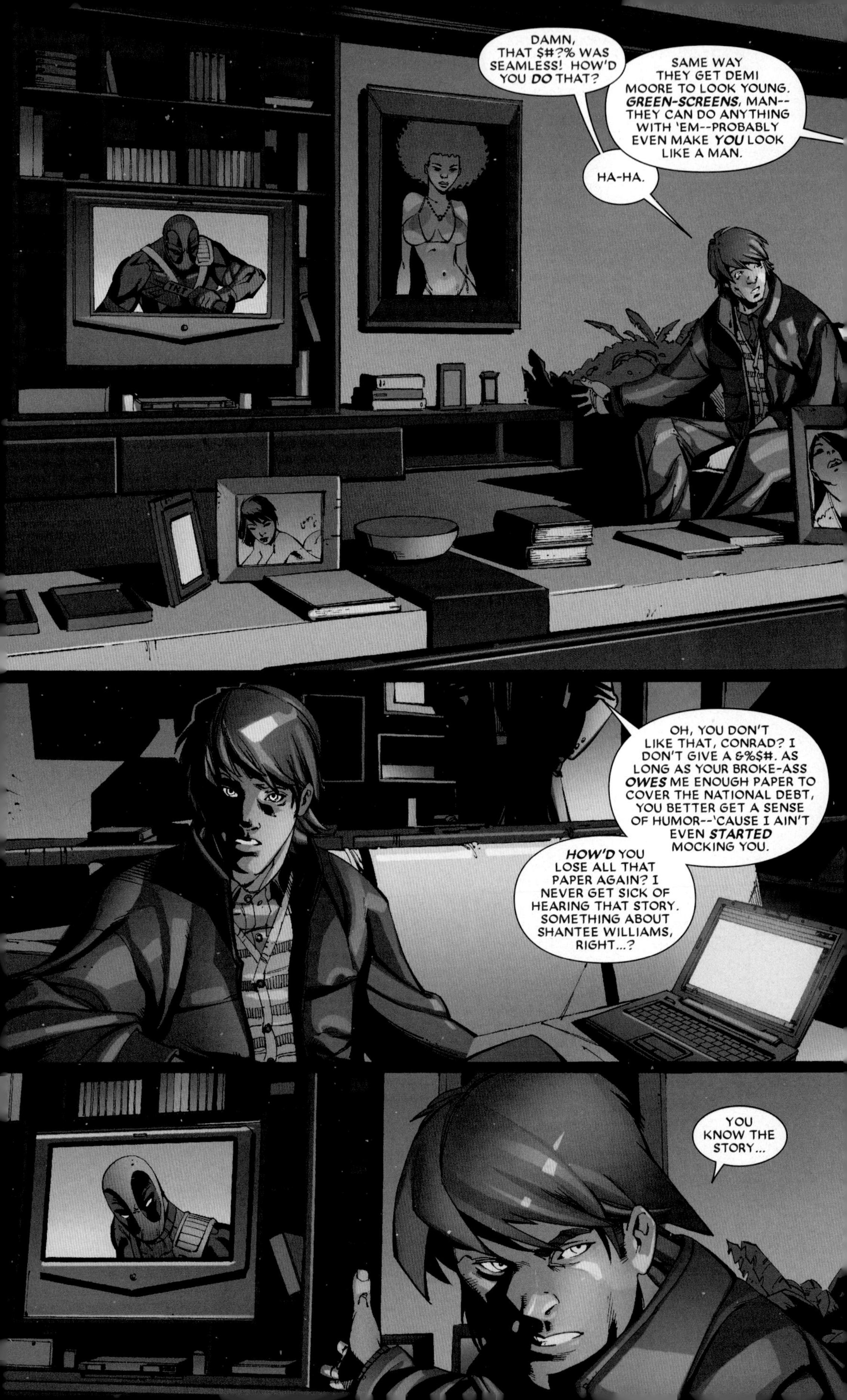
DAMN, THAT $#?% WAS SEAMLESS! HOW'D YOU *DO* THAT?
SAME WAY THEY GET DEMI MOORE TO LOOK YOUNG. *GREEN-SCREENS*, MAN--THEY CAN DO ANYTHING WITH 'EM--PROBABLY EVEN MAKE *YOU* LOOK LIKE A MAN.
HA-HA.
OH, YOU DON'T LIKE THAT, CONRAD? I DON'T GIVE A &%$#. AS LONG AS YOUR BROKE-ASS *OWES* ME ENOUGH PAPER TO COVER THE NATIONAL DEBT, YOU BETTER GET A SENSE OF HUMOR--'CAUSE I AIN'T EVEN *STARTED* MOCKING YOU.
HOW'D YOU LOSE ALL THAT PAPER AGAIN? I NEVER GET SICK OF HEARING THAT STORY. SOMETHING ABOUT SHANTEE WILLIAMS, RIGHT...?
YOU KNOW THE STORY...

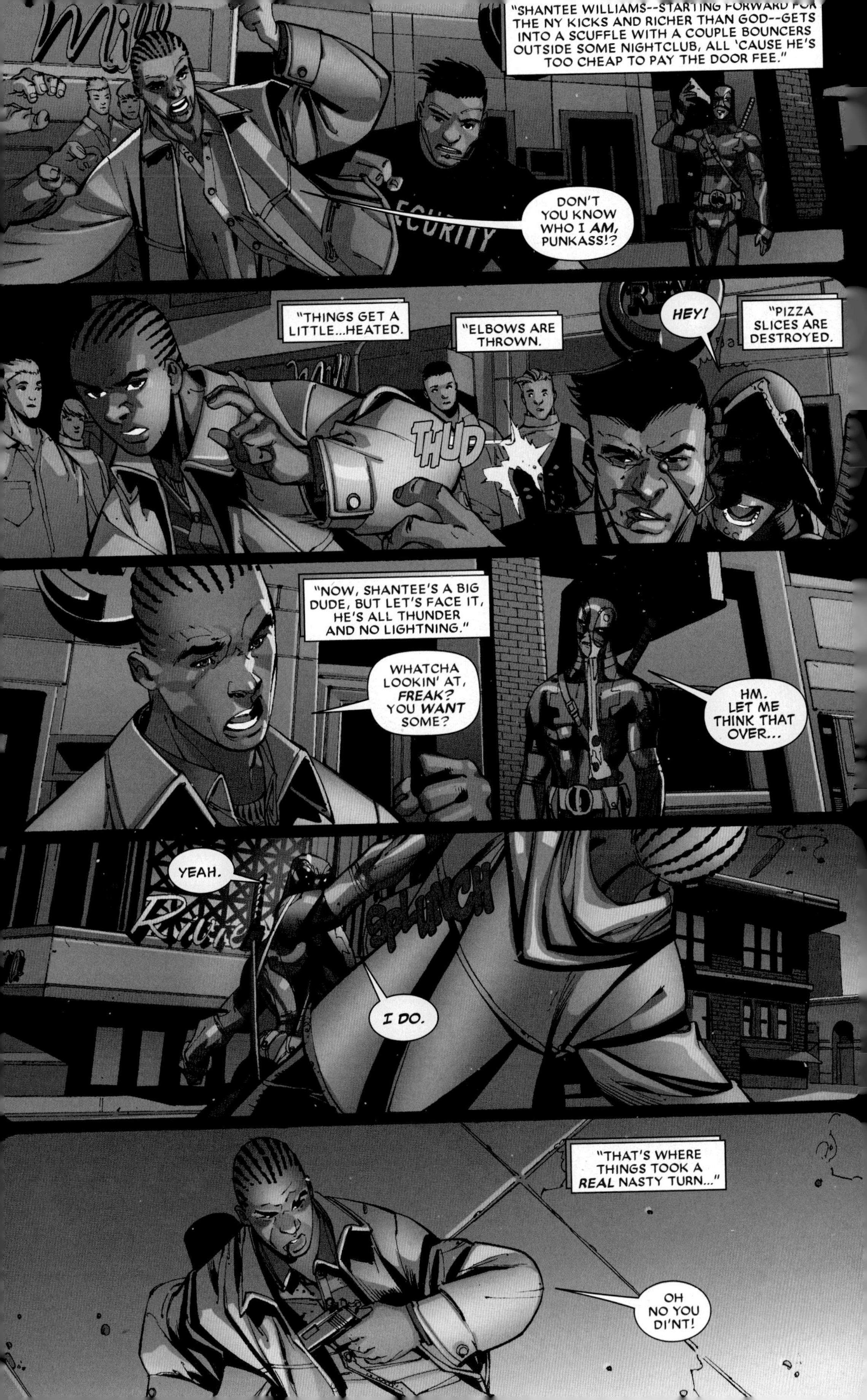
"SHANTEE WILLIAMS--STARTING FORWARD FOR THE NY KICKS AND RICHER THAN GOD--GETS INTO A SCUFFLE WITH A COUPLE BOUNCERS OUTSIDE SOME NIGHTCLUB, ALL 'CAUSE HE'S TOO CHEAP TO PAY THE DOOR FEE."
DON'T YOU KNOW WHO I AM, PUNKASS!?
SECURITY
"THINGS GET A LITTLE...HEATED.
"ELBOWS ARE THROWN.
HEY!
"PIZZA SLICES ARE DESTROYED.
THUD
"NOW, SHANTEE'S A BIG DUDE, BUT LET'S FACE IT, HE'S ALL THUNDER AND NO LIGHTNING."
WHATCHA LOOKIN' AT, FREAK? YOU WANT SOME?
HM. LET ME THINK THAT OVER...
YEAH.
SPLUNCH
I DO.
"THAT'S WHERE THINGS TOOK A REAL NASTY TURN..."
OH NO YOU DI'NT!

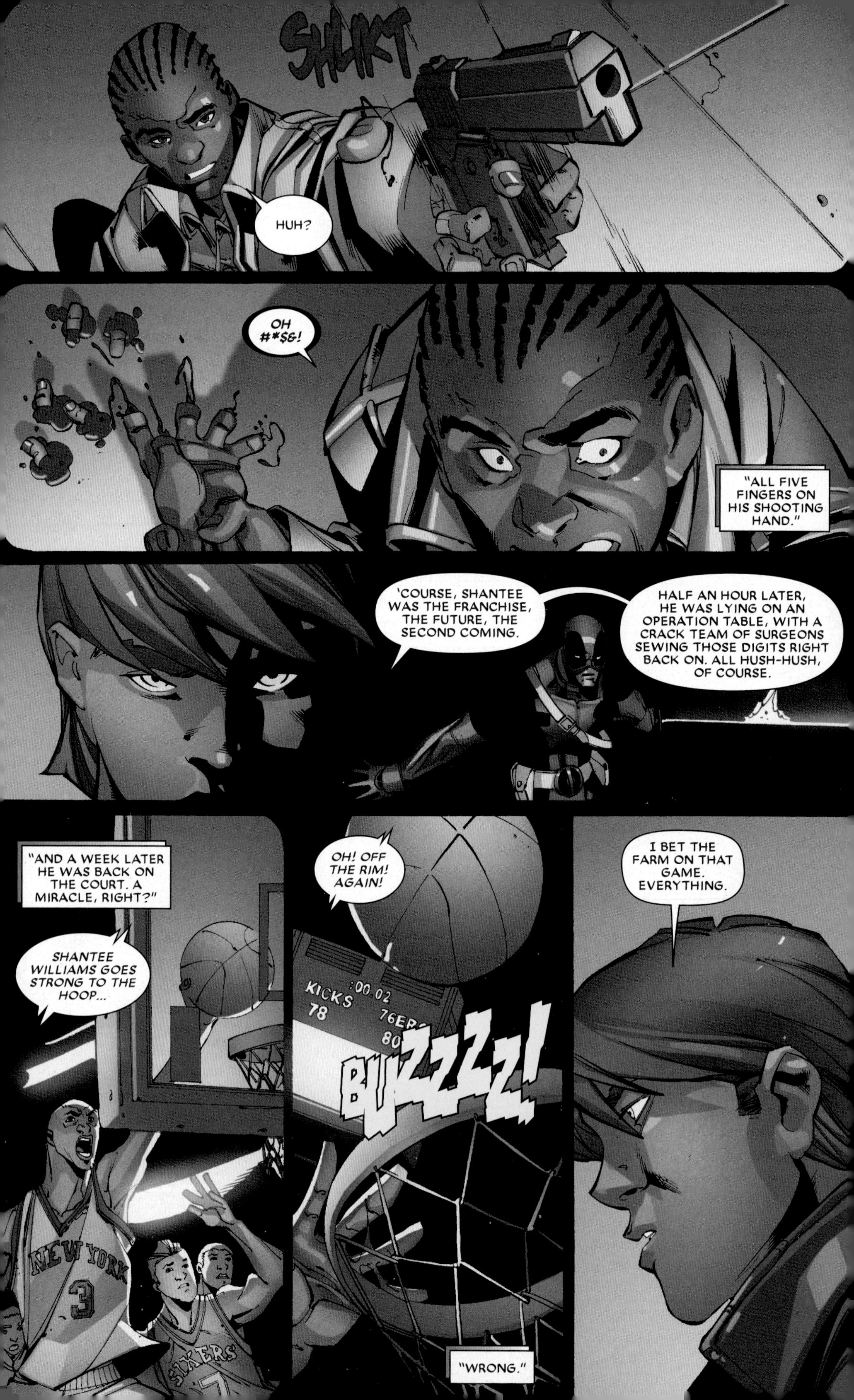
SHLIKT
HUH?
OH #*$&!
"ALL FIVE FINGERS ON HIS SHOOTING HAND."
'COURSE, SHANTEE WAS THE FRANCHISE, THE FUTURE, THE SECOND COMING.
HALF AN HOUR LATER, HE WAS LYING ON AN OPERATION TABLE, WITH A CRACK TEAM OF SURGEONS SEWING THOSE DIGITS RIGHT BACK ON. ALL HUSH-HUSH, OF COURSE.
"AND A WEEK LATER HE WAS BACK ON THE COURT. A MIRACLE, RIGHT?"
SHANTEE WILLIAMS GOES STRONG TO THE HOOP...
NEW YORK
3
SIXERS
7
OH! OFF THE RIM! AGAIN!
:00.02
KICKS 78
76ERS 80
BUZZZZ!
"WRONG."
I BET THE FARM ON THAT GAME. EVERYTHING.

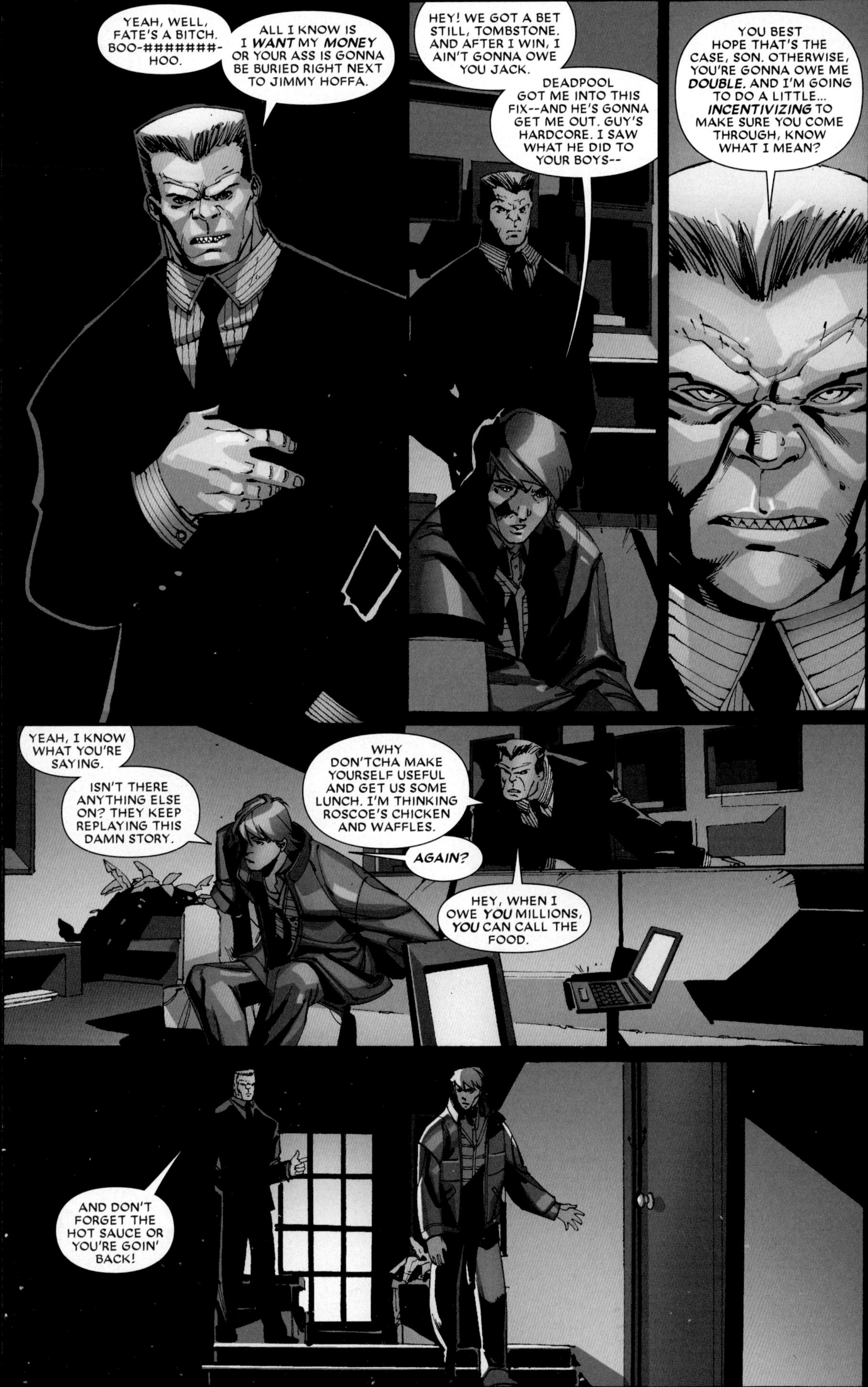

YEAH, WELL, FATE'S A BITCH. BOO-#######-HOO.
ALL I KNOW IS I WANT MY MONEY OR YOUR ASS IS GONNA BE BURIED RIGHT NEXT TO JIMMY HOFFA.
HEY! WE GOT A BET STILL, TOMBSTONE. AND AFTER I WIN, I AIN'T GONNA OWE YOU JACK.
DEADPOOL GOT ME INTO THIS FIX--AND HE'S GONNA GET ME OUT. GUY'S HARDCORE. I SAW WHAT HE DID TO YOUR BOYS--
YOU BEST HOPE THAT'S THE CASE, SON. OTHERWISE, YOU'RE GONNA OWE ME DOUBLE. AND I'M GOING TO DO A LITTLE... INCENTIVIZING TO MAKE SURE YOU COME THROUGH, KNOW WHAT I MEAN?
YEAH, I KNOW WHAT YOU'RE SAYING.
ISN'T THERE ANYTHING ELSE ON? THEY KEEP REPLAYING THIS DAMN STORY.
WHY DON'TCHA MAKE YOURSELF USEFUL AND GET US SOME LUNCH. I'M THINKING ROSCOE'S CHICKEN AND WAFFLES.
AGAIN?
HEY, WHEN I OWE YOU MILLIONS, YOU CAN CALL THE FOOD.
AND DON'T FORGET THE HOT SAUCE OR YOU'RE GOIN' BACK!

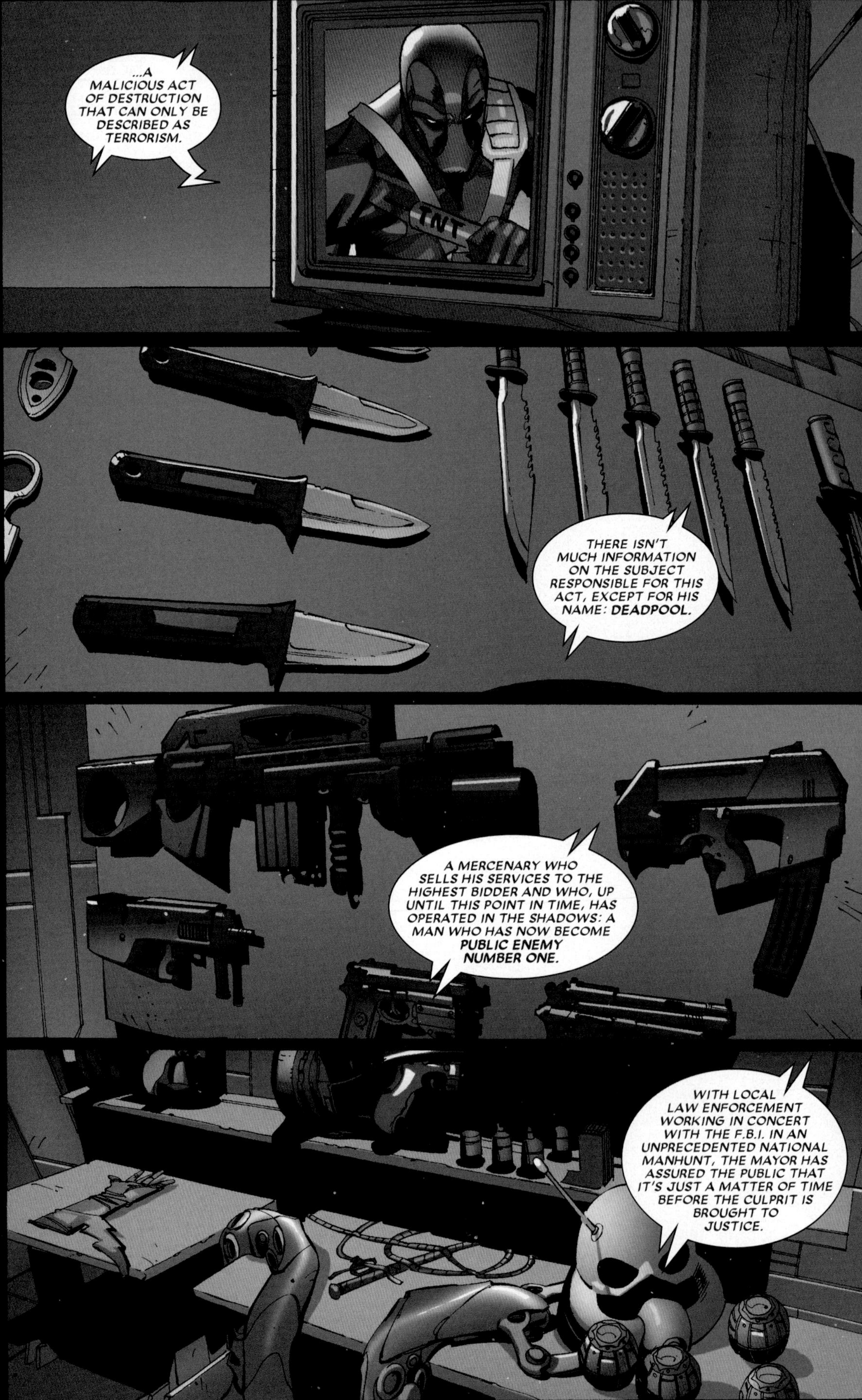
...A MALICIOUS ACT OF DESTRUCTION THAT CAN ONLY BE DESCRIBED AS TERRORISM.
TNT
THERE ISN'T MUCH INFORMATION ON THE SUBJECT RESPONSIBLE FOR THIS ACT, EXCEPT FOR HIS NAME: **DEADPOOL.**
A MERCENARY WHO SELLS HIS SERVICES TO THE HIGHEST BIDDER AND WHO, UP UNTIL THIS POINT IN TIME, HAS OPERATED IN THE SHADOWS: A MAN WHO HAS NOW BECOME **PUBLIC ENEMY NUMBER ONE.**
WITH LOCAL LAW ENFORCEMENT WORKING IN CONCERT WITH THE F.B.I. IN AN UNPRECEDENTED NATIONAL MANHUNT, THE MAYOR HAS ASSURED THE PUBLIC THAT IT'S JUST A MATTER OF TIME BEFORE THE CULPRIT IS BROUGHT TO JUSTICE.

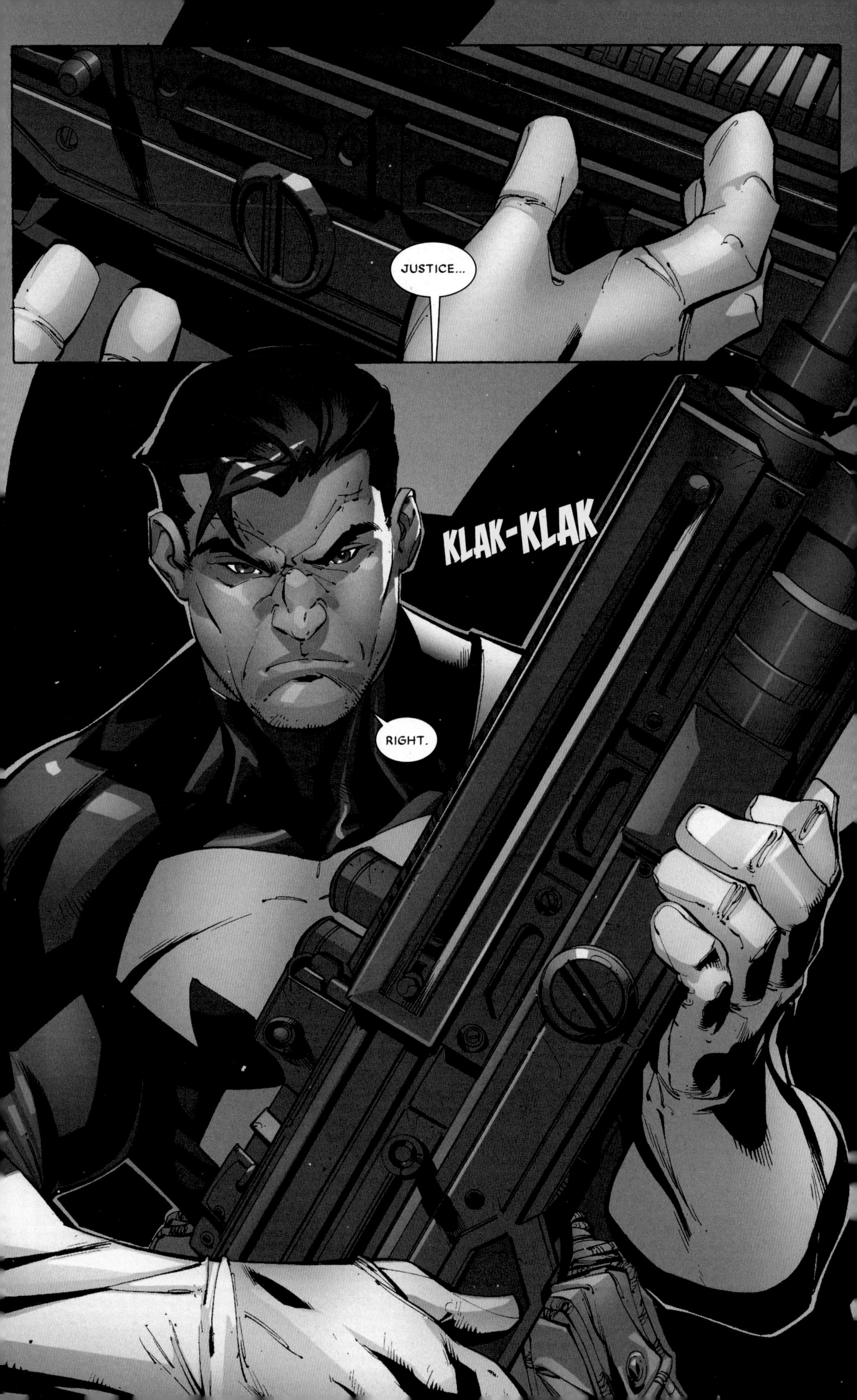
JUSTICE...
KLAK-KLAK
RIGHT.

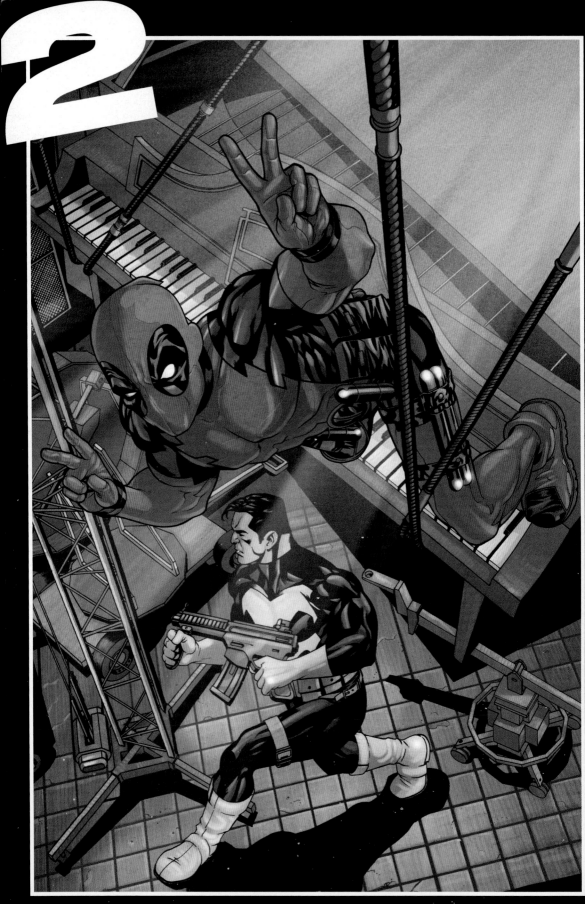

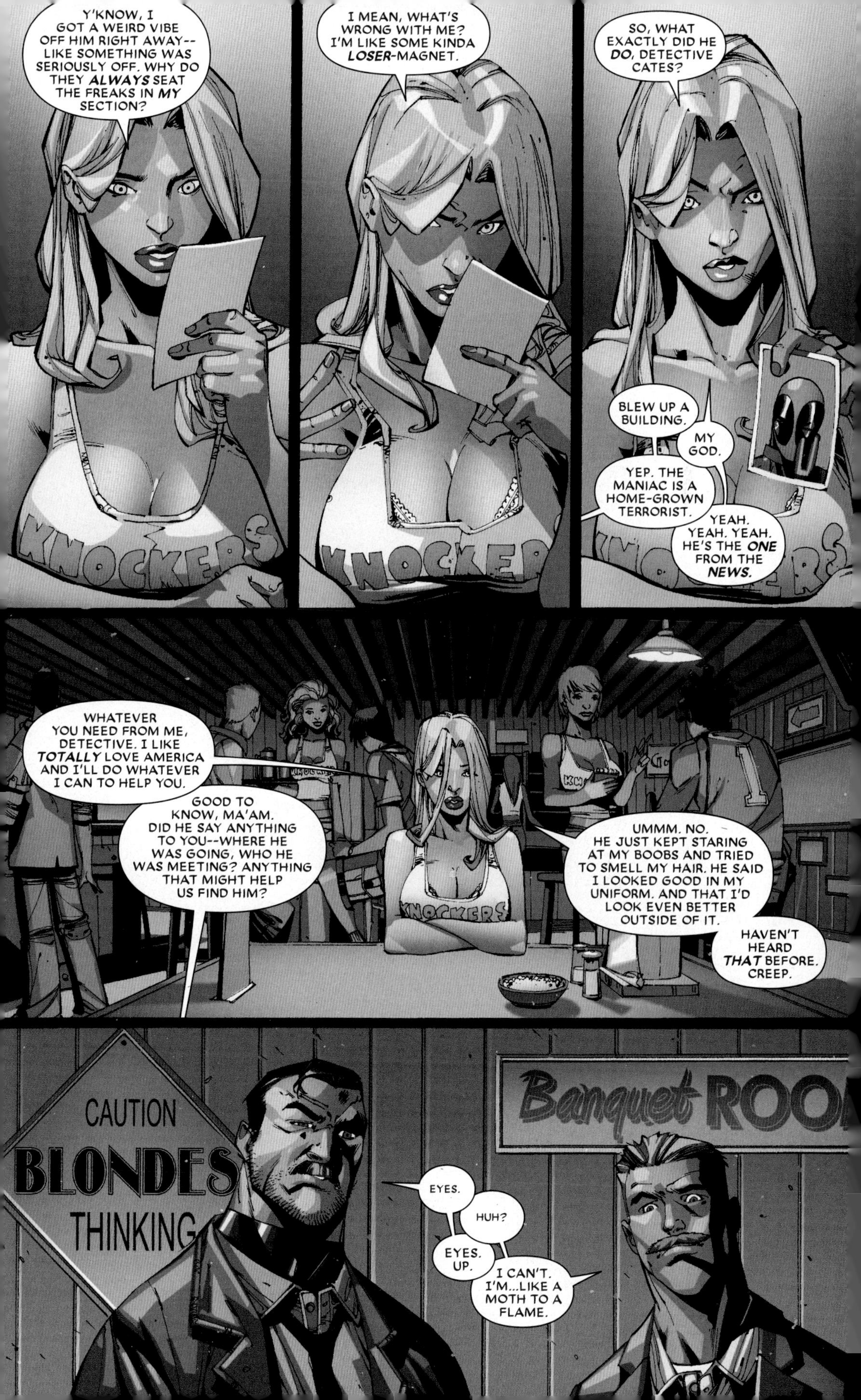

Y'KNOW, I GOT A WEIRD VIBE OFF HIM RIGHT AWAY--LIKE SOMETHING WAS SERIOUSLY OFF. WHY DO THEY *ALWAYS* SEAT THE FREAKS IN *MY* SECTION?
KNOCKERS
I MEAN, WHAT'S WRONG WITH ME? I'M LIKE SOME KINDA *LOSER*-MAGNET.
KNOCKERS
SO, WHAT EXACTLY DID HE *DO*, DETECTIVE CATES?
BLEW UP A BUILDING.
MY GOD.
YEP. THE MANIAC IS A HOME-GROWN TERRORIST.
YEAH. YEAH. YEAH. HE'S THE *ONE* FROM THE *NEWS.*
WHATEVER YOU NEED FROM ME, DETECTIVE. I LIKE *TOTALLY* LOVE AMERICA AND I'LL DO WHATEVER I CAN TO HELP YOU.
GOOD TO KNOW, MA'AM. DID HE SAY ANYTHING TO YOU--WHERE HE WAS GOING, WHO HE WAS MEETING? ANYTHING THAT MIGHT HELP US FIND HIM?
KNOCKERS
UMMM. NO. HE JUST KEPT STARING AT MY BOOBS AND TRIED TO SMELL MY HAIR. HE SAID I LOOKED GOOD IN MY UNIFORM. AND THAT I'D LOOK EVEN BETTER OUTSIDE OF IT.
HAVEN'T HEARD *THAT* BEFORE. CREEP.
CAUTION
BLONDES
THINKING
Banquet ROO
EYES.
HUH?
EYES. UP.
I CAN'T. I'M...LIKE A MOTH TO A FLAME.

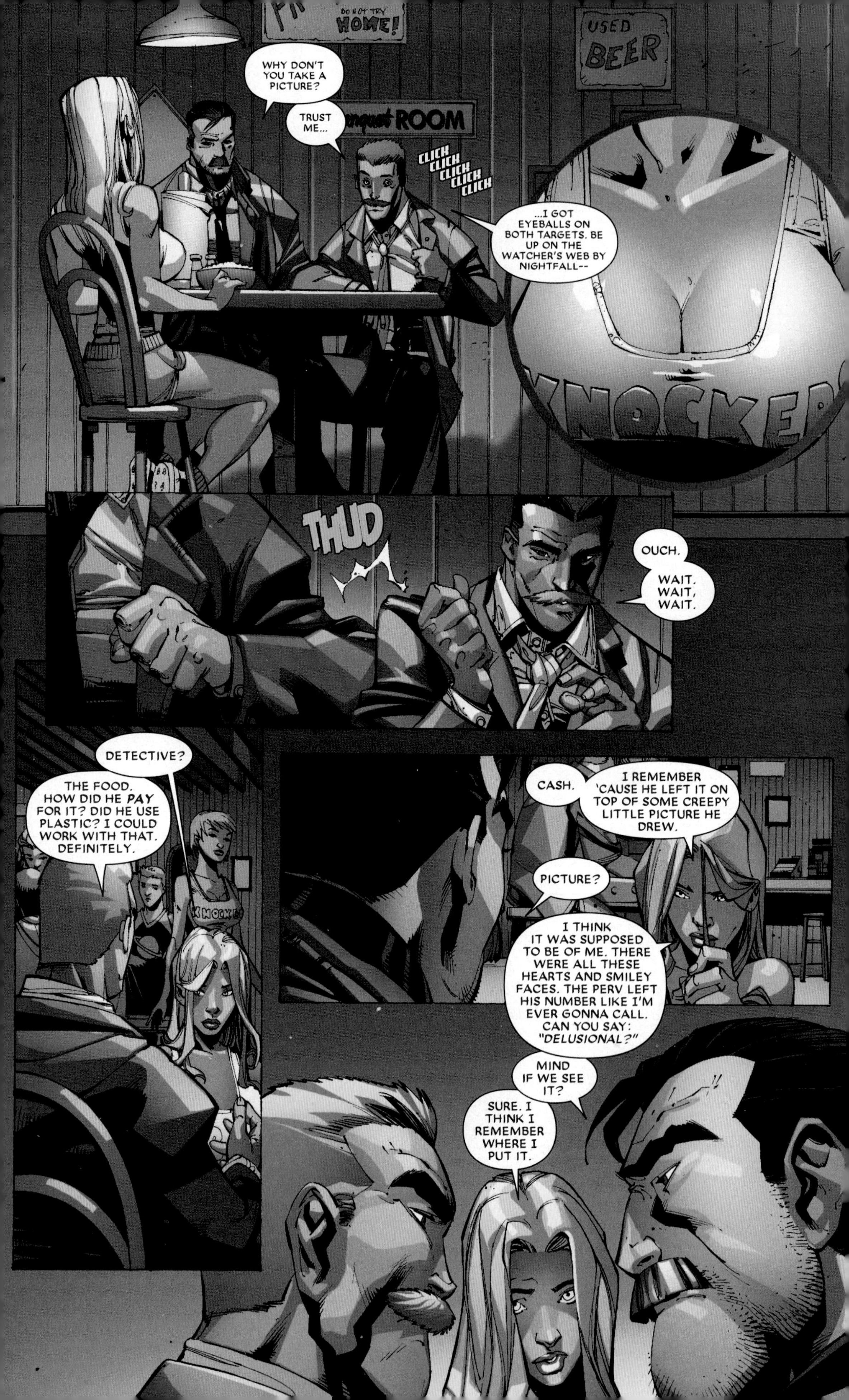
DO NOT TRY
HOME!
USED BEER
WHY DON'T YOU TAKE A PICTURE?
TRUST ME...
ROOM
CLICK CLICK CLICK CLICK CLICK
...I GOT EYEBALLS ON BOTH TARGETS. BE UP ON THE WATCHER'S WEB BY NIGHTFALL--
THUD
OUCH.
WAIT. WAIT, WAIT.
DETECTIVE?
THE FOOD. HOW DID HE *PAY* FOR IT? DID HE USE PLASTIC? I COULD WORK WITH THAT. DEFINITELY.
CASH.
I REMEMBER 'CAUSE HE LEFT IT ON TOP OF SOME CREEPY LITTLE PICTURE HE DREW.
PICTURE?
I THINK IT WAS SUPPOSED TO BE OF ME. THERE WERE ALL THESE HEARTS AND SMILEY FACES. THE PERV LEFT HIS NUMBER LIKE I'M EVER GONNA CALL. CAN YOU SAY: *"DELUSIONAL?"*
MIND IF WE SEE IT?
SURE. I THINK I REMEMBER WHERE I PUT IT.

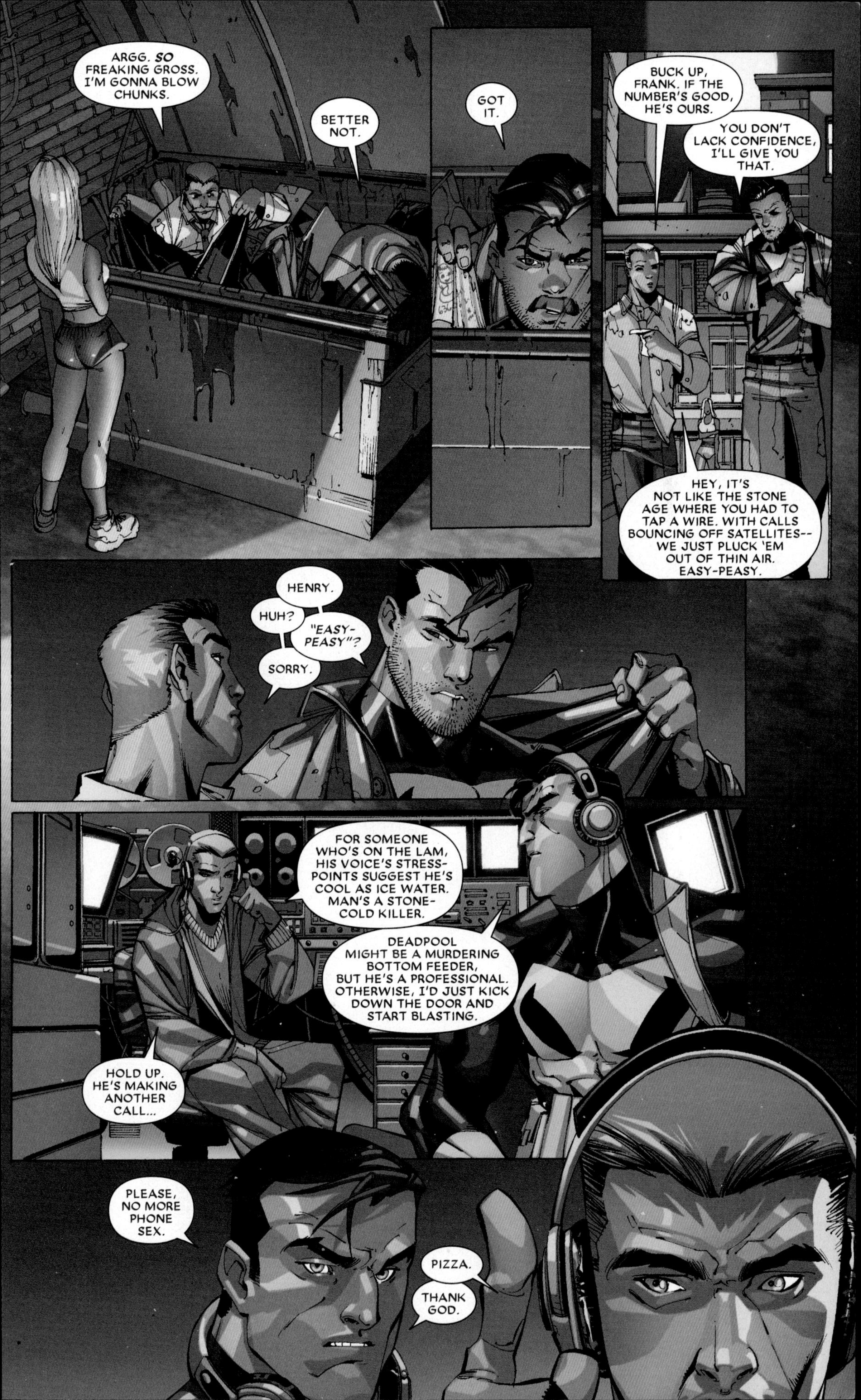
ARGG. SO FREAKING GROSS. I'M GONNA BLOW CHUNKS.
BETTER NOT.
GOT IT.
BUCK UP, FRANK. IF THE NUMBER'S GOOD, HE'S OURS.
YOU DON'T LACK CONFIDENCE, I'LL GIVE YOU THAT.
HEY, IT'S NOT LIKE THE STONE AGE WHERE YOU HAD TO TAP A WIRE. WITH CALLS BOUNCING OFF SATELLITES-- WE JUST PLUCK 'EM OUT OF THIN AIR. EASY-PEASY.
HENRY.
HUH?
"EASY-PEASY"?
SORRY.
FOR SOMEONE WHO'S ON THE LAM, HIS VOICE'S STRESS-POINTS SUGGEST HE'S COOL AS ICE WATER. MAN'S A STONE-COLD KILLER.
DEADPOOL MIGHT BE A MURDERING BOTTOM FEEDER, BUT HE'S A PROFESSIONAL. OTHERWISE, I'D JUST KICK DOWN THE DOOR AND START BLASTING.
HOLD UP. HE'S MAKING ANOTHER CALL...
PLEASE, NO MORE PHONE SEX.
PIZZA.
THANK GOD.

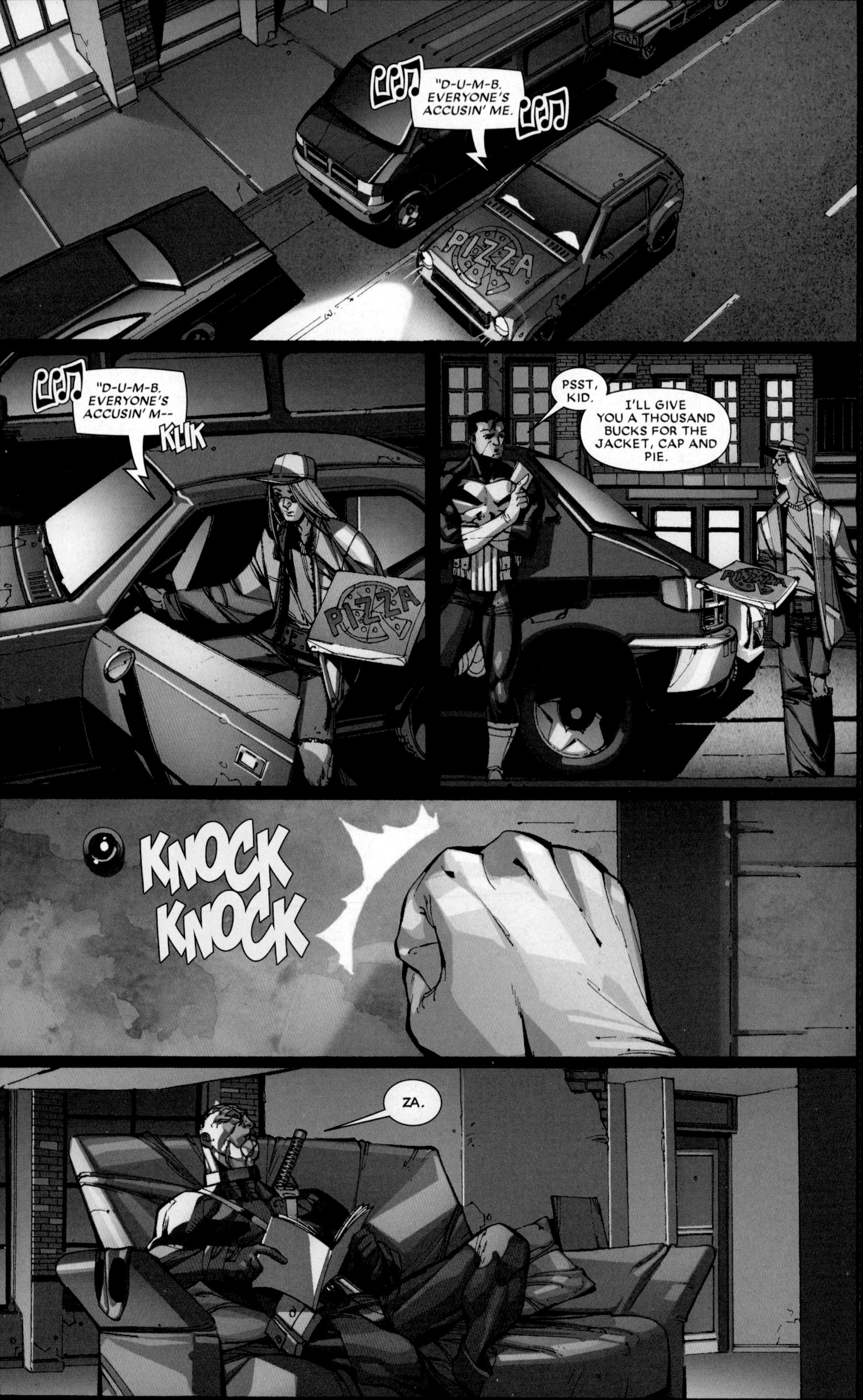
"D-U-M-B, EVERYONE'S ACCUSIN' ME.
"D-U-M-B, EVERYONE'S ACCUSIN' M--
KLIK
PSST, KID.
I'LL GIVE YOU A THOUSAND BUCKS FOR THE JACKET, CAP AND PIE.
KNOCK KNOCK
ZA.

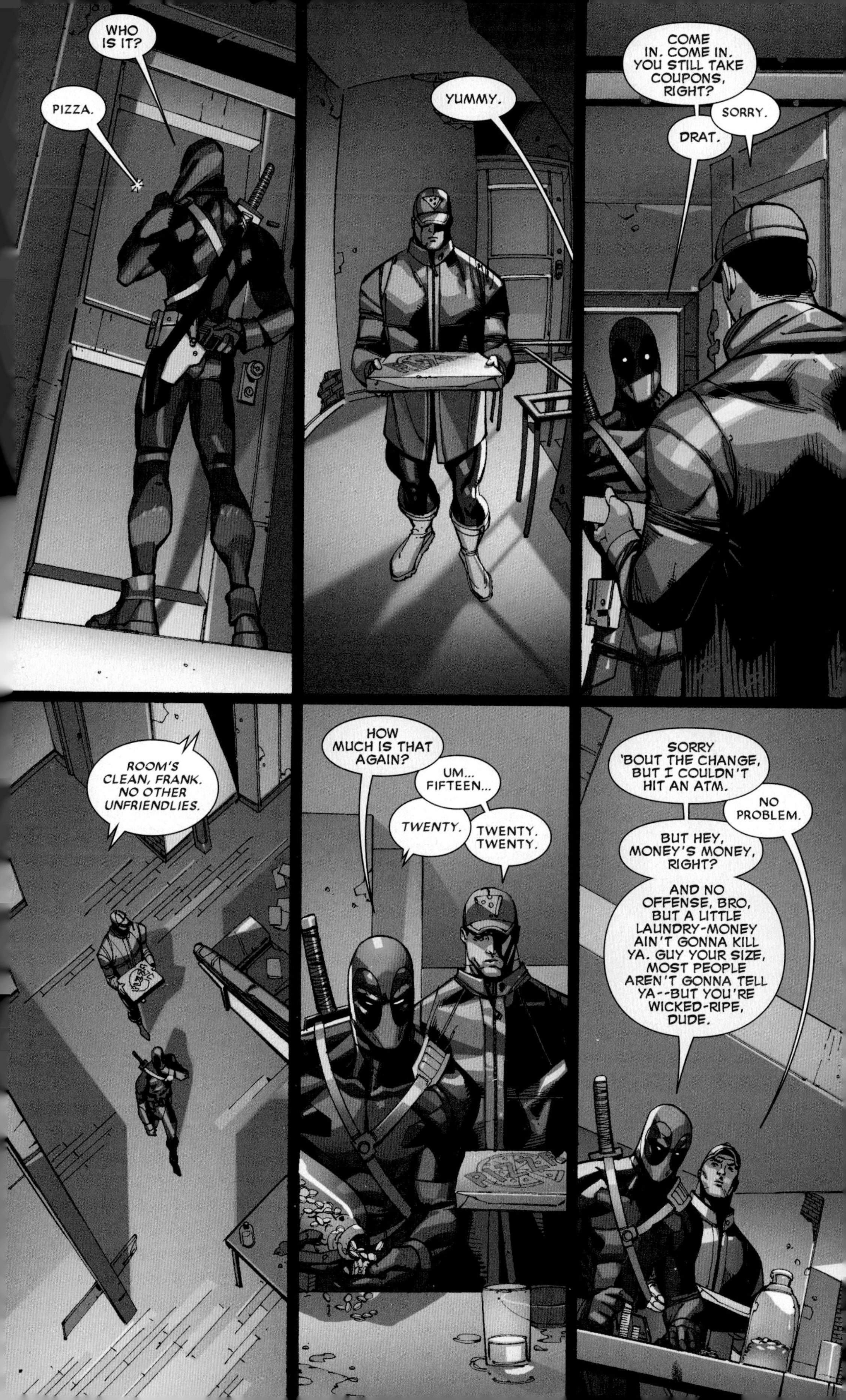
WHO IS IT?
PIZZA.
YUMMY.
COME IN. COME IN. YOU STILL TAKE COUPONS, RIGHT?
DRAT.
SORRY.
ROOM'S CLEAN, FRANK. NO OTHER UNFRIENDLIES.
HOW MUCH IS THAT AGAIN?
UM... FIFTEEN...
TWENTY.
TWENTY. TWENTY.
SORRY 'BOUT THE CHANGE, BUT I COULDN'T HIT AN ATM.
NO PROBLEM.
BUT HEY, MONEY'S MONEY, RIGHT?
AND NO OFFENSE, BRO, BUT A LITTLE LAUNDRY-MONEY AIN'T GONNA KILL YA. GUY YOUR SIZE, MOST PEOPLE AREN'T GONNA TELL YA--BUT YOU'RE WICKED-RIPE, DUDE.

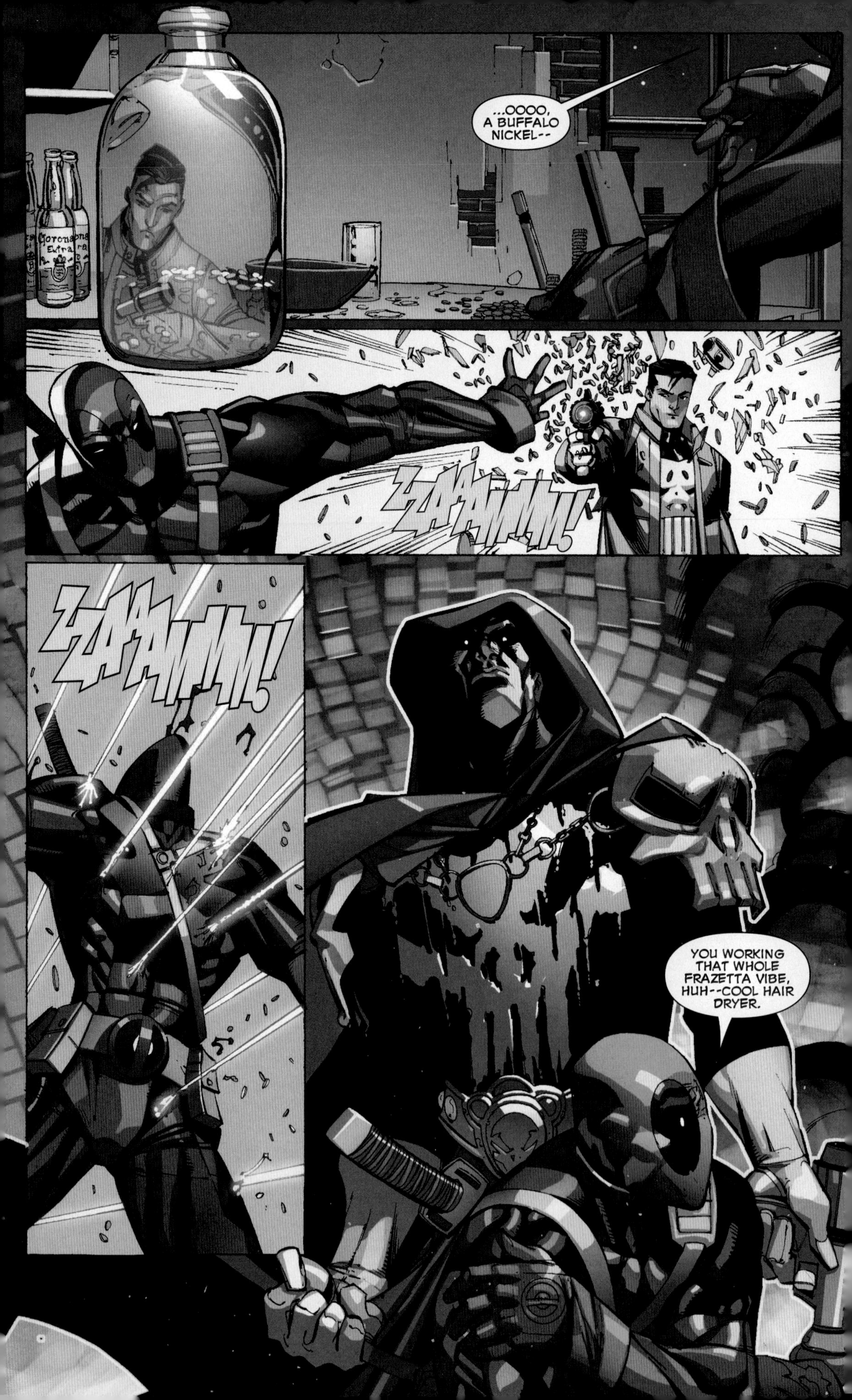
...OOOO, A BUFFALO NICKEL--
ZZAAMMM!
ZZAAMMM!
YOU WORKING THAT WHOLE FRAZETTA VIBE, HUH--COOL HAIR DRYER.

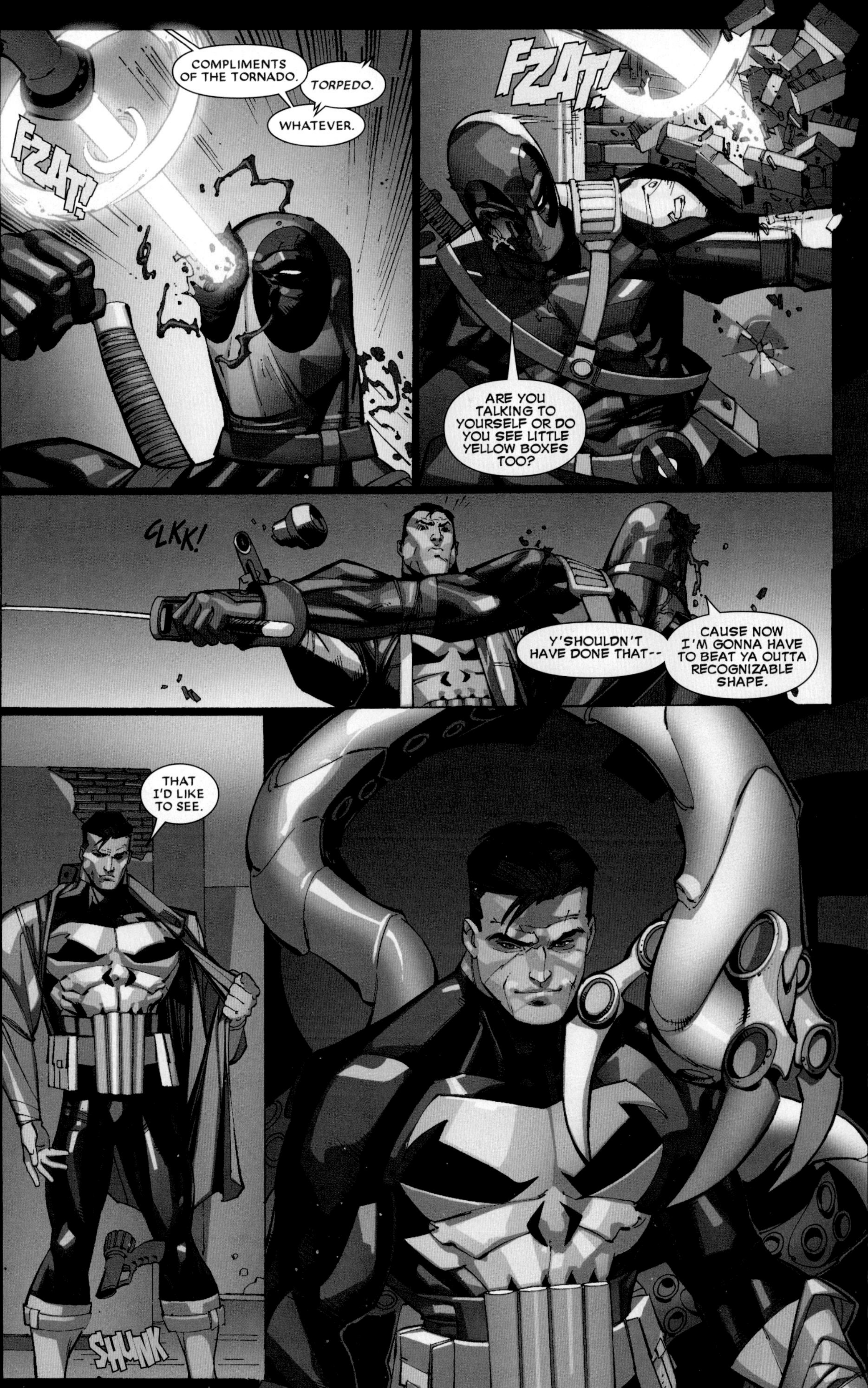

COMPLIMENTS OF THE TORNADO.
TORPEDO.
WHATEVER.
FZAT!
FZAT!
ARE YOU TALKING TO YOURSELF OR DO YOU SEE LITTLE YELLOW BOXES TOO?
CLKK!
Y'SHOULDN'T HAVE DONE THAT--
CAUSE NOW I'M GONNA HAVE TO BEAT YA OUTTA RECOGNIZABLE SHAPE.
THAT I'D LIKE TO SEE.
SHUNK

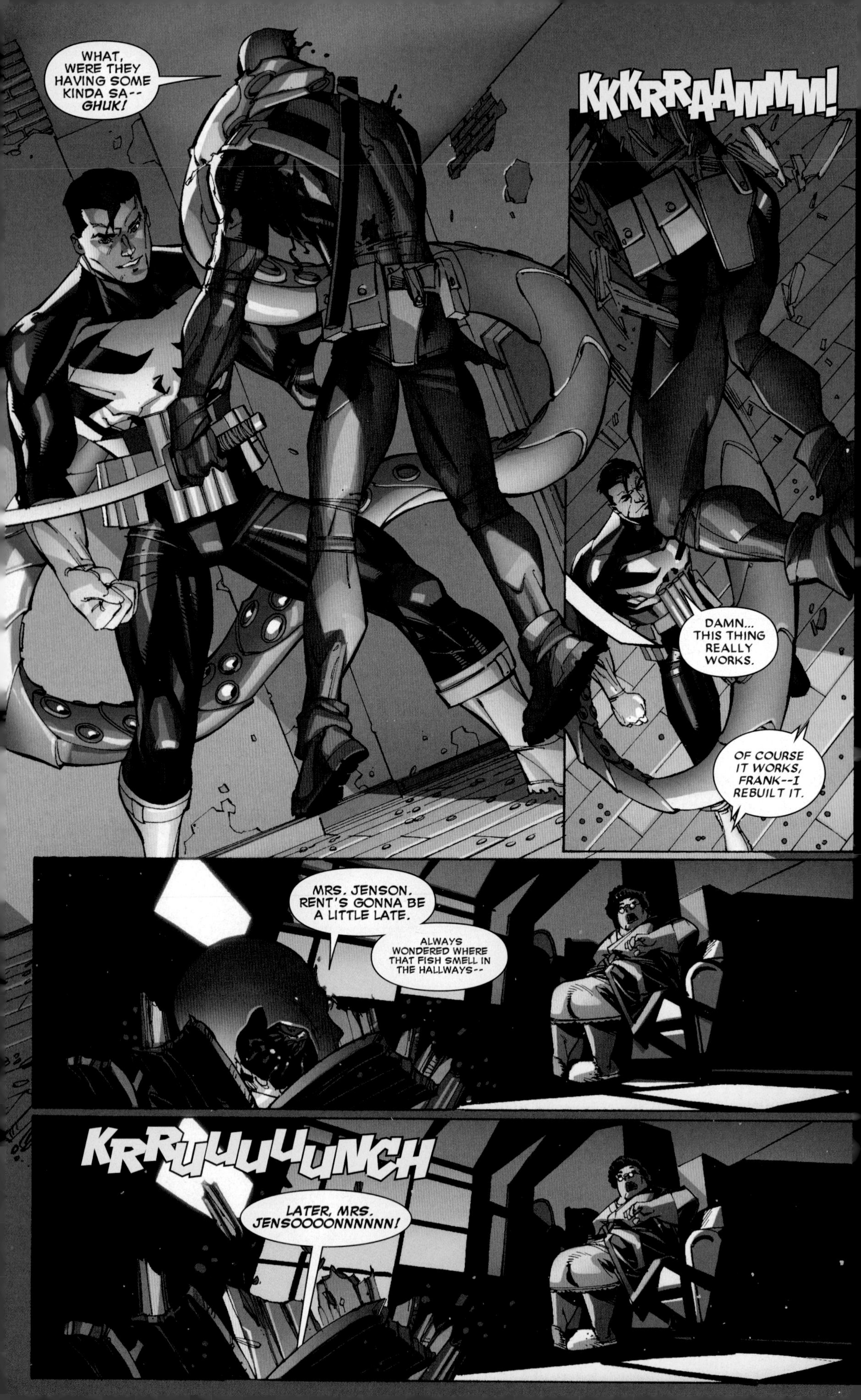
WHAT, WERE THEY HAVING SOME KINDA SA-- GHUK!
KKKRRAAMMM!
DAMN... THIS THING REALLY WORKS.
OF COURSE IT WORKS, FRANK--I REBUILT IT.
MRS. JENSON. RENT'S GONNA BE A LITTLE LATE.
ALWAYS WONDERED WHERE THAT FISH SMELL IN THE HALLWAYS--
KRRUUUUUNCH
LATER, MRS. JENSOOOONNNNNN!

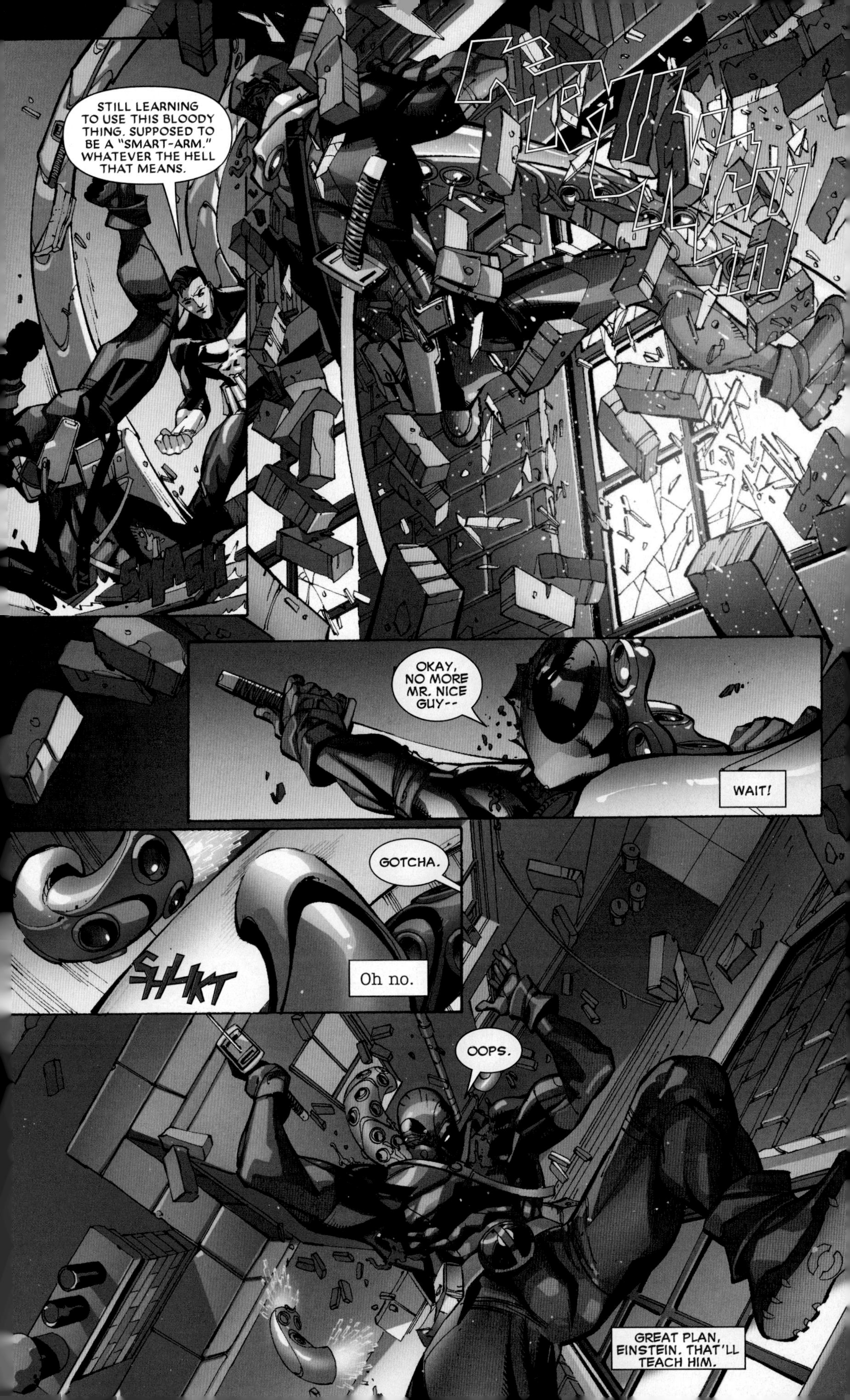

STILL LEARNING TO USE THIS BLOODY THING. SUPPOSED TO BE A "SMART-ARM." WHATEVER THE HELL THAT MEANS.
SMASH
OKAY, NO MORE MR. NICE GUY--
WAIT!
GOTCHA.
SHLIKT
Oh no.
OOPS.
GREAT PLAN, EINSTEIN. THAT'LL TEACH HIM.

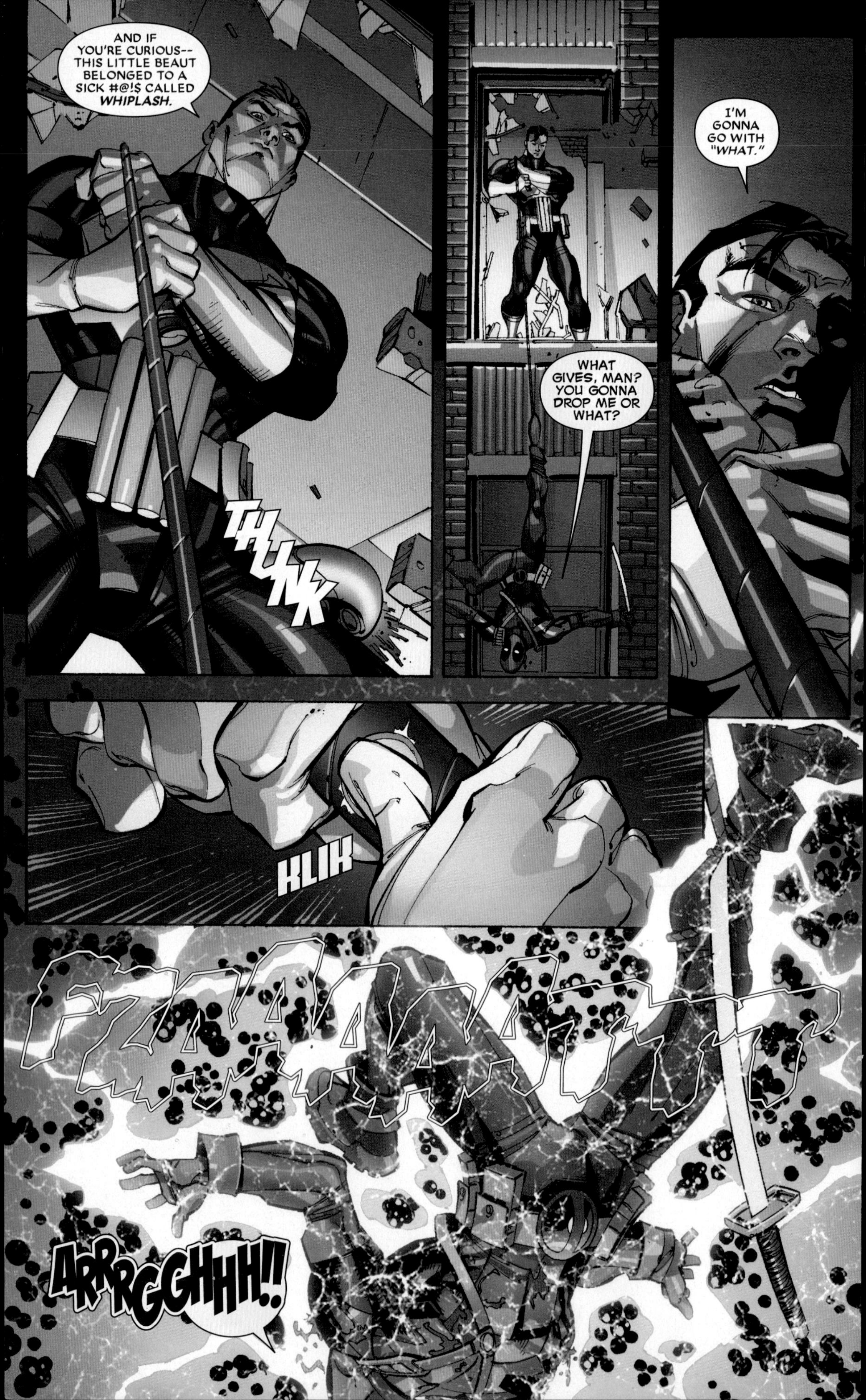
AND IF YOU'RE CURIOUS-- THIS LITTLE BEAUT BELONGED TO A SICK #@!$ CALLED WHIPLASH.
THUNK
WHAT GIVES, MAN? YOU GONNA DROP ME OR WHAT?
I'M GONNA GO WITH "WHAT."
KLIK
FZZAAAAZZT
ARRRGGHHH!!

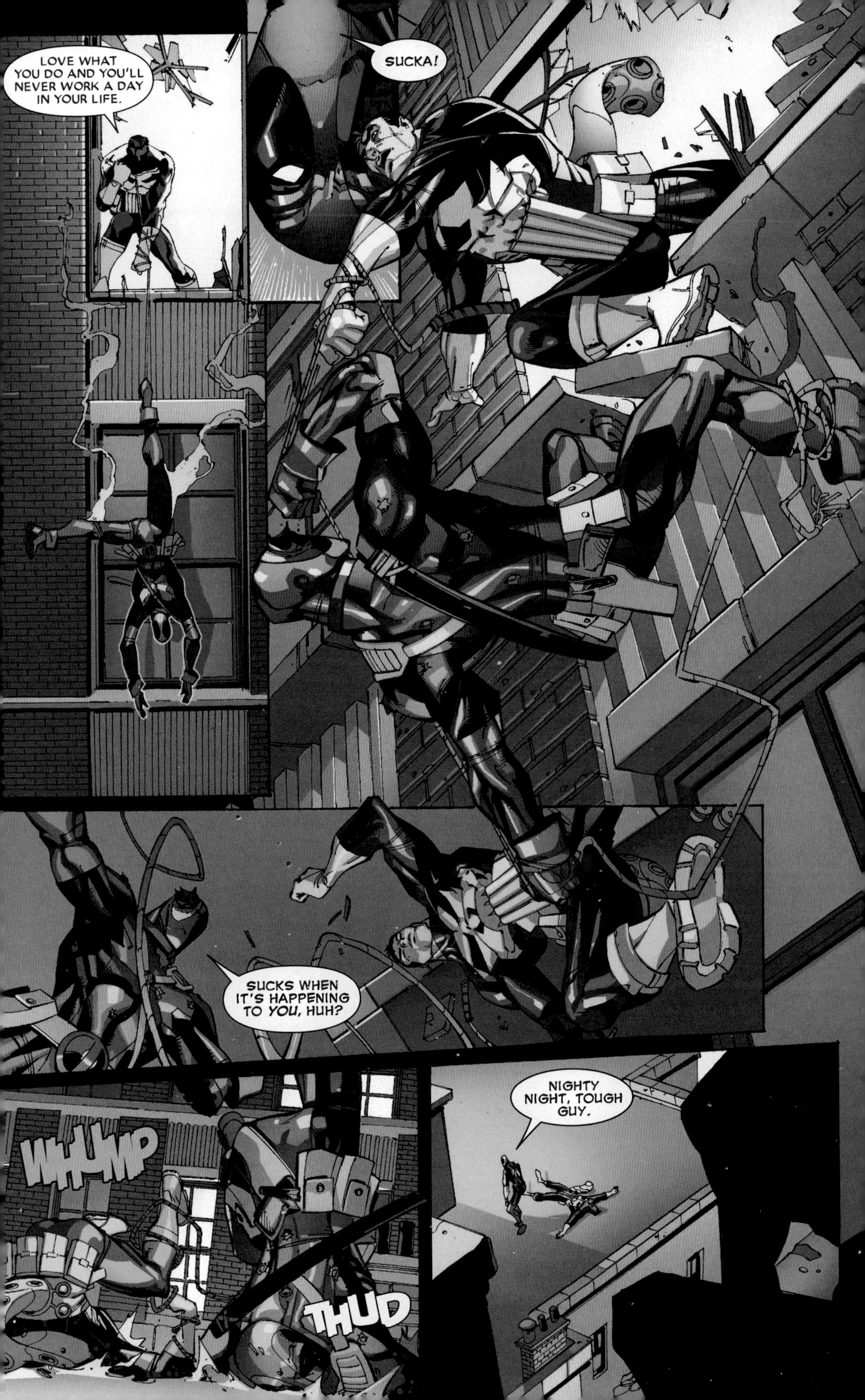
LOVE WHAT YOU DO AND YOU'LL NEVER WORK A DAY IN YOUR LIFE.
SUCKA!
SUCKS WHEN IT'S HAPPENING TO *YOU*, HUH?
WHUMP
THUD
NIGHTY NIGHT, TOUGH GUY.

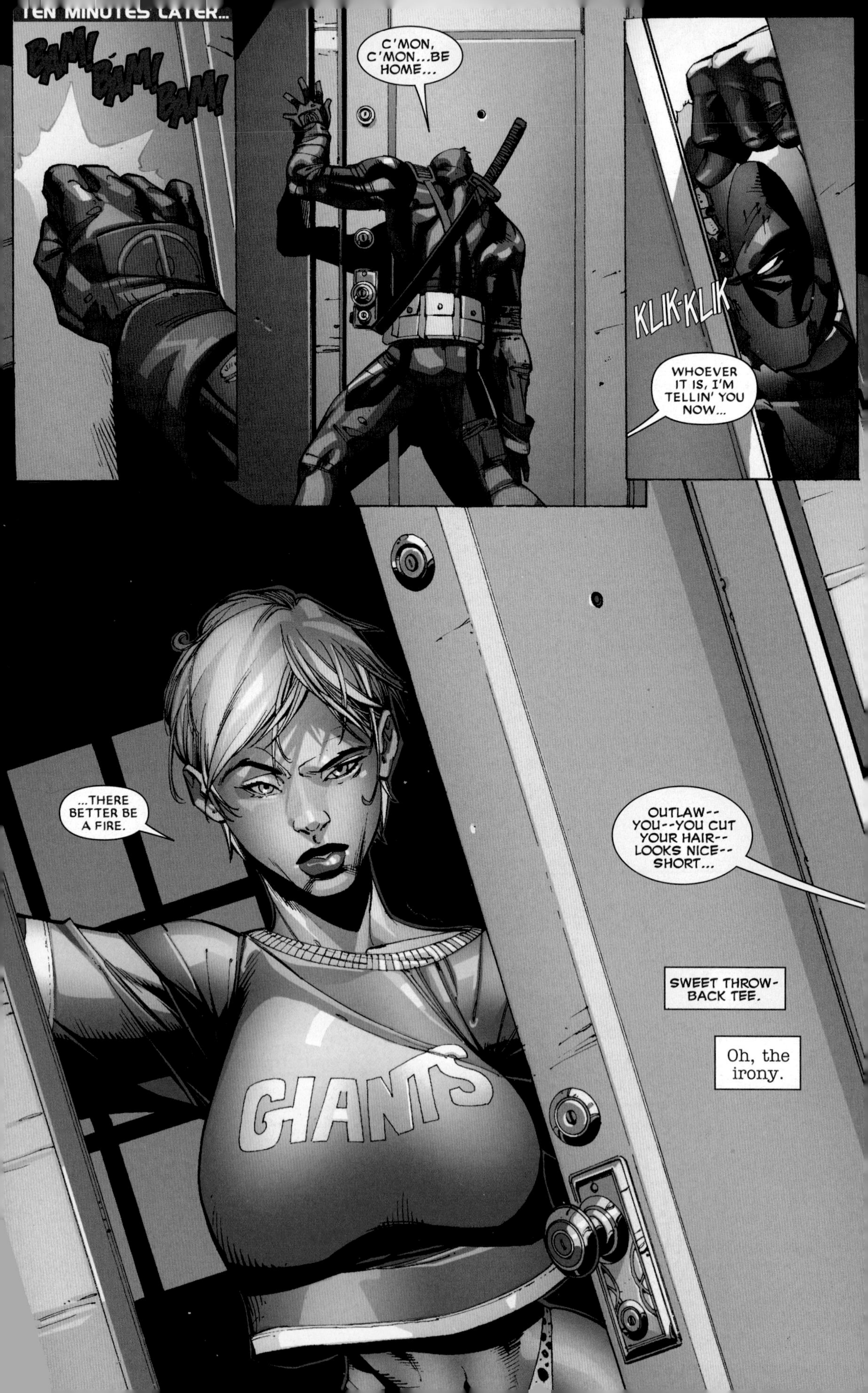

TEN MINUTES LATER...
BAM! BAM! BAM!
C'MON, C'MON...BE HOME...
KLIK-KLIK
WHOEVER IT IS, I'M TELLIN' YOU NOW...
...THERE BETTER BE A FIRE.
OUTLAW-- YOU--YOU CUT YOUR HAIR-- LOOKS NICE-- SHORT...
SWEET THROW-BACK TEE.
Oh, the irony.
GIANTS

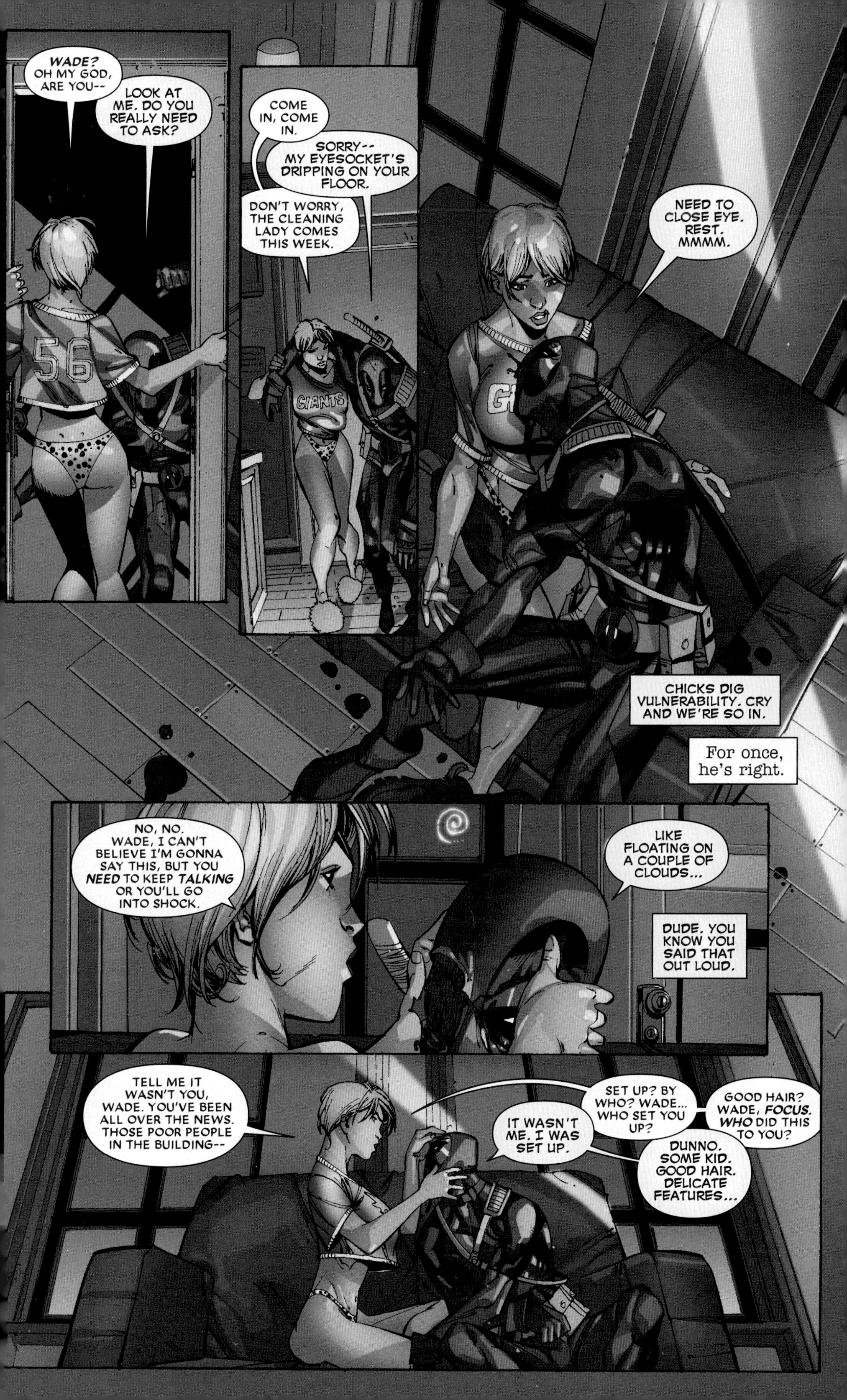

WADE? OH MY GOD, ARE YOU--
LOOK AT ME. DO YOU REALLY NEED TO ASK?
COME IN, COME IN.
SORRY-- MY EYESOCKET'S DRIPPING ON YOUR FLOOR.
DON'T WORRY, THE CLEANING LADY COMES THIS WEEK.
NEED TO CLOSE EYE. REST. MMMM.
CHICKS DIG VULNERABILITY. CRY AND WE'RE SO IN.
For once, he's right.
NO, NO. WADE, I CAN'T BELIEVE I'M GONNA SAY THIS, BUT YOU NEED TO KEEP TALKING OR YOU'LL GO INTO SHOCK.
LIKE FLOATING ON A COUPLE OF CLOUDS...
DUDE. YOU KNOW YOU SAID THAT OUT LOUD.
TELL ME IT WASN'T YOU, WADE. YOU'VE BEEN ALL OVER THE NEWS. THOSE POOR PEOPLE IN THE BUILDING--
IT WASN'T ME. I WAS SET UP.
SET UP? BY WHO? WADE... WHO SET YOU UP?
DUNNO. SOME KID. GOOD HAIR. DELICATE FEATURES...
GOOD HAIR? WADE, FOCUS. WHO DID THIS TO YOU?

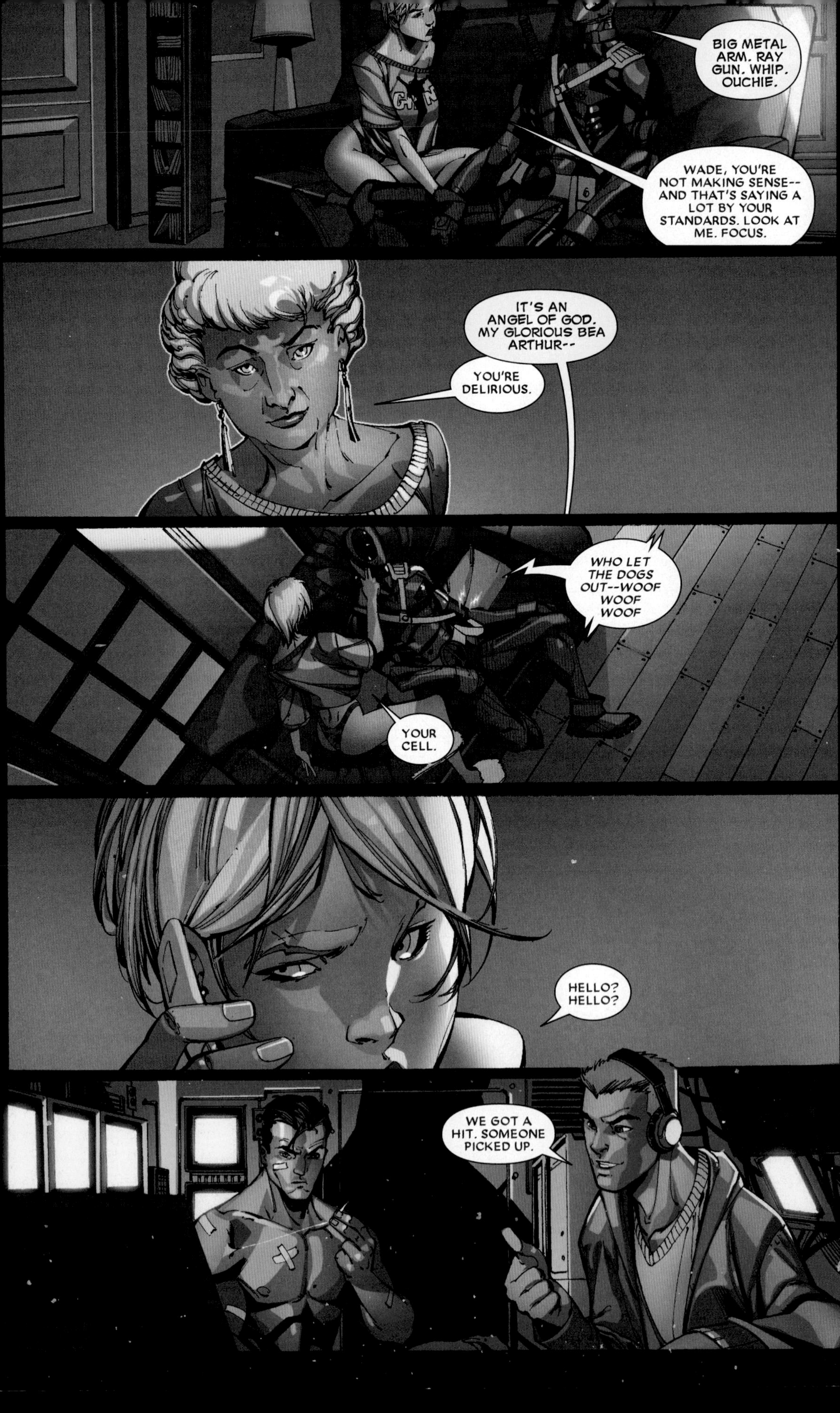
BIG METAL ARM. RAY GUN. WHIP. OUCHIE.
WADE, YOU'RE NOT MAKING SENSE-- AND THAT'S SAYING A LOT BY YOUR STANDARDS. LOOK AT ME. FOCUS.
IT'S AN ANGEL OF GOD. MY GLORIOUS BEA ARTHUR--
YOU'RE DELIRIOUS.
WHO LET THE DOGS OUT--WOOF WOOF WOOF
YOUR CELL.
HELLO? HELLO?
WE GOT A HIT. SOMEONE PICKED UP.

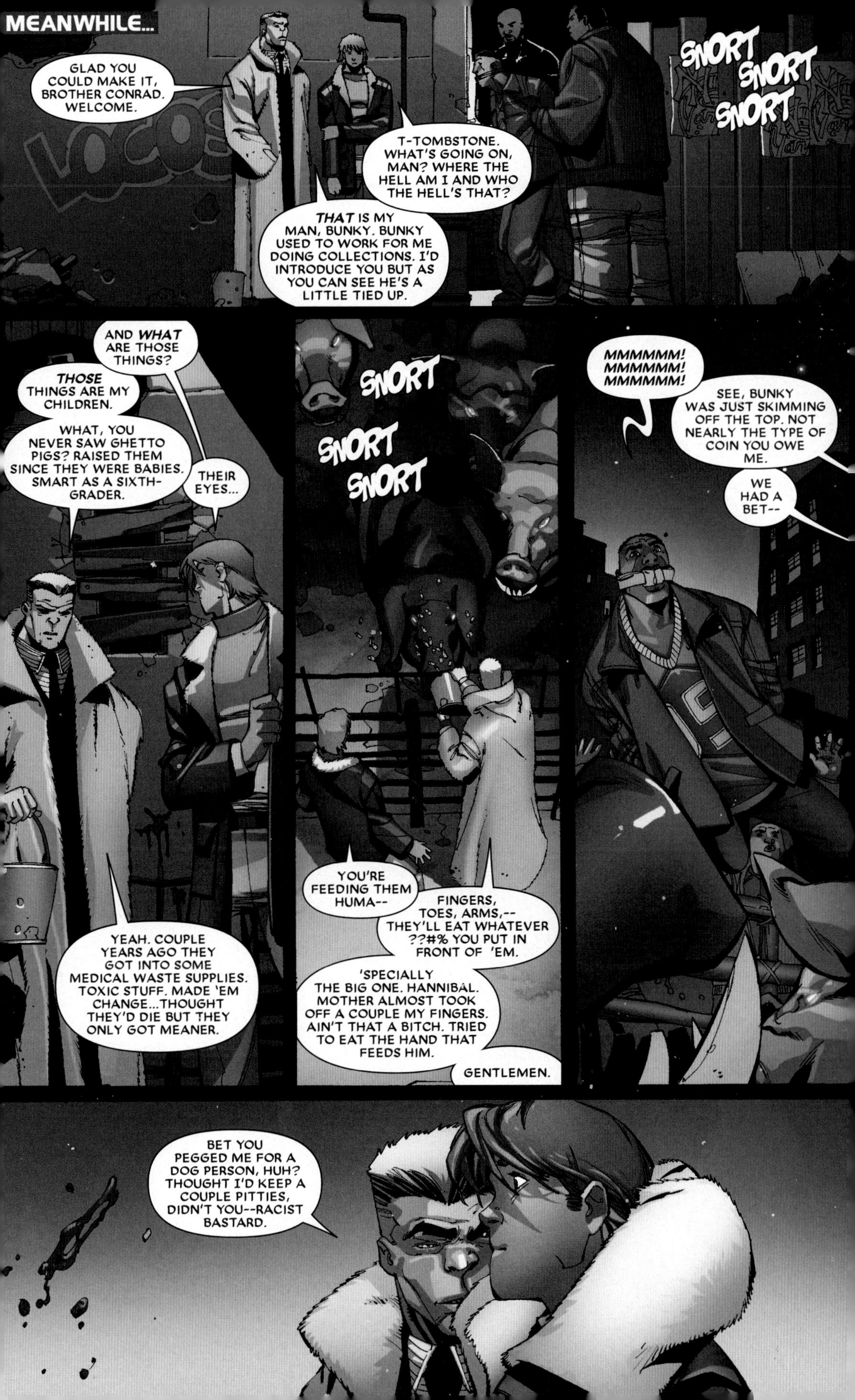
MEANWHILE...
GLAD YOU COULD MAKE IT, BROTHER CONRAD. WELCOME.
T-TOMBSTONE. WHAT'S GOING ON, MAN? WHERE THE HELL AM I AND WHO THE HELL'S THAT?
THAT IS MY MAN, BUNKY. BUNKY USED TO WORK FOR ME DOING COLLECTIONS. I'D INTRODUCE YOU BUT AS YOU CAN SEE HE'S A LITTLE TIED UP.
SNORT SNORT SNORT
AND *WHAT* ARE THOSE THINGS?
THOSE THINGS ARE MY CHILDREN.
WHAT, YOU NEVER SAW GHETTO PIGS? RAISED THEM SINCE THEY WERE BABIES. SMART AS A SIXTH-GRADER.
THEIR EYES...
YEAH. COUPLE YEARS AGO THEY GOT INTO SOME MEDICAL WASTE SUPPLIES. TOXIC STUFF. MADE 'EM CHANGE...THOUGHT THEY'D DIE BUT THEY ONLY GOT MEANER.
SNORT
SNORT
SNORT
YOU'RE FEEDING THEM HUMA--
FINGERS, TOES, ARMS,-- THEY'LL EAT WHATEVER ??#% YOU PUT IN FRONT OF 'EM.
'SPECIALLY THE BIG ONE. HANNIBAL. MOTHER ALMOST TOOK OFF A COUPLE MY FINGERS. AIN'T THAT A BITCH. TRIED TO EAT THE HAND THAT FEEDS HIM.
GENTLEMEN.
MMMMMM! MMMMMM! MMMMMM!
SEE, BUNKY WAS JUST SKIMMING OFF THE TOP. NOT NEARLY THE TYPE OF COIN YOU OWE ME.
WE HAD A BET--
BET YOU PEGGED ME FOR A DOG PERSON, HUH? THOUGHT I'D KEEP A COUPLE PITTIES, DIDN'T YOU--RACIST BASTARD.

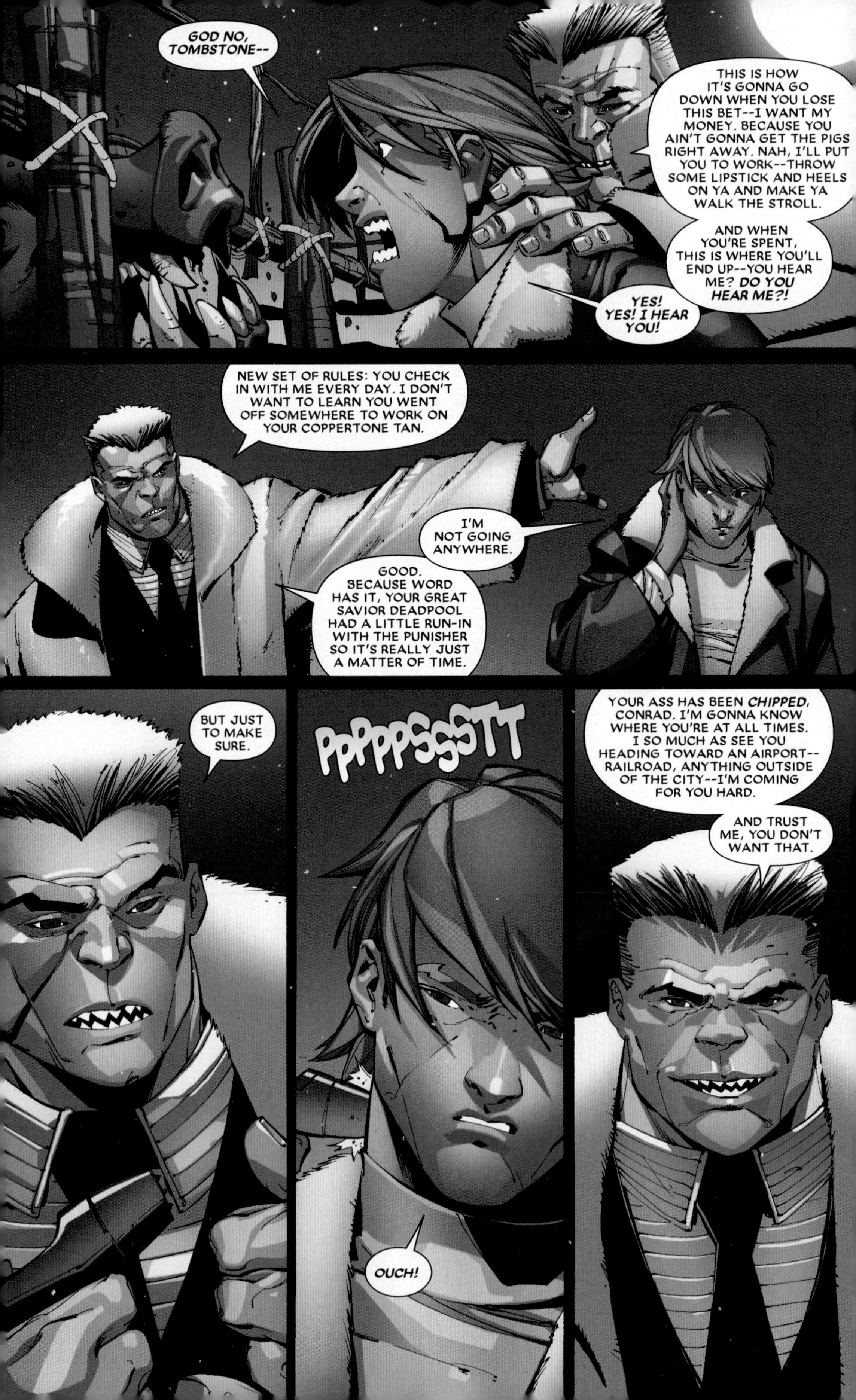
GOD NO, TOMBSTONE--
THIS IS HOW IT'S GONNA GO DOWN WHEN YOU LOSE THIS BET--I WANT MY MONEY. BECAUSE YOU AIN'T GONNA GET THE PIGS RIGHT AWAY. NAH, I'LL PUT YOU TO WORK--THROW SOME LIPSTICK AND HEELS ON YA AND MAKE YA WALK THE STROLL.
AND WHEN YOU'RE SPENT, THIS IS WHERE YOU'LL END UP--YOU HEAR ME? DO YOU HEAR ME?!
YES! YES! I HEAR YOU!
NEW SET OF RULES: YOU CHECK IN WITH ME EVERY DAY. I DON'T WANT TO LEARN YOU WENT OFF SOMEWHERE TO WORK ON YOUR COPPERTONE TAN.
I'M NOT GOING ANYWHERE.
GOOD. BECAUSE WORD HAS IT, YOUR GREAT SAVIOR DEADPOOL HAD A LITTLE RUN-IN WITH THE PUNISHER SO IT'S REALLY JUST A MATTER OF TIME.
BUT JUST TO MAKE SURE.
PPPPPSSSSTT
OUCH!
YOUR ASS HAS BEEN CHIPPED, CONRAD. I'M GONNA KNOW WHERE YOU'RE AT ALL TIMES. I SO MUCH AS SEE YOU HEADING TOWARD AN AIRPORT--RAILROAD, ANYTHING OUTSIDE OF THE CITY--I'M COMING FOR YOU HARD.
AND TRUST ME, YOU DON'T WANT THAT.

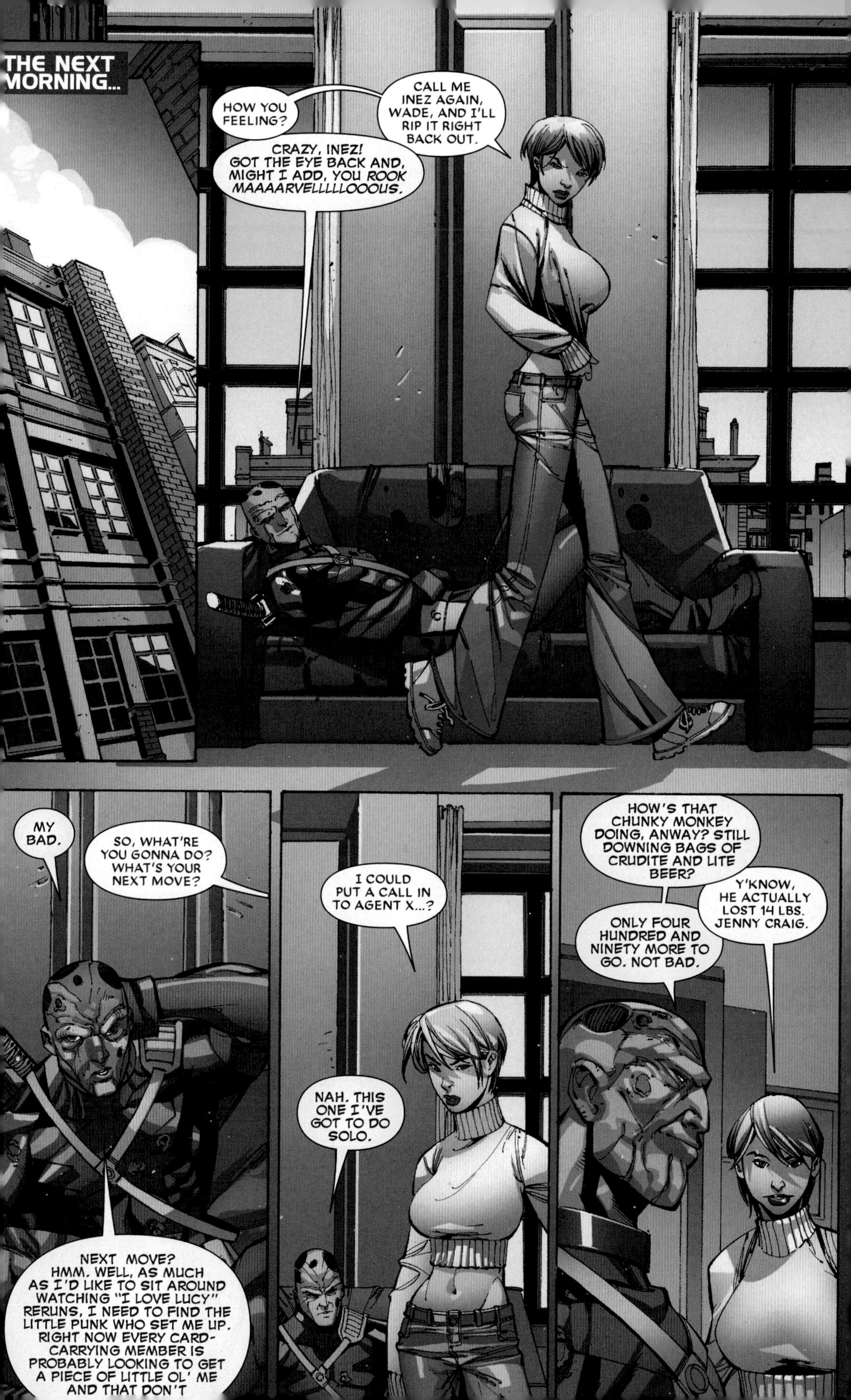
THE NEXT MORNING...
HOW YOU FEELING?
CRAZY, INEZ! GOT THE EYE BACK AND, MIGHT I ADD, YOU ROOK MAAAARVELLLLLOOOUS.
CALL ME INEZ AGAIN, WADE, AND I'LL RIP IT RIGHT BACK OUT.
MY BAD.
SO, WHAT'RE YOU GONNA DO? WHAT'S YOUR NEXT MOVE?
NEXT MOVE? HMM. WELL, AS MUCH AS I'D LIKE TO SIT AROUND WATCHING "I LOVE LUCY" RERUNS, I NEED TO FIND THE LITTLE PUNK WHO SET ME UP. RIGHT NOW EVERY CARD-CARRYING MEMBER IS PROBABLY LOOKING TO GET A PIECE OF LITTLE OL' ME AND THAT DON'T
I COULD PUT A CALL IN TO AGENT X...?
NAH. THIS ONE I'VE GOT TO DO SOLO.
HOW'S THAT CHUNKY MONKEY DOING, ANWAY? STILL DOWNING BAGS OF CRUDITE AND LITE BEER?
Y'KNOW, HE ACTUALLY LOST 14 LBS. JENNY CRAIG.
ONLY FOUR HUNDRED AND NINETY MORE TO GO. NOT BAD.

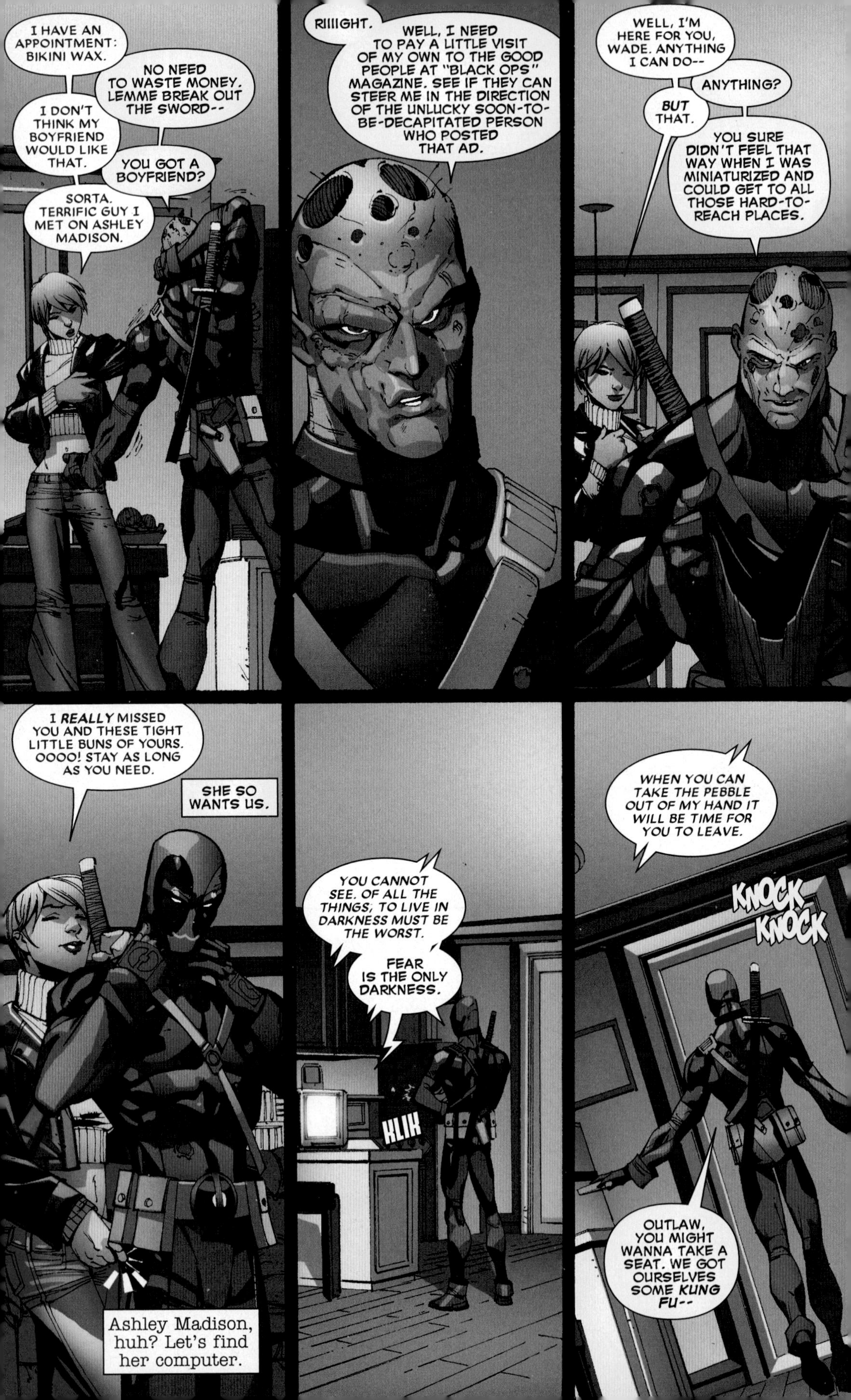
I HAVE AN APPOINTMENT: BIKINI WAX.
NO NEED TO WASTE MONEY. LEMME BREAK OUT THE SWORD--
I DON'T THINK MY BOYFRIEND WOULD LIKE THAT.
YOU GOT A BOYFRIEND?
SORTA. TERRIFIC GUY I MET ON ASHLEY MADISON.
RIIIIGHT.
WELL, I NEED TO PAY A LITTLE VISIT OF MY OWN TO THE GOOD PEOPLE AT "BLACK OPS" MAGAZINE. SEE IF THEY CAN STEER ME IN THE DIRECTION OF THE UNLUCKY SOON-TO-BE-DECAPITATED PERSON WHO POSTED THAT AD.
WELL, I'M HERE FOR YOU, WADE. ANYTHING I CAN DO--
BUT THAT.
ANYTHING?
YOU SURE DIDN'T FEEL THAT WAY WHEN I WAS MINIATURIZED AND COULD GET TO ALL THOSE HARD-TO-REACH PLACES.
I REALLY MISSED YOU AND THESE TIGHT LITTLE BUNS OF YOURS. OOOO! STAY AS LONG AS YOU NEED.
SHE SO WANTS US.
Ashley Madison, huh? Let's find her computer.
YOU CANNOT SEE. OF ALL THE THINGS, TO LIVE IN DARKNESS MUST BE THE WORST.
FEAR IS THE ONLY DARKNESS.
KLIK
WHEN YOU CAN TAKE THE PEBBLE OUT OF MY HAND IT WILL BE TIME FOR YOU TO LEAVE.
KNOCK KNOCK
OUTLAW, YOU MIGHT WANNA TAKE A SEAT. WE GOT OURSELVES SOME KUNG FU--

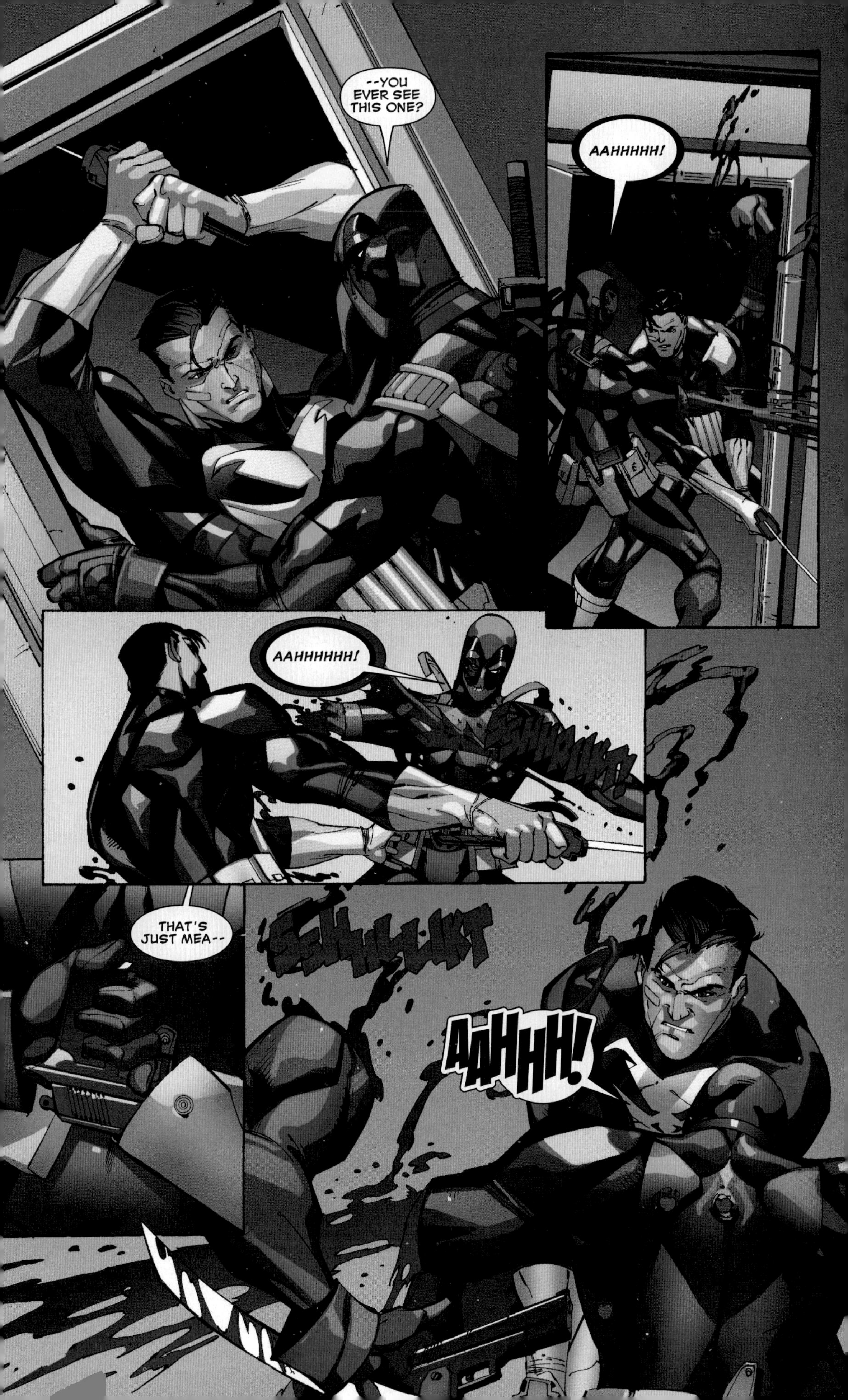
--YOU EVER SEE THIS ONE?
AAHHHHH!
AAHHHHHH!
THAT'S JUST MEA--
AAHHH!

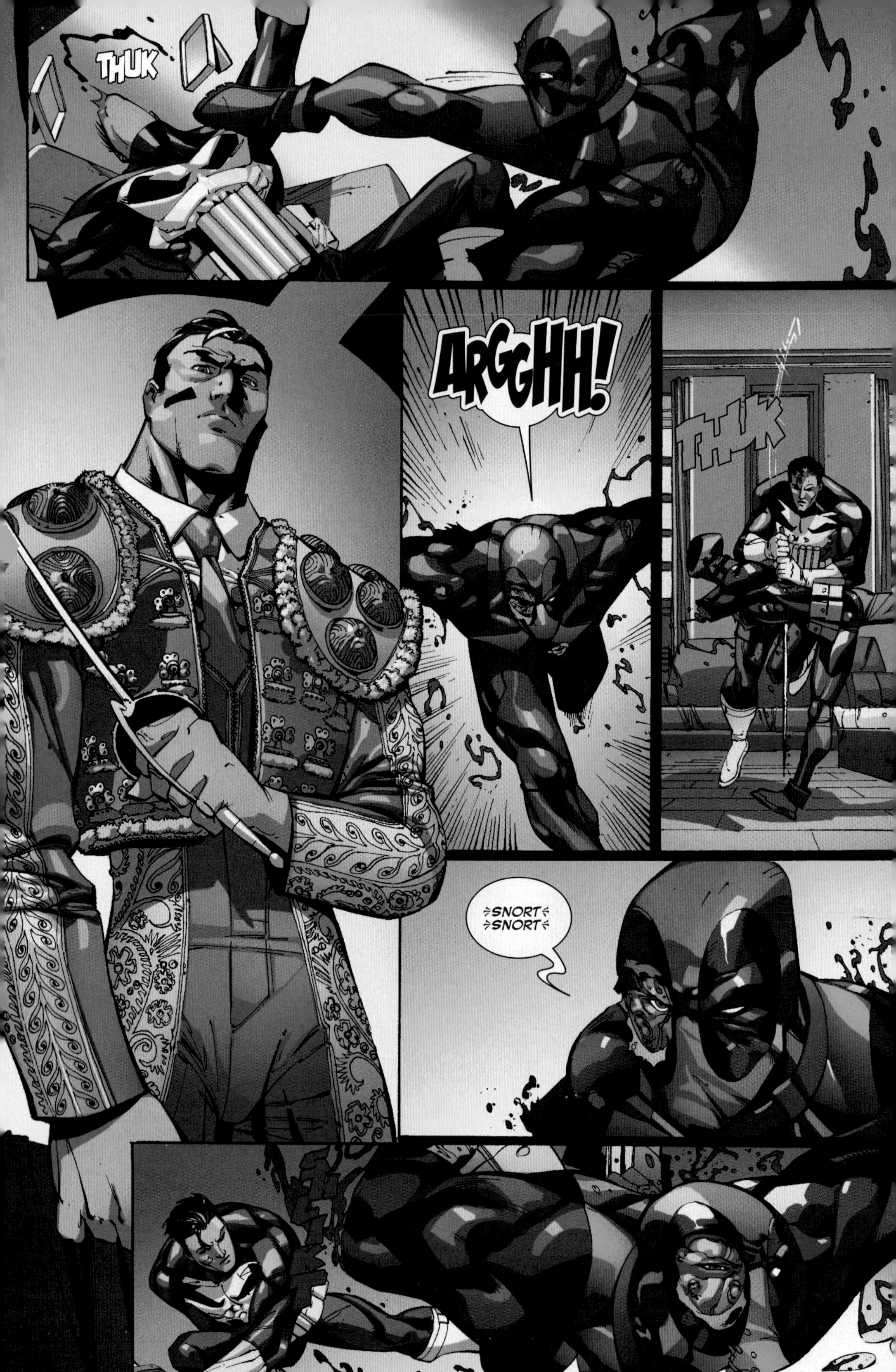
THUK
ARGGHH!
THUK
SNORT
SNORT

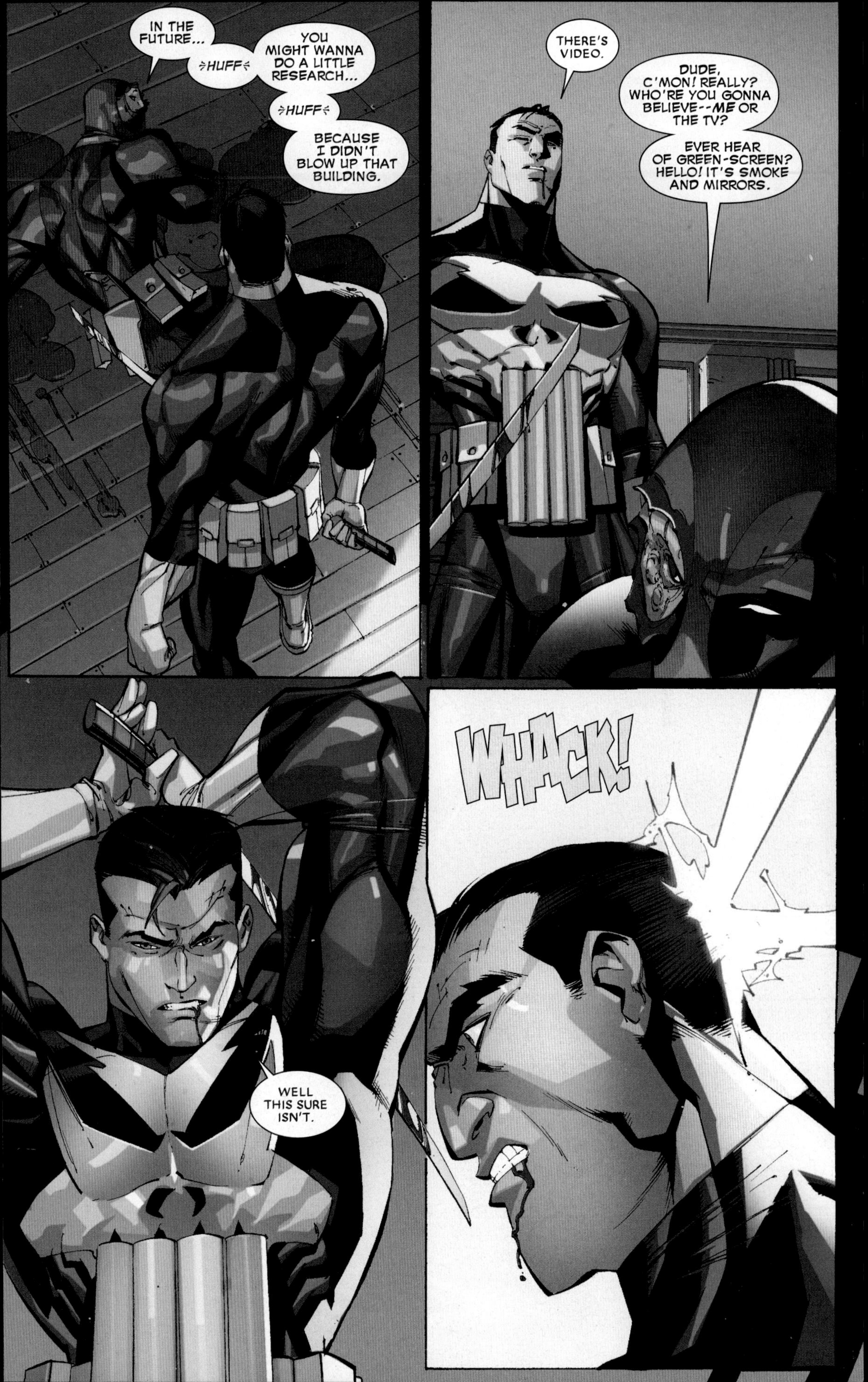
IN THE FUTURE...
HUFF
YOU MIGHT WANNA DO A LITTLE RESEARCH...
HUFF
BECAUSE I DIDN'T BLOW UP THAT BUILDING.
THERE'S VIDEO.
DUDE, C'MON! REALLY? WHO'RE YOU GONNA BELIEVE--ME OR THE TV?
EVER HEAR OF GREEN-SCREEN? HELLO! IT'S SMOKE AND MIRRORS.
WELL THIS SURE ISN'T.
WHACK!

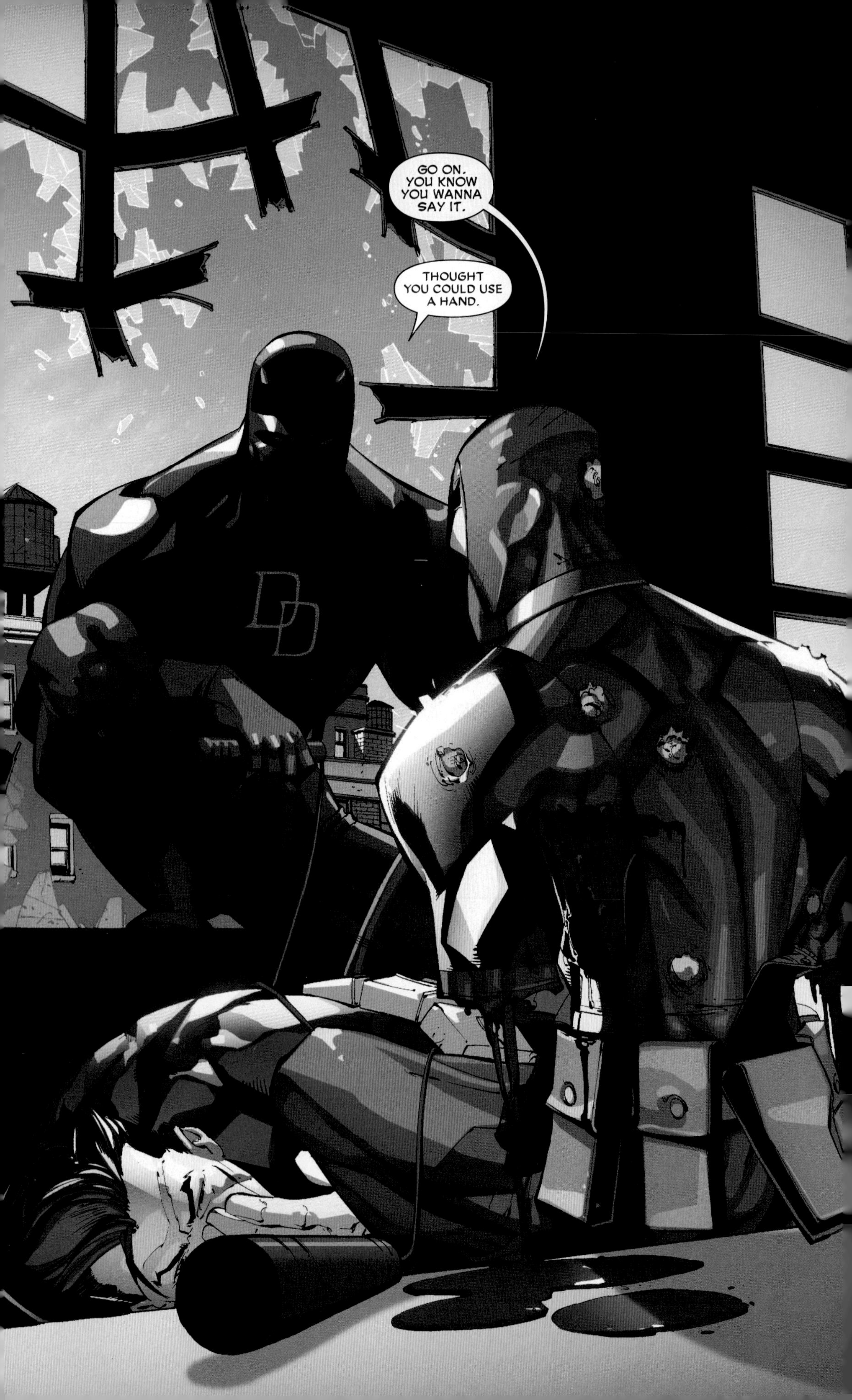
GO ON. YOU KNOW YOU WANNA SAY IT.
THOUGHT YOU COULD USE A HAND.

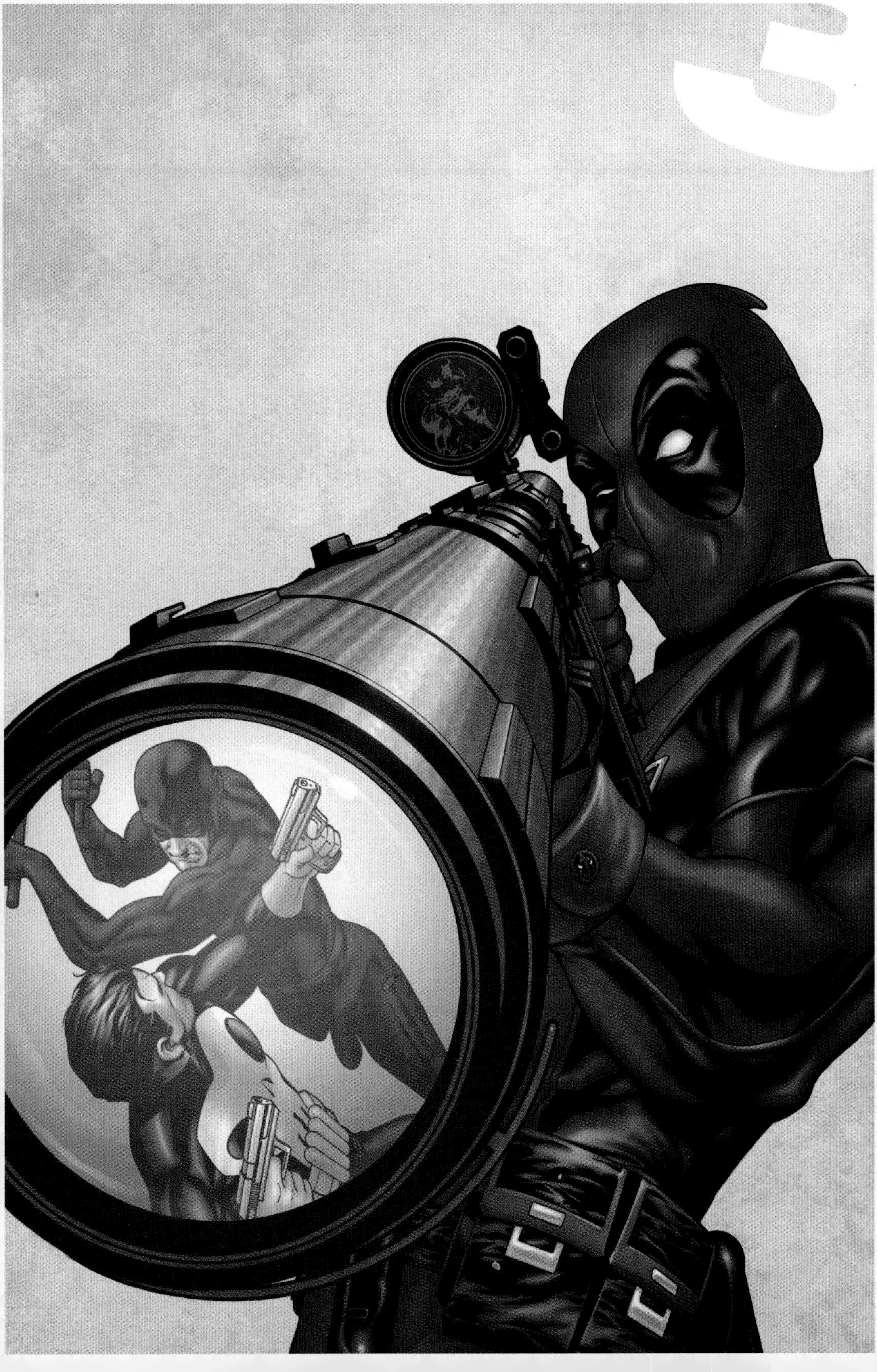
3

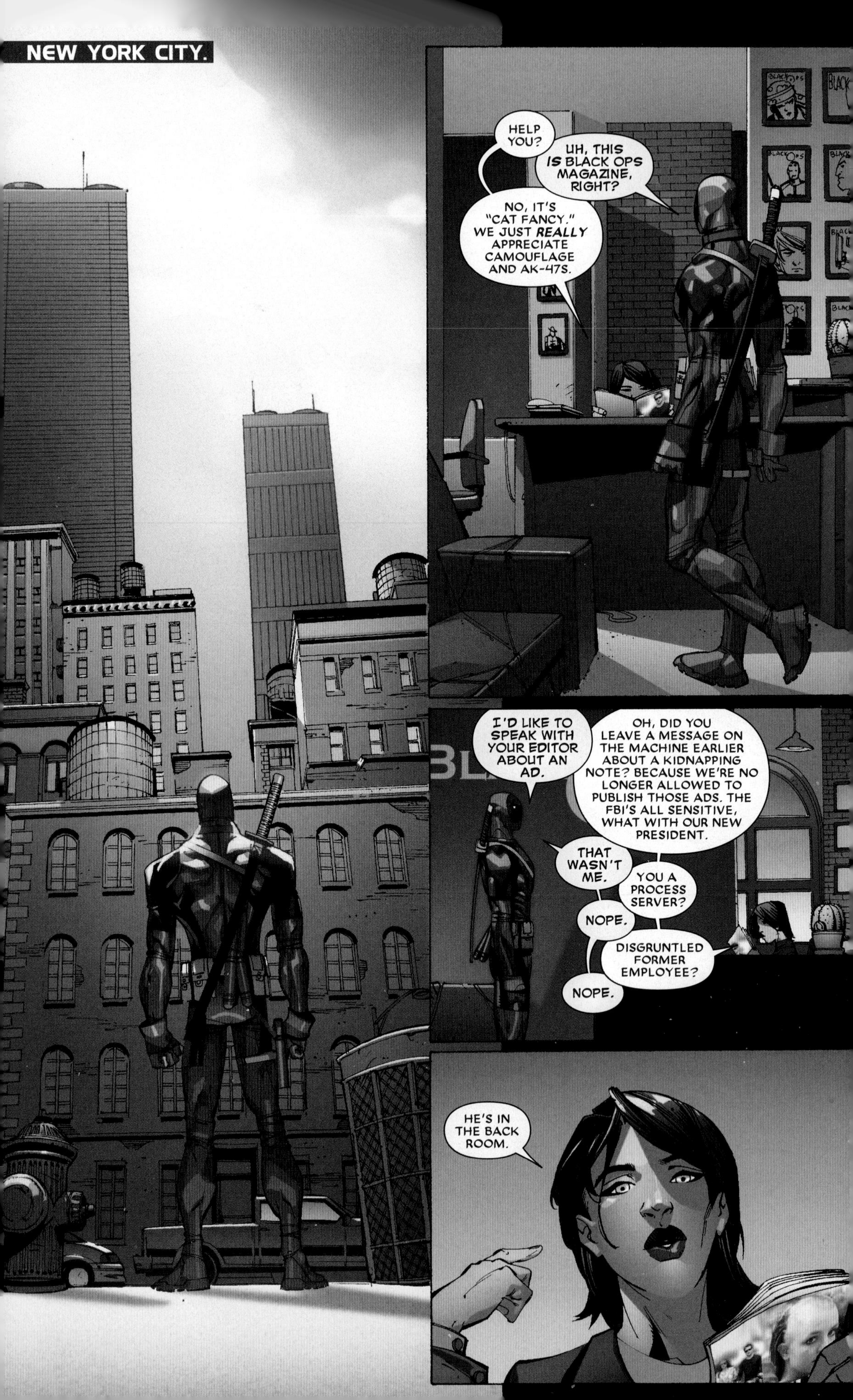
NEW YORK CITY.
HELP YOU?
UH, THIS IS BLACK OPS MAGAZINE, RIGHT?
NO, IT'S "CAT FANCY." WE JUST REALLY APPRECIATE CAMOUFLAGE AND AK-47S.
I'D LIKE TO SPEAK WITH YOUR EDITOR ABOUT AN AD.
OH, DID YOU LEAVE A MESSAGE ON THE MACHINE EARLIER ABOUT A KIDNAPPING NOTE? BECAUSE WE'RE NO LONGER ALLOWED TO PUBLISH THOSE ADS. THE FBI'S ALL SENSITIVE, WHAT WITH OUR NEW PRESIDENT.
THAT WASN'T ME.
YOU A PROCESS SERVER?
NOPE.
DISGRUNTLED FORMER EMPLOYEE?
NOPE.
HE'S IN THE BACK ROOM.

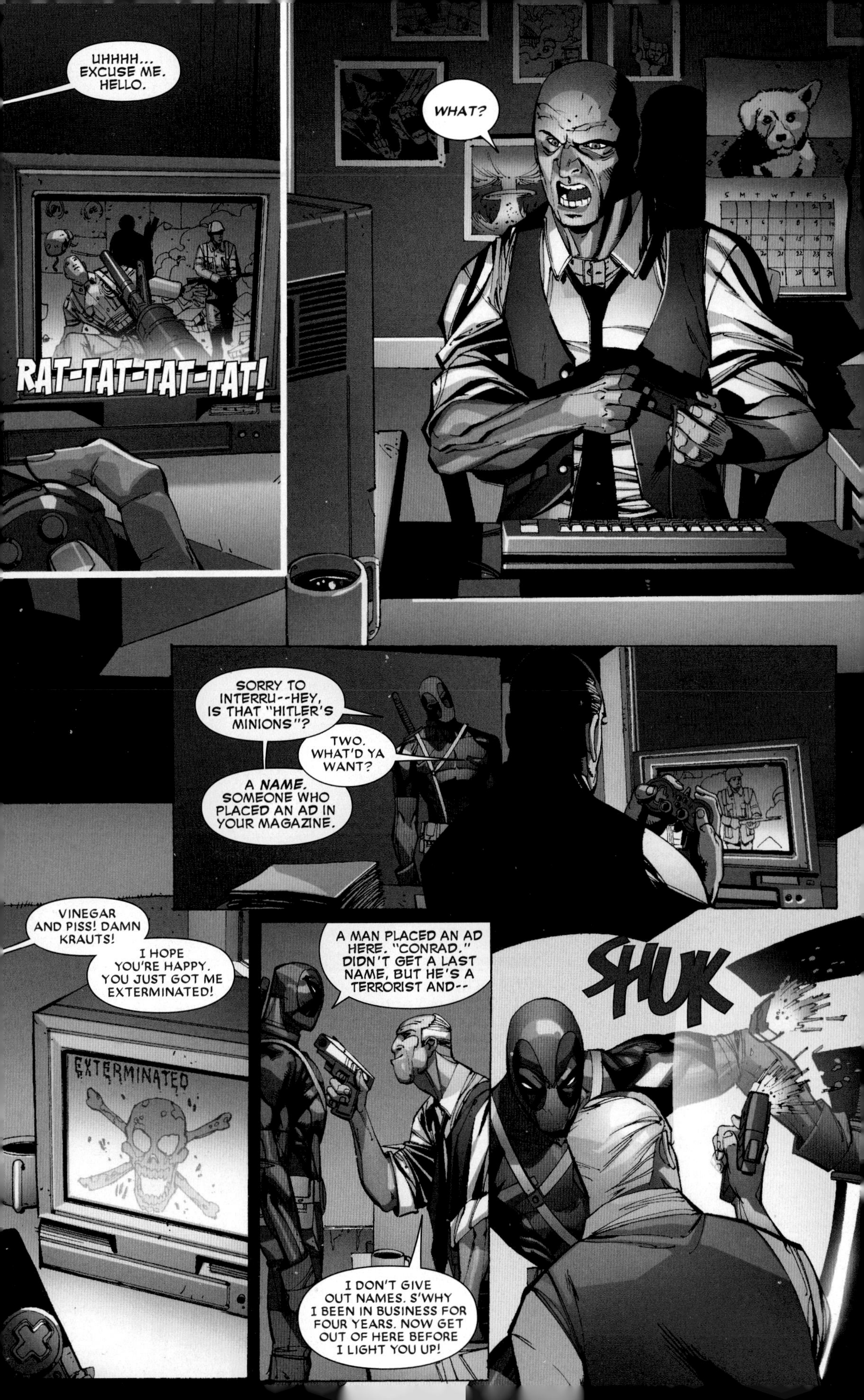
UHHHH... EXCUSE ME. HELLO.
WHAT?
RAT-TAT-TAT-TAT!
SORRY TO INTERRU--HEY, IS THAT "HITLER'S MINIONS"?
TWO. WHAT'D YA WANT?
A NAME. SOMEONE WHO PLACED AN AD IN YOUR MAGAZINE.
VINEGAR AND PISS! DAMN KRAUTS!
I HOPE YOU'RE HAPPY. YOU JUST GOT ME EXTERMINATED!
EXTERMINATED
A MAN PLACED AN AD HERE. "CONRAD." DIDN'T GET A LAST NAME, BUT HE'S A TERRORIST AND--
I DON'T GIVE OUT NAMES. S'WHY I BEEN IN BUSINESS FOR FOUR YEARS. NOW GET OUT OF HERE BEFORE I LIGHT YOU UP!
SHUK

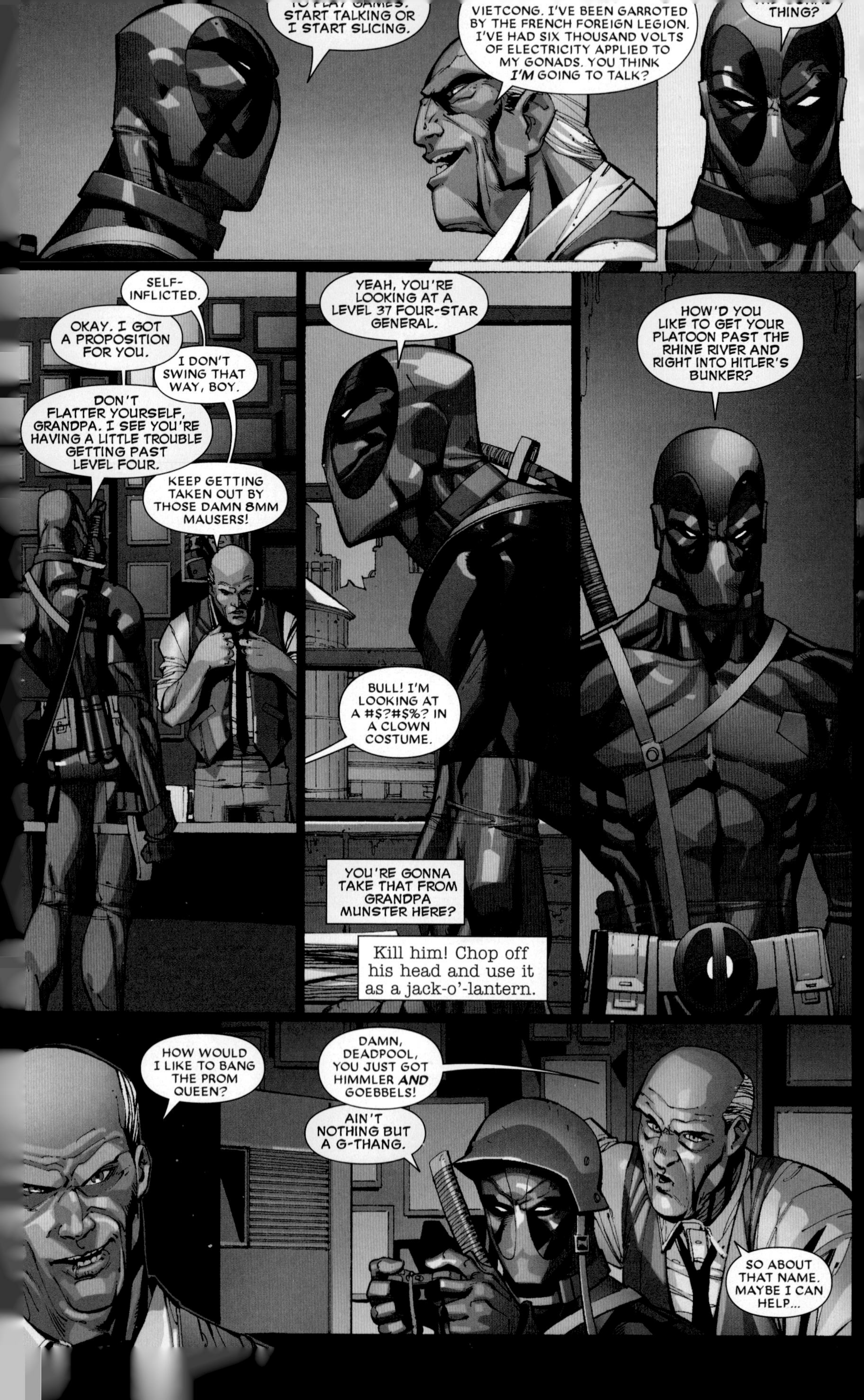
START TALKING OR I START SLICING.
VIETCONG. I'VE BEEN GARROTED BY THE FRENCH FOREIGN LEGION. I'VE HAD SIX THOUSAND VOLTS OF ELECTRICITY APPLIED TO MY GONADS. YOU THINK I'M GOING TO TALK?
THING?
SELF-INFLICTED.
OKAY. I GOT A PROPOSITION FOR YOU.
I DON'T SWING THAT WAY, BOY.
DON'T FLATTER YOURSELF, GRANDPA. I SEE YOU'RE HAVING A LITTLE TROUBLE GETTING PAST LEVEL FOUR.
KEEP GETTING TAKEN OUT BY THOSE DAMN 8MM MAUSERS!
YEAH, YOU'RE LOOKING AT A LEVEL 37 FOUR-STAR GENERAL.
BULL! I'M LOOKING AT A #$?#$%? IN A CLOWN COSTUME.
YOU'RE GONNA TAKE THAT FROM GRANDPA MUNSTER HERE?
Kill him! Chop off his head and use it as a jack-o'-lantern.
HOW'D YOU LIKE TO GET YOUR PLATOON PAST THE RHINE RIVER AND RIGHT INTO HITLER'S BUNKER?
HOW WOULD I LIKE TO BANG THE PROM QUEEN?
DAMN, DEADPOOL, YOU JUST GOT HIMMLER AND GOEBBELS!
AIN'T NOTHING BUT A G-THANG.
SO ABOUT THAT NAME. MAYBE I CAN HELP...

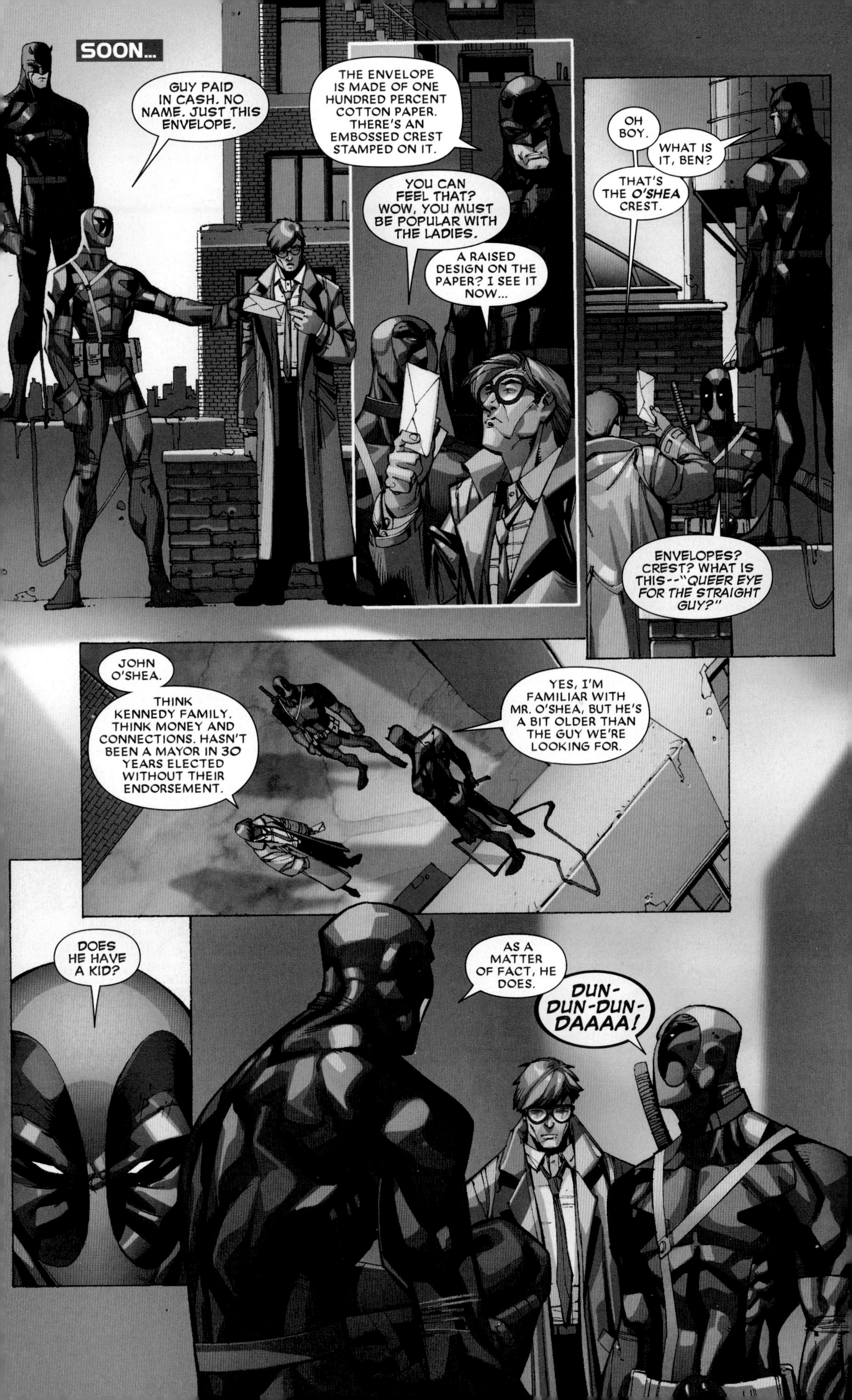
SOON...
GUY PAID IN CASH. NO NAME. JUST THIS ENVELOPE.
THE ENVELOPE IS MADE OF ONE HUNDRED PERCENT COTTON PAPER. THERE'S AN EMBOSSED CREST STAMPED ON IT.
YOU CAN FEEL THAT? WOW, YOU MUST BE POPULAR WITH THE LADIES.
A RAISED DESIGN ON THE PAPER? I SEE IT NOW...
OH BOY.
WHAT IS IT, BEN?
THAT'S THE O'SHEA CREST.
ENVELOPES? CREST? WHAT IS THIS--"QUEER EYE FOR THE STRAIGHT GUY?"
JOHN O'SHEA.
THINK KENNEDY FAMILY. THINK MONEY AND CONNECTIONS. HASN'T BEEN A MAYOR IN 30 YEARS ELECTED WITHOUT THEIR ENDORSEMENT.
YES, I'M FAMILIAR WITH MR. O'SHEA, BUT HE'S A BIT OLDER THAN THE GUY WE'RE LOOKING FOR.
DOES HE HAVE A KID?
AS A MATTER OF FACT, HE DOES.
DUN-DUN-DUN-DAAAA!

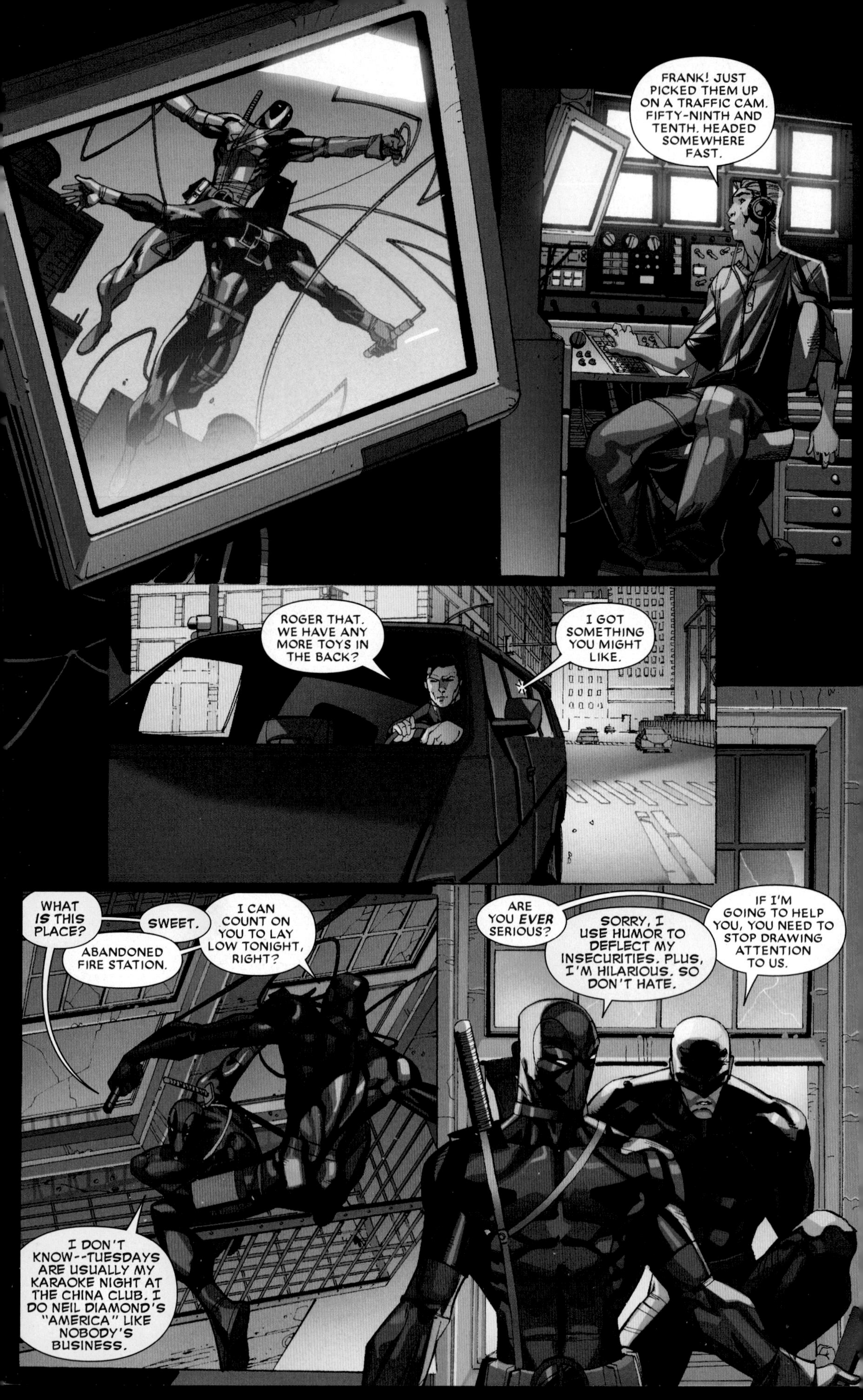
FRANK! JUST PICKED THEM UP ON A TRAFFIC CAM. FIFTY-NINTH AND TENTH. HEADED SOMEWHERE FAST.
ROGER THAT. WE HAVE ANY MORE TOYS IN THE BACK?
I GOT SOMETHING YOU MIGHT LIKE.
WHAT *IS* THIS PLACE?
ABANDONED FIRE STATION.
SWEET.
I CAN COUNT ON YOU TO LAY LOW TONIGHT, RIGHT?
I DON'T KNOW--TUESDAYS ARE USUALLY MY KARAOKE NIGHT AT THE CHINA CLUB. I DO NEIL DIAMOND'S "AMERICA" LIKE NOBODY'S BUSINESS.
ARE YOU *EVER* SERIOUS?
SORRY, I USE HUMOR TO DEFLECT MY INSECURITIES. PLUS, I'M HILARIOUS. SO DON'T HATE.
IF I'M GOING TO HELP YOU, YOU NEED TO STOP DRAWING ATTENTION TO US.

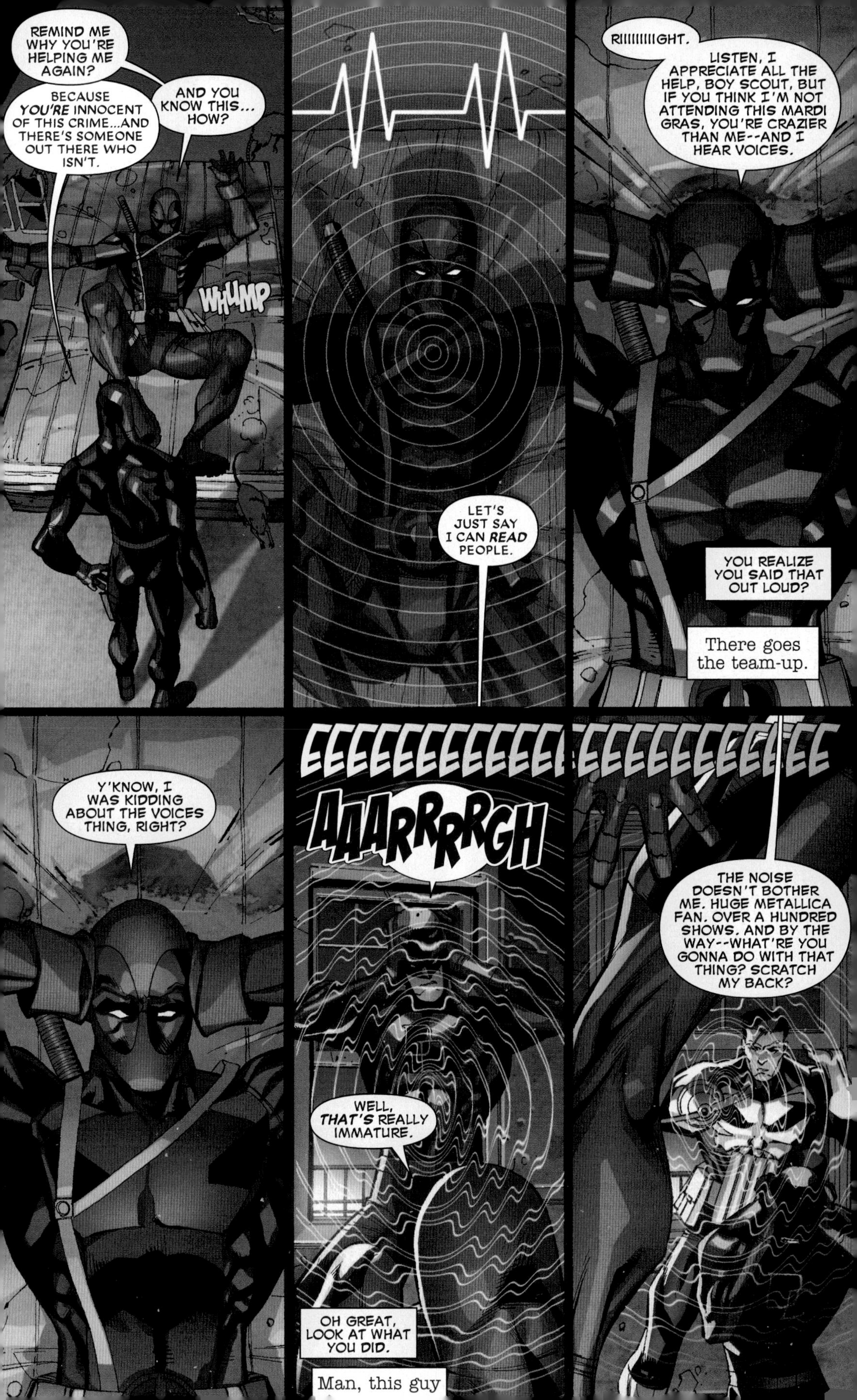
REMIND ME WHY YOU'RE HELPING ME AGAIN?
BECAUSE YOU'RE INNOCENT OF THIS CRIME...AND THERE'S SOMEONE OUT THERE WHO ISN'T.
AND YOU KNOW THIS... HOW?
WHUMP
LET'S JUST SAY I CAN READ PEOPLE.
RIIIIIIIIGHT.
LISTEN, I APPRECIATE ALL THE HELP, BOY SCOUT, BUT IF YOU THINK I'M NOT ATTENDING THIS MARDI GRAS, YOU'RE CRAZIER THAN ME--AND I HEAR VOICES.
YOU REALIZE YOU SAID THAT OUT LOUD?
There goes the team-up.
Y'KNOW, I WAS KIDDING ABOUT THE VOICES THING, RIGHT?
EEEEEEEEEEEEEEEEEEEEEEEEEEE
AAARRRRGH
WELL, THAT'S REALLY IMMATURE.
OH GREAT, LOOK AT WHAT YOU DID.
Man, this guy
THE NOISE DOESN'T BOTHER ME. HUGE METALLICA FAN. OVER A HUNDRED SHOWS. AND BY THE WAY--WHAT'RE YOU GONNA DO WITH THAT THING? SCRATCH MY BACK?

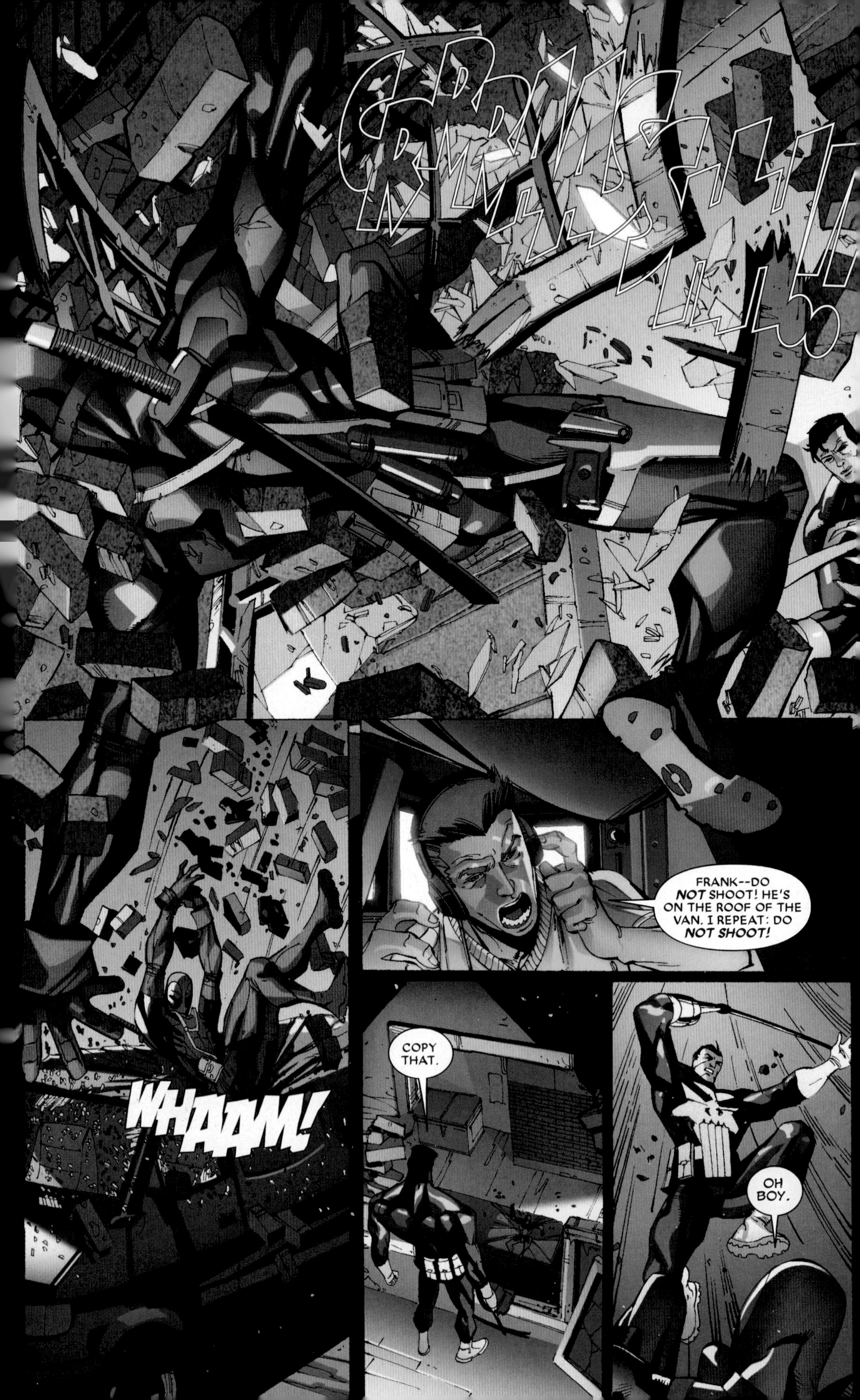
WHAAM!
FRANK--DO NOT SHOOT! HE'S ON THE ROOF OF THE VAN. I REPEAT: DO NOT SHOOT!
COPY THAT.
OH BOY.

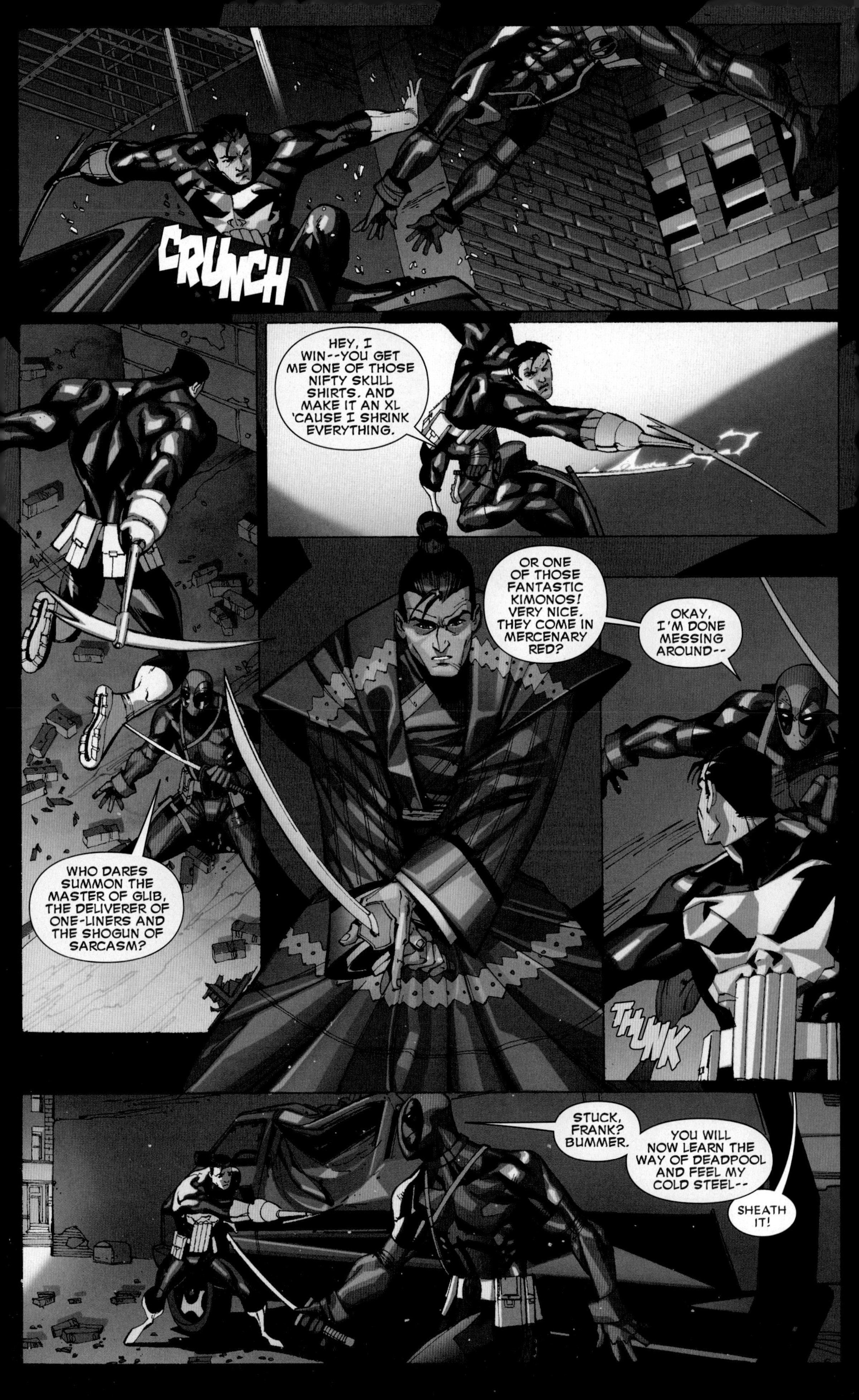
CRUNCH
HEY, I WIN--YOU GET ME ONE OF THOSE NIFTY SKULL SHIRTS. AND MAKE IT AN XL 'CAUSE I SHRINK EVERYTHING.
WHO DARES SUMMON THE MASTER OF GLIB, THE DELIVERER OF ONE-LINERS AND THE SHOGUN OF SARCASM?
OR ONE OF THOSE FANTASTIC KIMONOS! VERY NICE. THEY COME IN MERCENARY RED?
OKAY, I'M DONE MESSING AROUND--
THUNK
STUCK, FRANK? BUMMER.
YOU WILL NOW LEARN THE WAY OF DEADPOOL AND FEEL MY COLD STEEL--
SHEATH IT!

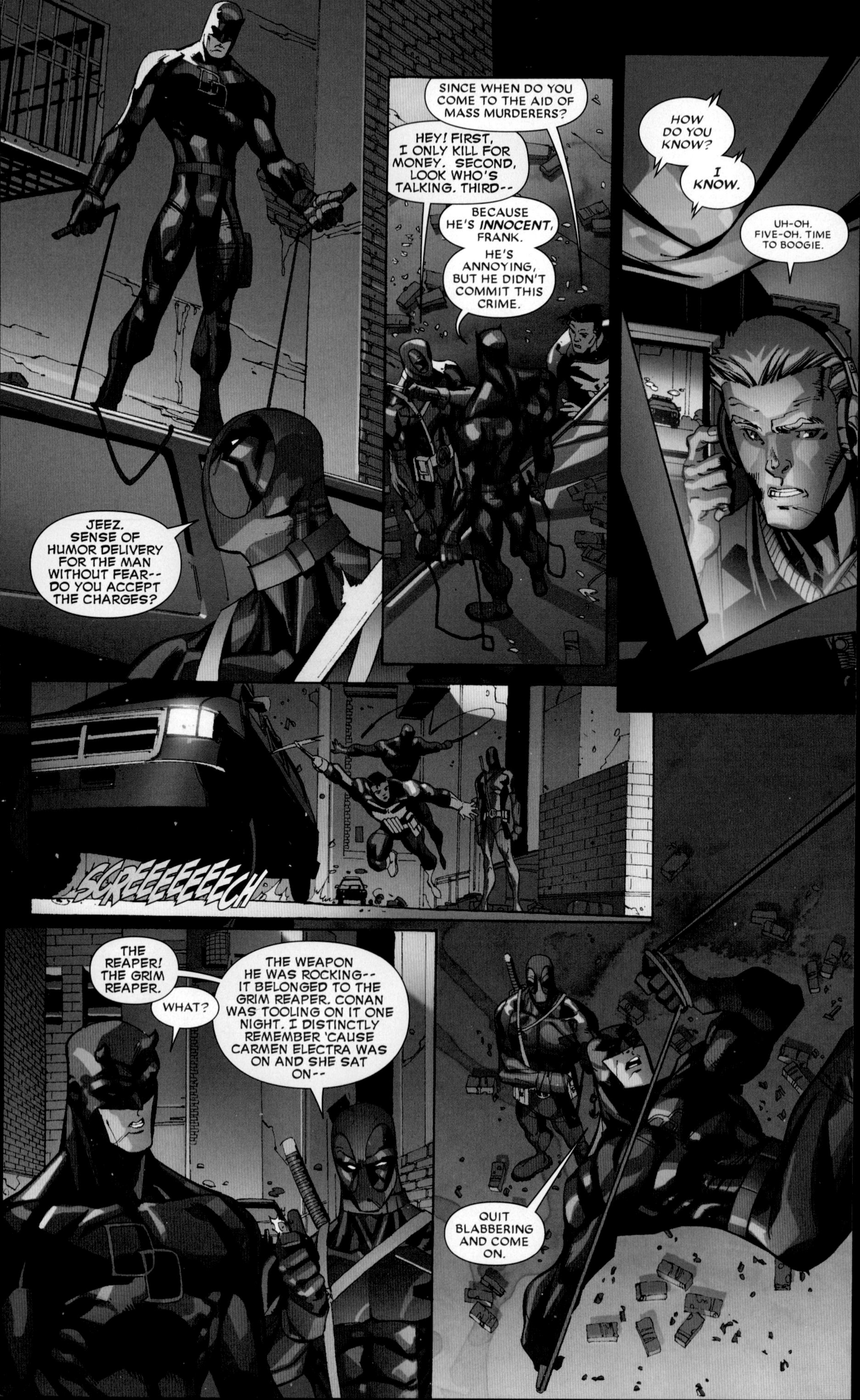
JEEZ. SENSE OF HUMOR DELIVERY FOR THE MAN WITHOUT FEAR-- DO YOU ACCEPT THE CHARGES?
SINCE WHEN DO YOU COME TO THE AID OF MASS MURDERERS?
HEY! FIRST, I ONLY KILL FOR MONEY. SECOND, LOOK WHO'S TALKING. THIRD--
BECAUSE HE'S INNOCENT, FRANK.
HE'S ANNOYING, BUT HE DIDN'T COMMIT THIS CRIME.
HOW DO YOU KNOW?
I KNOW.
UH-OH. FIVE-OH. TIME TO BOOGIE.
SCREEEEEEEECH
THE REAPER! THE GRIM REAPER.
WHAT?
THE WEAPON HE WAS ROCKING-- IT BELONGED TO THE GRIM REAPER. CONAN WAS TOOLING ON IT ONE NIGHT. I DISTINCTLY REMEMBER 'CAUSE CARMEN ELECTRA WAS ON AND SHE SAT ON--
QUIT BLABBERING AND COME ON.

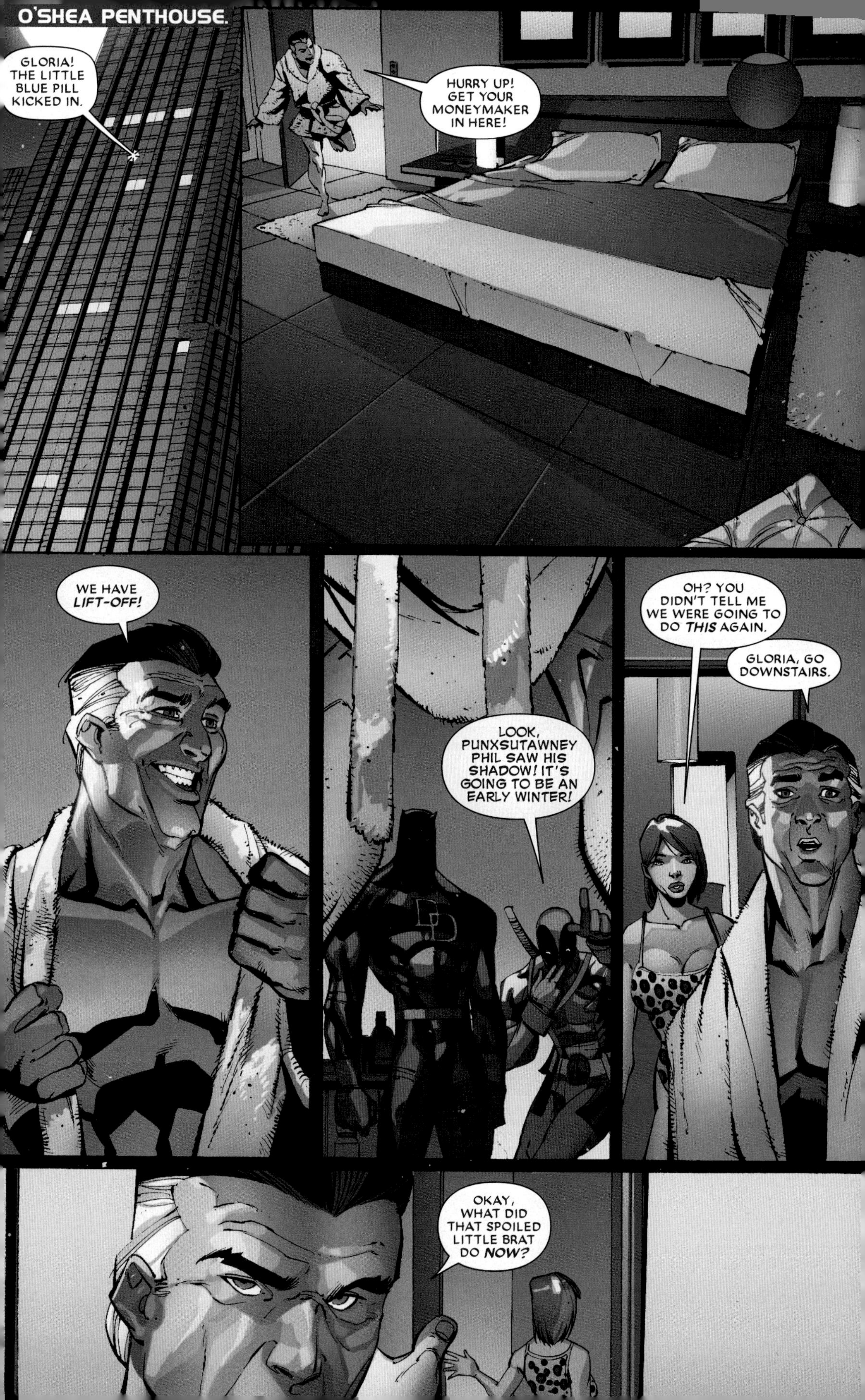
O'SHEA PENTHOUSE.
GLORIA! THE LITTLE BLUE PILL KICKED IN.
HURRY UP! GET YOUR MONEYMAKER IN HERE!
WE HAVE LIFT-OFF!
LOOK, PUNXSUTAWNEY PHIL SAW HIS SHADOW! IT'S GOING TO BE AN EARLY WINTER!
OH? YOU DIDN'T TELL ME WE WERE GOING TO DO THIS AGAIN.
GLORIA, GO DOWNSTAIRS.
OKAY, WHAT DID THAT SPOILED LITTLE BRAT DO NOW?

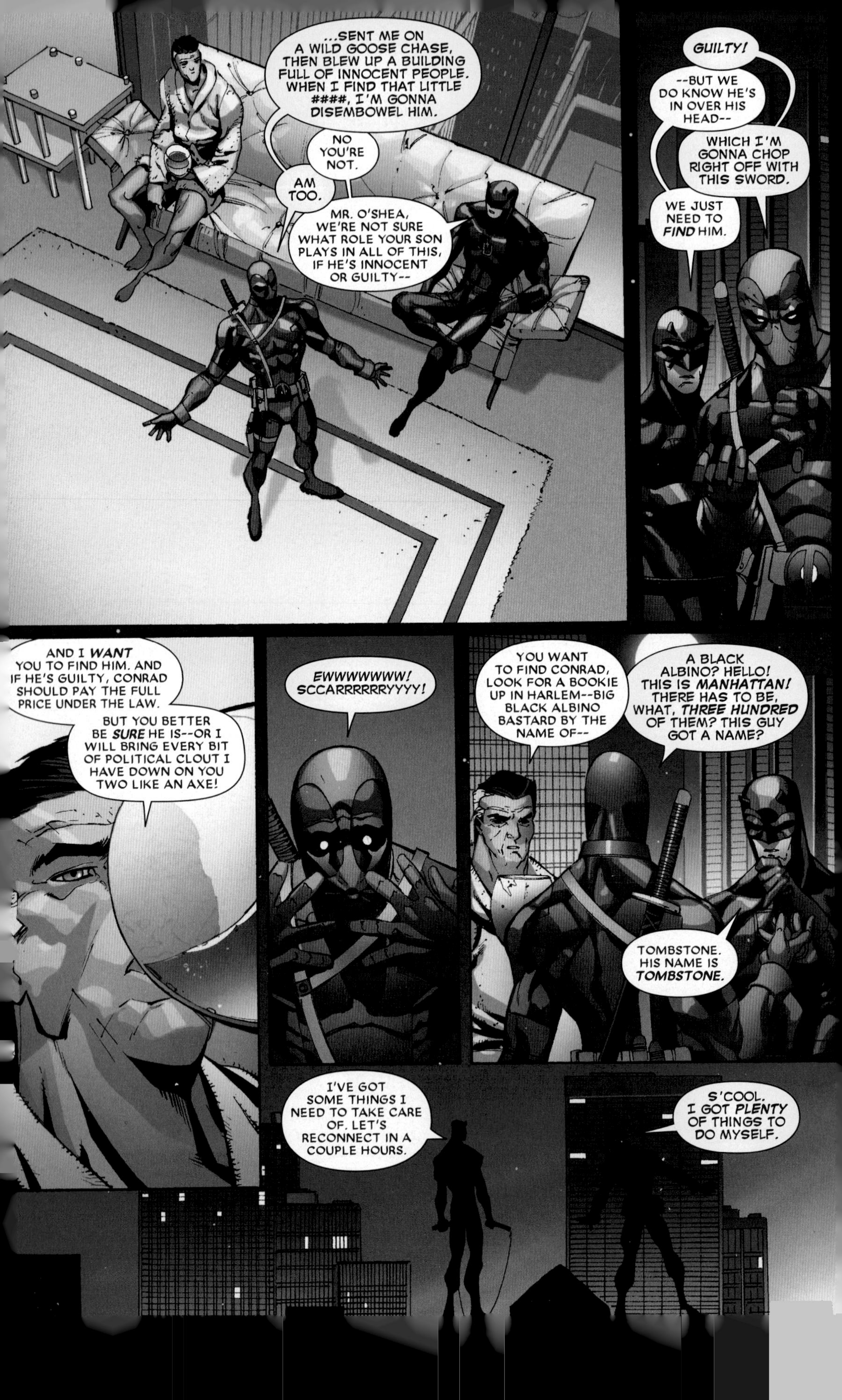
...SENT ME ON A WILD GOOSE CHASE, THEN BLEW UP A BUILDING FULL OF INNOCENT PEOPLE. WHEN I FIND THAT LITTLE ####, I'M GONNA DISEMBOWEL HIM.
NO YOU'RE NOT.
AM TOO.
MR. O'SHEA, WE'RE NOT SURE WHAT ROLE YOUR SON PLAYS IN ALL OF THIS, IF HE'S INNOCENT OR GUILTY--
GUILTY!
--BUT WE DO KNOW HE'S IN OVER HIS HEAD--
WHICH I'M GONNA CHOP RIGHT OFF WITH THIS SWORD.
WE JUST NEED TO FIND HIM.
AND I WANT YOU TO FIND HIM. AND IF HE'S GUILTY, CONRAD SHOULD PAY THE FULL PRICE UNDER THE LAW.
BUT YOU BETTER BE SURE HE IS--OR I WILL BRING EVERY BIT OF POLITICAL CLOUT I HAVE DOWN ON YOU TWO LIKE AN AXE!
EWWWWWWW! SCCARRRRRRYYYY!
YOU WANT TO FIND CONRAD, LOOK FOR A BOOKIE UP IN HARLEM--BIG BLACK ALBINO BASTARD BY THE NAME OF--
A BLACK ALBINO? HELLO! THIS IS MANHATTAN! THERE HAS TO BE, WHAT, THREE HUNDRED OF THEM? THIS GUY GOT A NAME?
TOMBSTONE. HIS NAME IS TOMBSTONE.
I'VE GOT SOME THINGS I NEED TO TAKE CARE OF. LET'S RECONNECT IN A COUPLE HOURS.
S'COOL. I GOT PLENTY OF THINGS TO DO MYSELF.

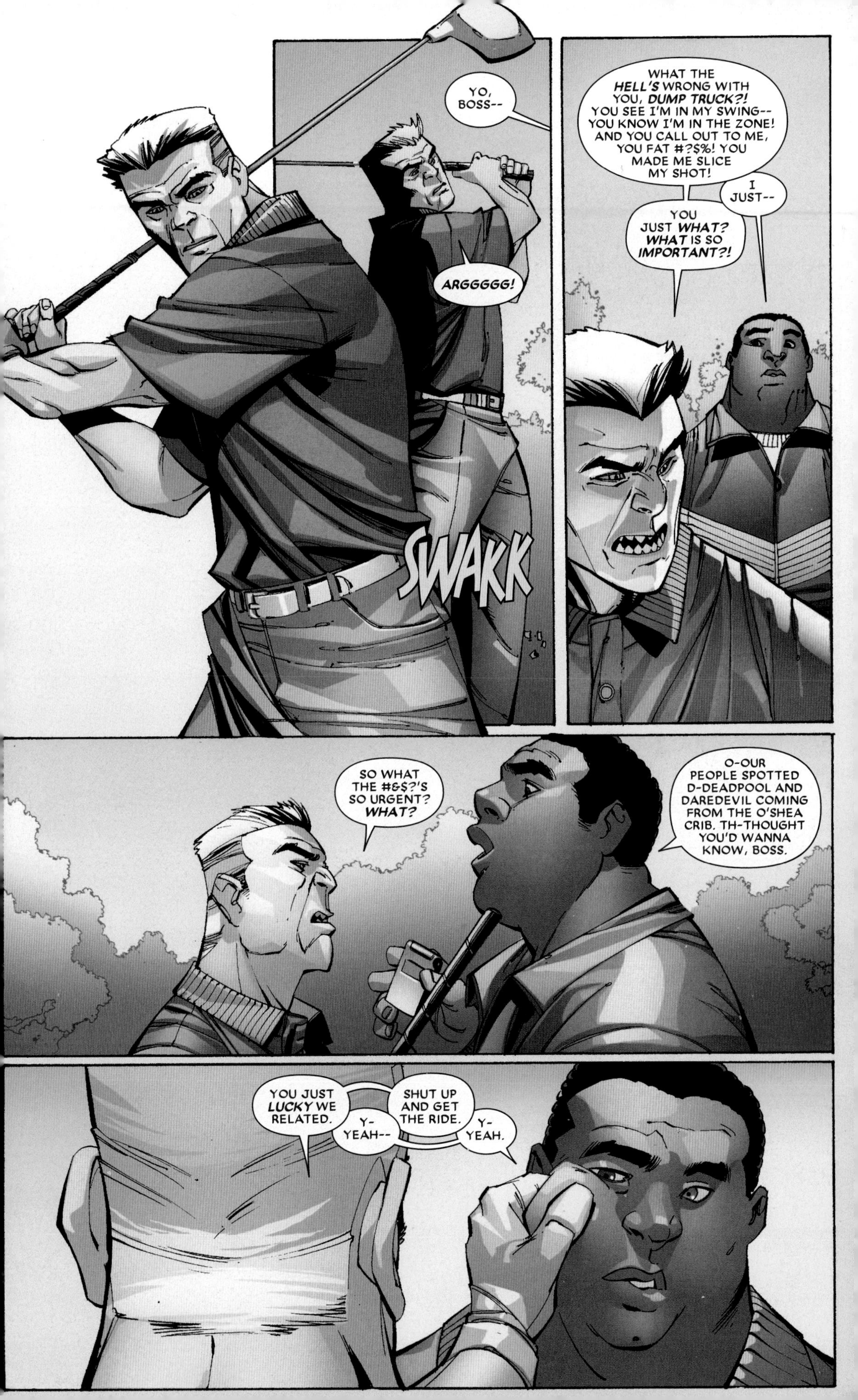
YO, BOSS--
ARGGGGG!
SWAKK
WHAT THE HELL'S WRONG WITH YOU, DUMP TRUCK?! YOU SEE I'M IN MY SWING-- YOU KNOW I'M IN THE ZONE! AND YOU CALL OUT TO ME, YOU FAT #?$%! YOU MADE ME SLICE MY SHOT!
I JUST--
YOU JUST WHAT? WHAT IS SO IMPORTANT?!
SO WHAT THE #&$?'S SO URGENT? WHAT?
O-OUR PEOPLE SPOTTED D-DEADPOOL AND DAREDEVIL COMING FROM THE O'SHEA CRIB. TH-THOUGHT YOU'D WANNA KNOW, BOSS.
YOU JUST LUCKY WE RELATED.
Y-YEAH--
SHUT UP AND GET THE RIDE.
Y-YEAH.

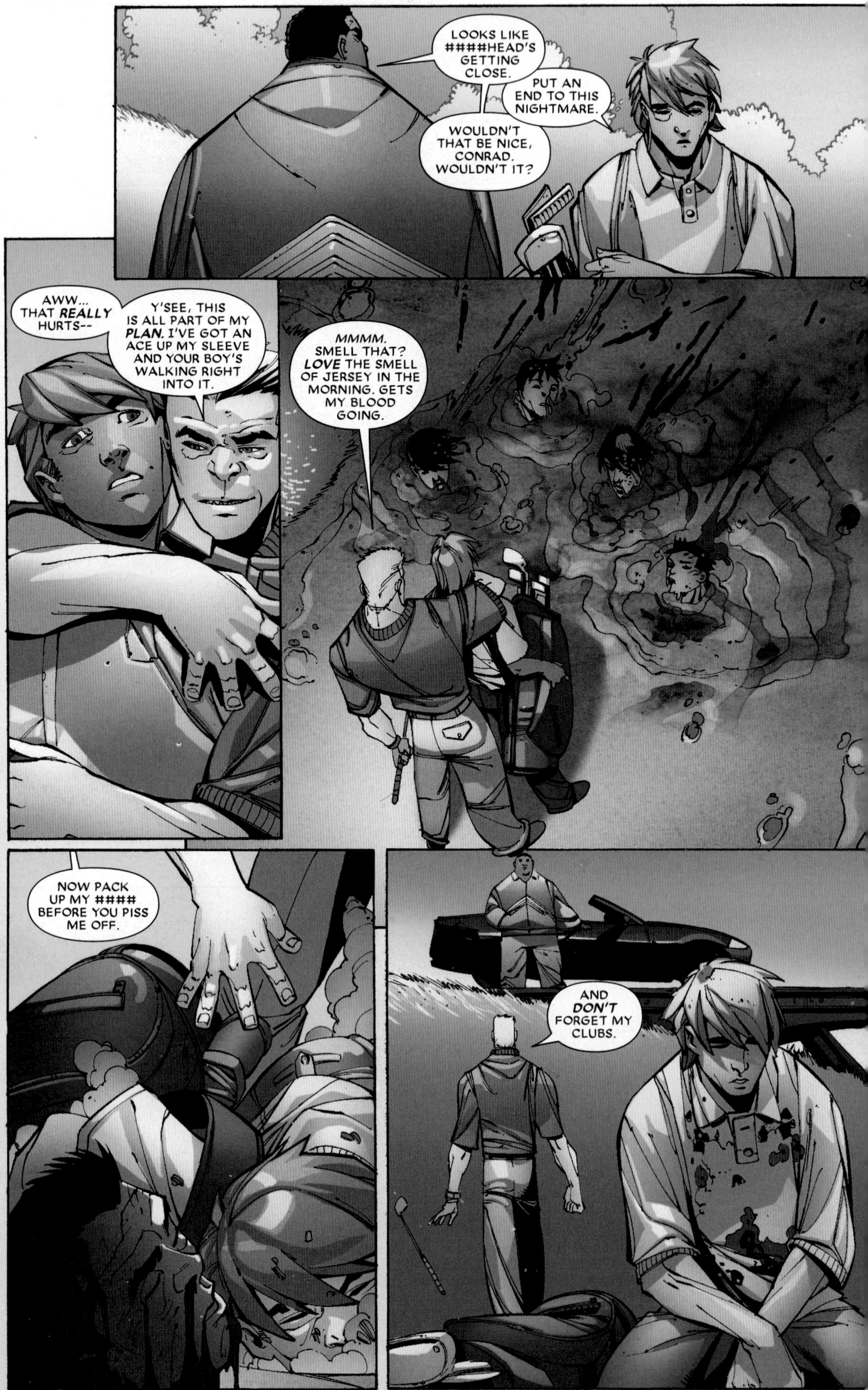
LOOKS LIKE ####HEAD'S GETTING CLOSE.
PUT AN END TO THIS NIGHTMARE.
WOULDN'T THAT BE NICE, CONRAD. WOULDN'T IT?
AWW... THAT **REALLY** HURTS--
Y'SEE, THIS IS ALL PART OF MY **PLAN.** I'VE GOT AN ACE UP MY SLEEVE AND YOUR BOY'S WALKING RIGHT INTO IT.
MMMM. SMELL THAT? **LOVE** THE SMELL OF JERSEY IN THE MORNING. GETS MY BLOOD GOING.
NOW PACK UP MY #### BEFORE YOU PISS ME OFF.
AND **DON'T** FORGET MY CLUBS.

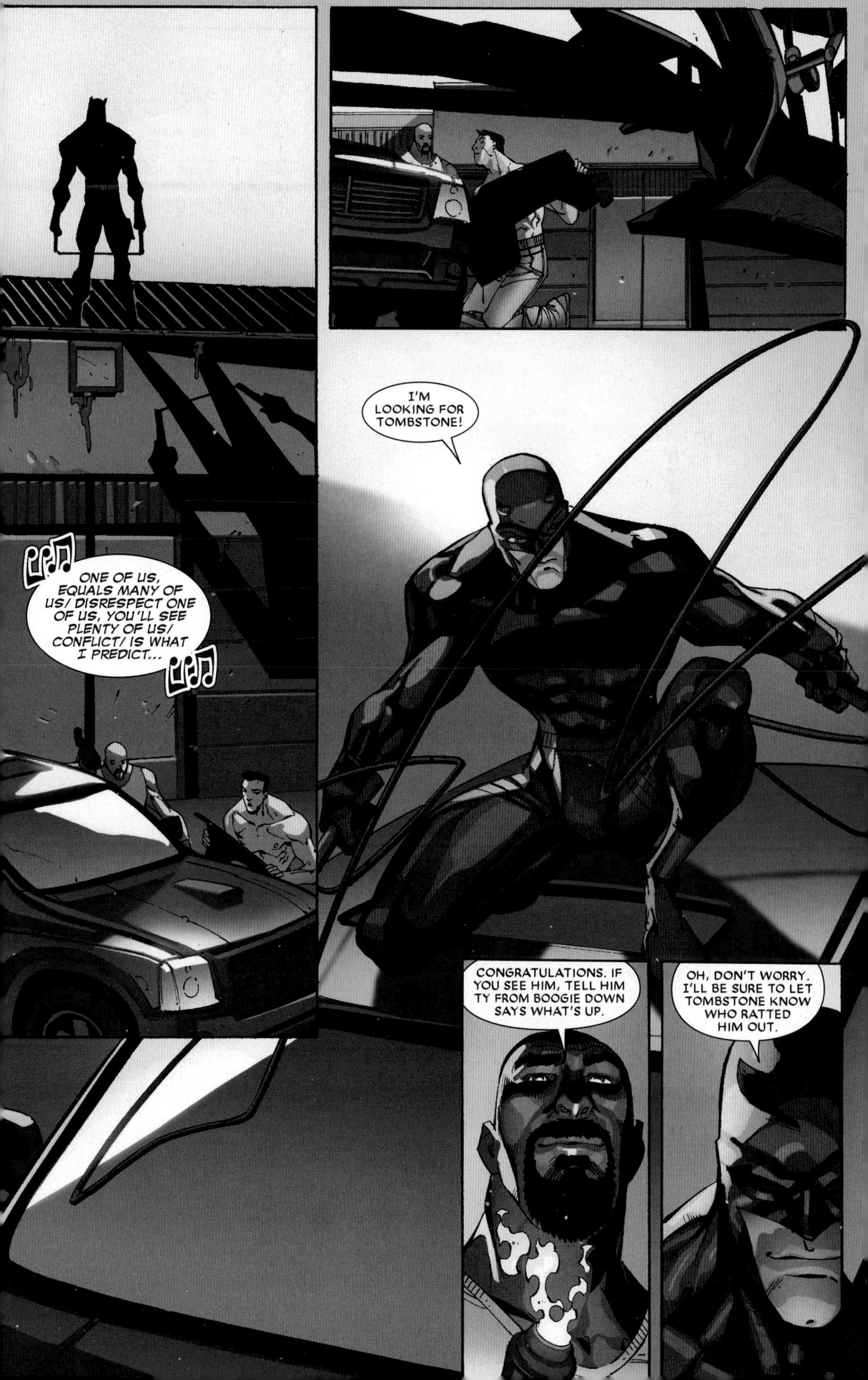
ONE OF US, EQUALS MANY OF US/ DISRESPECT ONE OF US, YOU'LL SEE PLENTY OF US/ CONFLICT/ IS WHAT I PREDICT...
I'M LOOKING FOR TOMBSTONE!
CONGRATULATIONS. IF YOU SEE HIM, TELL HIM TY FROM BOOGIE DOWN SAYS WHAT'S UP.
OH, DON'T WORRY. I'LL BE SURE TO LET TOMBSTONE KNOW WHO RATTED HIM OUT.

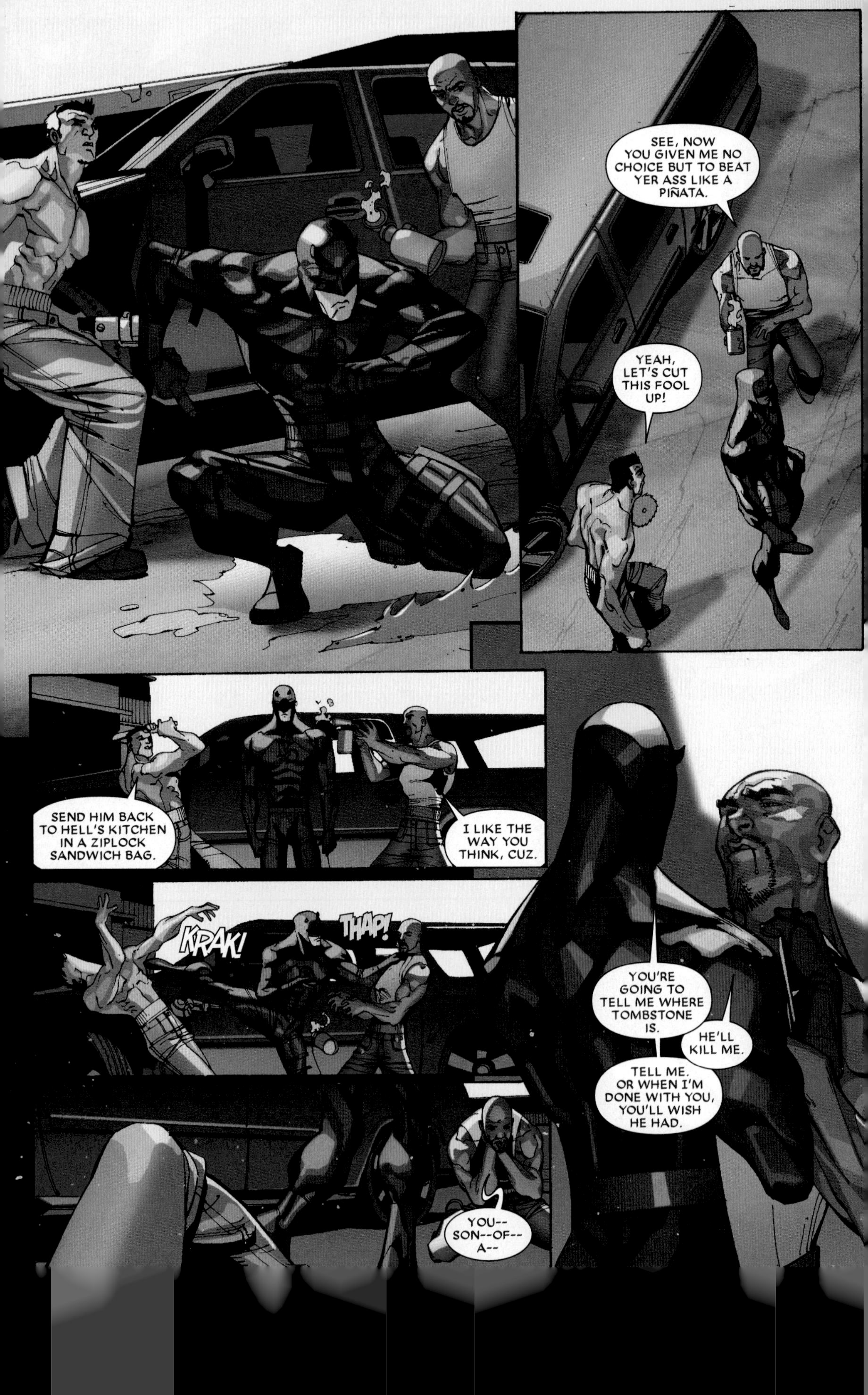
SEE, NOW YOU GIVEN ME NO CHOICE BUT TO BEAT YER ASS LIKE A PIÑATA.
YEAH, LET'S CUT THIS FOOL UP!
SEND HIM BACK TO HELL'S KITCHEN IN A ZIPLOCK SANDWICH BAG.
I LIKE THE WAY YOU THINK, CUZ.
KRAK!
THAP!
YOU--SON--OF--A--
YOU'RE GOING TO TELL ME WHERE TOMBSTONE IS.
HE'LL KILL ME.
TELL ME. OR WHEN I'M DONE WITH YOU, YOU'LL WISH HE HAD.

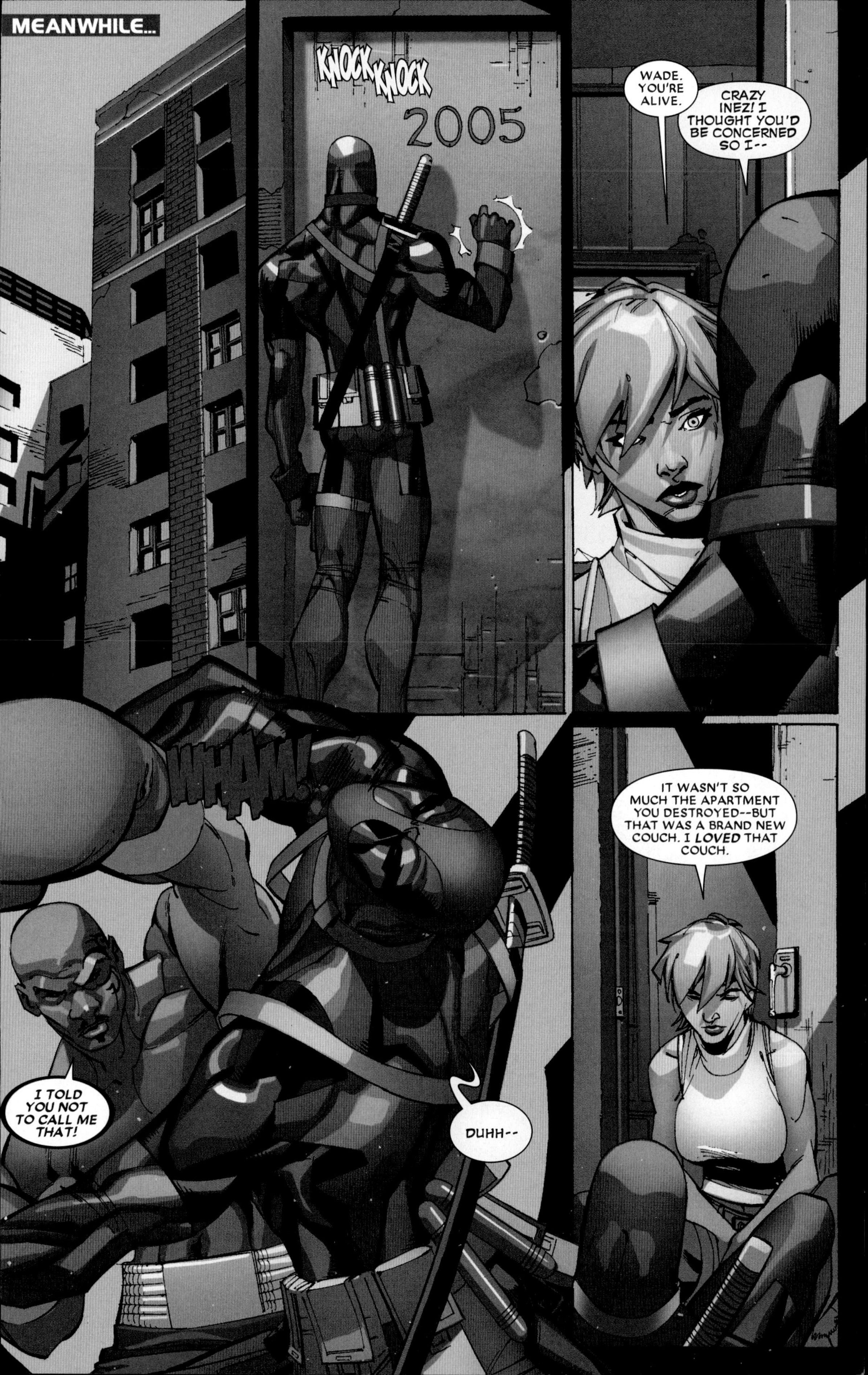
MEANWHILE...
KNOCK KNOCK
2005
WADE. YOU'RE ALIVE.
CRAZY INEZ! I THOUGHT YOU'D BE CONCERNED SO I--
WHAM!
I TOLD YOU NOT TO CALL ME THAT!
DUHH--
IT WASN'T SO MUCH THE APARTMENT YOU DESTROYED--BUT THAT WAS A BRAND NEW COUCH. I LOVED THAT COUCH.

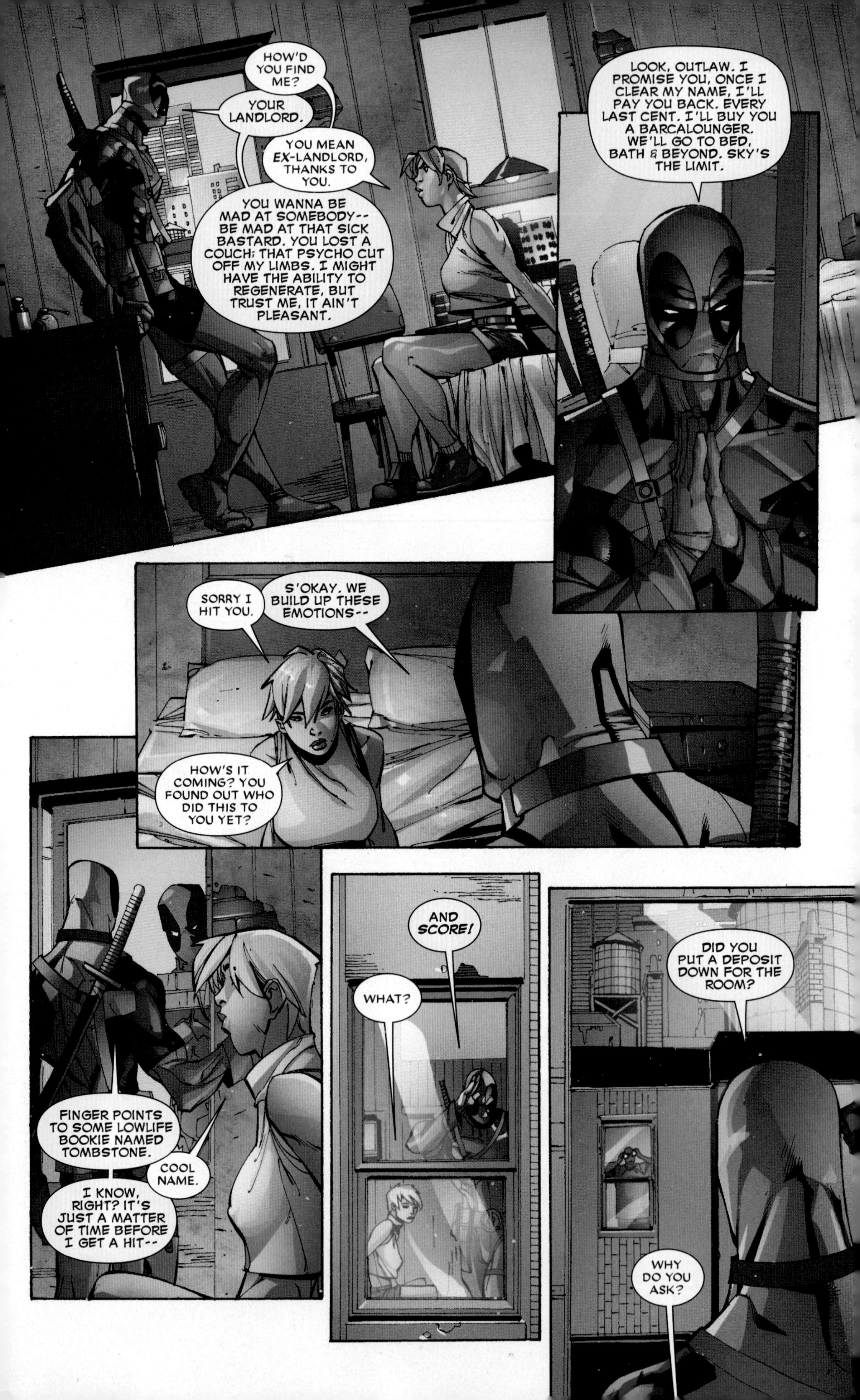
HOW'D YOU FIND ME?
YOUR LANDLORD.
YOU MEAN *EX*-LANDLORD, THANKS TO YOU.
YOU WANNA BE MAD AT SOMEBODY-- BE MAD AT THAT SICK BASTARD. YOU LOST A COUCH; THAT PSYCHO CUT OFF MY LIMBS. I MIGHT HAVE THE ABILITY TO REGENERATE, BUT TRUST ME, IT AIN'T PLEASANT.
LOOK, OUTLAW. I PROMISE YOU, ONCE I CLEAR MY NAME, I'LL PAY YOU BACK. EVERY LAST CENT. I'LL BUY YOU A BARCALOUNGER. WE'LL GO TO BED, BATH & BEYOND. SKY'S THE LIMIT.
SORRY I HIT YOU.
S'OKAY. WE BUILD UP THESE EMOTIONS--
HOW'S IT COMING? YOU FOUND OUT WHO DID THIS TO YOU YET?
FINGER POINTS TO SOME LOWLIFE BOOKIE NAMED TOMBSTONE.
COOL NAME.
I KNOW, RIGHT? IT'S JUST A MATTER OF TIME BEFORE I GET A HIT--
AND *SCORE!*
WHAT?
DID YOU PUT A DEPOSIT DOWN FOR THE ROOM?
WHY DO YOU ASK?

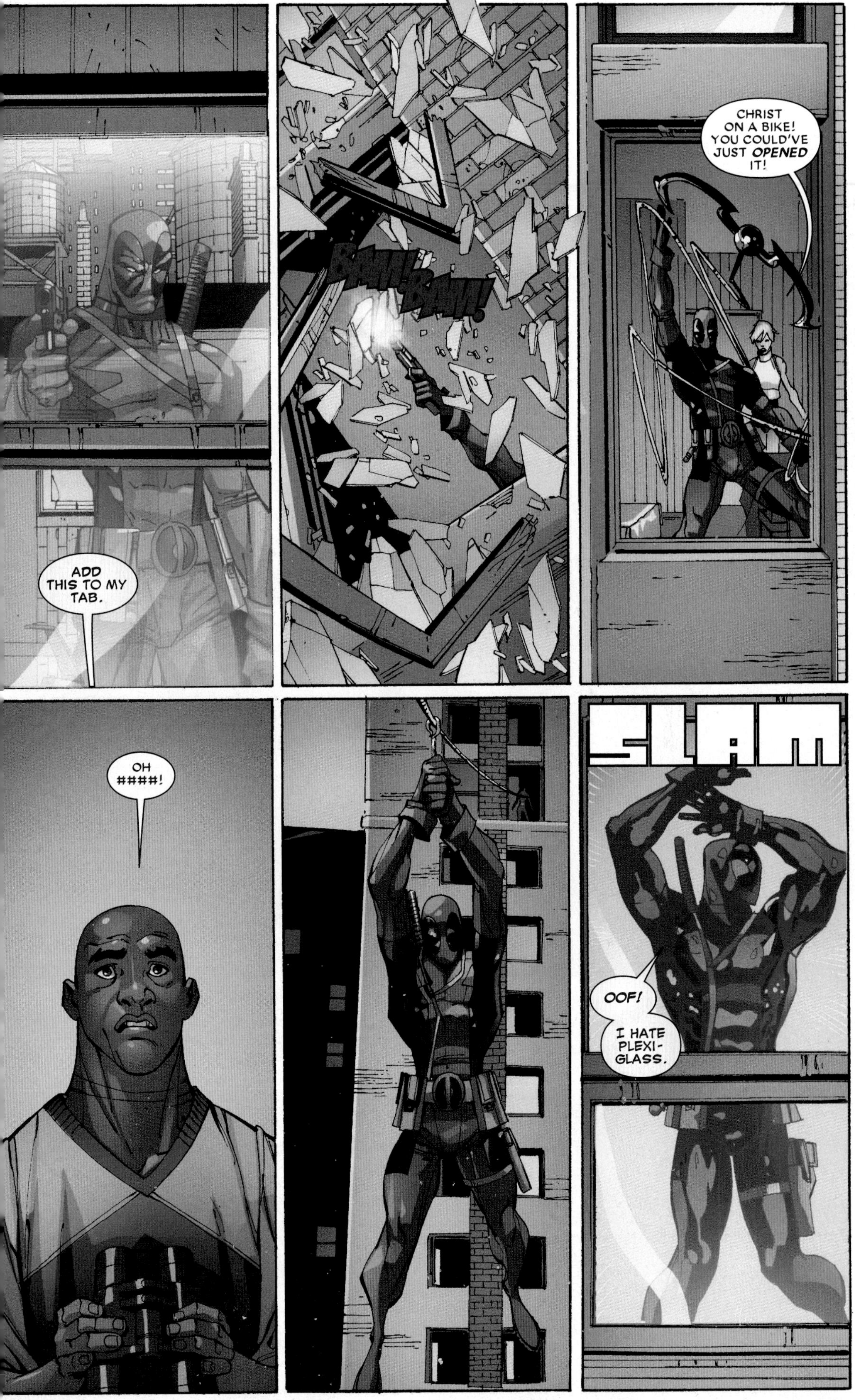

ADD THIS TO MY TAB.
BAM! BAM!
CHRIST ON A BIKE! YOU COULD'VE JUST OPENED IT!
OH ####!
SLAM
OOF!
I HATE PLEXI-GLASS.

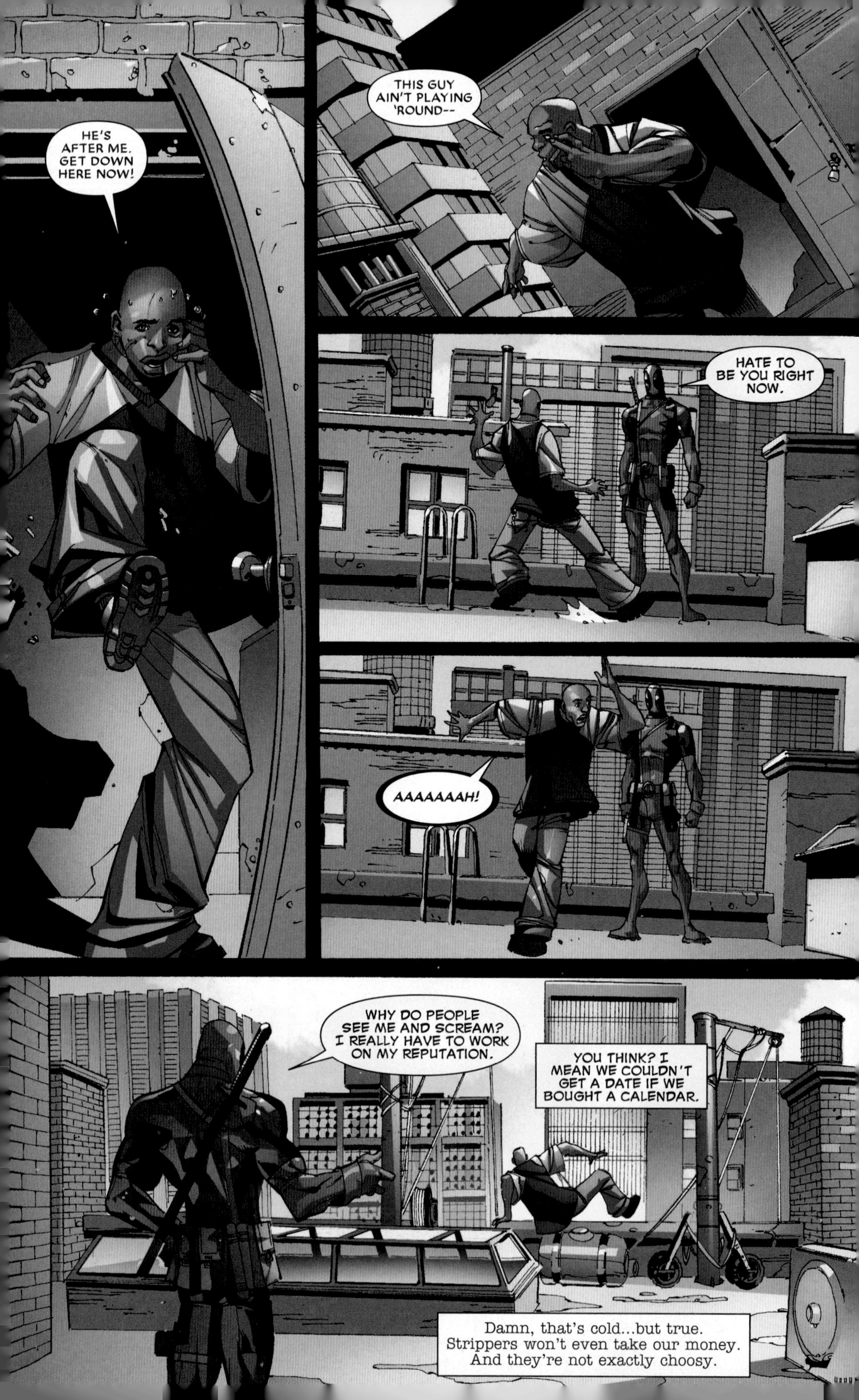

HE'S AFTER ME. GET DOWN HERE NOW!
THIS GUY AIN'T PLAYING 'ROUND--
HATE TO BE YOU RIGHT NOW.
AAAAAAAH!
WHY DO PEOPLE SEE ME AND SCREAM? I REALLY HAVE TO WORK ON MY REPUTATION.
YOU THINK? I MEAN WE COULDN'T GET A DATE IF WE BOUGHT A CALENDAR.
Damn, that's cold...but true. Strippers won't even take our money. And they're not exactly choosy.

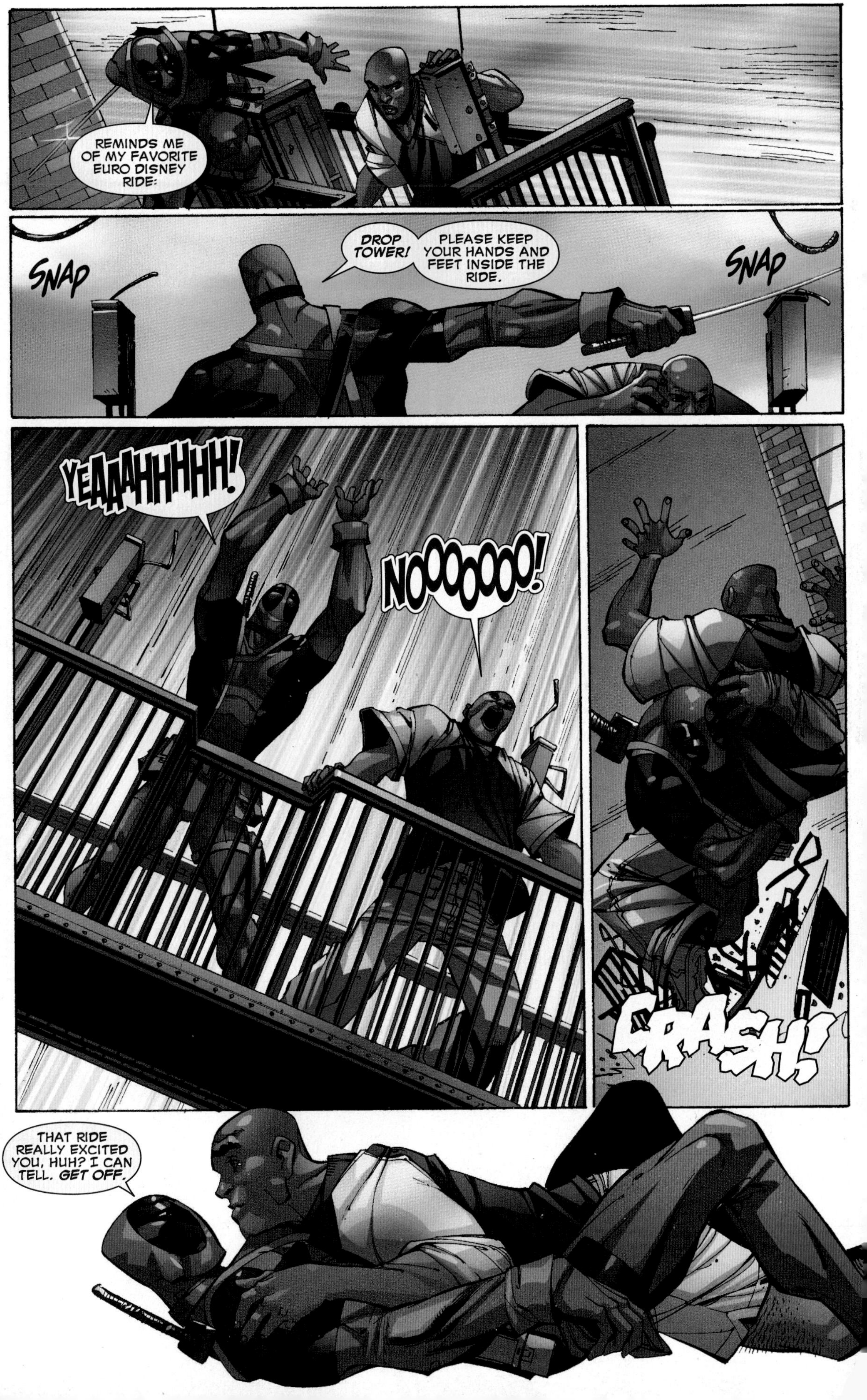
REMINDS ME OF MY FAVORITE EURO DISNEY RIDE:
SNAP
DROP TOWER!
PLEASE KEEP YOUR HANDS AND FEET INSIDE THE RIDE.
SNAP
YEAAAHHHHH!
NOOOOOOO!
CRASH!
THAT RIDE REALLY EXCITED YOU, HUH? I CAN TELL. GET OFF.

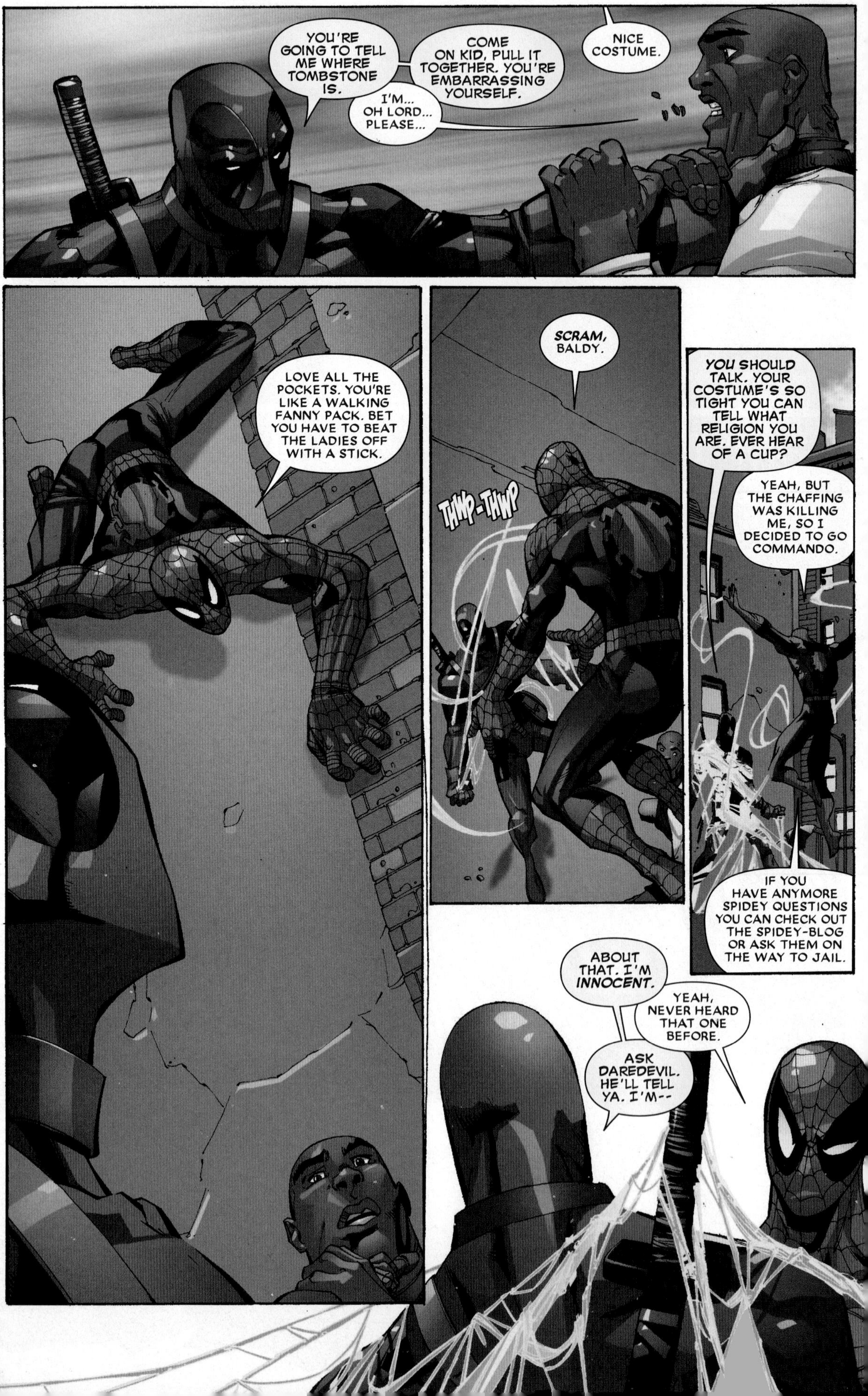
YOU'RE GOING TO TELL ME WHERE TOMBSTONE IS.
COME ON KID, PULL IT TOGETHER. YOU'RE EMBARRASSING YOURSELF.
I'M... OH LORD... PLEASE...
NICE COSTUME.
LOVE ALL THE POCKETS. YOU'RE LIKE A WALKING FANNY PACK. BET YOU HAVE TO BEAT THE LADIES OFF WITH A STICK.
SCRAM, BALDY.
THWP-THWP
YOU SHOULD TALK. YOUR COSTUME'S SO TIGHT YOU CAN TELL WHAT RELIGION YOU ARE. EVER HEAR OF A CUP?
YEAH, BUT THE CHAFFING WAS KILLING ME, SO I DECIDED TO GO COMMANDO.
IF YOU HAVE ANYMORE SPIDEY QUESTIONS YOU CAN CHECK OUT THE SPIDEY-BLOG OR ASK THEM ON THE WAY TO JAIL.
ABOUT THAT. I'M INNOCENT.
YEAH, NEVER HEARD THAT ONE BEFORE.
ASK DAREDEVIL. HE'LL TELL YA. I'M--

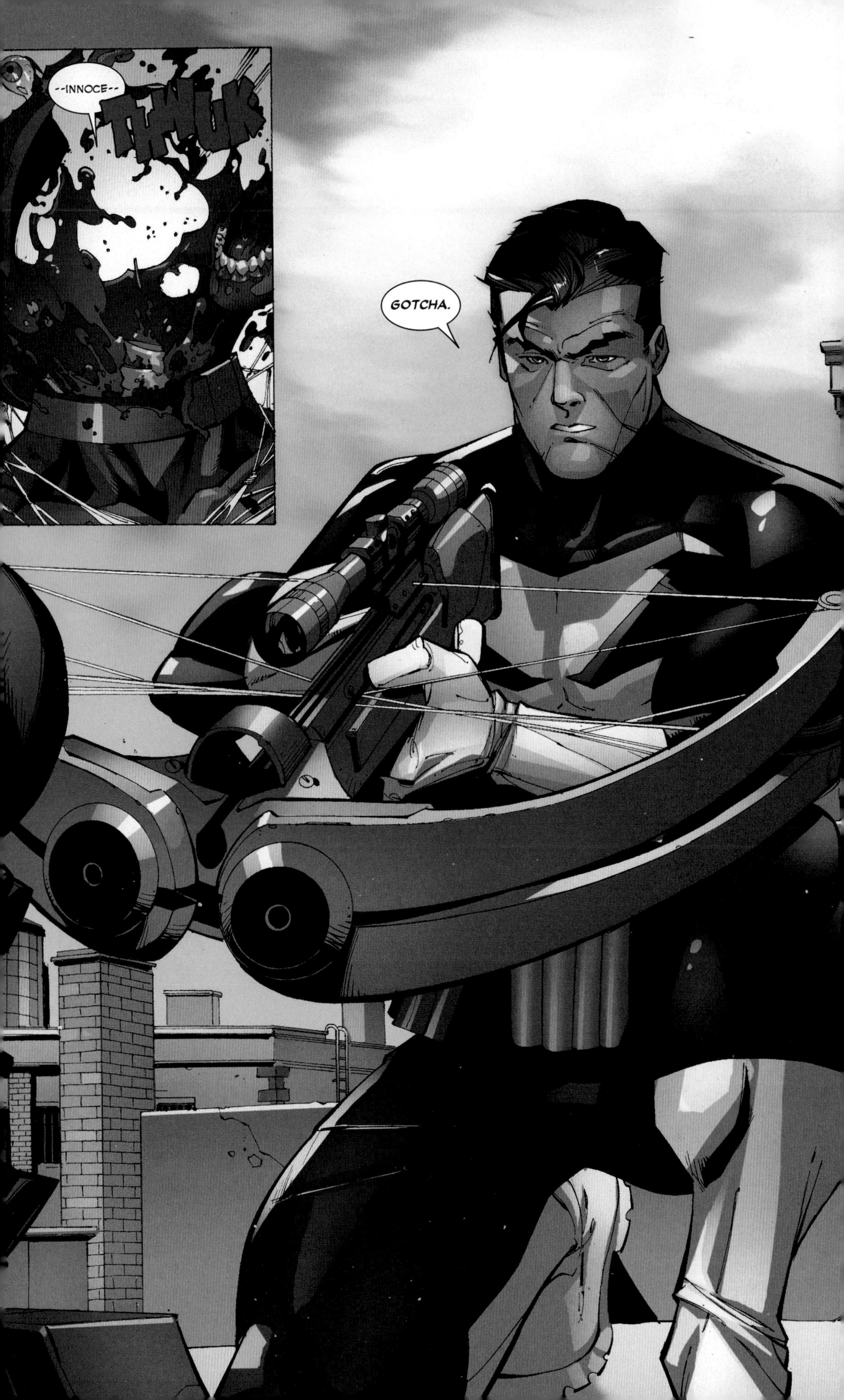
--INNOCE--
THWUK
GOTCHA.

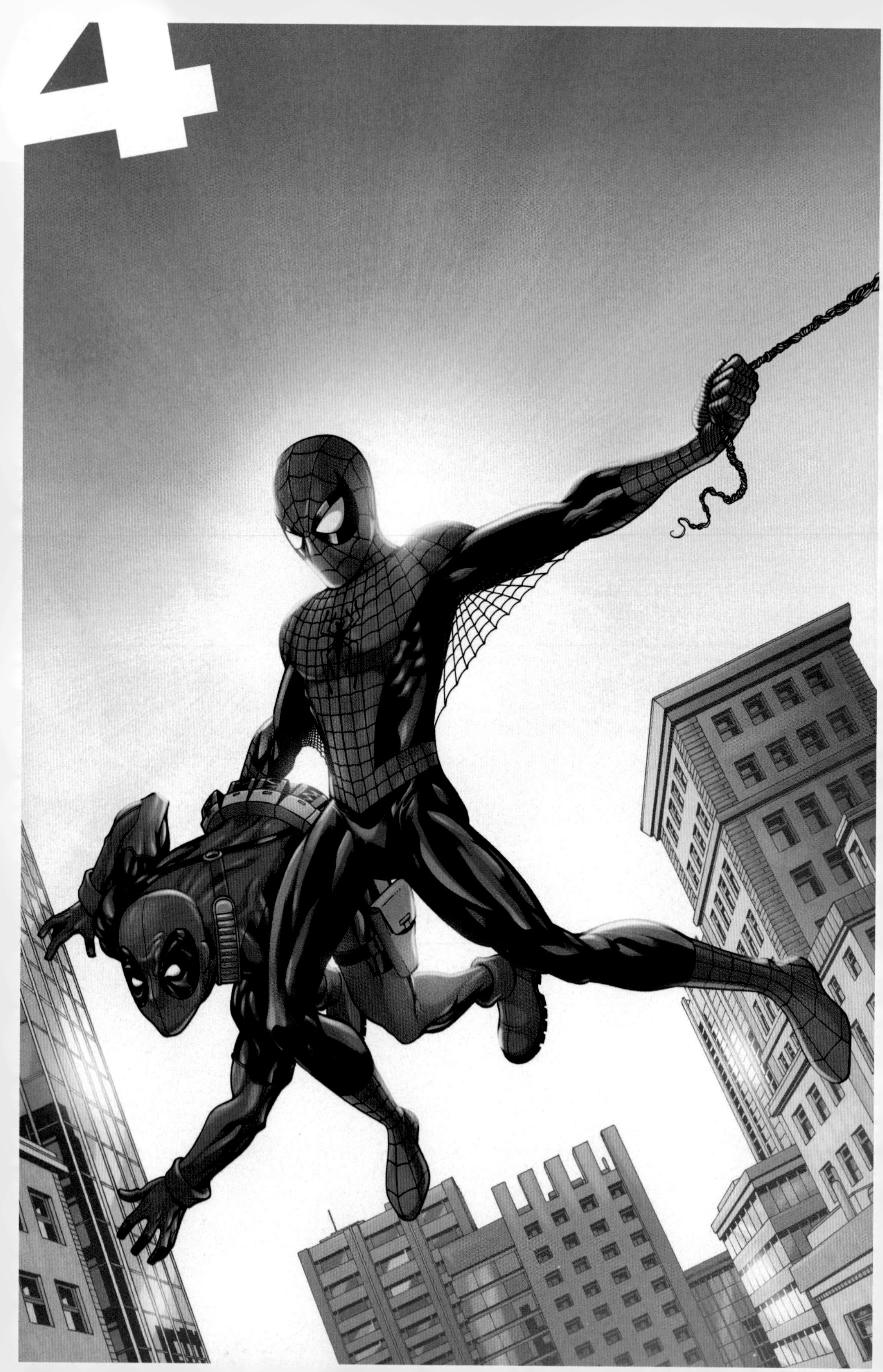
4

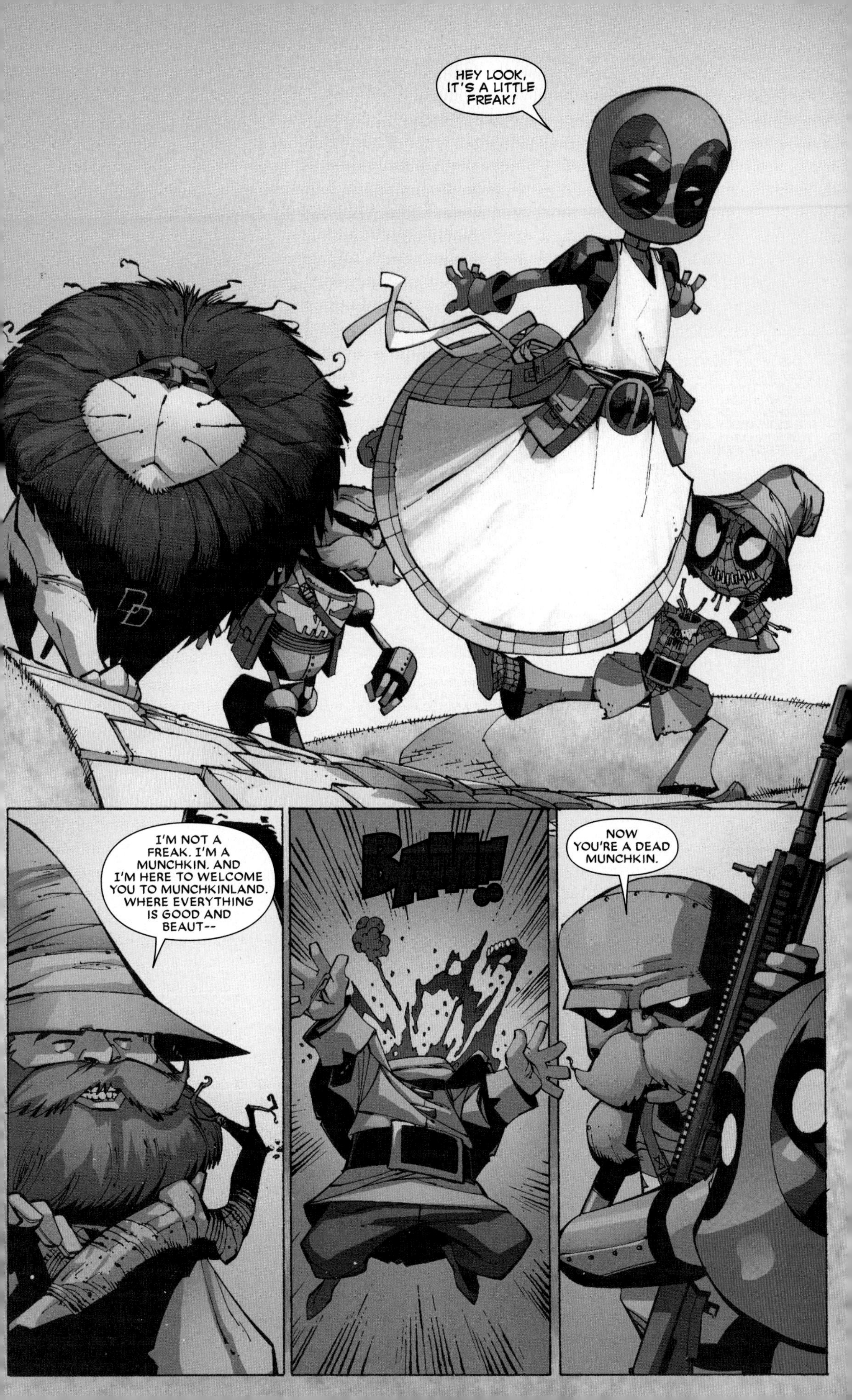
HEY LOOK, IT'S A LITTLE FREAK!
I'M NOT A FREAK. I'M A MUNCHKIN, AND I'M HERE TO WELCOME YOU TO MUNCHKINLAND. WHERE EVERYTHING IS GOOD AND BEAUT--
NOW YOU'RE A DEAD MUNCHKIN.

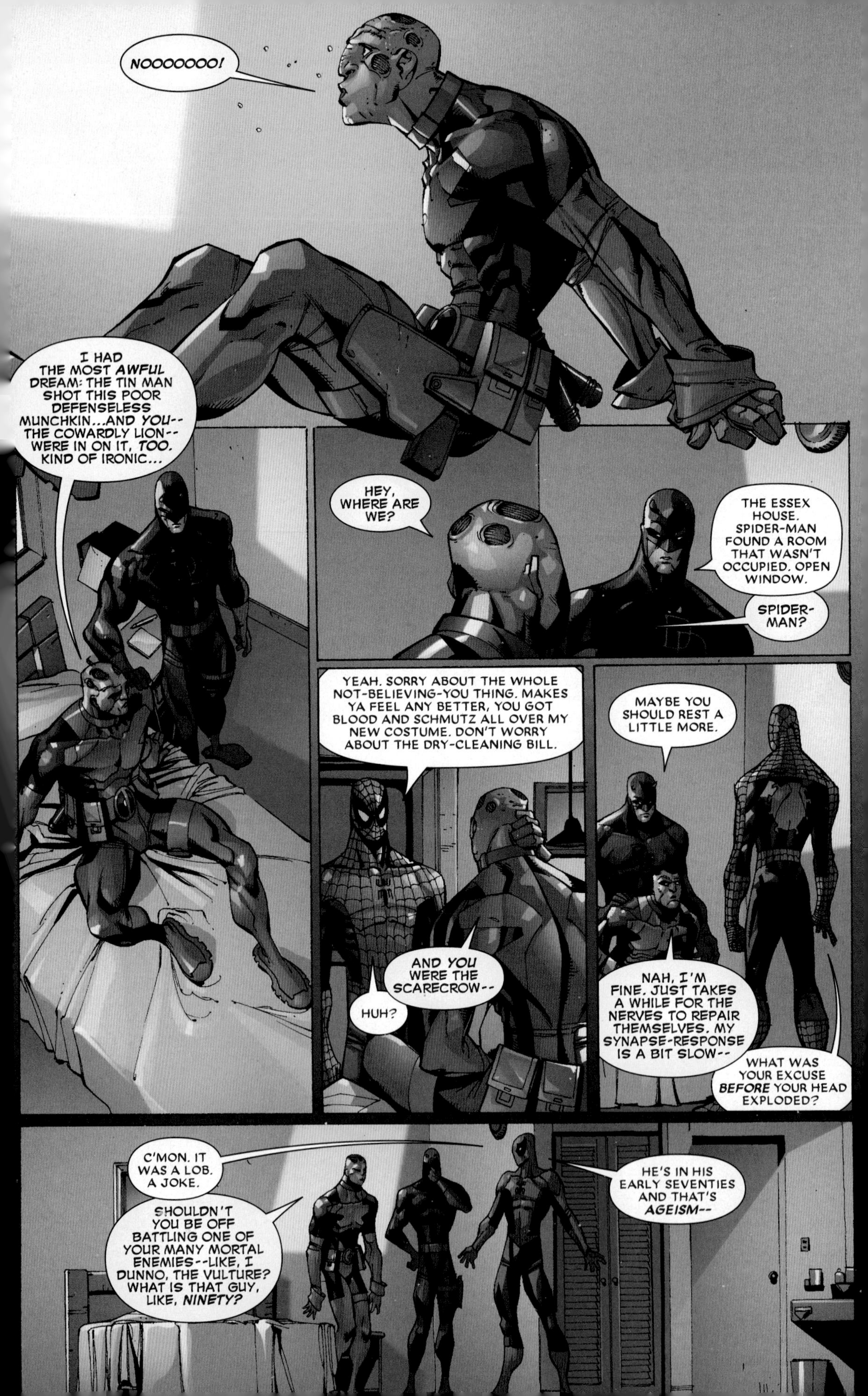
NOOOOOOO!
I HAD THE MOST AWFUL DREAM: THE TIN MAN SHOT THIS POOR DEFENSELESS MUNCHKIN...AND YOU-- THE COWARDLY LION-- WERE IN ON IT, TOO. KIND OF IRONIC...
HEY, WHERE ARE WE?
THE ESSEX HOUSE. SPIDER-MAN FOUND A ROOM THAT WASN'T OCCUPIED. OPEN WINDOW.
SPIDER-MAN?
YEAH. SORRY ABOUT THE WHOLE NOT-BELIEVING-YOU THING. MAKES YA FEEL ANY BETTER, YOU GOT BLOOD AND SCHMUTZ ALL OVER MY NEW COSTUME. DON'T WORRY ABOUT THE DRY-CLEANING BILL.
AND YOU WERE THE SCARECROW--
HUH?
MAYBE YOU SHOULD REST A LITTLE MORE.
NAH, I'M FINE. JUST TAKES A WHILE FOR THE NERVES TO REPAIR THEMSELVES. MY SYNAPSE-RESPONSE IS A BIT SLOW--
WHAT WAS YOUR EXCUSE BEFORE YOUR HEAD EXPLODED?
C'MON. IT WAS A LOB. A JOKE.
SHOULDN'T YOU BE OFF BATTLING ONE OF YOUR MANY MORTAL ENEMIES--LIKE, I DUNNO, THE VULTURE? WHAT IS THAT GUY, LIKE, NINETY?
HE'S IN HIS EARLY SEVENTIES AND THAT'S AGEISM--

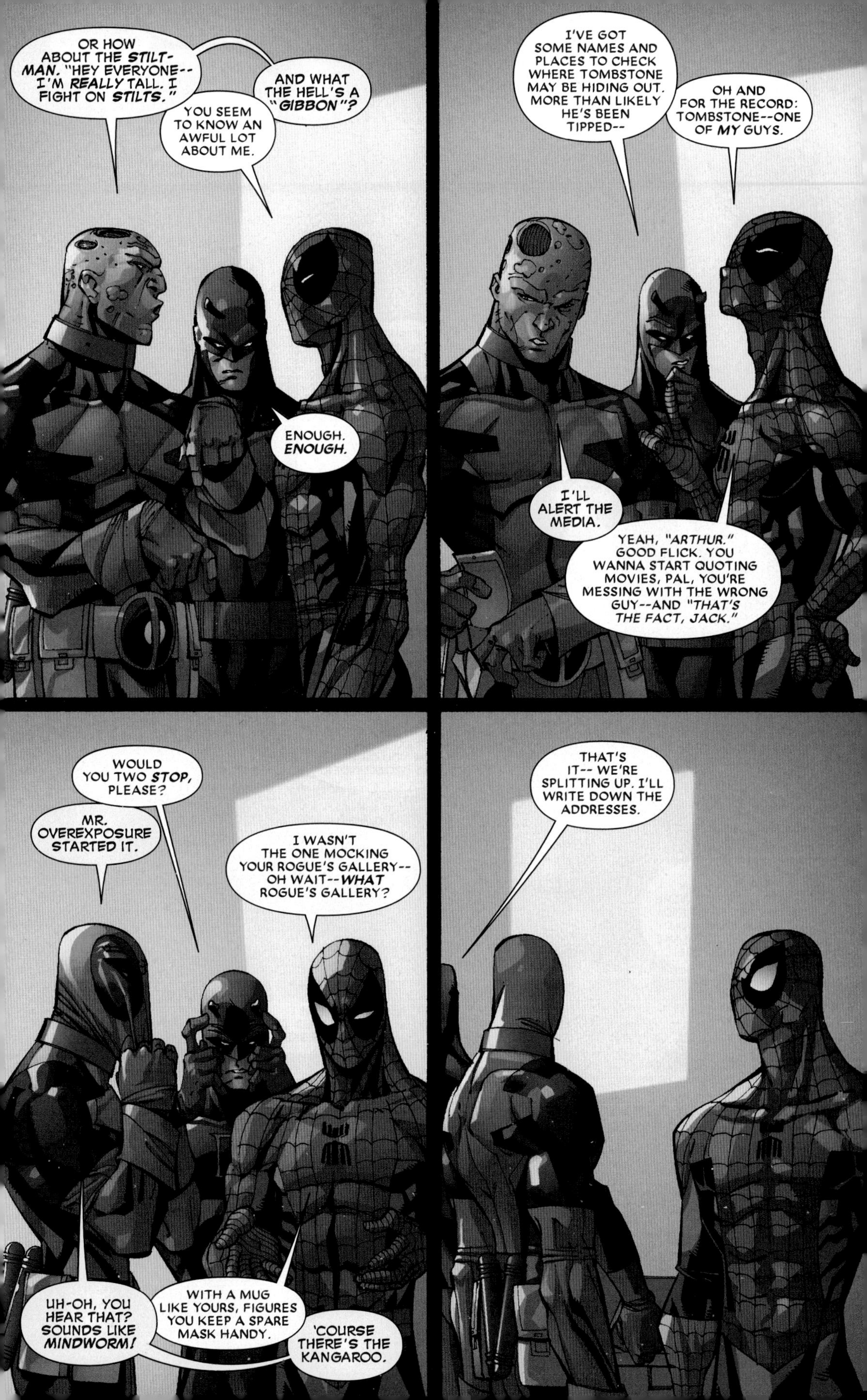
OR HOW ABOUT THE STILT-MAN. "HEY EVERYONE-- I'M REALLY TALL. I FIGHT ON STILTS."
AND WHAT THE HELL'S A "GIBBON"?
YOU SEEM TO KNOW AN AWFUL LOT ABOUT ME.
ENOUGH. ENOUGH.
I'VE GOT SOME NAMES AND PLACES TO CHECK WHERE TOMBSTONE MAY BE HIDING OUT. MORE THAN LIKELY HE'S BEEN TIPPED--
OH AND FOR THE RECORD: TOMBSTONE--ONE OF MY GUYS.
I'LL ALERT THE MEDIA.
YEAH, "ARTHUR." GOOD FLICK. YOU WANNA START QUOTING MOVIES, PAL, YOU'RE MESSING WITH THE WRONG GUY--AND "THAT'S THE FACT, JACK."
WOULD YOU TWO STOP, PLEASE?
MR. OVEREXPOSURE STARTED IT.
I WASN'T THE ONE MOCKING YOUR ROGUE'S GALLERY-- OH WAIT--WHAT ROGUE'S GALLERY?
UH-OH, YOU HEAR THAT? SOUNDS LIKE MINDWORM!
WITH A MUG LIKE YOURS, FIGURES YOU KEEP A SPARE MASK HANDY.
'COURSE THERE'S THE KANGAROO.
THAT'S IT-- WE'RE SPLITTING UP. I'LL WRITE DOWN THE ADDRESSES.

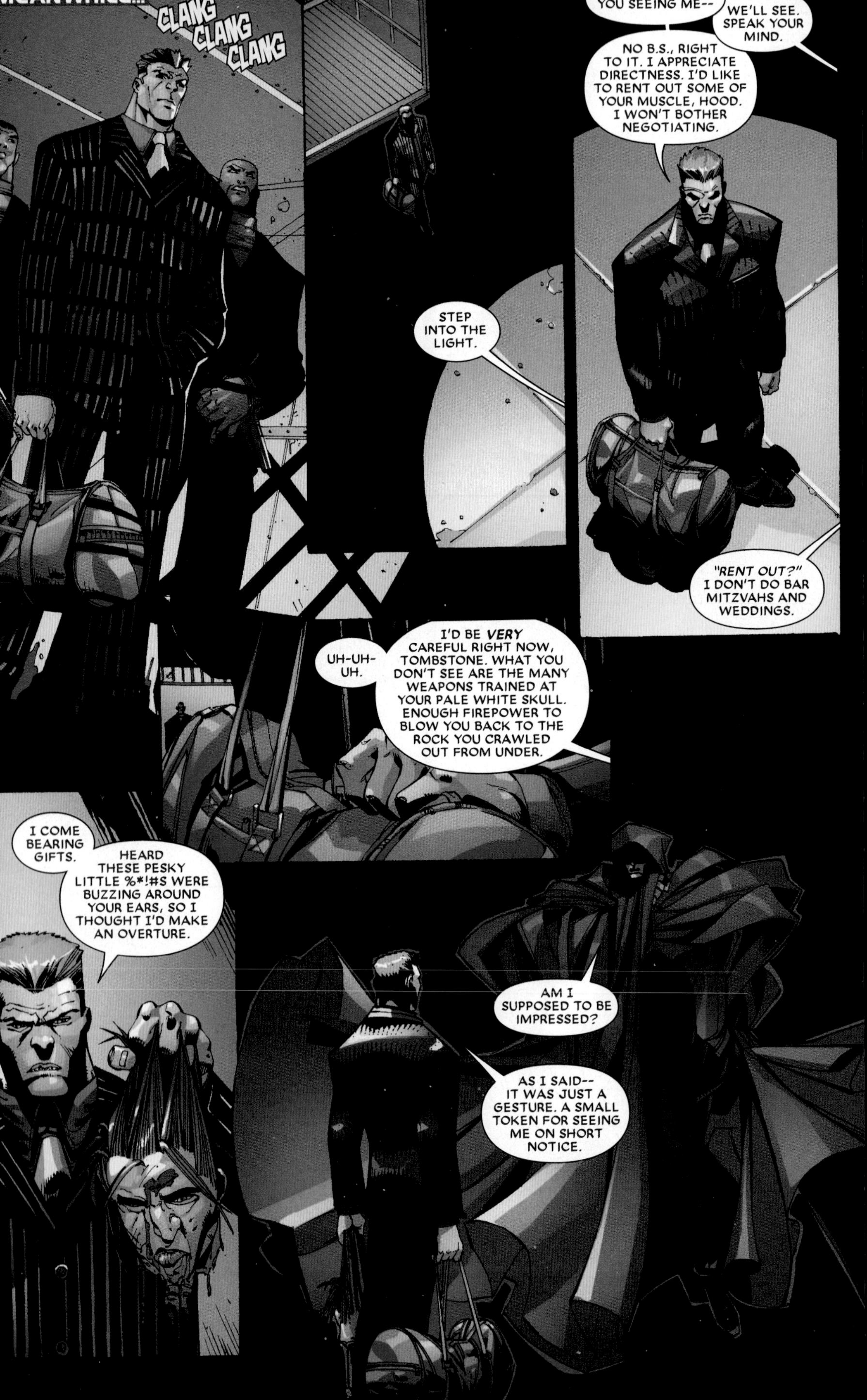
CLANG CLANG CLANG
STEP INTO THE LIGHT.
YOU SEEING ME--
WE'LL SEE. SPEAK YOUR MIND.
NO B.S., RIGHT TO IT. I APPRECIATE DIRECTNESS. I'D LIKE TO RENT OUT SOME OF YOUR MUSCLE, HOOD. I WON'T BOTHER NEGOTIATING.
"RENT OUT?" I DON'T DO BAR MITZVAHS AND WEDDINGS.
UH-UH-UH.
I'D BE VERY CAREFUL RIGHT NOW, TOMBSTONE. WHAT YOU DON'T SEE ARE THE MANY WEAPONS TRAINED AT YOUR PALE WHITE SKULL. ENOUGH FIREPOWER TO BLOW YOU BACK TO THE ROCK YOU CRAWLED OUT FROM UNDER.
I COME BEARING GIFTS.
HEARD THESE PESKY LITTLE %*!#S WERE BUZZING AROUND YOUR EARS, SO I THOUGHT I'D MAKE AN OVERTURE.
AM I SUPPOSED TO BE IMPRESSED?
AS I SAID-- IT WAS JUST A GESTURE. A SMALL TOKEN FOR SEEING ME ON SHORT NOTICE.

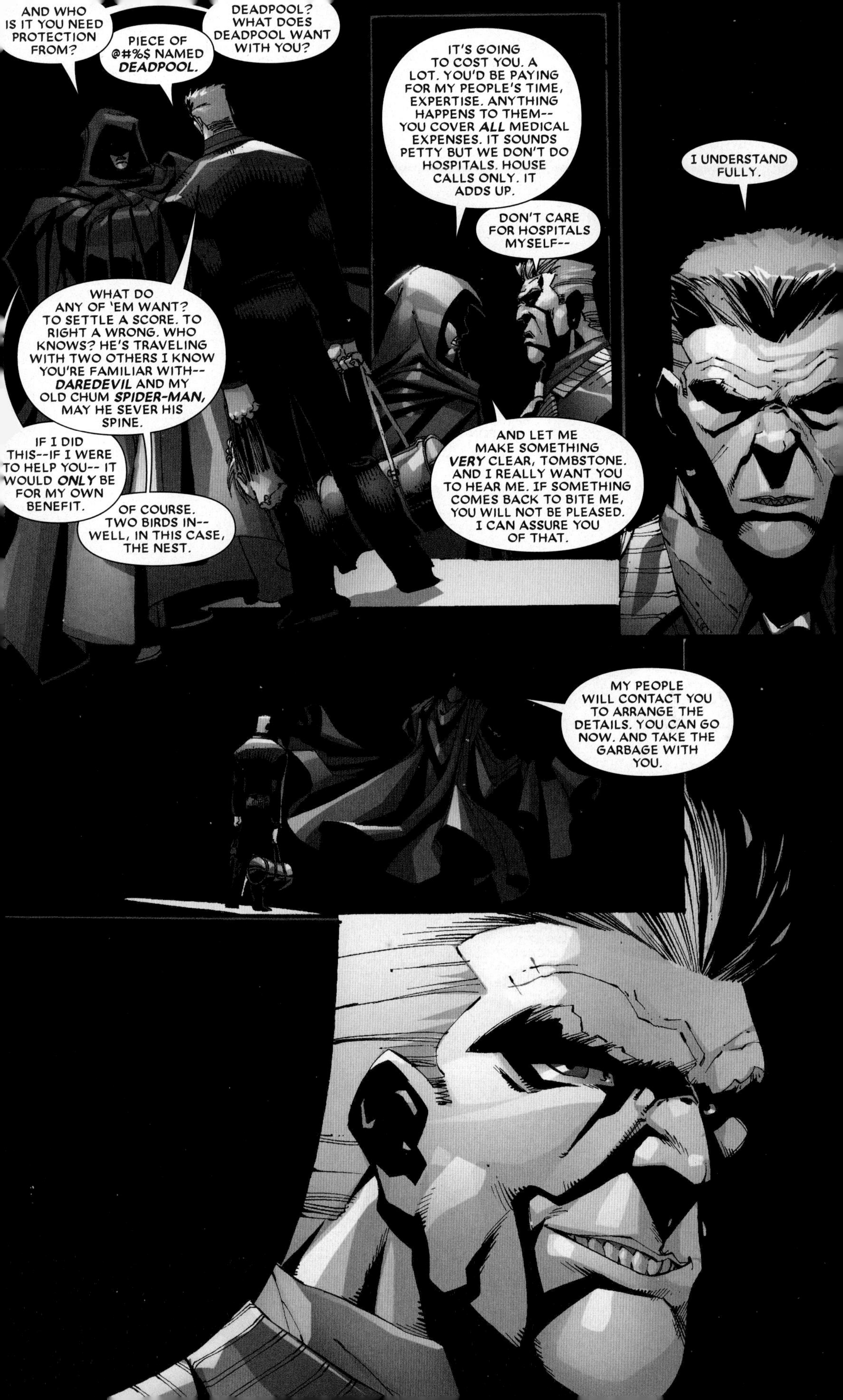
AND WHO IS IT YOU NEED PROTECTION FROM?
PIECE OF @#%$ NAMED DEADPOOL.
DEADPOOL? WHAT DOES DEADPOOL WANT WITH YOU?
WHAT DO ANY OF 'EM WANT? TO SETTLE A SCORE. TO RIGHT A WRONG. WHO KNOWS? HE'S TRAVELING WITH TWO OTHERS I KNOW YOU'RE FAMILIAR WITH-- DAREDEVIL AND MY OLD CHUM SPIDER-MAN, MAY HE SEVER HIS SPINE.
IF I DID THIS--IF I WERE TO HELP YOU-- IT WOULD ONLY BE FOR MY OWN BENEFIT.
OF COURSE. TWO BIRDS IN-- WELL, IN THIS CASE, THE NEST.
IT'S GOING TO COST YOU. A LOT. YOU'D BE PAYING FOR MY PEOPLE'S TIME, EXPERTISE. ANYTHING HAPPENS TO THEM-- YOU COVER ALL MEDICAL EXPENSES. IT SOUNDS PETTY BUT WE DON'T DO HOSPITALS. HOUSE CALLS ONLY. IT ADDS UP.
DON'T CARE FOR HOSPITALS MYSELF--
AND LET ME MAKE SOMETHING VERY CLEAR, TOMBSTONE. AND I REALLY WANT YOU TO HEAR ME. IF SOMETHING COMES BACK TO BITE ME, YOU WILL NOT BE PLEASED. I CAN ASSURE YOU OF THAT.
I UNDERSTAND FULLY.
MY PEOPLE WILL CONTACT YOU TO ARRANGE THE DETAILS. YOU CAN GO NOW. AND TAKE THE GARBAGE WITH YOU.

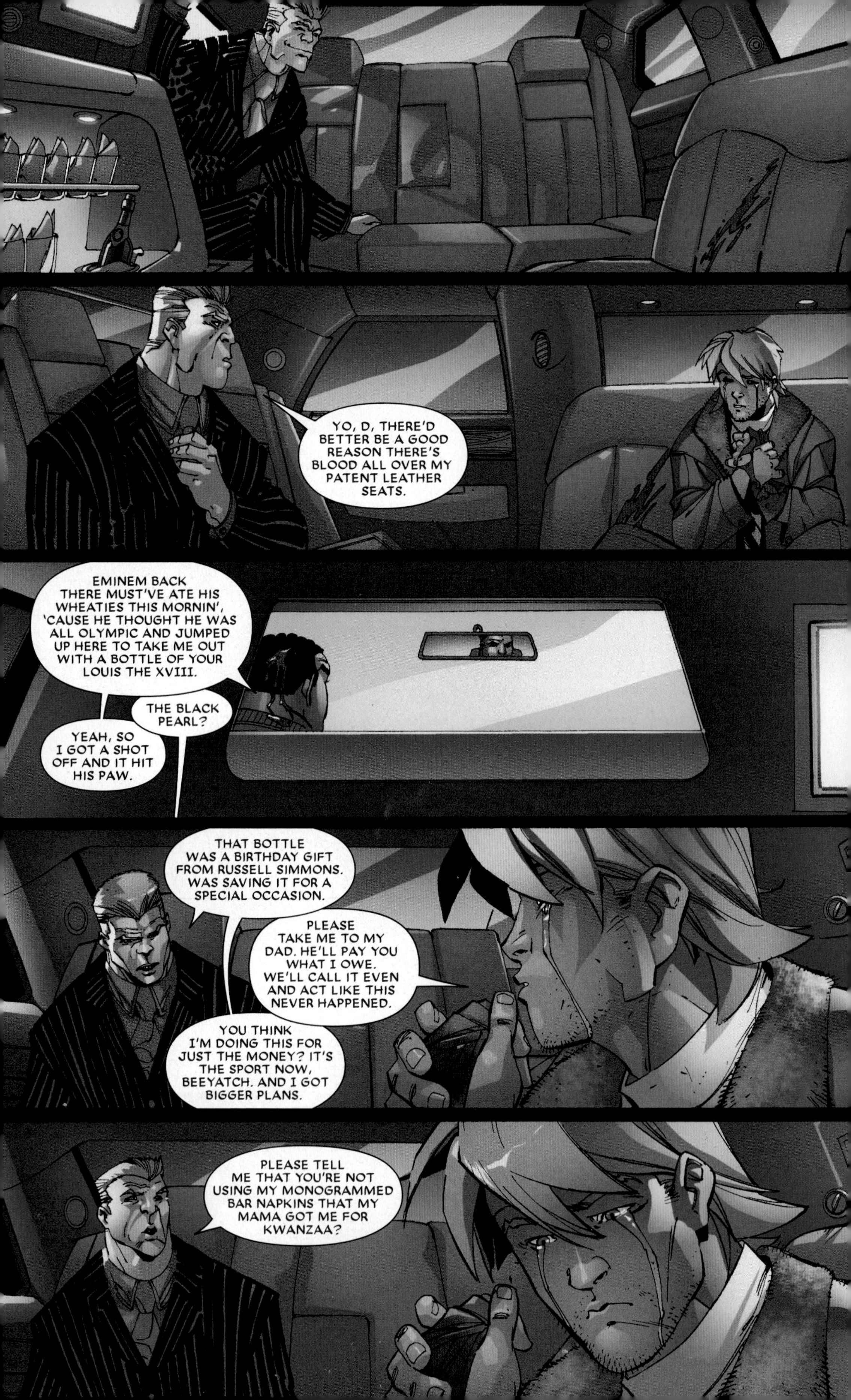
YO, D, THERE'D BETTER BE A GOOD REASON THERE'S BLOOD ALL OVER MY PATENT LEATHER SEATS.
EMINEM BACK THERE MUST'VE ATE HIS WHEATIES THIS MORNIN', 'CAUSE HE THOUGHT HE WAS ALL OLYMPIC AND JUMPED UP HERE TO TAKE ME OUT WITH A BOTTLE OF YOUR LOUIS THE XVIII.
THE BLACK PEARL?
YEAH, SO I GOT A SHOT OFF AND IT HIT HIS PAW.
THAT BOTTLE WAS A BIRTHDAY GIFT FROM RUSSELL SIMMONS. WAS SAVING IT FOR A SPECIAL OCCASION.
PLEASE TAKE ME TO MY DAD. HE'LL PAY YOU WHAT I OWE. WE'LL CALL IT EVEN AND ACT LIKE THIS NEVER HAPPENED.
YOU THINK I'M DOING THIS FOR JUST THE MONEY? IT'S THE SPORT NOW, BEEYATCH. AND I GOT BIGGER PLANS.
PLEASE TELL ME THAT YOU'RE NOT USING MY MONOGRAMMED BAR NAPKINS THAT MY MAMA GOT ME FOR KWANZAA?

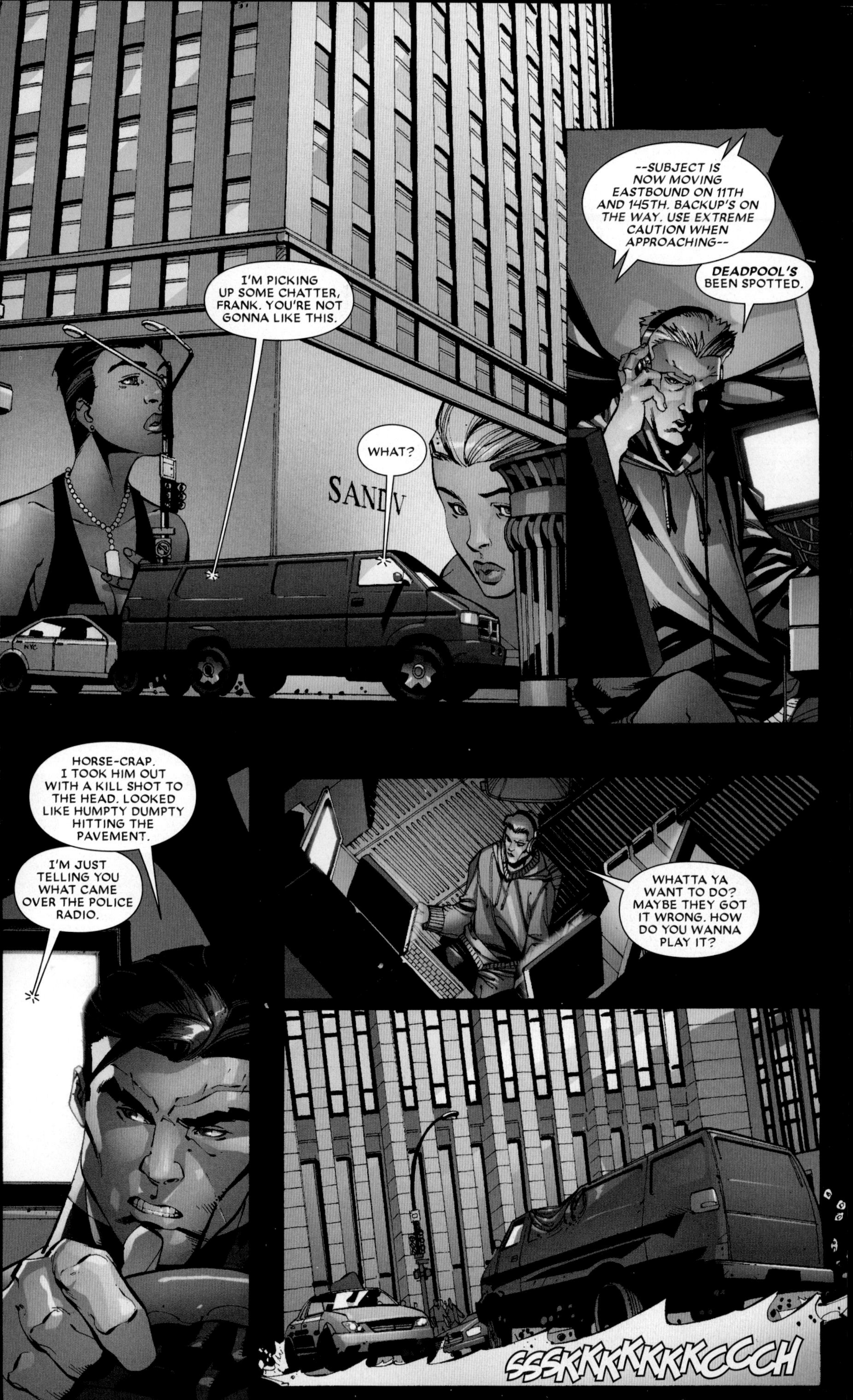
I'M PICKING UP SOME CHATTER, FRANK. YOU'RE NOT GONNA LIKE THIS.
WHAT?
SAND V
--SUBJECT IS NOW MOVING EASTBOUND ON 11TH AND 145TH. BACKUP'S ON THE WAY. USE EXTREME CAUTION WHEN APPROACHING--
DEADPOOL'S BEEN SPOTTED.
HORSE-CRAP. I TOOK HIM OUT WITH A KILL SHOT TO THE HEAD. LOOKED LIKE HUMPTY DUMPTY HITTING THE PAVEMENT.
I'M JUST TELLING YOU WHAT CAME OVER THE POLICE RADIO.
WHATTA YA WANT TO DO? MAYBE THEY GOT IT WRONG. HOW DO YOU WANNA PLAY IT?
SSSKKKKKKKCCCH

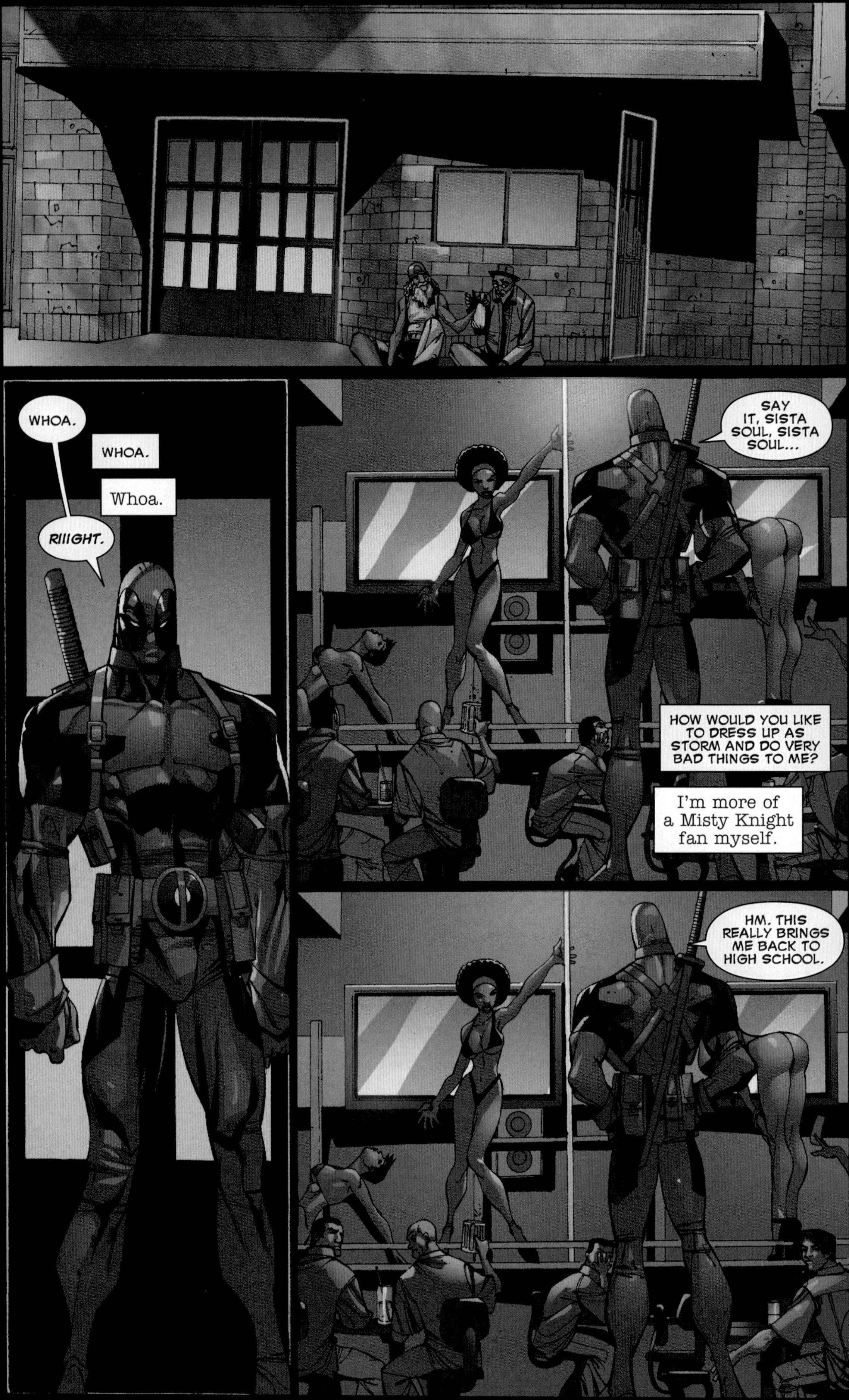
WHOA.
WHOA.
Whoa.
RIIIGHT.
SAY IT, SISTA SOUL, SISTA SOUL...
HOW WOULD YOU LIKE TO DRESS UP AS STORM AND DO VERY BAD THINGS TO ME?
I'm more of a Misty Knight fan myself.
HM. THIS REALLY BRINGS ME BACK TO HIGH SCHOOL.

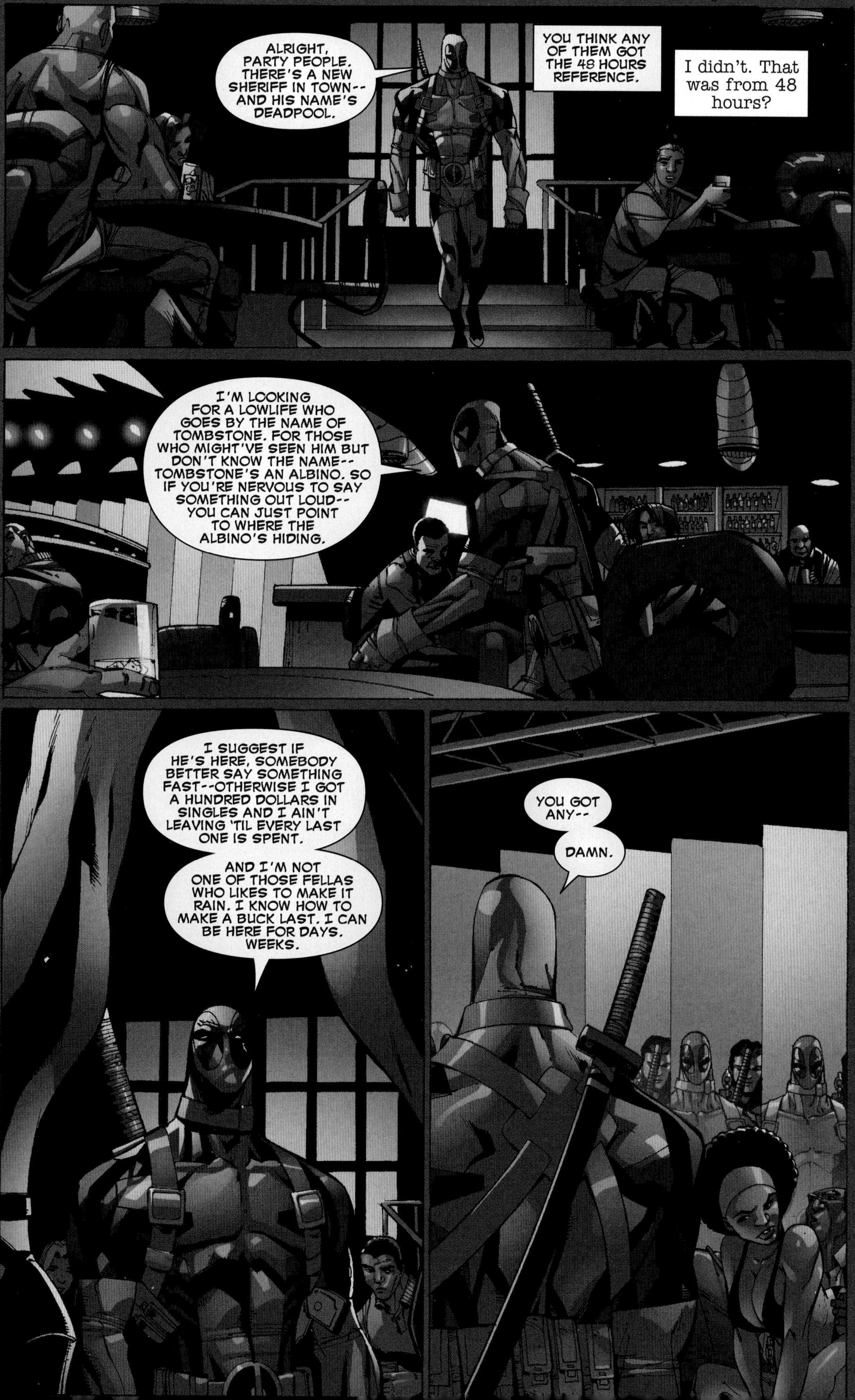

ALRIGHT, PARTY PEOPLE. THERE'S A NEW SHERIFF IN TOWN--AND HIS NAME'S DEADPOOL.
YOU THINK ANY OF THEM GOT THE 48 HOURS REFERENCE.
I didn't. That was from 48 hours?
I'M LOOKING FOR A LOWLIFE WHO GOES BY THE NAME OF TOMBSTONE. FOR THOSE WHO MIGHT'VE SEEN HIM BUT DON'T KNOW THE NAME--TOMBSTONE'S AN ALBINO. SO IF YOU'RE NERVOUS TO SAY SOMETHING OUT LOUD--YOU CAN JUST POINT TO WHERE THE ALBINO'S HIDING.
I SUGGEST IF HE'S HERE, SOMEBODY BETTER SAY SOMETHING FAST--OTHERWISE I GOT A HUNDRED DOLLARS IN SINGLES AND I AIN'T LEAVING 'TIL EVERY LAST ONE IS SPENT.
AND I'M NOT ONE OF THOSE FELLAS WHO LIKES TO MAKE IT RAIN. I KNOW HOW TO MAKE A BUCK LAST. I CAN BE HERE FOR DAYS. WEEKS.
YOU GOT ANY--
DAMN.

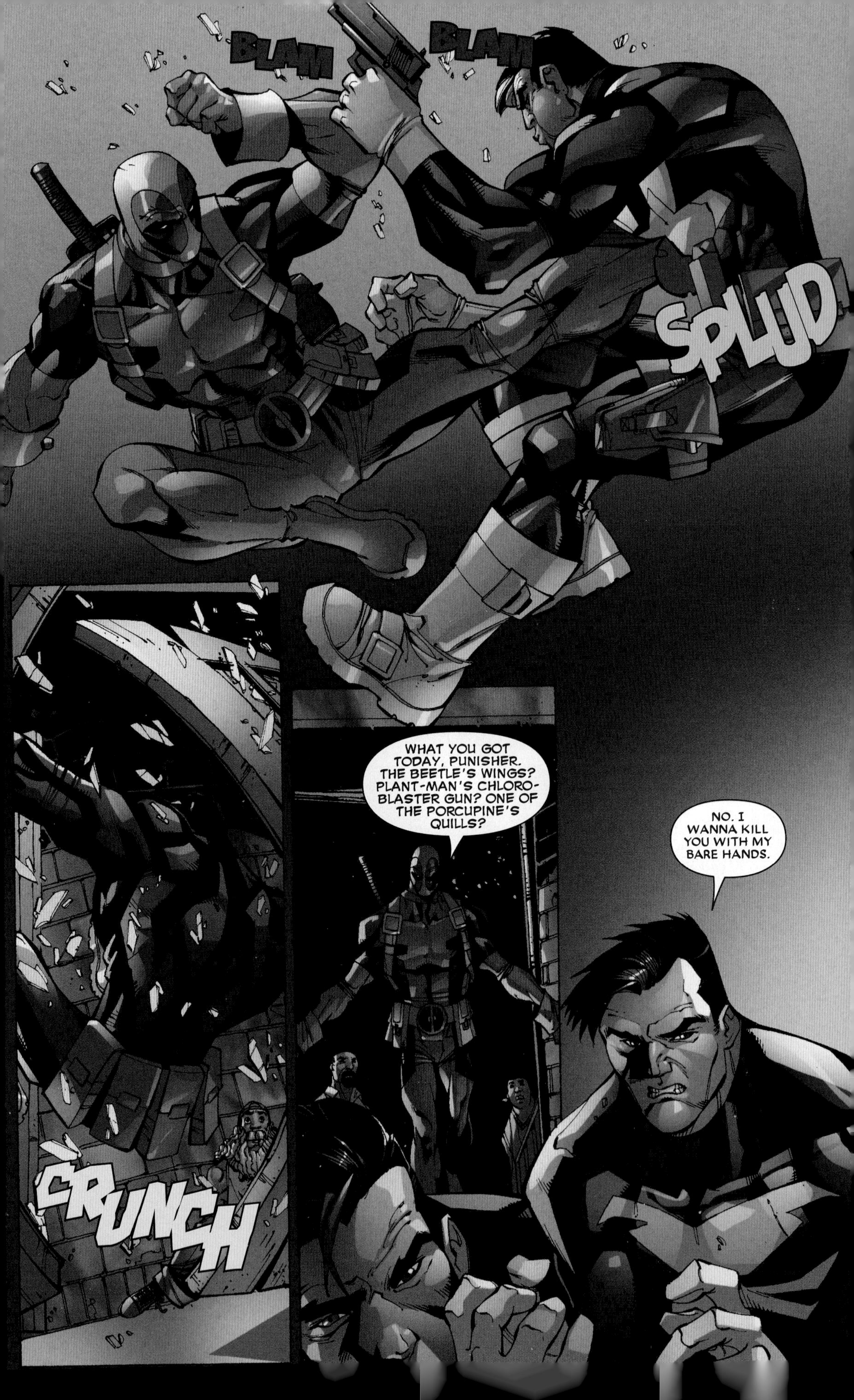
BLAM
BLAM
SPLUD
CRUNCH
WHAT YOU GOT TODAY, PUNISHER. THE BEETLE'S WINGS? PLANT-MAN'S CHLORO-BLASTER GUN? ONE OF THE PORCUPINE'S QUILLS?
NO. I WANNA KILL YOU WITH MY BARE HANDS.

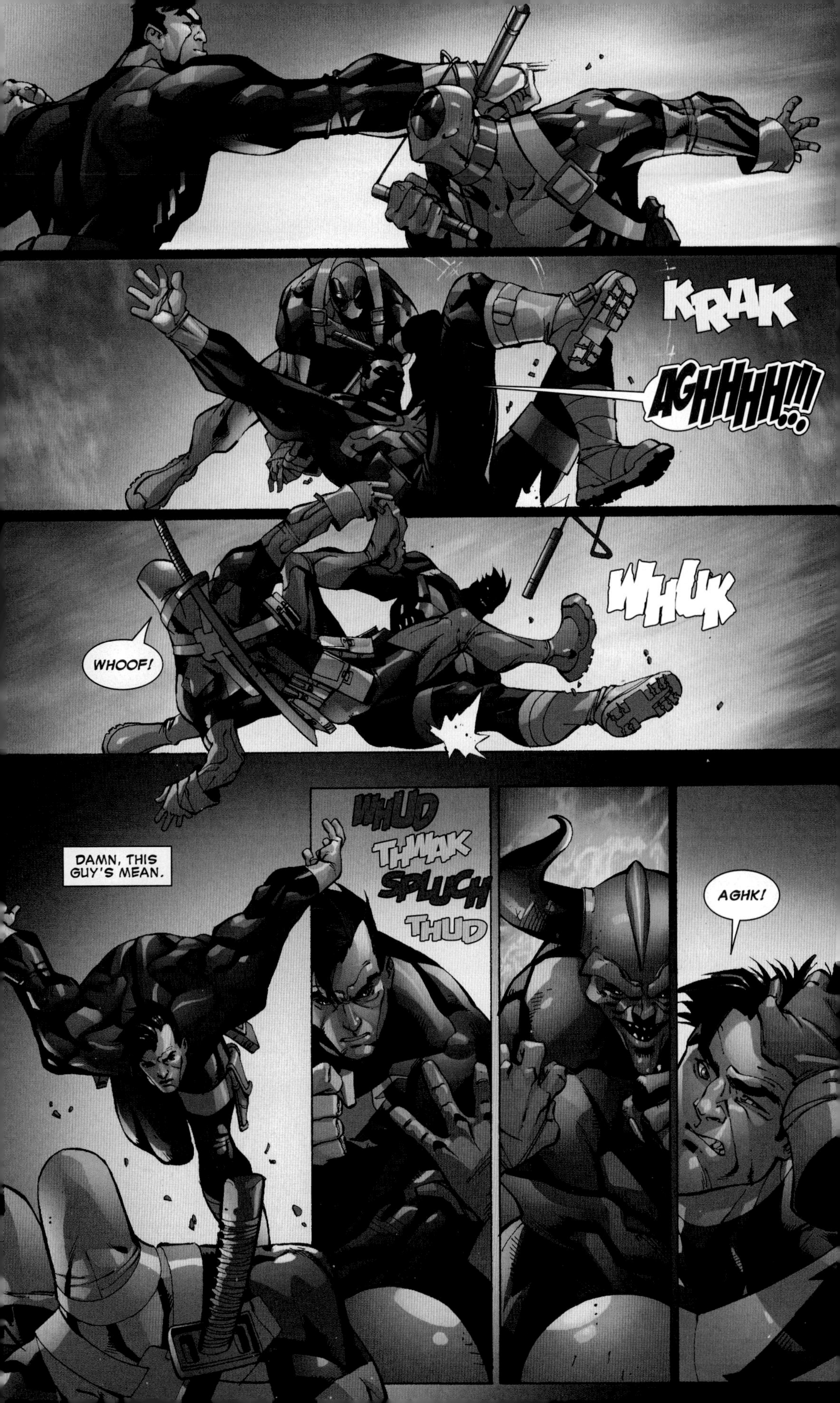
KRAK
AGHHHH!!!
WHUK
WHOOF!
DAMN, THIS GUY'S MEAN.
WHUD
THWAK
SPLUCH
THUD
AGHK!

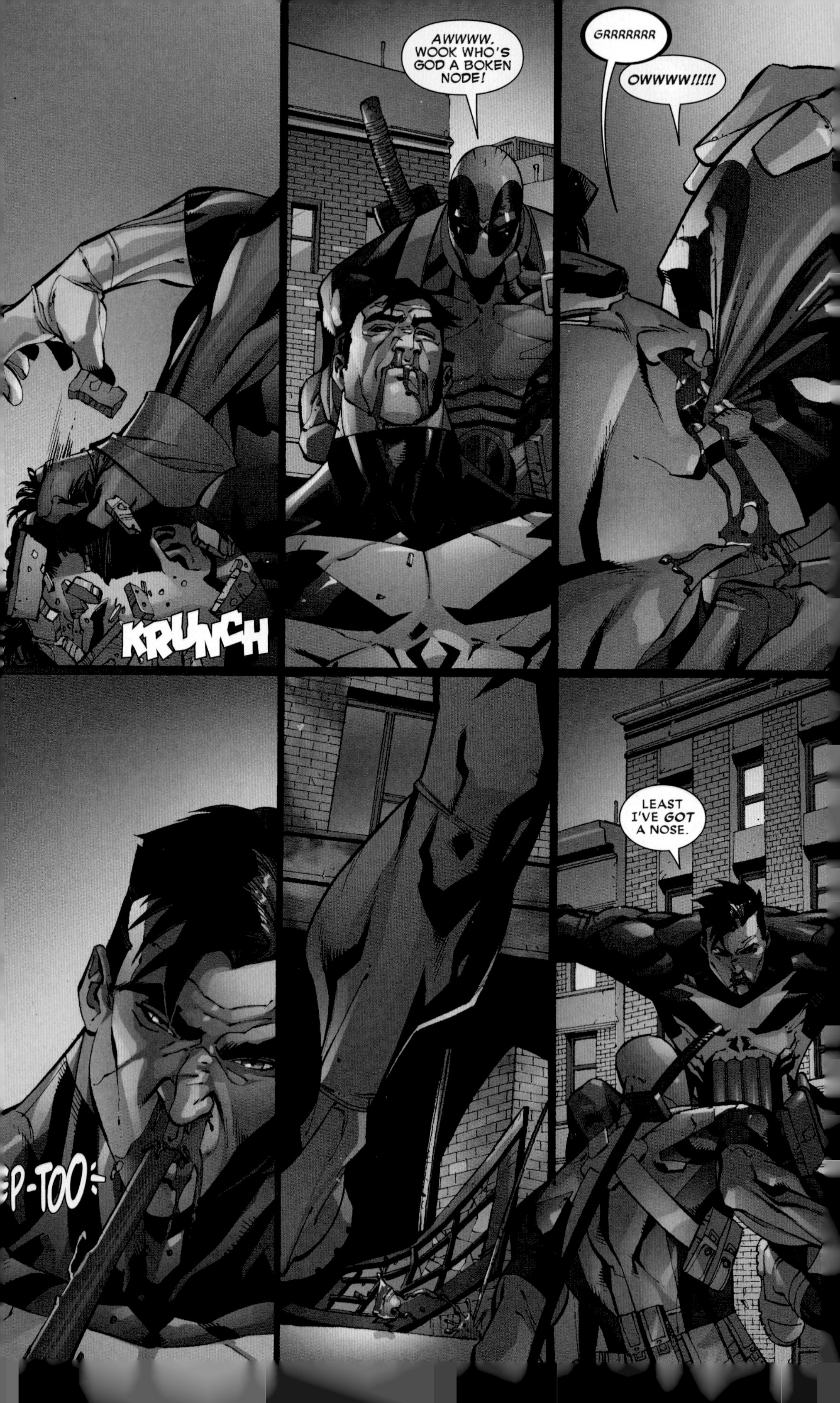
KRUNCH
AWWWW. WOOK WHO'S GOD A BOKEN NODE!
GRRRRRRR
OWWWW!!!!!
P-TOO
LEAST I'VE GOT A NOSE.

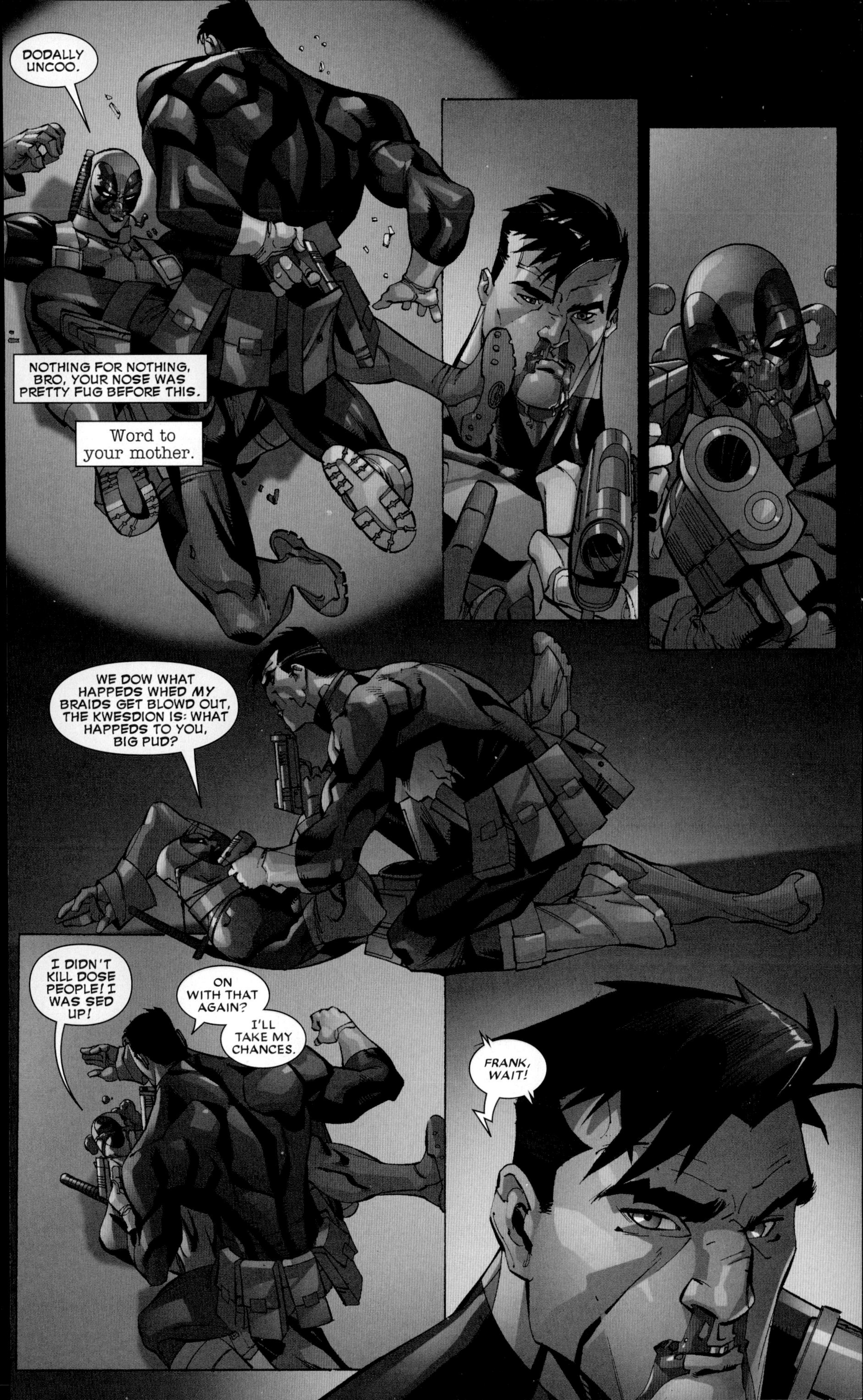
DODALLY UNCOO.
NOTHING FOR NOTHING, BRO, YOUR NOSE WAS PRETTY FUG BEFORE THIS.
Word to your mother.
WE DOW WHAT HAPPEDS WHED MY BRAIDS GET BLOWD OUT, THE KWESDION IS: WHAT HAPPEDS TO YOU, BIG PUD?
I DIDN'T KILL DOSE PEOPLE! I WAS SED UP!
ON WITH THAT AGAIN?
I'LL TAKE MY CHANCES.
FRANK, WAIT!

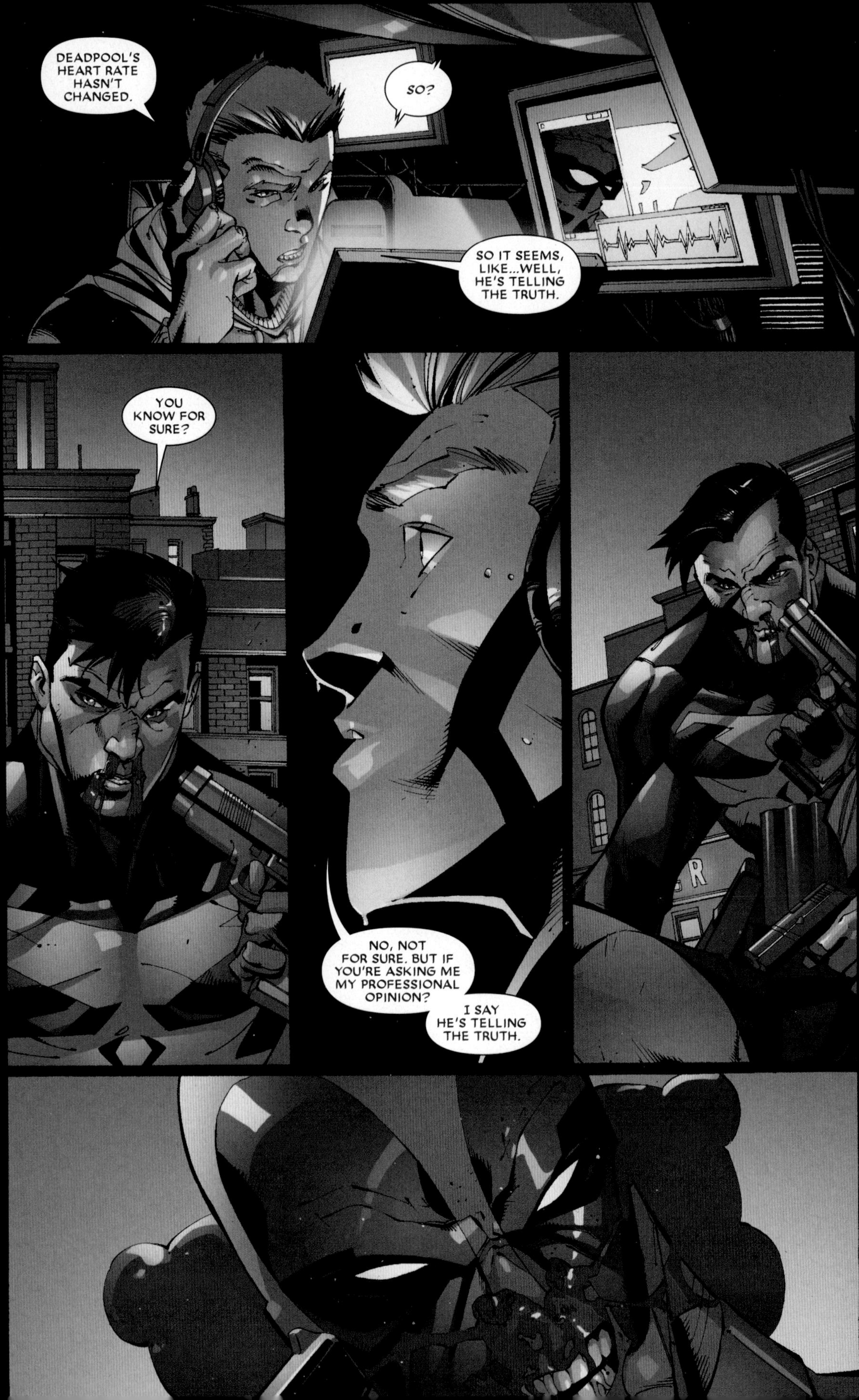
DEADPOOL'S HEART RATE HASN'T CHANGED.
SO?
SO IT SEEMS, LIKE...WELL, HE'S TELLING THE TRUTH.
YOU KNOW FOR SURE?
NO, NOT FOR SURE. BUT IF YOU'RE ASKING ME MY PROFESSIONAL OPINION?
I SAY HE'S TELLING THE TRUTH.

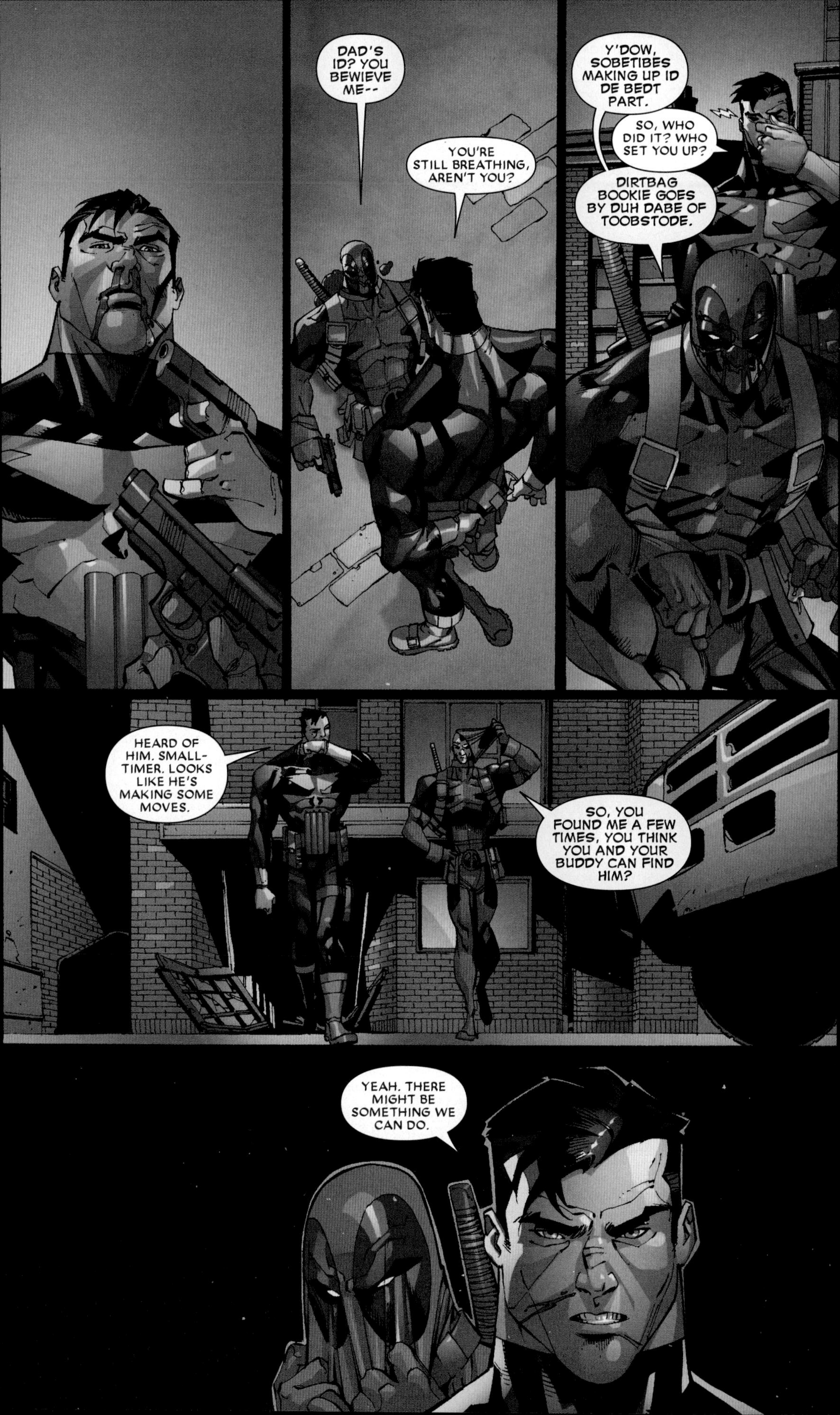
DAD'S ID? YOU BEWIEVE ME--
YOU'RE STILL BREATHING, AREN'T YOU?
Y'DOW, SOBETIBES MAKING UP ID DE BEDT PART.
SO, WHO DID IT? WHO SET YOU UP?
DIRTBAG BOOKIE GOES BY DUH DABE OF TOOBSTODE.
HEARD OF HIM. SMALL-TIMER. LOOKS LIKE HE'S MAKING SOME MOVES.
SO, YOU FOUND ME A FEW TIMES, YOU THINK YOU AND YOUR BUDDY CAN FIND HIM?
YEAH. THERE MIGHT BE SOMETHING WE CAN DO.

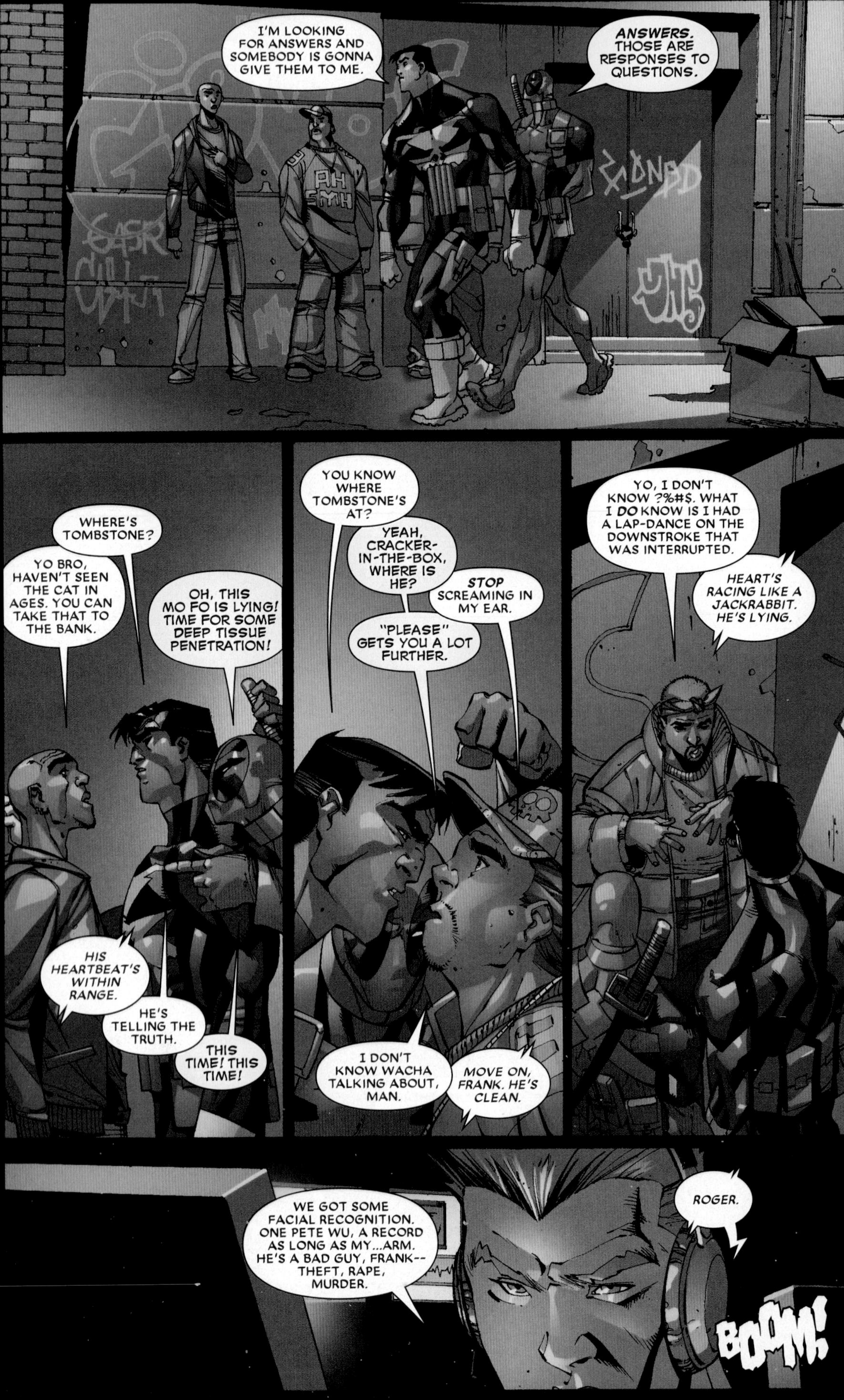
I'M LOOKING FOR ANSWERS AND SOMEBODY IS GONNA GIVE THEM TO ME.
ANSWERS. THOSE ARE RESPONSES TO QUESTIONS.
WHERE'S TOMBSTONE?
YO BRO, HAVEN'T SEEN THE CAT IN AGES. YOU CAN TAKE THAT TO THE BANK.
OH, THIS MO FO IS LYING! TIME FOR SOME DEEP TISSUE PENETRATION!
HIS HEARTBEAT'S WITHIN RANGE.
HE'S TELLING THE TRUTH.
THIS TIME! THIS TIME!
YOU KNOW WHERE TOMBSTONE'S AT?
YEAH, CRACKER-IN-THE-BOX, WHERE IS HE?
STOP SCREAMING IN MY EAR.
"PLEASE" GETS YOU A LOT FURTHER.
I DON'T KNOW WACHA TALKING ABOUT, MAN.
MOVE ON, FRANK. HE'S CLEAN.
YO, I DON'T KNOW ?%#$. WHAT I DO KNOW IS I HAD A LAP-DANCE ON THE DOWNSTROKE THAT WAS INTERRUPTED.
HEART'S RACING LIKE A JACKRABBIT. HE'S LYING.
WE GOT SOME FACIAL RECOGNITION. ONE PETE WU, A RECORD AS LONG AS MY...ARM. HE'S A BAD GUY, FRANK-- THEFT, RAPE, MURDER.
ROGER.
BOOM!

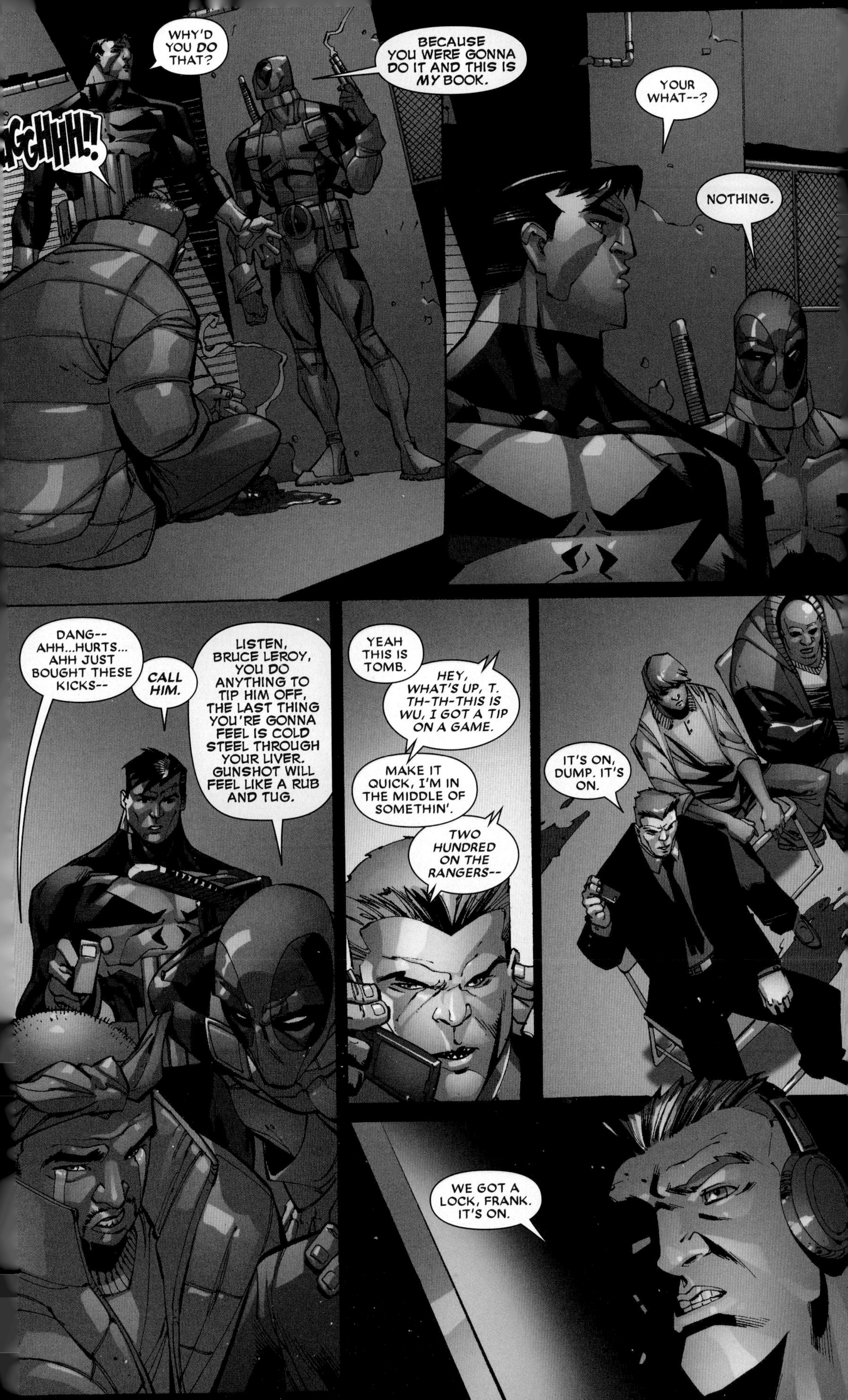

GGHHH!!
WHY'D YOU DO THAT?
BECAUSE YOU WERE GONNA DO IT AND THIS IS MY BOOK.
YOUR WHAT--?
NOTHING.
DANG-- AHH...HURTS... AHH JUST BOUGHT THESE KICKS--
CALL HIM.
LISTEN, BRUCE LEROY, YOU DO ANYTHING TO TIP HIM OFF, THE LAST THING YOU'RE GONNA FEEL IS COLD STEEL THROUGH YOUR LIVER. GUNSHOT WILL FEEL LIKE A RUB AND TUG.
YEAH THIS IS TOMB.
HEY, WHAT'S UP, T. TH-TH-THIS IS WU, I GOT A TIP ON A GAME.
MAKE IT QUICK, I'M IN THE MIDDLE OF SOMETHIN'.
TWO HUNDRED ON THE RANGERS--
IT'S ON, DUMP. IT'S ON.
WE GOT A LOCK, FRANK. IT'S ON.

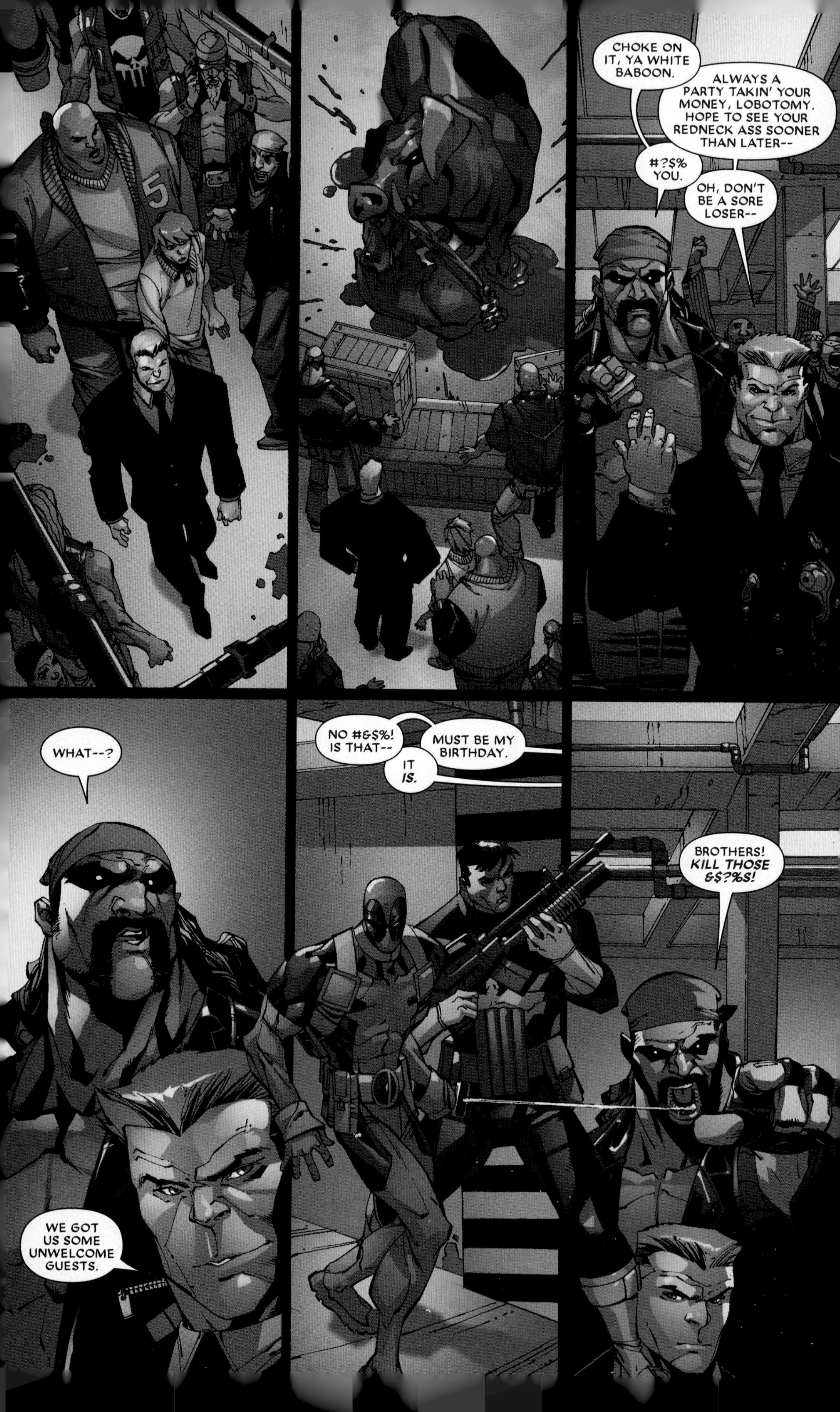
CHOKE ON IT, YA WHITE BABOON.
ALWAYS A PARTY TAKIN' YOUR MONEY, LOBOTOMY. HOPE TO SEE YOUR REDNECK ASS SOONER THAN LATER--
#?$% YOU.
OH, DON'T BE A SORE LOSER--
WHAT--?
WE GOT US SOME UNWELCOME GUESTS.
NO #&$%! IS THAT--
MUST BE MY BIRTHDAY.
IT *IS.*
BROTHERS! *KILL THOSE &$?%S!*

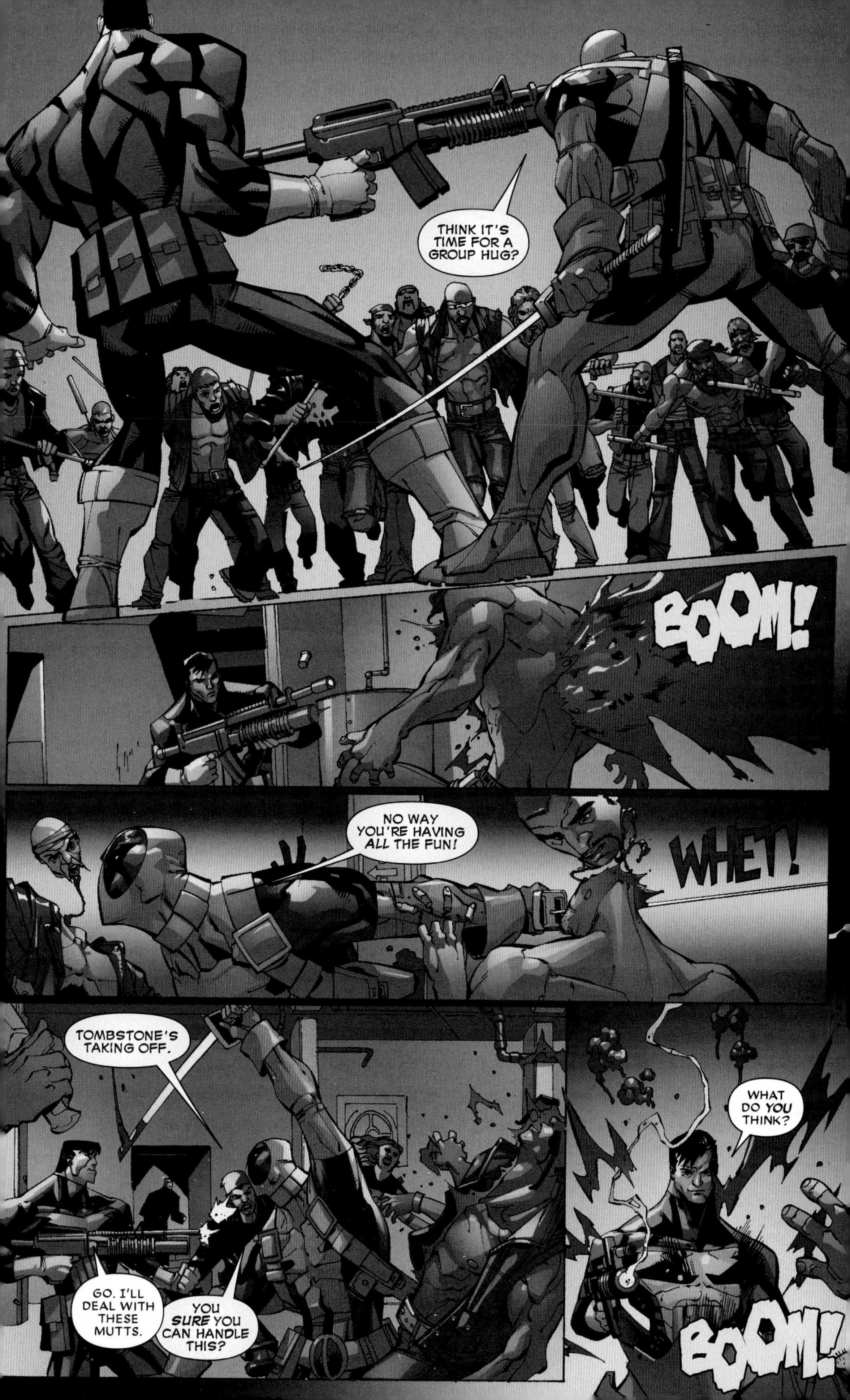
THINK IT'S TIME FOR A GROUP HUG?
BOOM!
NO WAY YOU'RE HAVING ALL THE FUN!
WHET!
TOMBSTONE'S TAKING OFF.
GO. I'LL DEAL WITH THESE MUTTS.
YOU SURE YOU CAN HANDLE THIS?
WHAT DO YOU THINK?
BOOM!

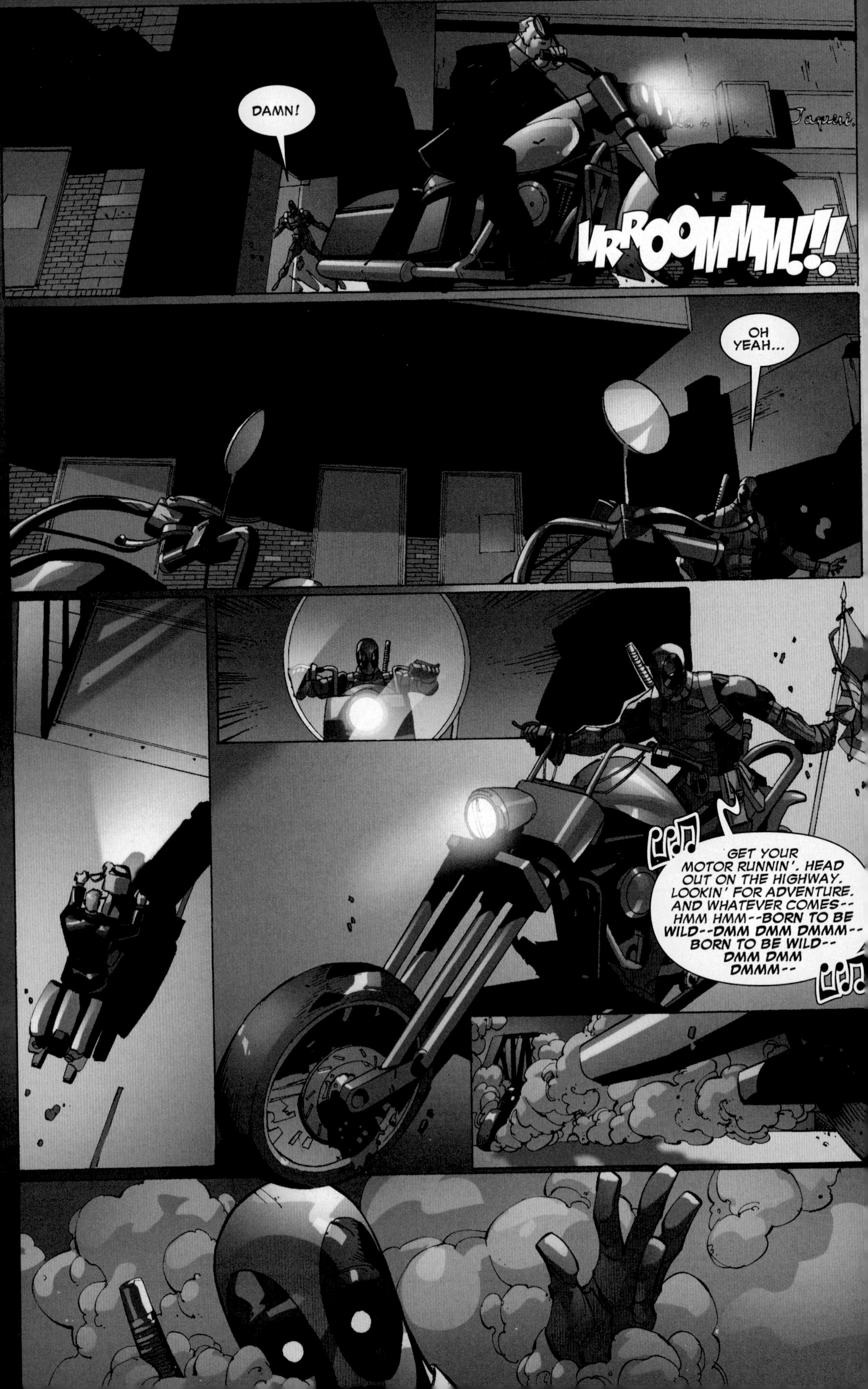
DAMN!
VRROOMMMM!!!
OH YEAH...
GET YOUR MOTOR RUNNIN'. HEAD OUT ON THE HIGHWAY. LOOKIN' FOR ADVENTURE. AND WHATEVER COMES-- HMM HMM--BORN TO BE WILD--DMM DMM DMMM-- BORN TO BE WILD-- DMM DMM DMMM--

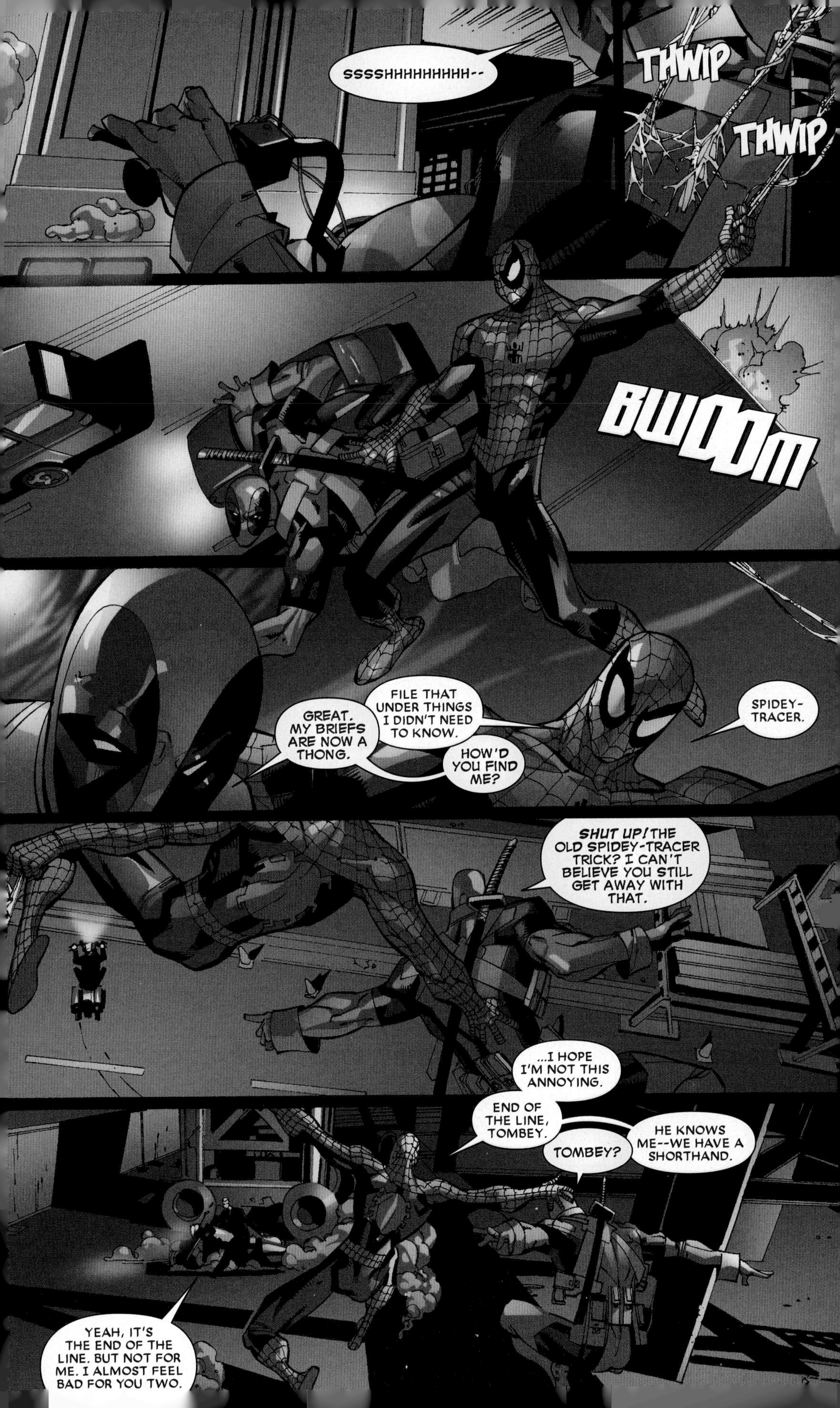
SSSSHHHHHHHHHH--
THWIP
THWIP
BWOOM
GREAT. MY BRIEFS ARE NOW A THONG.
FILE THAT UNDER THINGS I DIDN'T NEED TO KNOW.
HOW'D YOU FIND ME?
SPIDEY-TRACER.
SHUT UP! THE OLD SPIDEY-TRACER TRICK? I CAN'T BELIEVE YOU STILL GET AWAY WITH THAT.
...I HOPE I'M NOT THIS ANNOYING.
END OF THE LINE, TOMBEY.
TOMBEY?
HE KNOWS ME--WE HAVE A SHORTHAND.
YEAH, IT'S THE END OF THE LINE. BUT NOT FOR ME. I ALMOST FEEL BAD FOR YOU TWO.

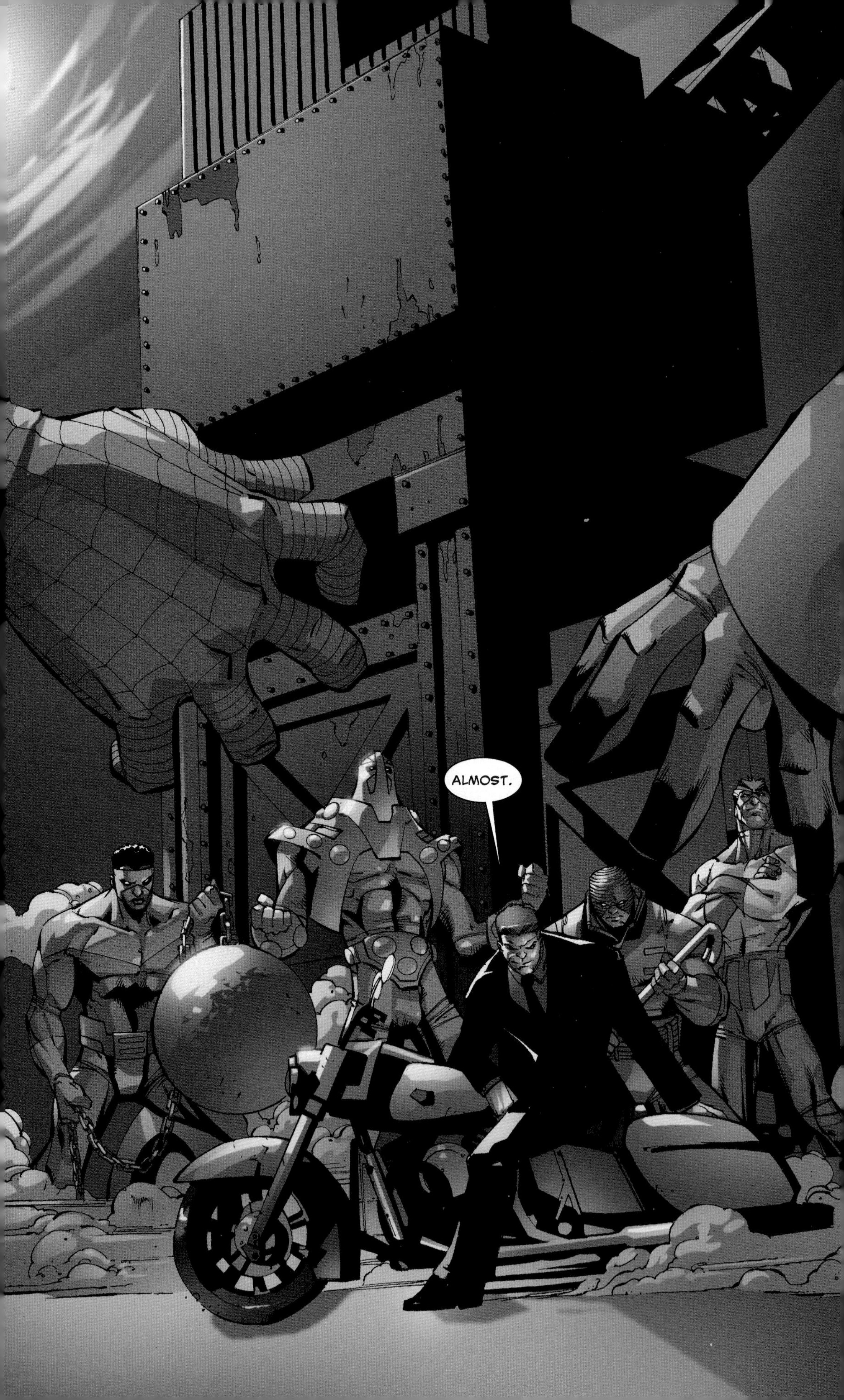
ALMOST.

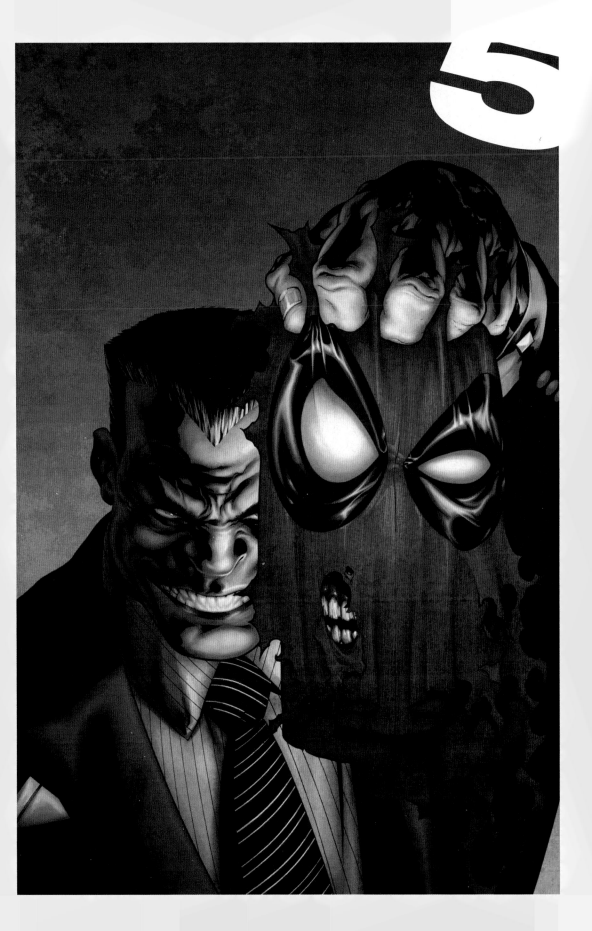

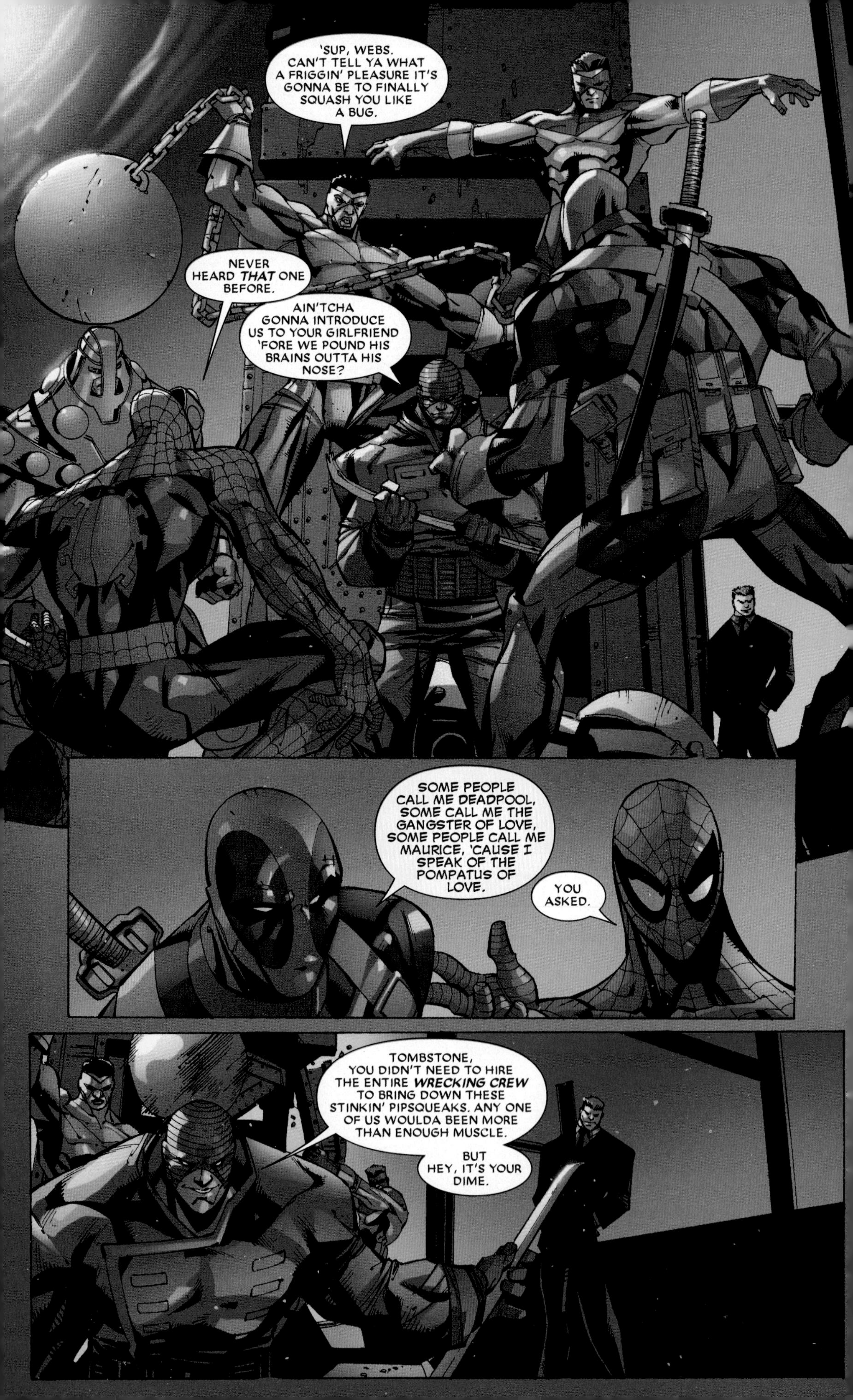
'SUP, WEBS. CAN'T TELL YA WHAT A FRIGGIN' PLEASURE IT'S GONNA BE TO FINALLY SQUASH YOU LIKE A BUG.
NEVER HEARD *THAT* ONE BEFORE.
AIN'TCHA GONNA INTRODUCE US TO YOUR GIRLFRIEND 'FORE WE POUND HIS BRAINS OUTTA HIS NOSE?
SOME PEOPLE CALL ME **DEADPOOL**, SOME CALL ME THE GANGSTER OF LOVE, SOME PEOPLE CALL ME MAURICE, 'CAUSE I SPEAK OF THE POMPATUS OF LOVE.
YOU ASKED.
TOMBSTONE, YOU DIDN'T NEED TO HIRE THE ENTIRE ***WRECKING CREW*** TO BRING DOWN THESE STINKIN' PIPSQUEAKS. ANY ONE OF US WOULDA BEEN MORE THAN ENOUGH MUSCLE.
BUT HEY, IT'S YOUR DIME.

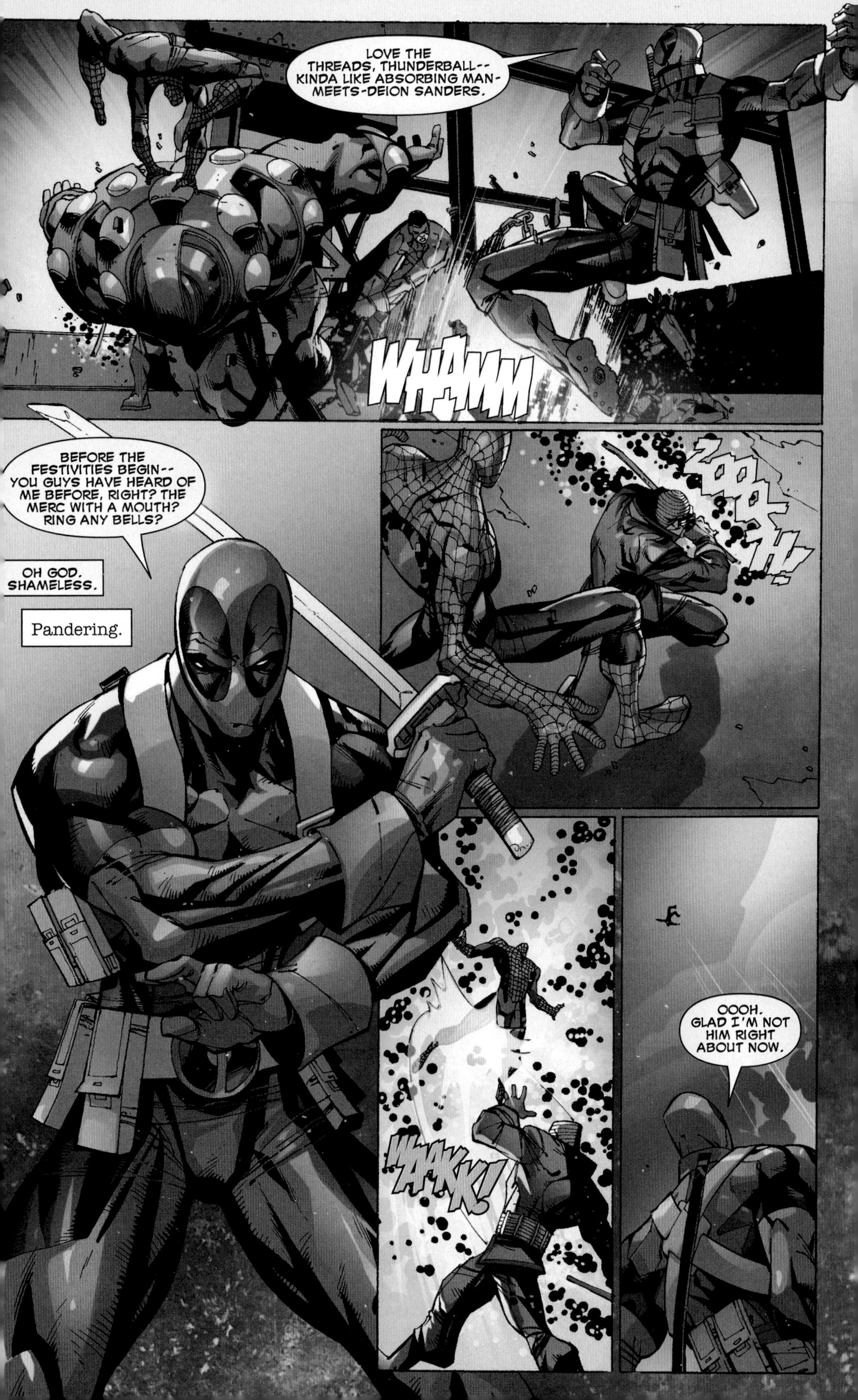
LOVE THE THREADS, THUNDERBALL-- KINDA LIKE ABSORBING MAN-MEETS-DEION SANDERS.
WHAMM
BEFORE THE FESTIVITIES BEGIN-- YOU GUYS HAVE HEARD OF ME BEFORE, RIGHT? THE MERC WITH A MOUTH? RING ANY BELLS?
OH GOD. SHAMELESS.
Pandering.
ZOOOCH!
WHAKK!
OOOH. GLAD I'M NOT HIM RIGHT ABOUT NOW.

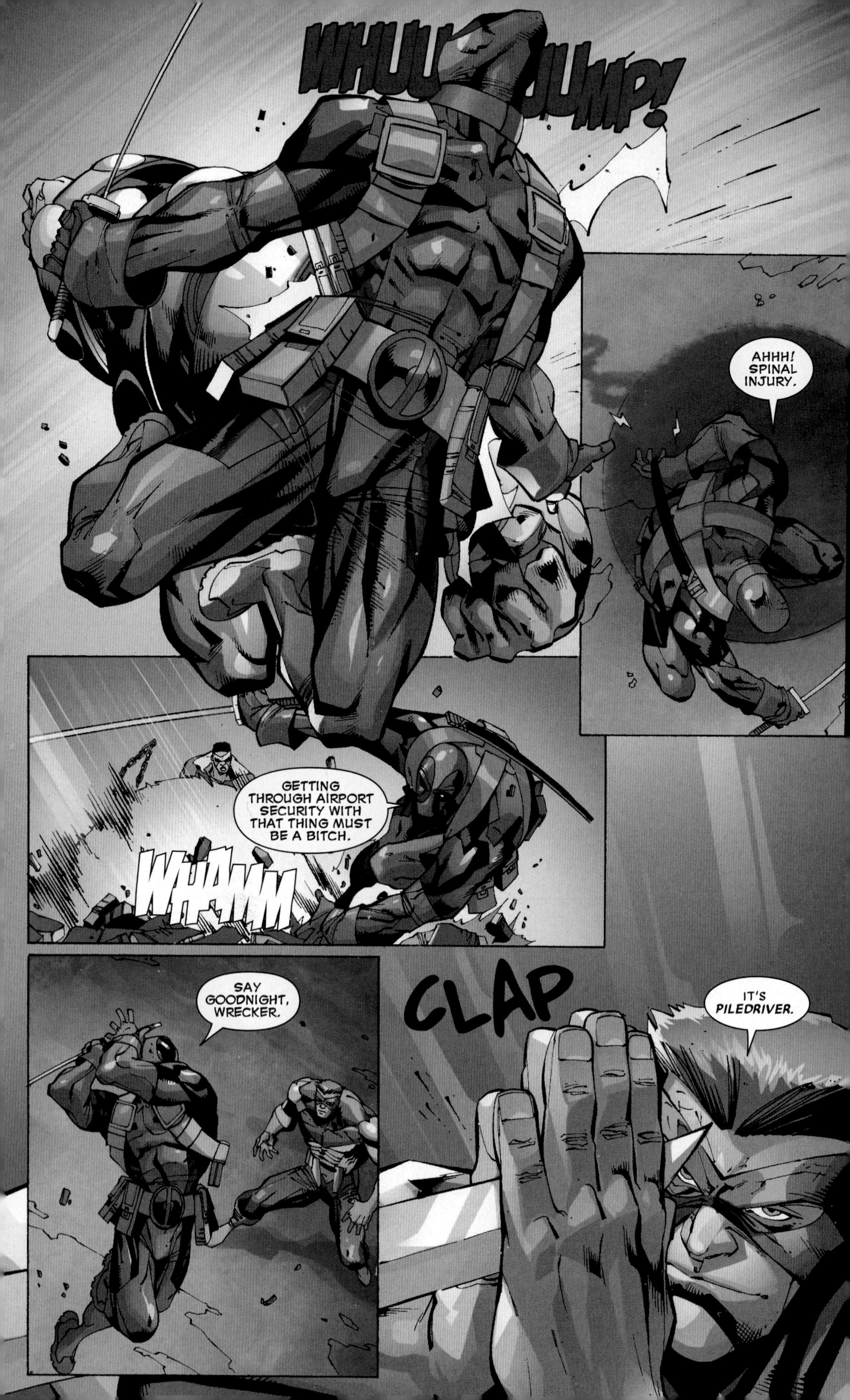
WHUUMP!
AHHH! SPINAL INJURY.
GETTING THROUGH AIRPORT SECURITY WITH THAT THING MUST BE A BITCH.
WHAMM
SAY GOODNIGHT, WRECKER.
CLAP
IT'S PILEDRIVER.

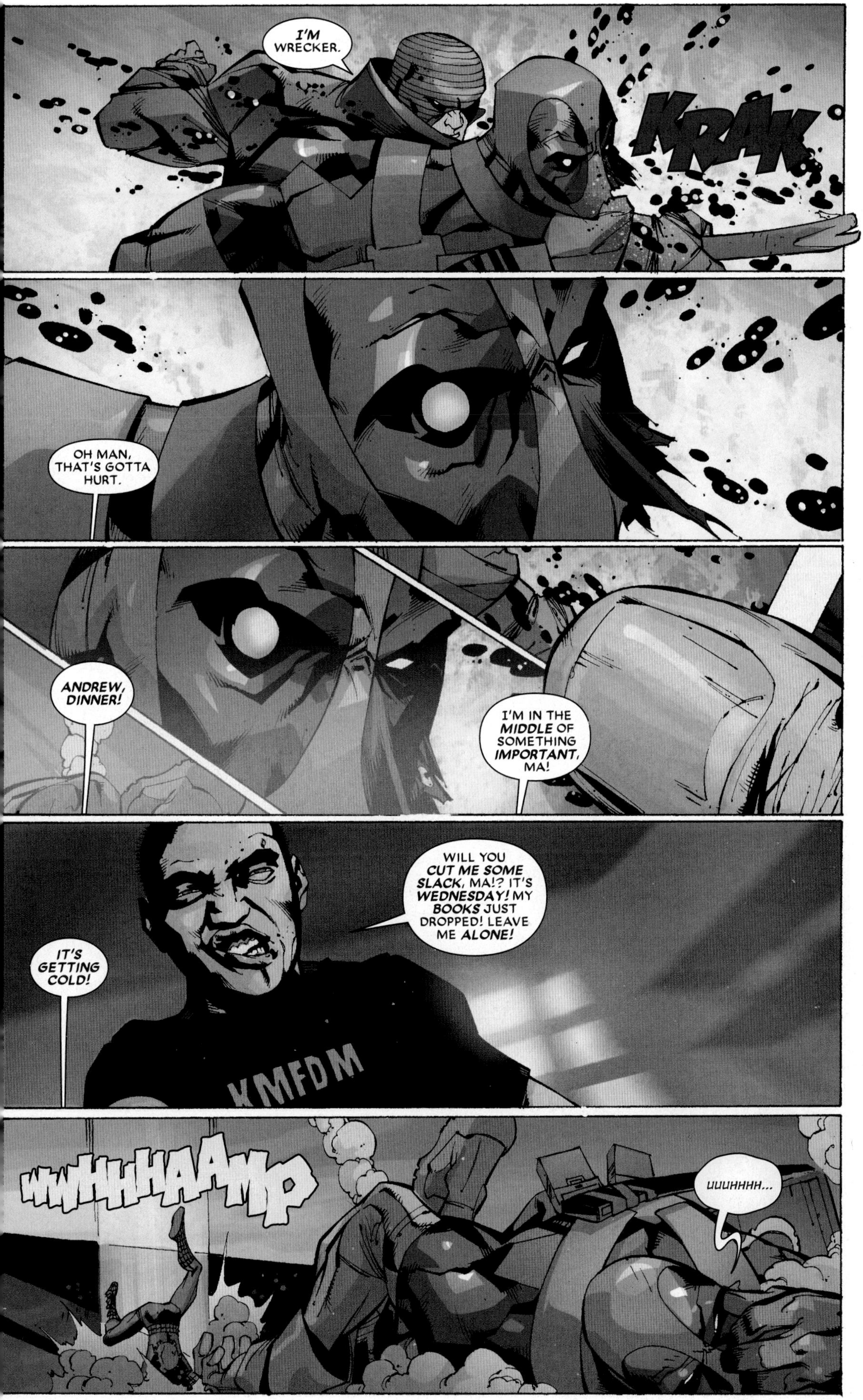
I'M WRECKER.
KRAK
OH MAN, THAT'S GOTTA HURT.
ANDREW, DINNER!
I'M IN THE MIDDLE OF SOMETHING IMPORTANT, MA!
IT'S GETTING COLD!
WILL YOU CUT ME SOME SLACK, MA!? IT'S WEDNESDAY! MY BOOKS JUST DROPPED! LEAVE ME ALONE!
KMFDM
WWHHHAAMP
UUUHHHH...

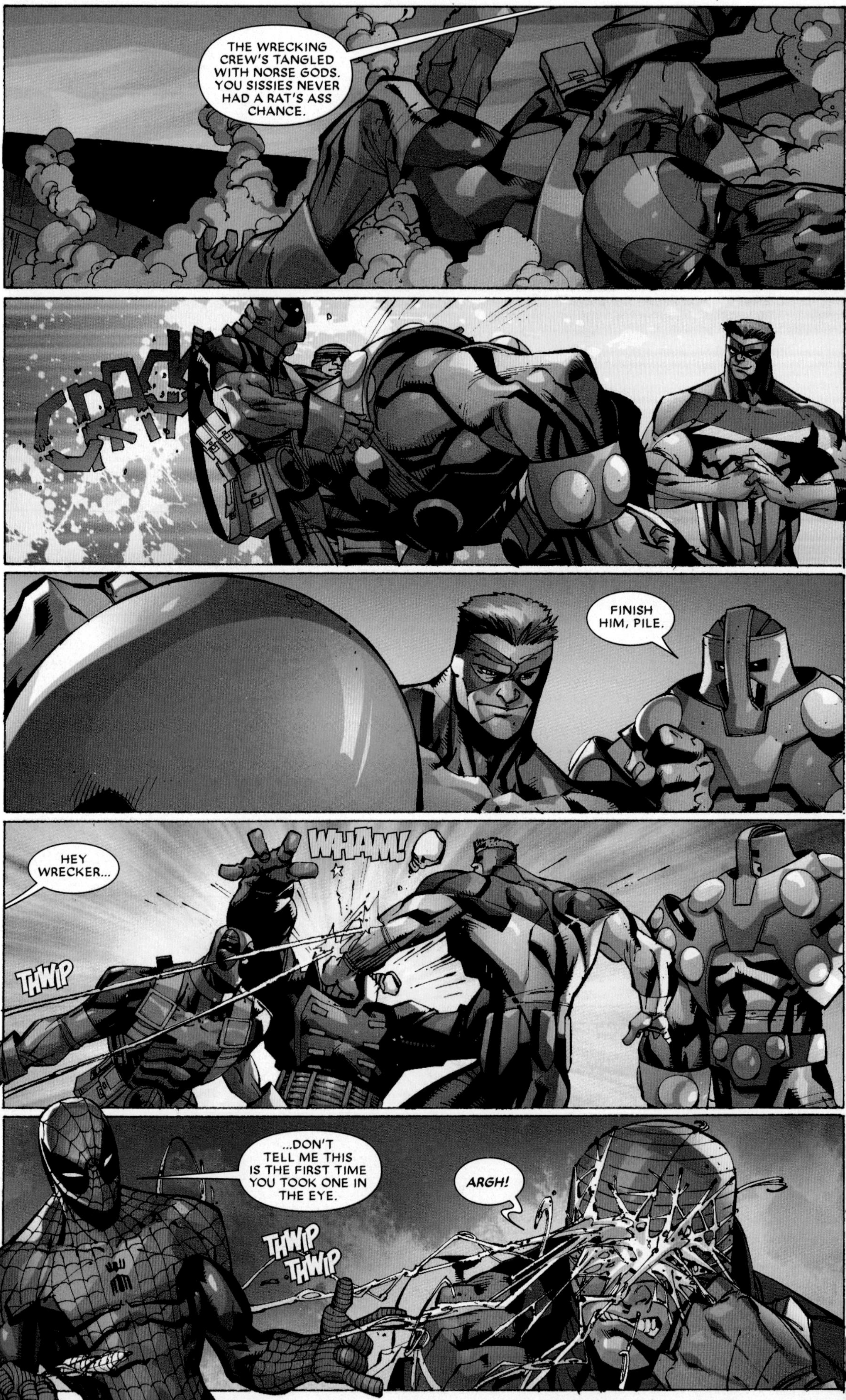
THE WRECKING CREW'S TANGLED WITH NORSE GODS. YOU SISSIES NEVER HAD A RAT'S ASS CHANCE.
FINISH HIM, PILE.
HEY WRECKER...
WHAM!
THWIP
...DON'T TELL ME THIS IS THE FIRST TIME YOU TOOK ONE IN THE EYE.
ARGH!
THWIP THWIP

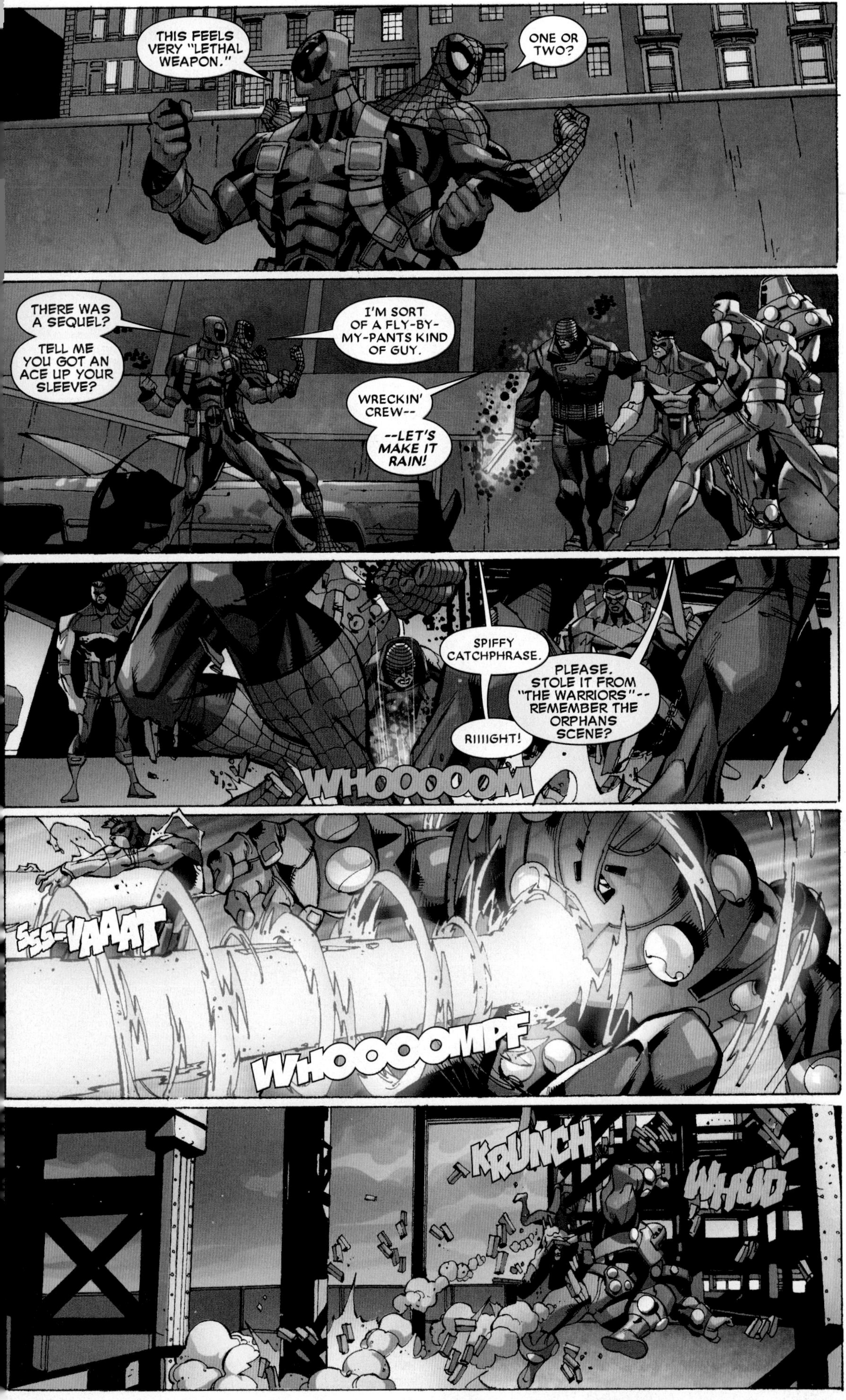
THIS FEELS VERY "LETHAL WEAPON."
ONE OR TWO?
THERE WAS A SEQUEL?
TELL ME YOU GOT AN ACE UP YOUR SLEEVE?
I'M SORT OF A FLY-BY-MY-PANTS KIND OF GUY.
WRECKIN' CREW--
--LET'S MAKE IT RAIN!
SPIFFY CATCHPHRASE.
PLEASE. STOLE IT FROM "THE WARRIORS"--REMEMBER THE ORPHANS SCENE?
RIIIIGHT!
WHOOOOOM
SSS-VAAAT
WHOOOOOMPF
KRUNCH
WHUD

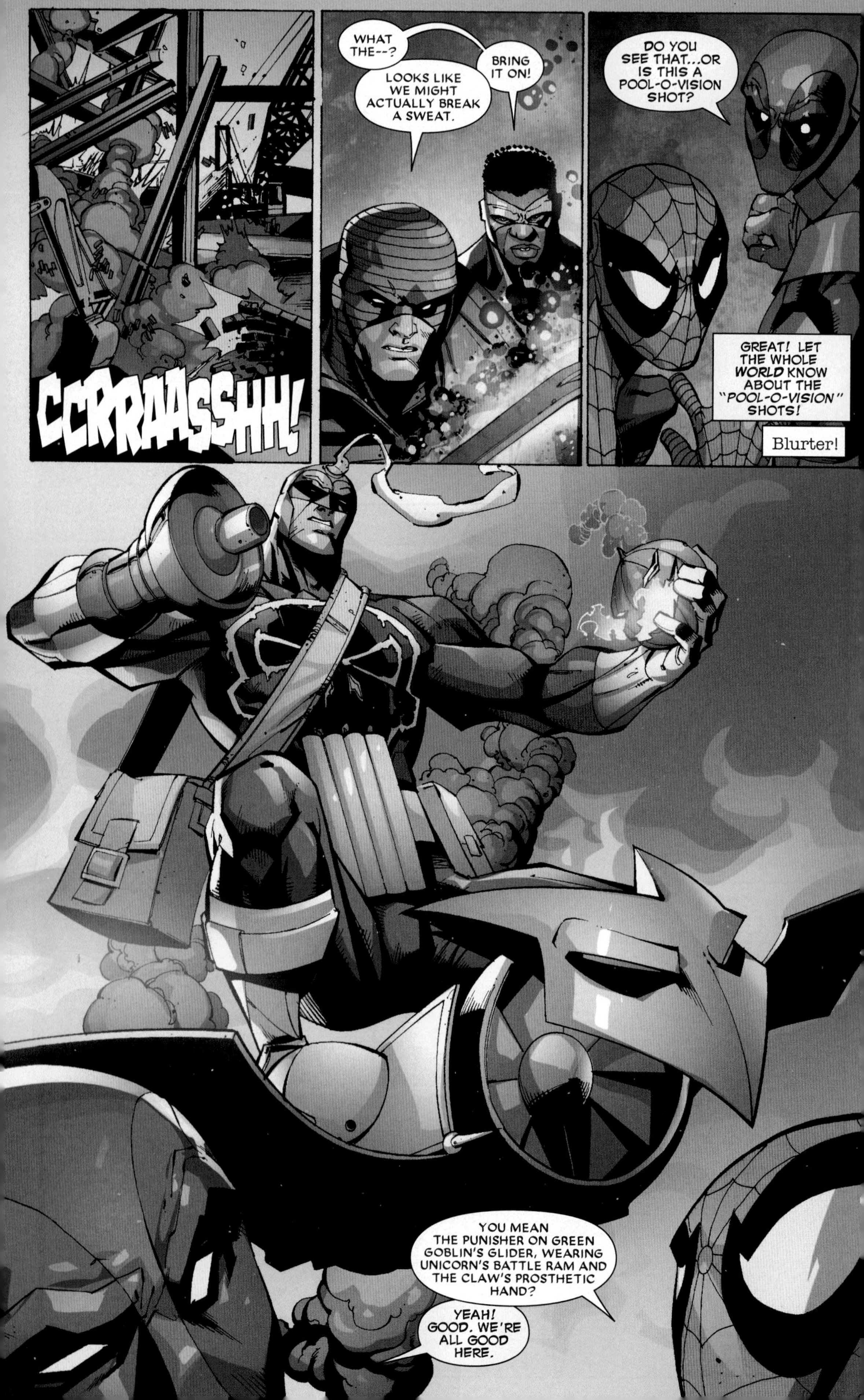
CCRRAASSHH!
WHAT THE--?
LOOKS LIKE WE MIGHT ACTUALLY BREAK A SWEAT.
BRING IT ON!
DO YOU SEE THAT...OR IS THIS A POOL-O-VISION SHOT?
GREAT! LET THE WHOLE WORLD KNOW ABOUT THE "POOL-O-VISION" SHOTS!
Blurter!
YOU MEAN THE PUNISHER ON GREEN GOBLIN'S GLIDER, WEARING UNICORN'S BATTLE RAM AND THE CLAW'S PROSTHETIC HAND?
YEAH! GOOD. WE'RE ALL GOOD HERE.

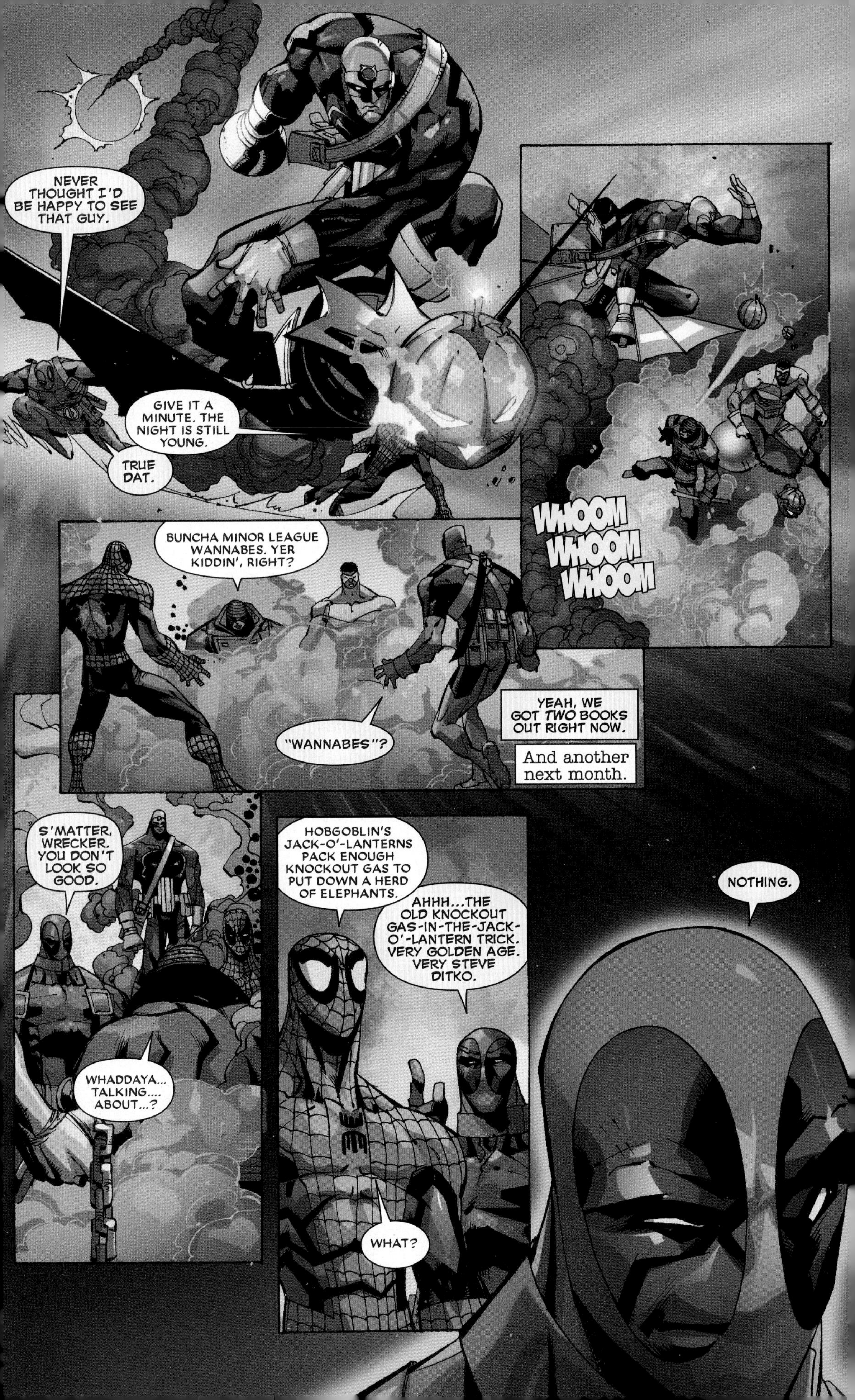
NEVER THOUGHT I'D BE HAPPY TO SEE THAT GUY.
GIVE IT A MINUTE. THE NIGHT IS STILL YOUNG.
TRUE DAT.
WHOOM WHOOM WHOOM
BUNCHA MINOR LEAGUE WANNABES. YER KIDDIN', RIGHT?
"WANNABES"?
YEAH, WE GOT TWO BOOKS OUT RIGHT NOW.
And another next month.
S'MATTER, WRECKER. YOU DON'T LOOK SO GOOD.
WHADDAYA... TALKING.... ABOUT...?
HOBGOBLIN'S JACK-O'-LANTERNS PACK ENOUGH KNOCKOUT GAS TO PUT DOWN A HERD OF ELEPHANTS.
AHHH...THE OLD KNOCKOUT GAS-IN-THE-JACK-O'-LANTERN TRICK. VERY GOLDEN AGE. VERY STEVE DITKO.
WHAT?
NOTHING.

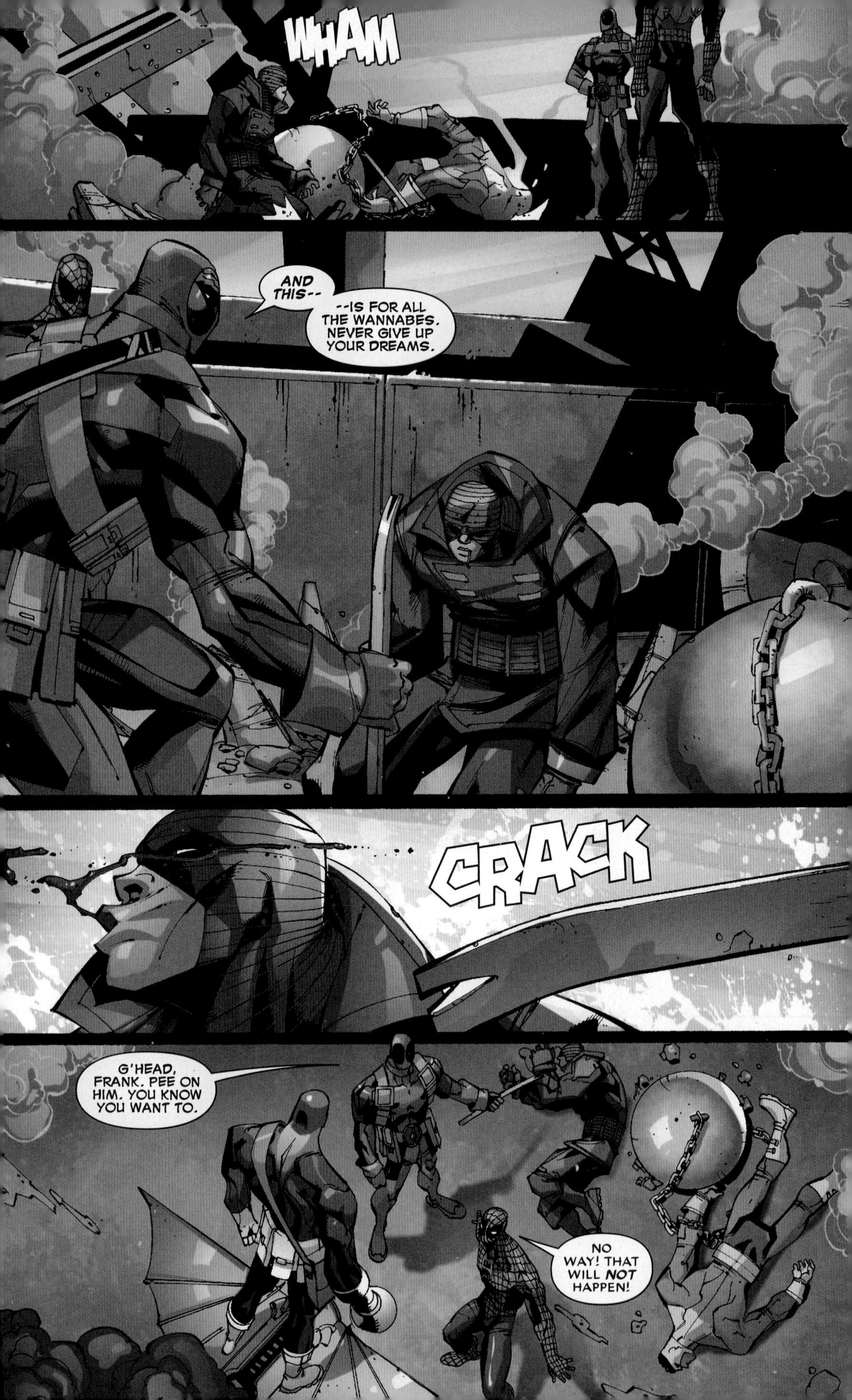
WHAM
AND THIS--
--IS FOR ALL THE WANNABES. NEVER GIVE UP YOUR DREAMS.
CRACK
G'HEAD, FRANK. PEE ON HIM. YOU KNOW YOU WANT TO.
NO WAY! THAT WILL NOT HAPPEN!

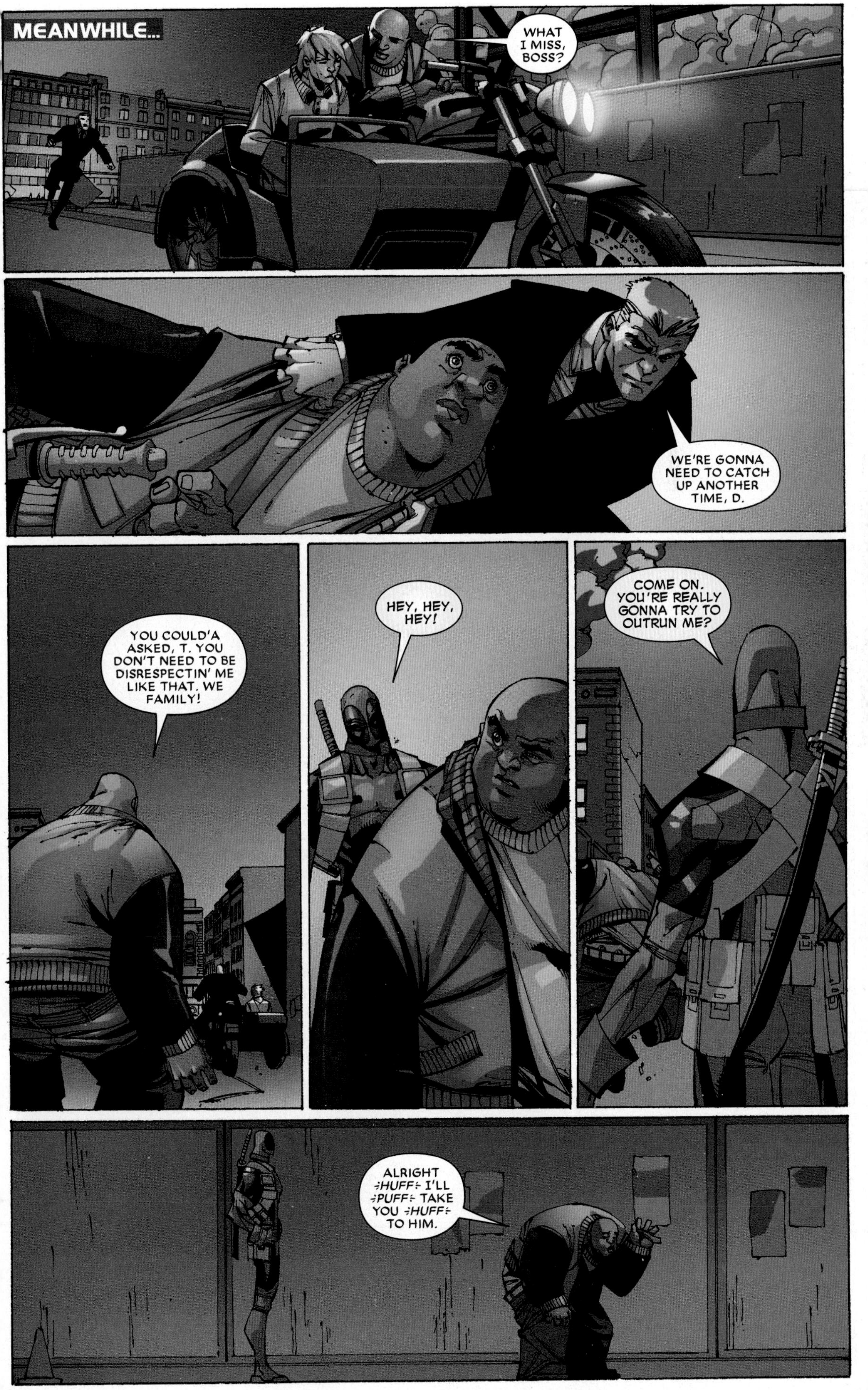
MEANWHILE...
WHAT I MISS, BOSS?
WE'RE GONNA NEED TO CATCH UP ANOTHER TIME, D.
YOU COULD'A ASKED, T. YOU DON'T NEED TO BE DISRESPECTIN' ME LIKE THAT. WE FAMILY!
HEY, HEY, HEY!
COME ON. YOU'RE REALLY GONNA TRY TO OUTRUN ME?
ALRIGHT ≑HUFF≑ I'LL ≑PUFF≑ TAKE YOU ≑HUFF≑ TO HIM.

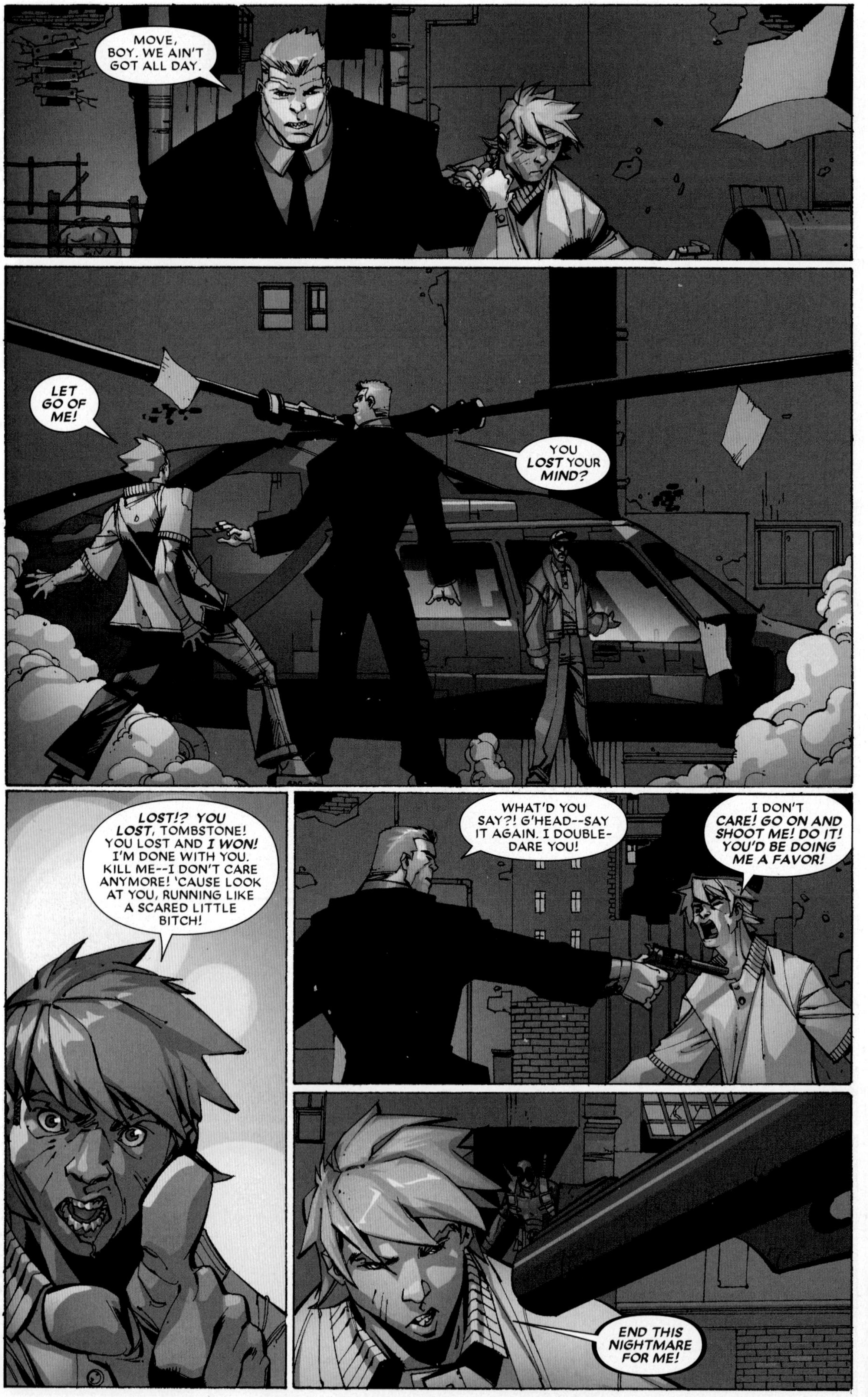
MOVE, BOY. WE AIN'T GOT ALL DAY.
LET GO OF ME!
YOU LOST YOUR MIND?
LOST!? YOU LOST, TOMBSTONE! YOU LOST AND I WON! I'M DONE WITH YOU. KILL ME--I DON'T CARE ANYMORE! 'CAUSE LOOK AT YOU, RUNNING LIKE A SCARED LITTLE BITCH!
WHAT'D YOU SAY?! G'HEAD--SAY IT AGAIN. I DOUBLE-DARE YOU!
I DON'T CARE! GO ON AND SHOOT ME! DO IT! YOU'D BE DOING ME A FAVOR!
END THIS NIGHTMARE FOR ME!

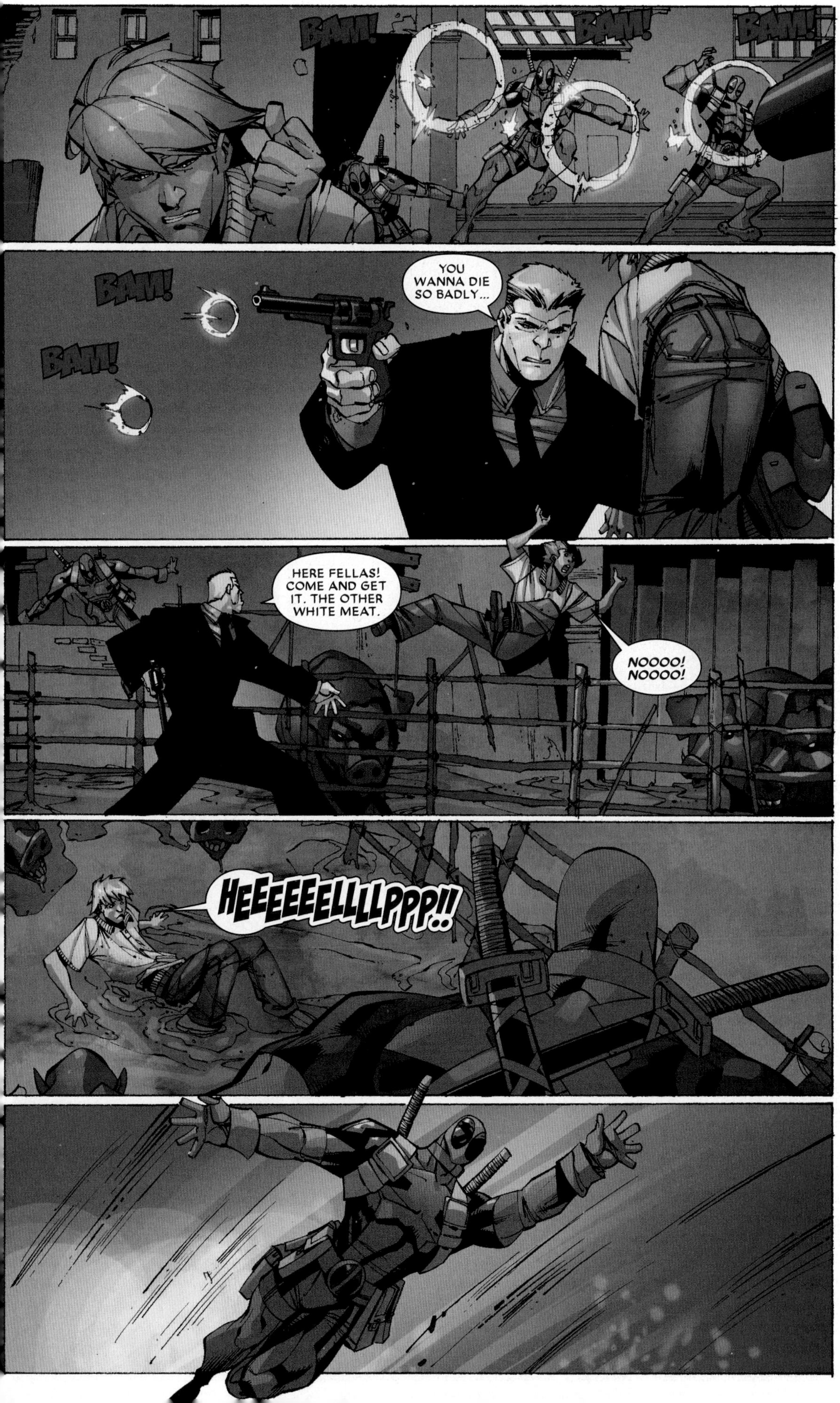
BAM!
BAM!
BAM!
BAM!
BAM!
YOU WANNA DIE SO BADLY...
HERE FELLAS! COME AND GET IT. THE OTHER WHITE MEAT.
NOOOO! NOOOO!
HEEEEEELLLLPPP!!

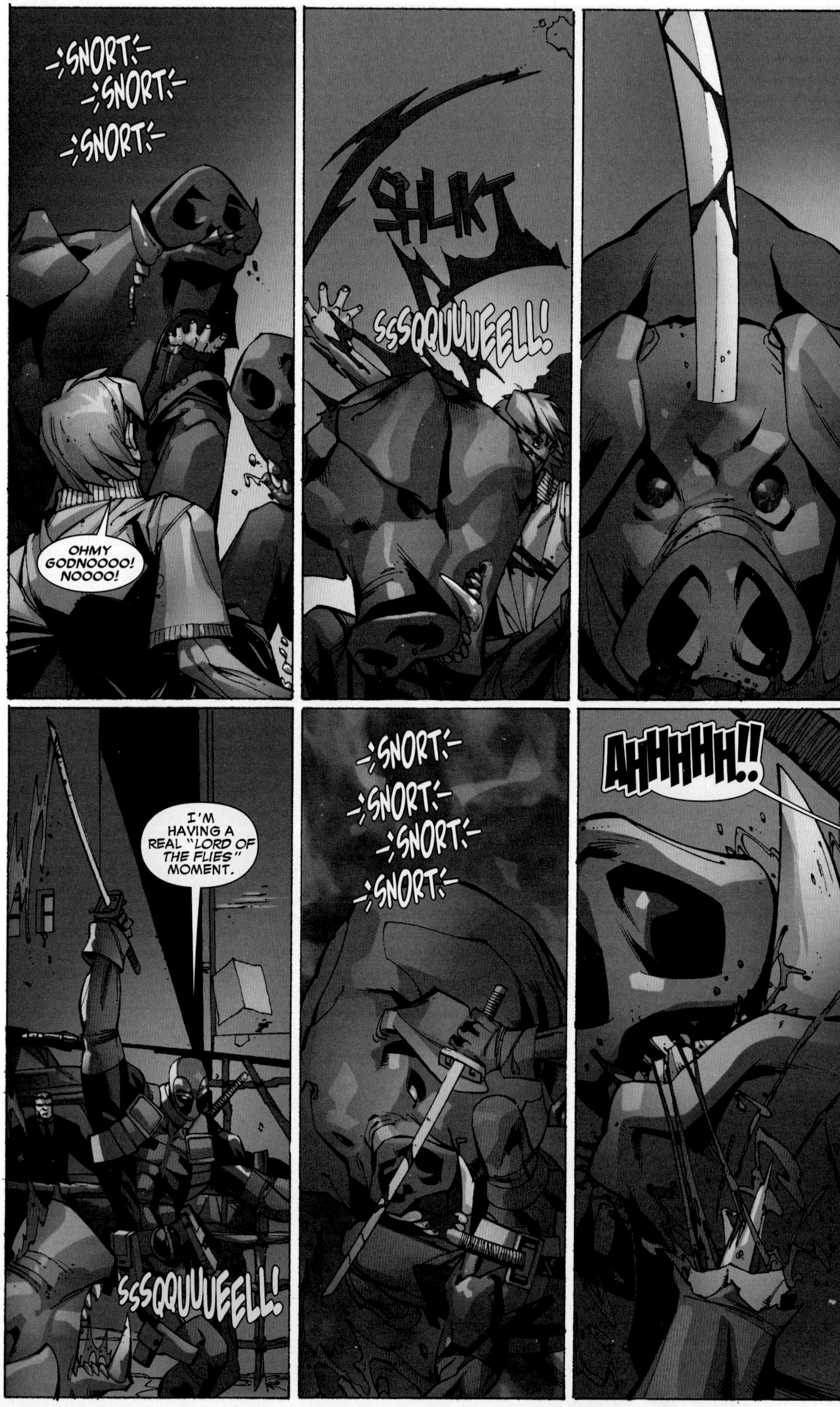
SNORT
SNORT
SNORT
OHMY GODNOOOO! NOOOO!
SHLIKT
SSSQQUUUEELL!
I'M HAVING A REAL "LORD OF THE FLIES" MOMENT.
SSSQQUUUEELL!
SNORT
SNORT
SNORT
SNORT
AHHHHH!!

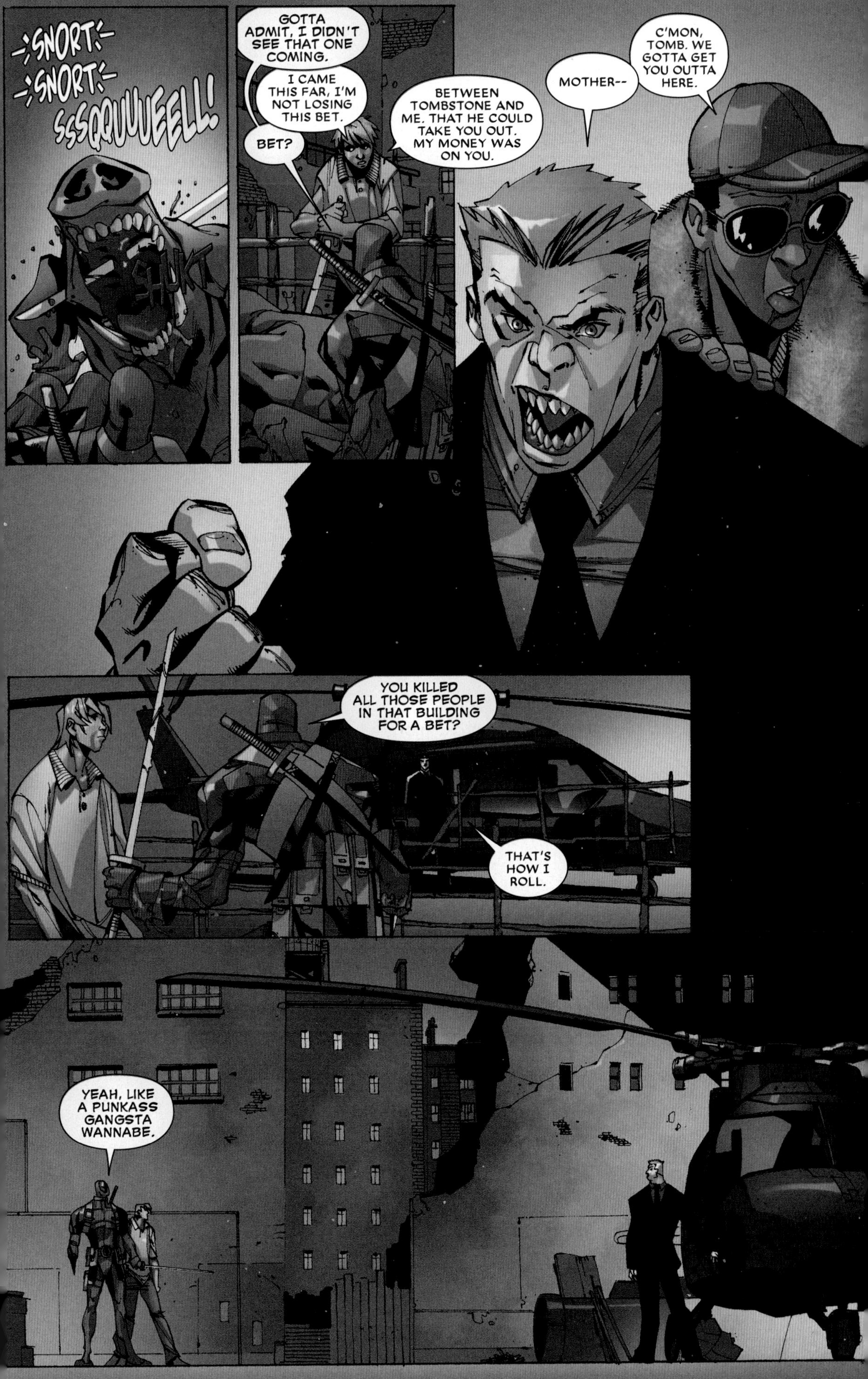
SNORT
SNORT
SSSQQUUUEELL!
SHUKT
GOTTA ADMIT, I DIDN'T SEE THAT ONE COMING.
I CAME THIS FAR, I'M NOT LOSING THIS BET.
BET?
BETWEEN TOMBSTONE AND ME. THAT HE COULD TAKE YOU OUT. MY MONEY WAS ON YOU.
MOTHER--
C'MON, TOMB. WE GOTTA GET YOU OUTTA HERE.
YOU KILLED ALL THOSE PEOPLE IN THAT BUILDING FOR A BET?
THAT'S HOW I ROLL.
YEAH, LIKE A PUNKASS GANGSTA WANNABE.

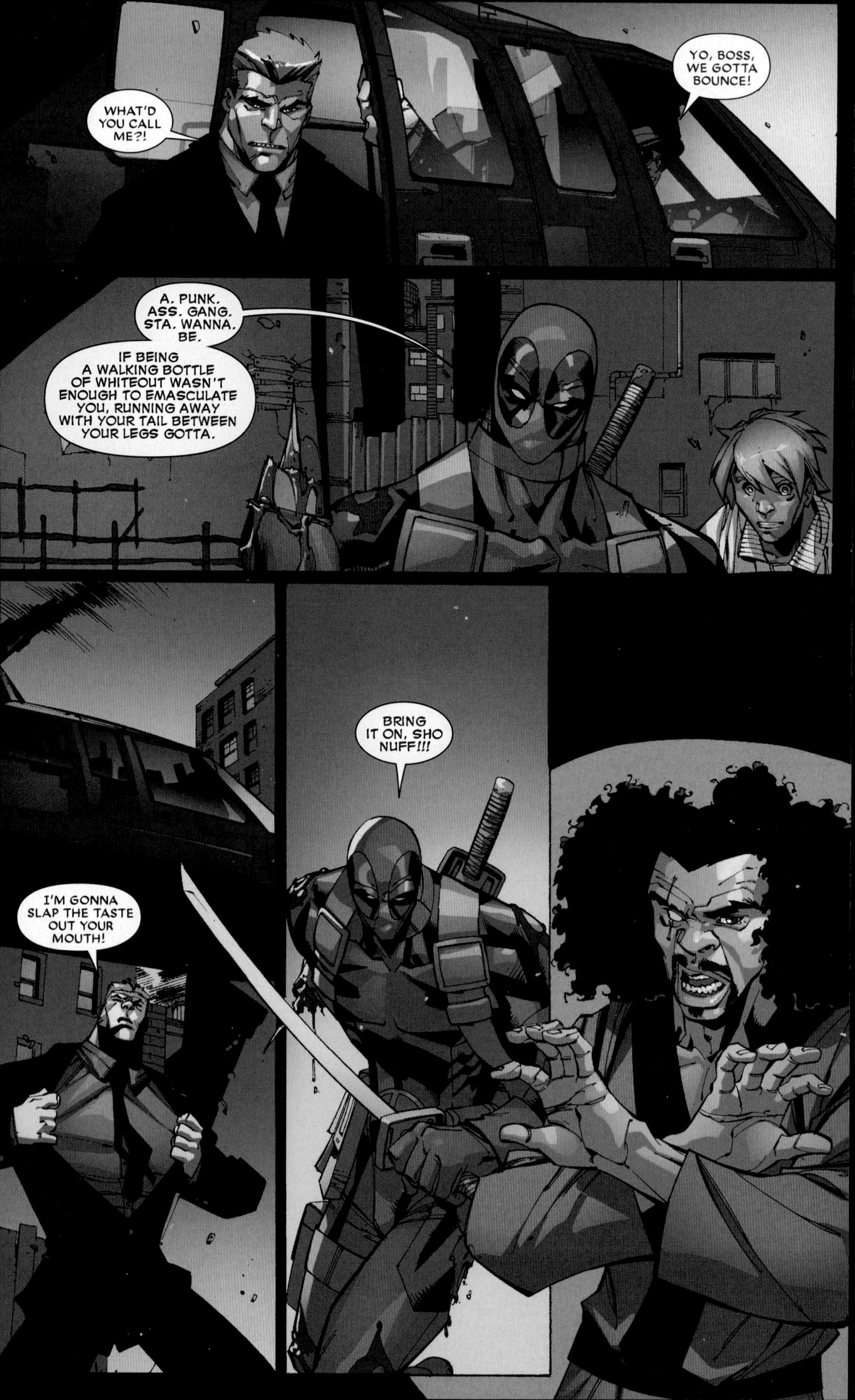
WHAT'D YOU CALL ME?!
YO, BOSS, WE GOTTA BOUNCE!
A. PUNK. ASS. GANG. STA. WANNA. BE.
IF BEING A WALKING BOTTLE OF WHITEOUT WASN'T ENOUGH TO EMASCULATE YOU, RUNNING AWAY WITH YOUR TAIL BETWEEN YOUR LEGS GOTTA.
I'M GONNA SLAP THE TASTE OUT YOUR MOUTH!
BRING IT ON, SHO NUFF!!!

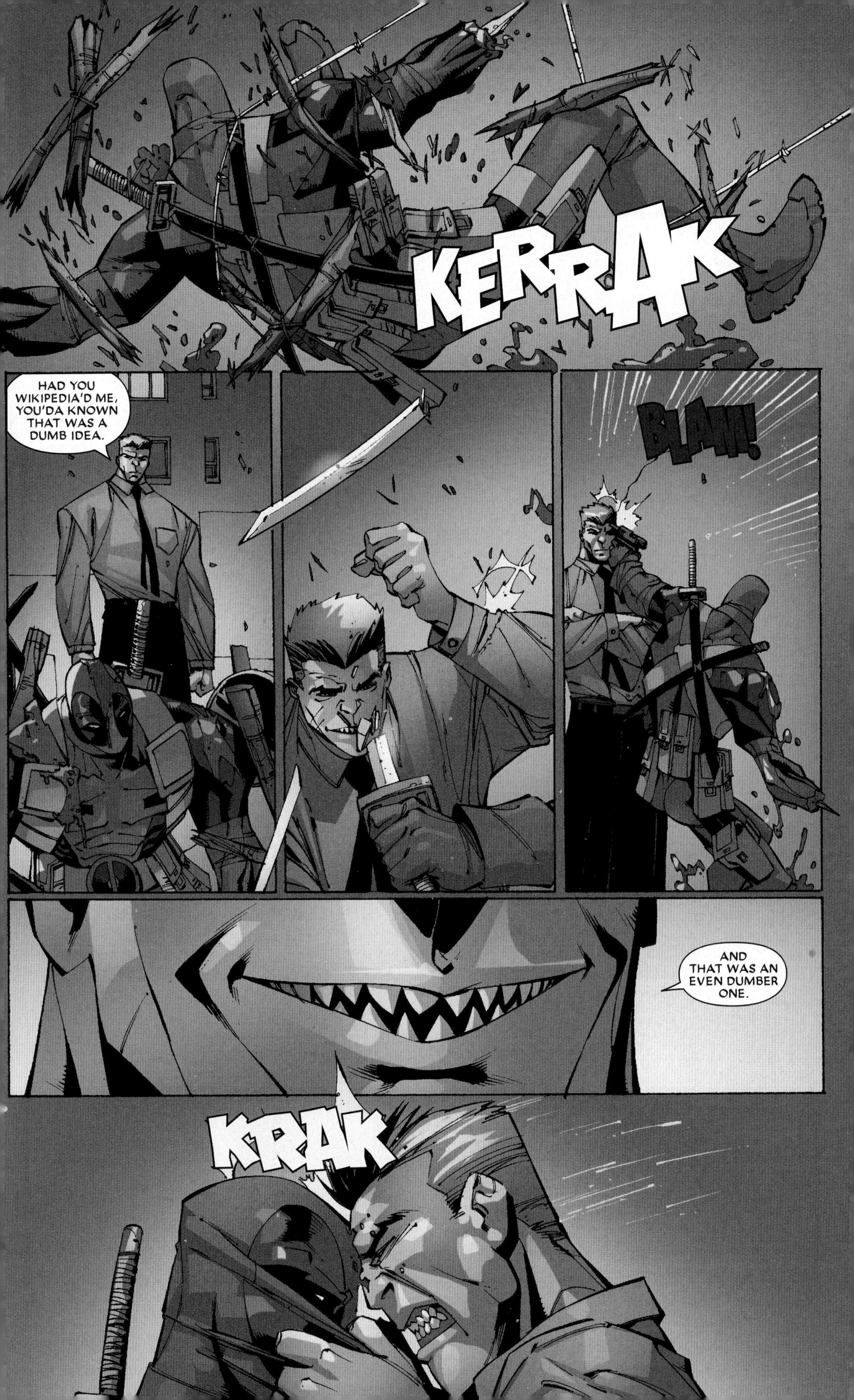
KERRAK
HAD YOU WIKIPEDIA'D ME, YOU'DA KNOWN THAT WAS A DUMB IDEA.
BLAM!
AND THAT WAS AN EVEN DUMBER ONE.
KRAK

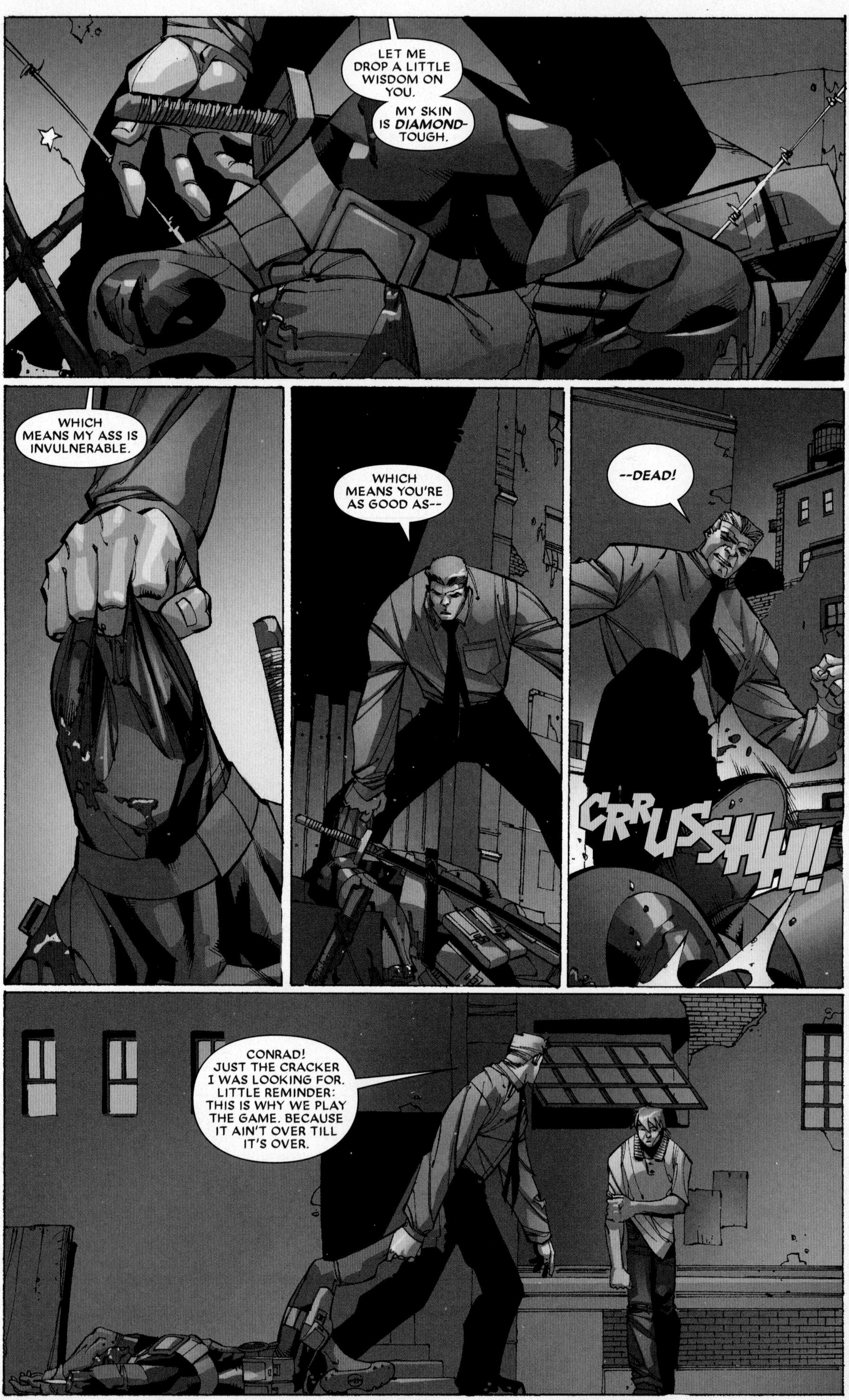
LET ME DROP A LITTLE WISDOM ON YOU.
MY SKIN IS *DIAMOND*-TOUGH.
WHICH MEANS MY ASS IS INVULNERABLE.
WHICH MEANS YOU'RE AS GOOD AS--
--*DEAD!*
CRRUSSHH!!
CONRAD! JUST THE CRACKER I WAS LOOKING FOR. LITTLE REMINDER: THIS IS WHY WE PLAY THE GAME. BECAUSE IT AIN'T OVER TILL IT'S OVER.

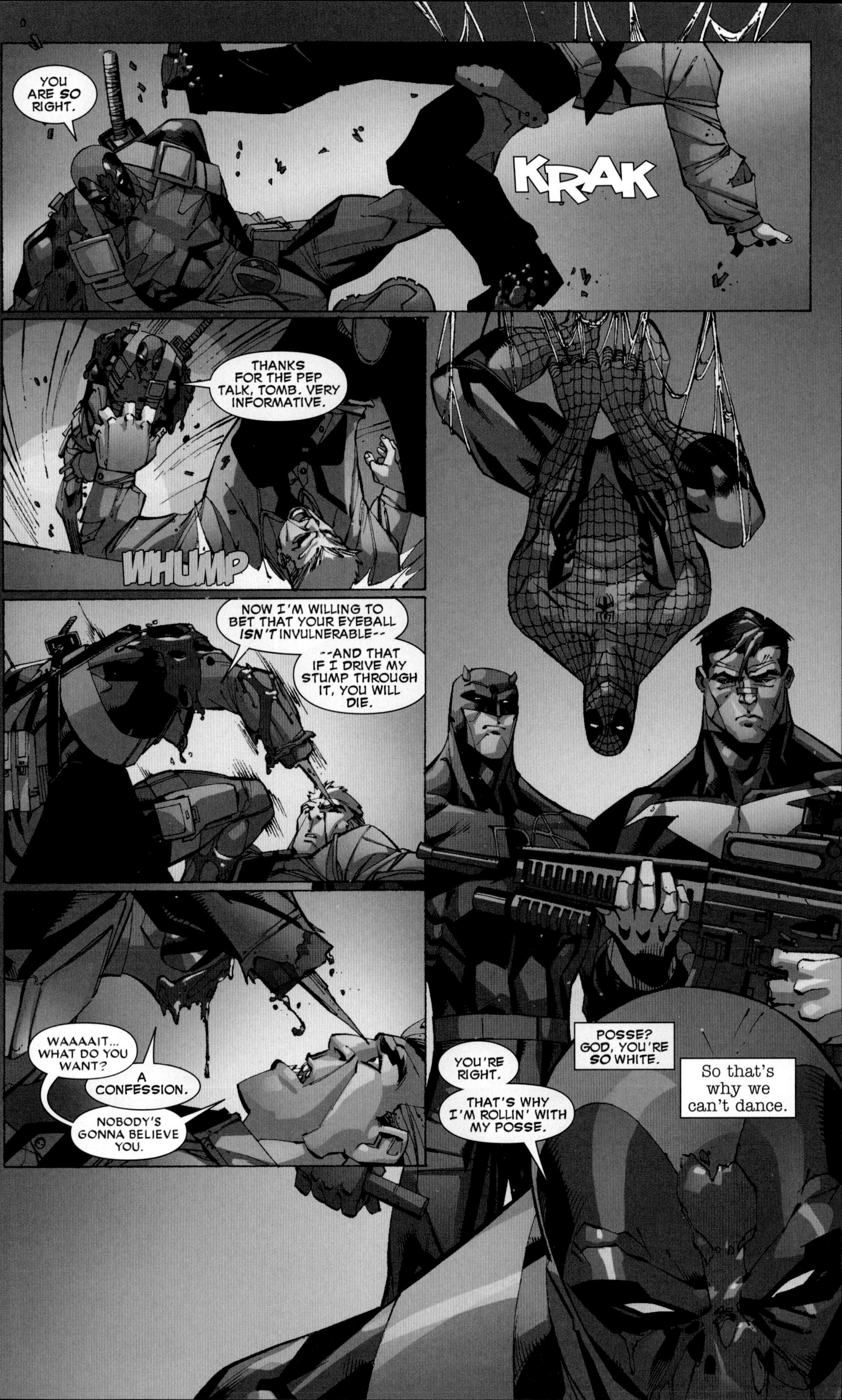

YOU ARE *SO* RIGHT.
KRAK
THANKS FOR THE PEP TALK, TOMB. VERY INFORMATIVE.
WHUMP
NOW I'M WILLING TO BET THAT YOUR EYEBALL *ISN'T* INVULNERABLE--
--AND THAT IF I DRIVE MY STUMP THROUGH IT, YOU WILL DIE.
WAAAAIT... WHAT DO YOU WANT?
A CONFESSION.
NOBODY'S GONNA BELIEVE YOU.
YOU'RE RIGHT.
THAT'S WHY I'M ROLLIN' WITH MY POSSE.
POSSE? GOD, YOU'RE *SO* WHITE.
So that's why we can't dance.

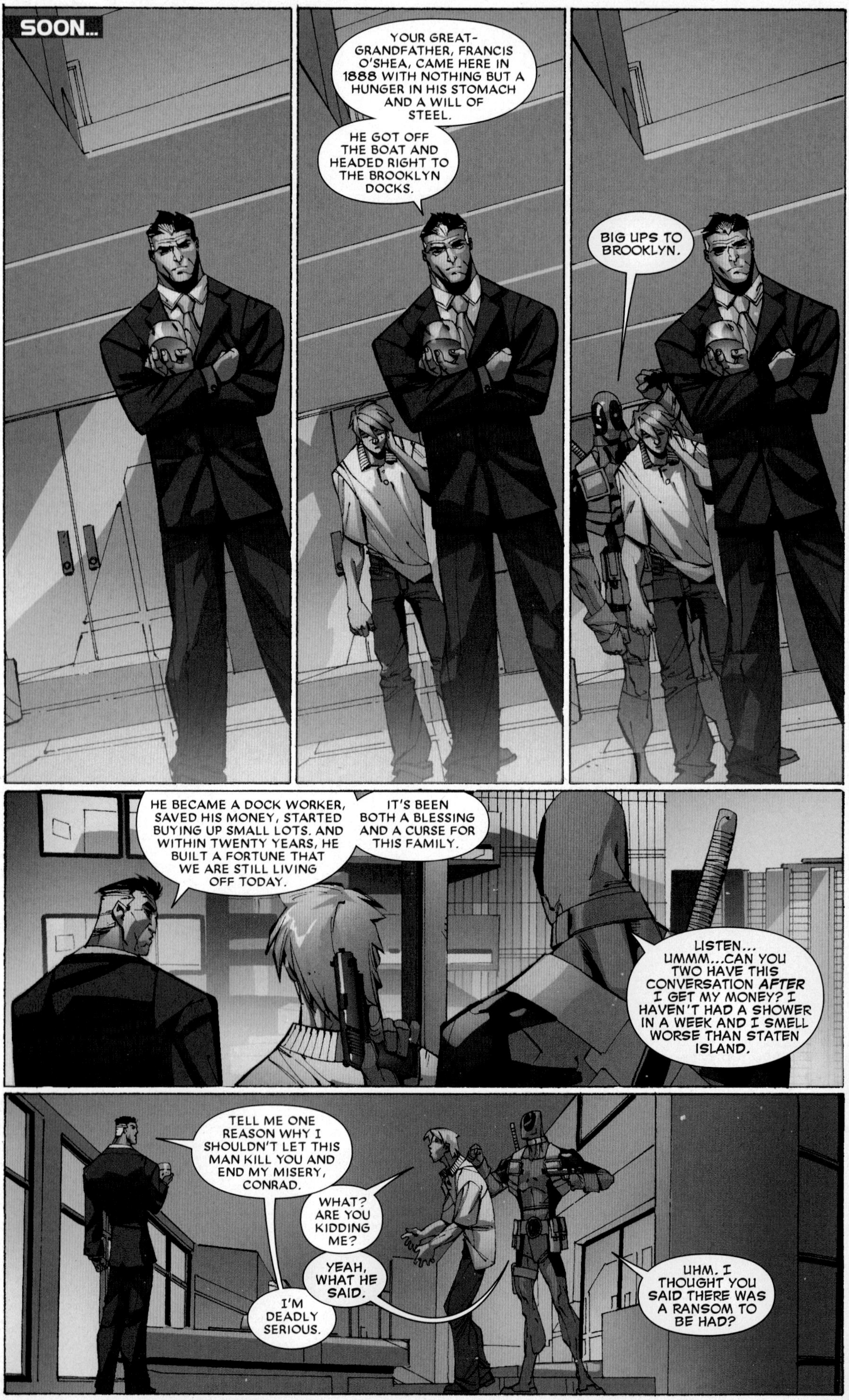
SOON...
YOUR GREAT-GRANDFATHER, FRANCIS O'SHEA, CAME HERE IN 1888 WITH NOTHING BUT A HUNGER IN HIS STOMACH AND A WILL OF STEEL.
HE GOT OFF THE BOAT AND HEADED RIGHT TO THE BROOKLYN DOCKS.
BIG UPS TO BROOKLYN.
HE BECAME A DOCK WORKER, SAVED HIS MONEY, STARTED BUYING UP SMALL LOTS. AND WITHIN TWENTY YEARS, HE BUILT A FORTUNE THAT WE ARE STILL LIVING OFF TODAY.
IT'S BEEN BOTH A BLESSING AND A CURSE FOR THIS FAMILY.
LISTEN... UMMM...CAN YOU TWO HAVE THIS CONVERSATION *AFTER* I GET MY MONEY? I HAVEN'T HAD A SHOWER IN A WEEK AND I SMELL WORSE THAN STATEN ISLAND.
TELL ME ONE REASON WHY I SHOULDN'T LET THIS MAN KILL YOU AND END MY MISERY, CONRAD.
WHAT? ARE YOU KIDDING ME?
YEAH, WHAT HE SAID.
I'M DEADLY SERIOUS.
UHM. I THOUGHT YOU SAID THERE WAS A RANSOM TO BE HAD?

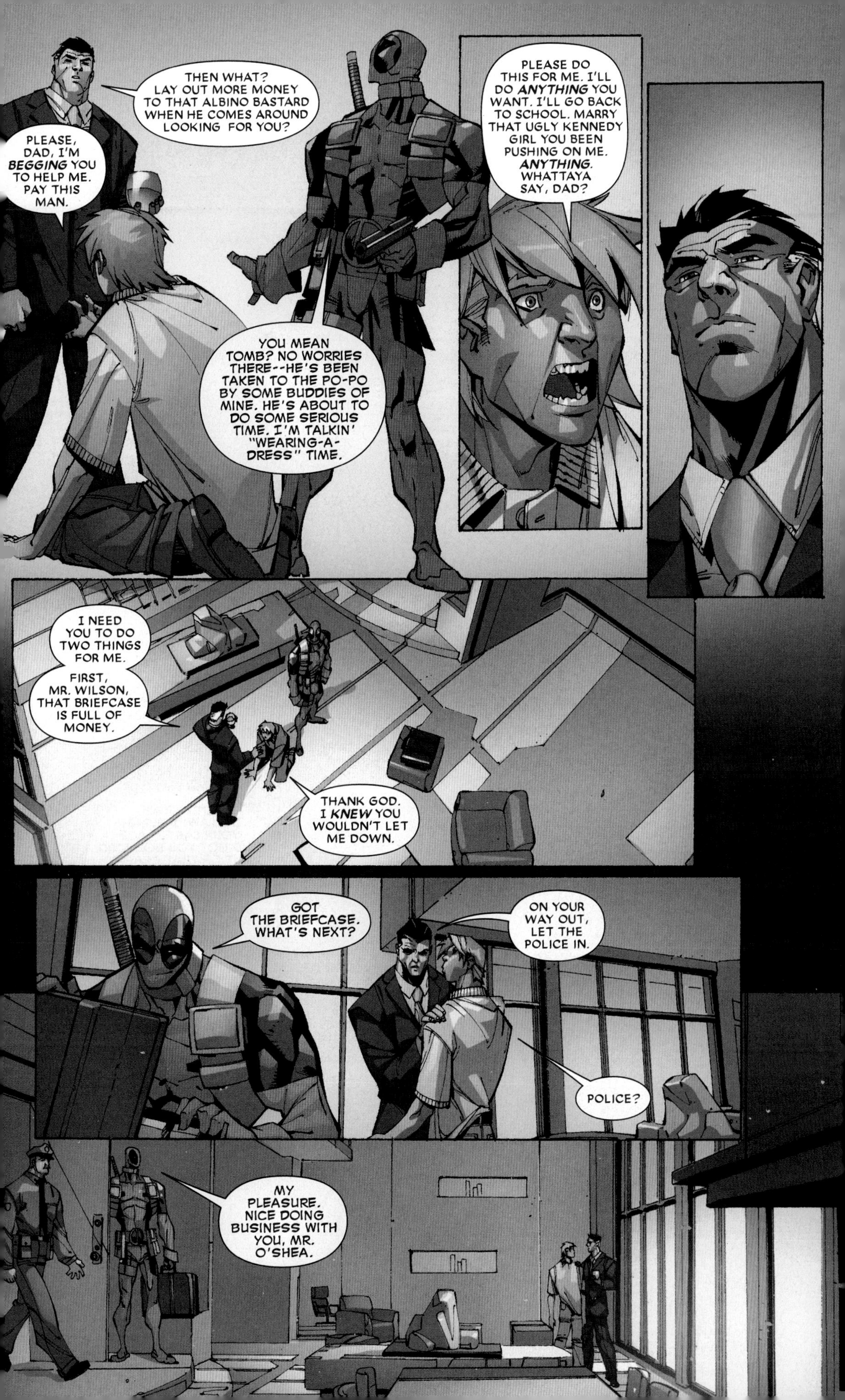

THEN WHAT? LAY OUT MORE MONEY TO THAT ALBINO BASTARD WHEN HE COMES AROUND LOOKING FOR YOU?
PLEASE, DAD, I'M *BEGGING* YOU TO HELP ME. PAY THIS MAN.
YOU MEAN TOMB? NO WORRIES THERE--HE'S BEEN TAKEN TO THE PO-PO BY SOME BUDDIES OF MINE. HE'S ABOUT TO DO SOME SERIOUS TIME. I'M TALKIN' "WEARING-A-DRESS" TIME.
PLEASE DO THIS FOR ME. I'LL DO *ANYTHING* YOU WANT. I'LL GO BACK TO SCHOOL. MARRY THAT UGLY KENNEDY GIRL YOU BEEN PUSHING ON ME. *ANYTHING*. WHATTAYA SAY, DAD?
I NEED YOU TO DO TWO THINGS FOR ME.
FIRST, MR. WILSON, THAT BRIEFCASE IS FULL OF MONEY.
THANK GOD. I *KNEW* YOU WOULDN'T LET ME DOWN.
GOT THE BRIEFCASE. WHAT'S NEXT?
ON YOUR WAY OUT, LET THE POLICE IN.
POLICE?
MY PLEASURE. NICE DOING BUSINESS WITH YOU, MR. O'SHEA.

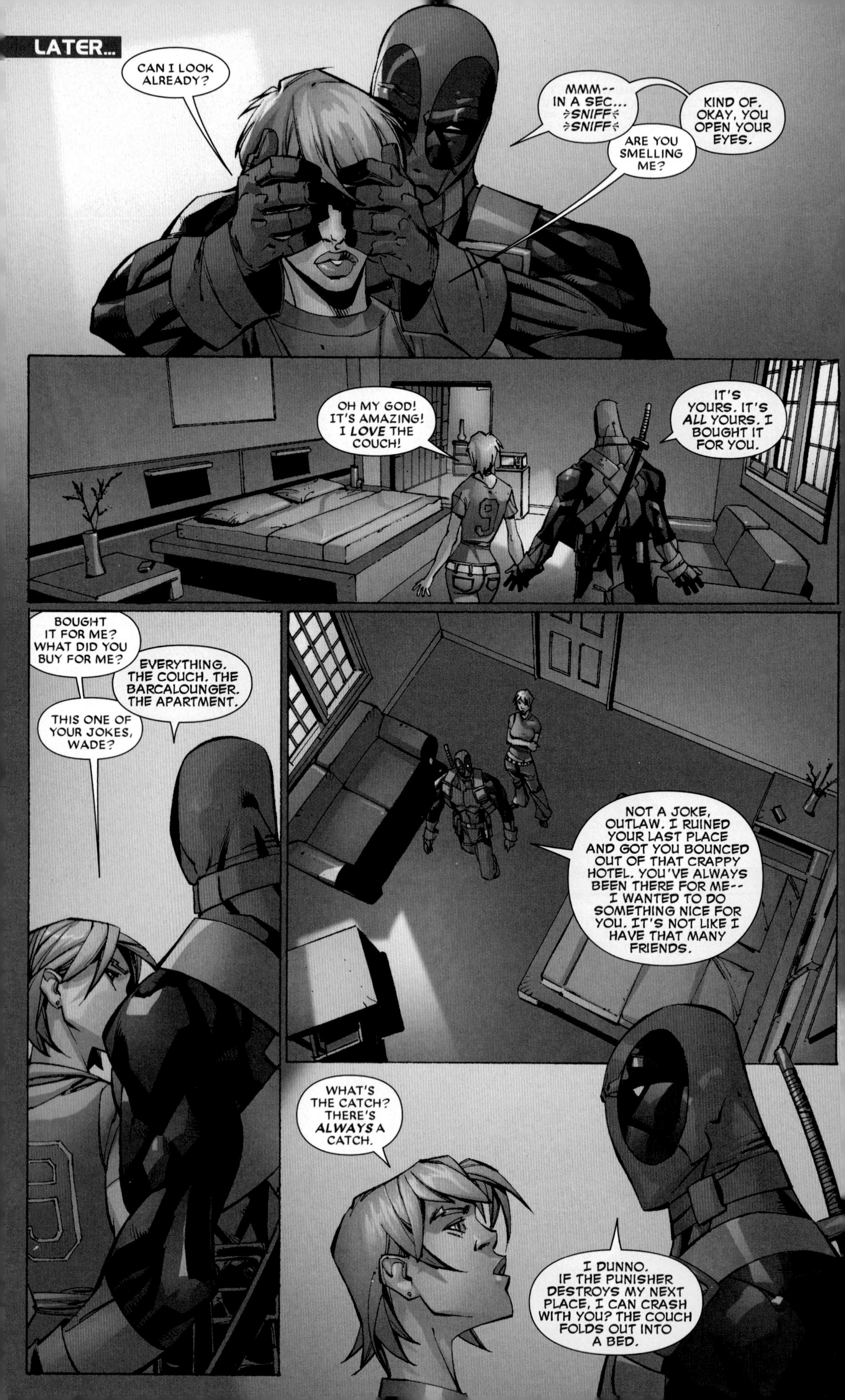
LATER...
CAN I LOOK ALREADY?
MMM-- IN A SEC... *SNIFF* *SNIFF*
ARE YOU SMELLING ME?
KIND OF. OKAY, YOU OPEN YOUR EYES.
OH MY GOD! IT'S AMAZING! I LOVE THE COUCH!
IT'S YOURS. IT'S ALL YOURS. I BOUGHT IT FOR YOU.
BOUGHT IT FOR ME? WHAT DID YOU BUY FOR ME?
EVERYTHING. THE COUCH. THE BARCALOUNGER. THE APARTMENT.
THIS ONE OF YOUR JOKES, WADE?
NOT A JOKE, OUTLAW. I RUINED YOUR LAST PLACE AND GOT YOU BOUNCED OUT OF THAT CRAPPY HOTEL. YOU'VE ALWAYS BEEN THERE FOR ME-- I WANTED TO DO SOMETHING NICE FOR YOU. IT'S NOT LIKE I HAVE THAT MANY FRIENDS.
WHAT'S THE CATCH? THERE'S ALWAYS A CATCH.
I DUNNO. IF THE PUNISHER DESTROYS MY NEXT PLACE, I CAN CRASH WITH YOU? THE COUCH FOLDS OUT INTO A BED.

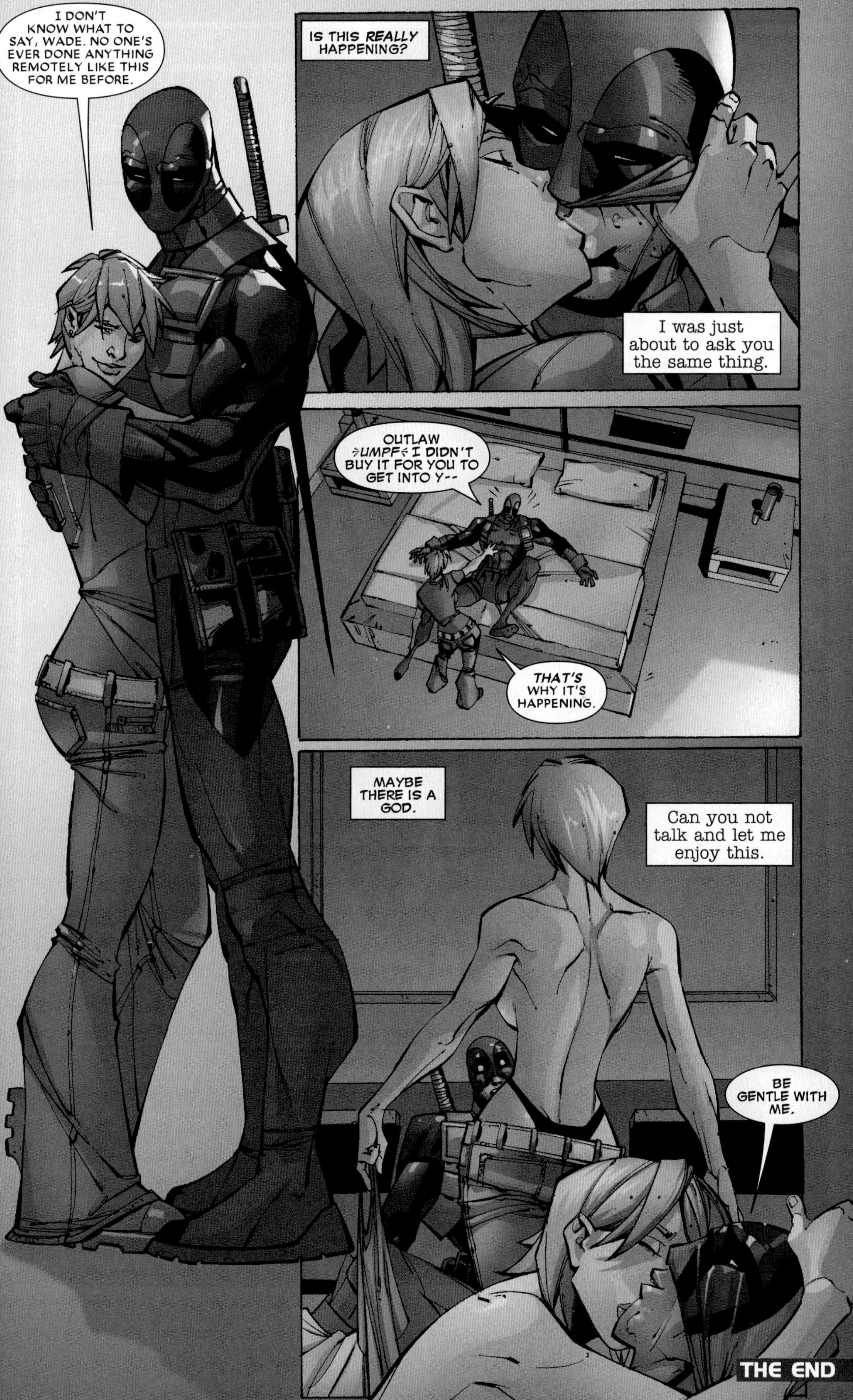
I DON'T KNOW WHAT TO SAY, WADE. NO ONE'S EVER DONE ANYTHING REMOTELY LIKE THIS FOR ME BEFORE.
IS THIS REALLY HAPPENING?
I was just about to ask you the same thing.
OUTLAW ≯UMPF≮ I DIDN'T BUY IT FOR YOU TO GET INTO Y--
THAT'S WHY IT'S HAPPENING.
MAYBE THERE IS A GOD.
Can you not talk and let me enjoy this.
BE GENTLE WITH ME.
THE END

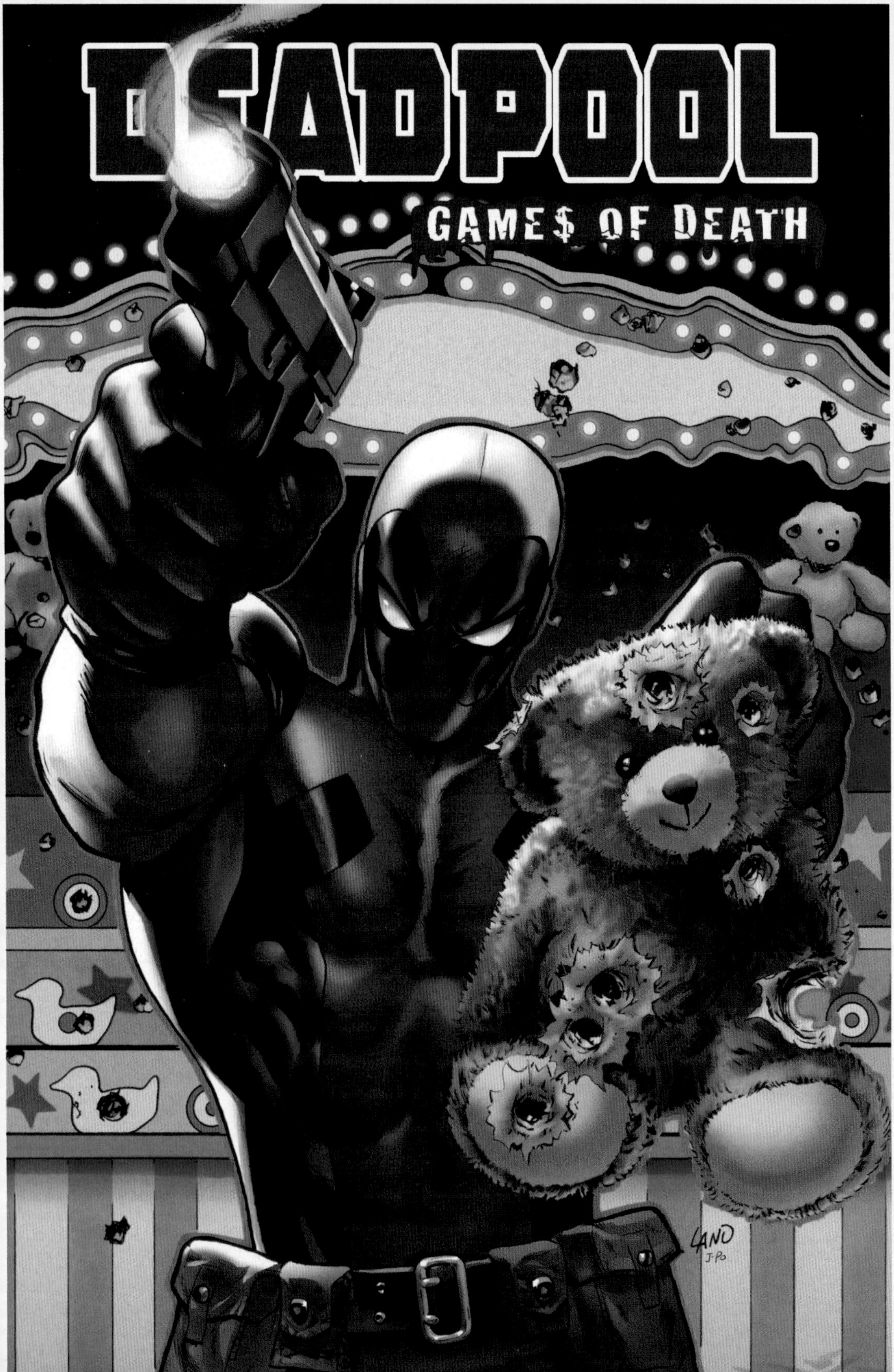
DEADPOOL
GAMES OF DEATH
LAND
J-Po

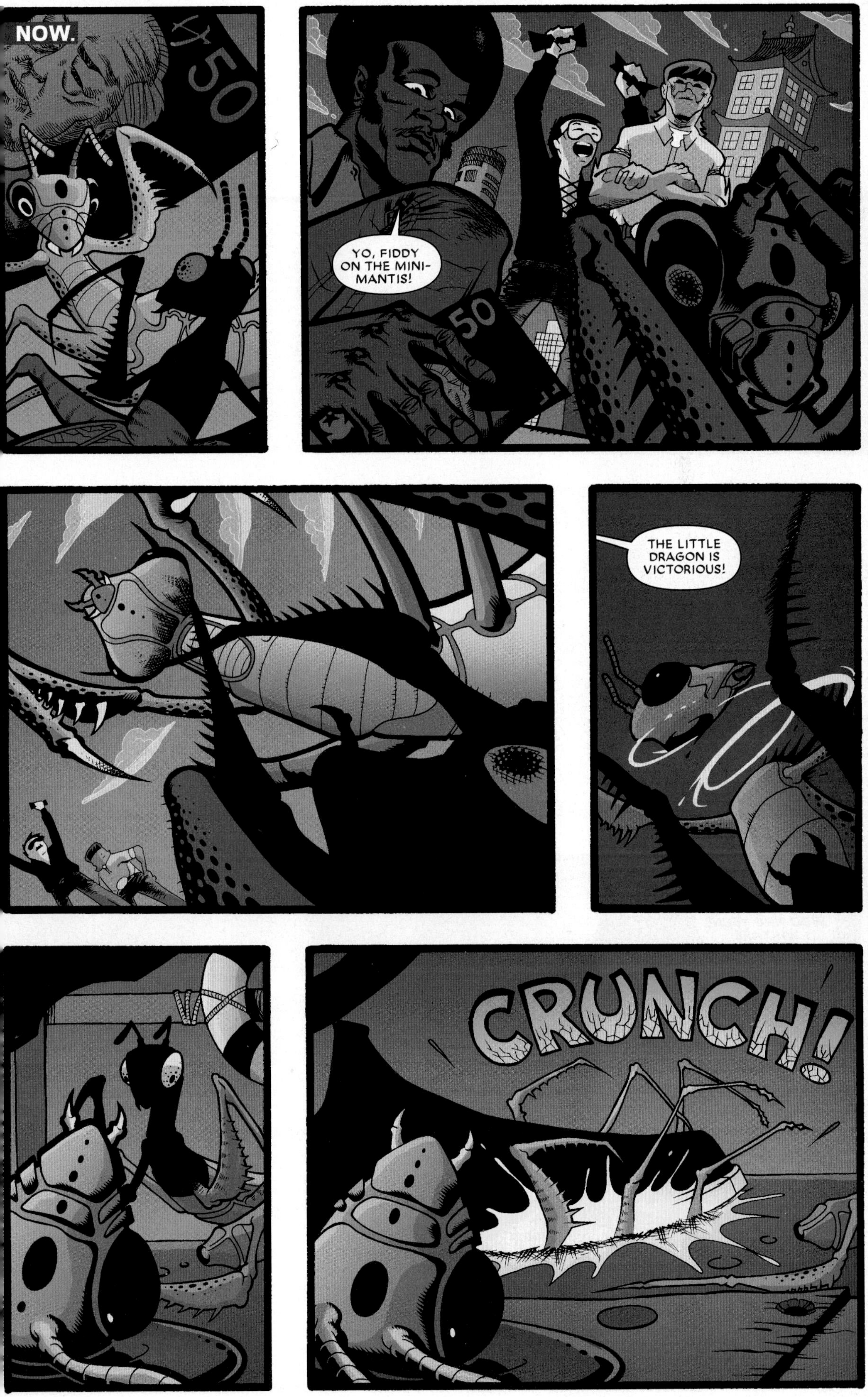
NOW.
50
YO, FIDDY ON THE MINI-MANTIS!
50
THE LITTLE DRAGON IS VICTORIOUS!
CRUNCH!

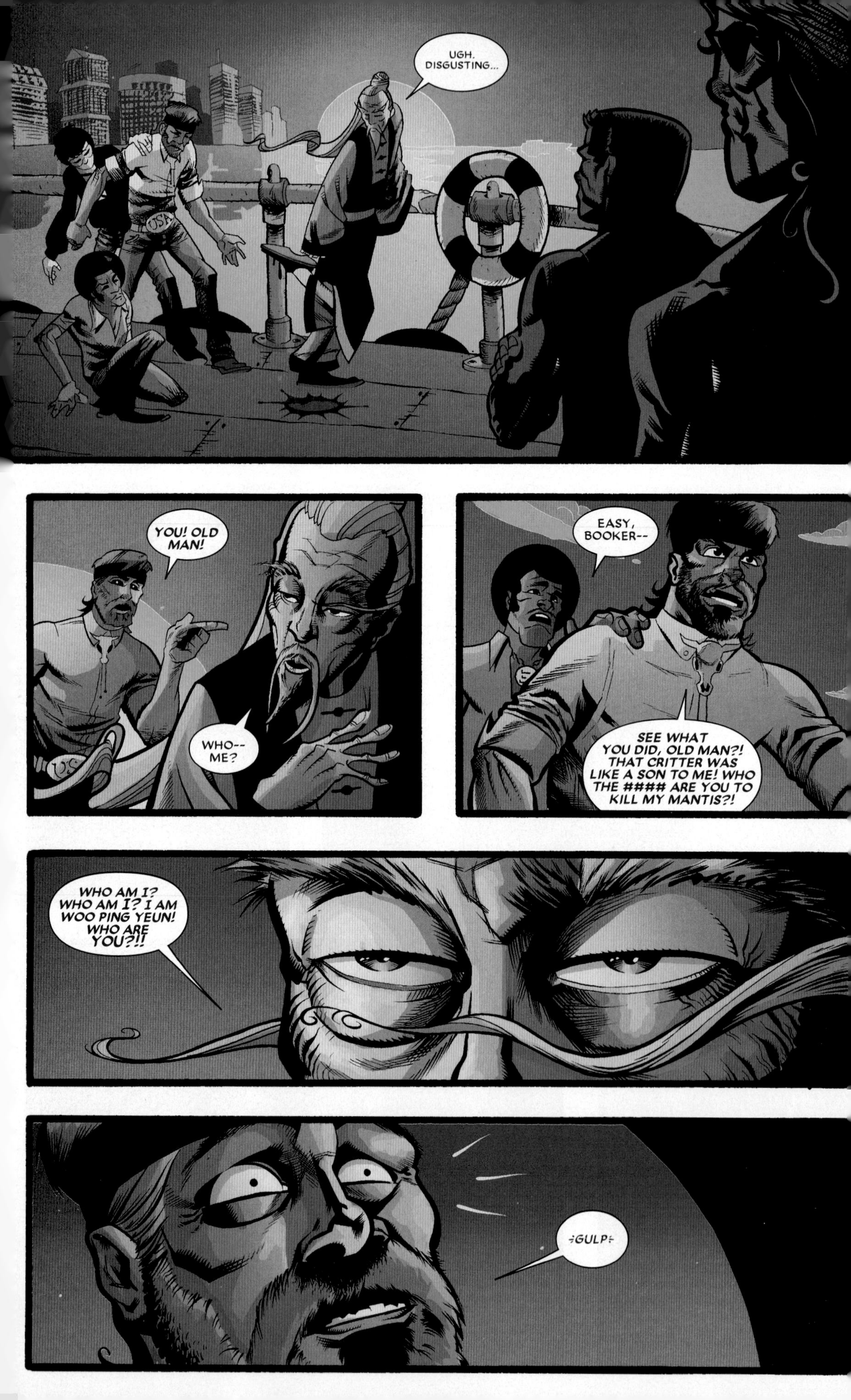
UGH. DISGUSTING...
YOU! OLD MAN!
WHO-- ME?
EASY, BOOKER--
SEE WHAT YOU DID, OLD MAN?! THAT CRITTER WAS LIKE A SON TO ME! WHO THE #### ARE YOU TO KILL MY MANTIS?!
WHO AM I? WHO AM I? I AM WOO PING YEUN! WHO ARE YOU?!!
÷GULP÷

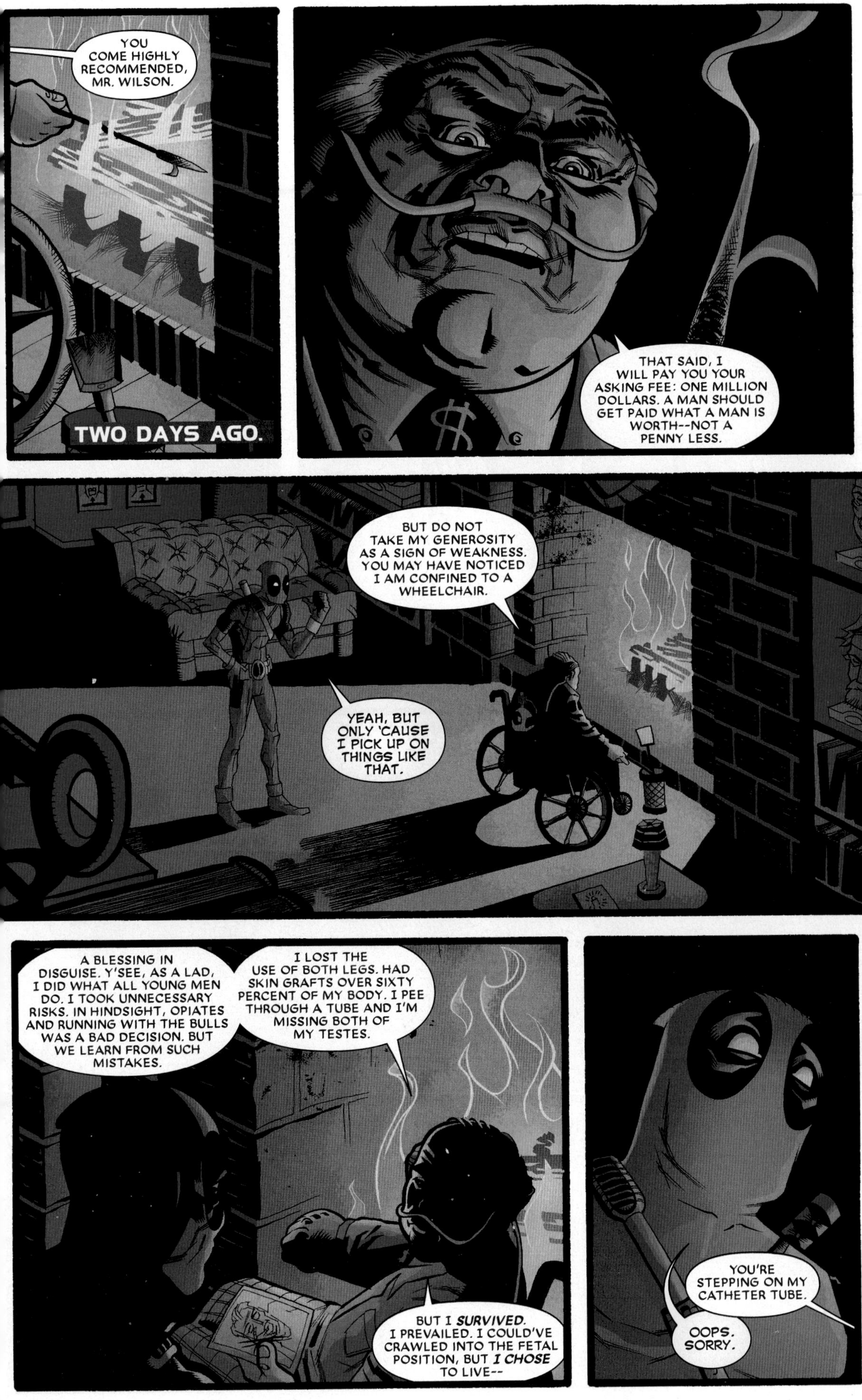
YOU COME HIGHLY RECOMMENDED, MR. WILSON.
TWO DAYS AGO.
THAT SAID, I WILL PAY YOU YOUR ASKING FEE: ONE MILLION DOLLARS. A MAN SHOULD GET PAID WHAT A MAN IS WORTH--NOT A PENNY LESS.
BUT DO NOT TAKE MY GENEROSITY AS A SIGN OF WEAKNESS. YOU MAY HAVE NOTICED I AM CONFINED TO A WHEELCHAIR.
YEAH, BUT ONLY 'CAUSE I PICK UP ON THINGS LIKE THAT.
A BLESSING IN DISGUISE. Y'SEE, AS A LAD, I DID WHAT ALL YOUNG MEN DO. I TOOK UNNECESSARY RISKS. IN HINDSIGHT, OPIATES AND RUNNING WITH THE BULLS WAS A BAD DECISION. BUT WE LEARN FROM SUCH MISTAKES.
I LOST THE USE OF BOTH LEGS. HAD SKIN GRAFTS OVER SIXTY PERCENT OF MY BODY. I PEE THROUGH A TUBE AND I'M MISSING BOTH OF MY TESTES.
BUT I *SURVIVED*. I PREVAILED. I COULD'VE CRAWLED INTO THE FETAL POSITION, BUT *I CHOSE* TO LIVE--
YOU'RE STEPPING ON MY CATHETER TUBE.
OOPS. SORRY.

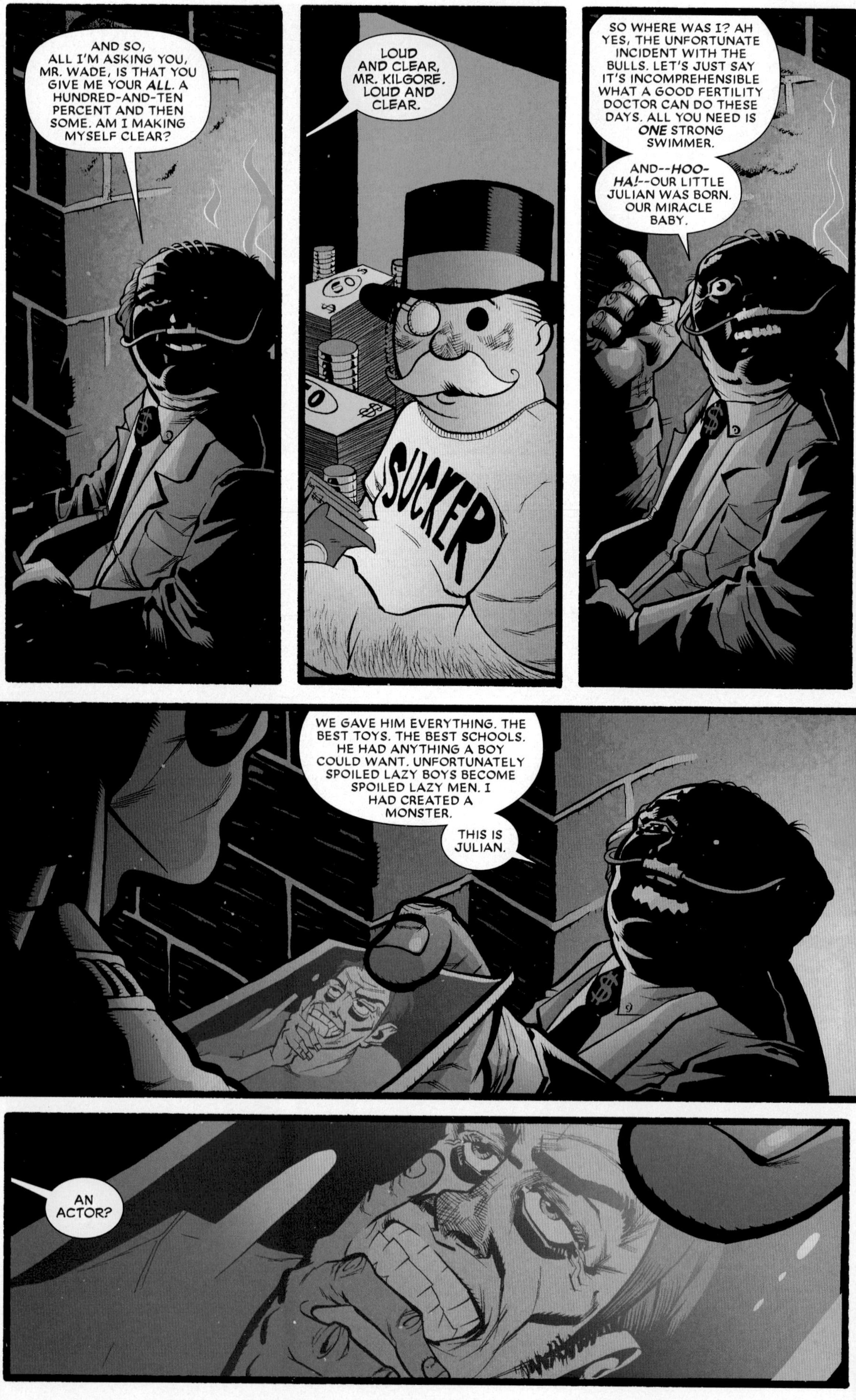
AND SO, ALL I'M ASKING YOU, MR. WADE, IS THAT YOU GIVE ME YOUR *ALL*. A HUNDRED-AND-TEN PERCENT AND THEN SOME. AM I MAKING MYSELF CLEAR?
LOUD AND CLEAR, MR. KILGORE. LOUD AND CLEAR.
SUCKER
SO WHERE WAS I? AH YES, THE UNFORTUNATE INCIDENT WITH THE BULLS. LET'S JUST SAY IT'S INCOMPREHENSIBLE WHAT A GOOD FERTILITY DOCTOR CAN DO THESE DAYS. ALL YOU NEED IS *ONE* STRONG SWIMMER.
AND--*HOO-HA!*--OUR LITTLE JULIAN WAS BORN. OUR MIRACLE BABY.
WE GAVE HIM EVERYTHING. THE BEST TOYS. THE BEST SCHOOLS. HE HAD ANYTHING A BOY COULD WANT. UNFORTUNATELY SPOILED LAZY BOYS BECOME SPOILED LAZY MEN. I HAD CREATED A MONSTER.
THIS IS JULIAN.
AN ACTOR?

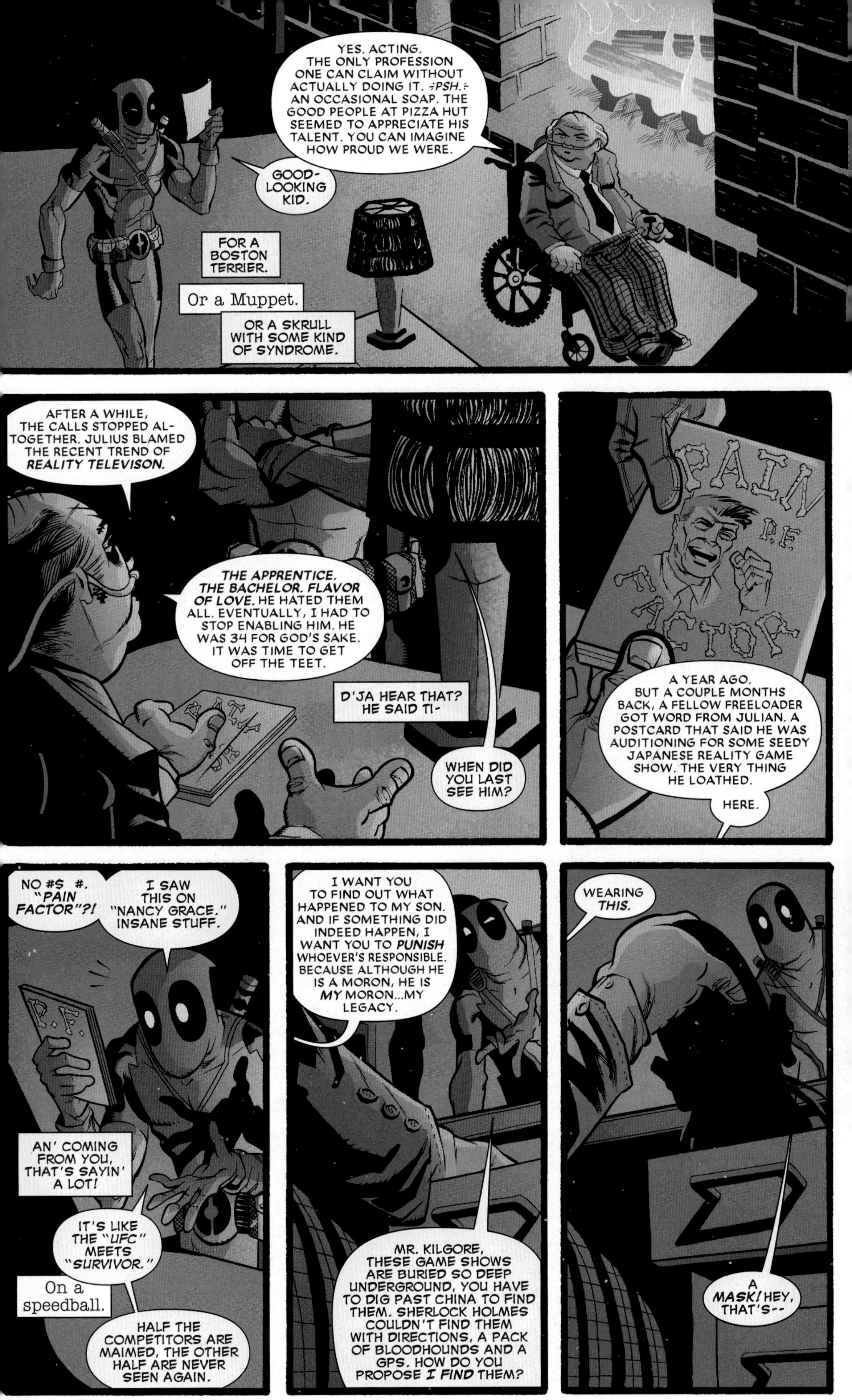

YES. ACTING. THE ONLY PROFESSION ONE CAN CLAIM WITHOUT ACTUALLY DOING IT. =PSH.= AN OCCASIONAL SOAP. THE GOOD PEOPLE AT PIZZA HUT SEEMED TO APPRECIATE HIS TALENT. YOU CAN IMAGINE HOW PROUD WE WERE.
GOOD-LOOKING KID.
FOR A BOSTON TERRIER.
Or a Muppet.
OR A SKRULL WITH SOME KIND OF SYNDROME.
AFTER A WHILE, THE CALLS STOPPED ALTOGETHER. JULIUS BLAMED THE RECENT TREND OF REALITY TELEVISON.
THE APPRENTICE. THE BACHELOR. FLAVOR OF LOVE. HE HATED THEM ALL. EVENTUALLY, I HAD TO STOP ENABLING HIM. HE WAS 34 FOR GOD'S SAKE. IT WAS TIME TO GET OFF THE TEET.
D'JA HEAR THAT? HE SAID TI-
WHEN DID YOU LAST SEE HIM?
PAIN P.F. FACTOR
A YEAR AGO. BUT A COUPLE MONTHS BACK, A FELLOW FREELOADER GOT WORD FROM JULIAN. A POSTCARD THAT SAID HE WAS AUDITIONING FOR SOME SEEDY JAPANESE REALITY GAME SHOW. THE VERY THING HE LOATHED.
HERE.
NO #$ #. "PAIN FACTOR"?!
I SAW THIS ON "NANCY GRACE." INSANE STUFF.
AN' COMING FROM YOU, THAT'S SAYIN' A LOT!
IT'S LIKE THE "UFC" MEETS "SURVIVOR."
On a speedball.
HALF THE COMPETITORS ARE MAIMED, THE OTHER HALF ARE NEVER SEEN AGAIN.
I WANT YOU TO FIND OUT WHAT HAPPENED TO MY SON. AND IF SOMETHING DID INDEED HAPPEN, I WANT YOU TO PUNISH WHOEVER'S RESPONSIBLE. BECAUSE ALTHOUGH HE IS A MORON, HE IS MY MORON...MY LEGACY.
MR. KILGORE, THESE GAME SHOWS ARE BURIED SO DEEP UNDERGROUND, YOU HAVE TO DIG PAST CHINA TO FIND THEM. SHERLOCK HOLMES COULDN'T FIND THEM WITH DIRECTIONS, A PACK OF BLOODHOUNDS AND A GPS. HOW DO YOU PROPOSE I FIND THEM?
WEARING THIS.
A MASK! HEY, THAT'S--

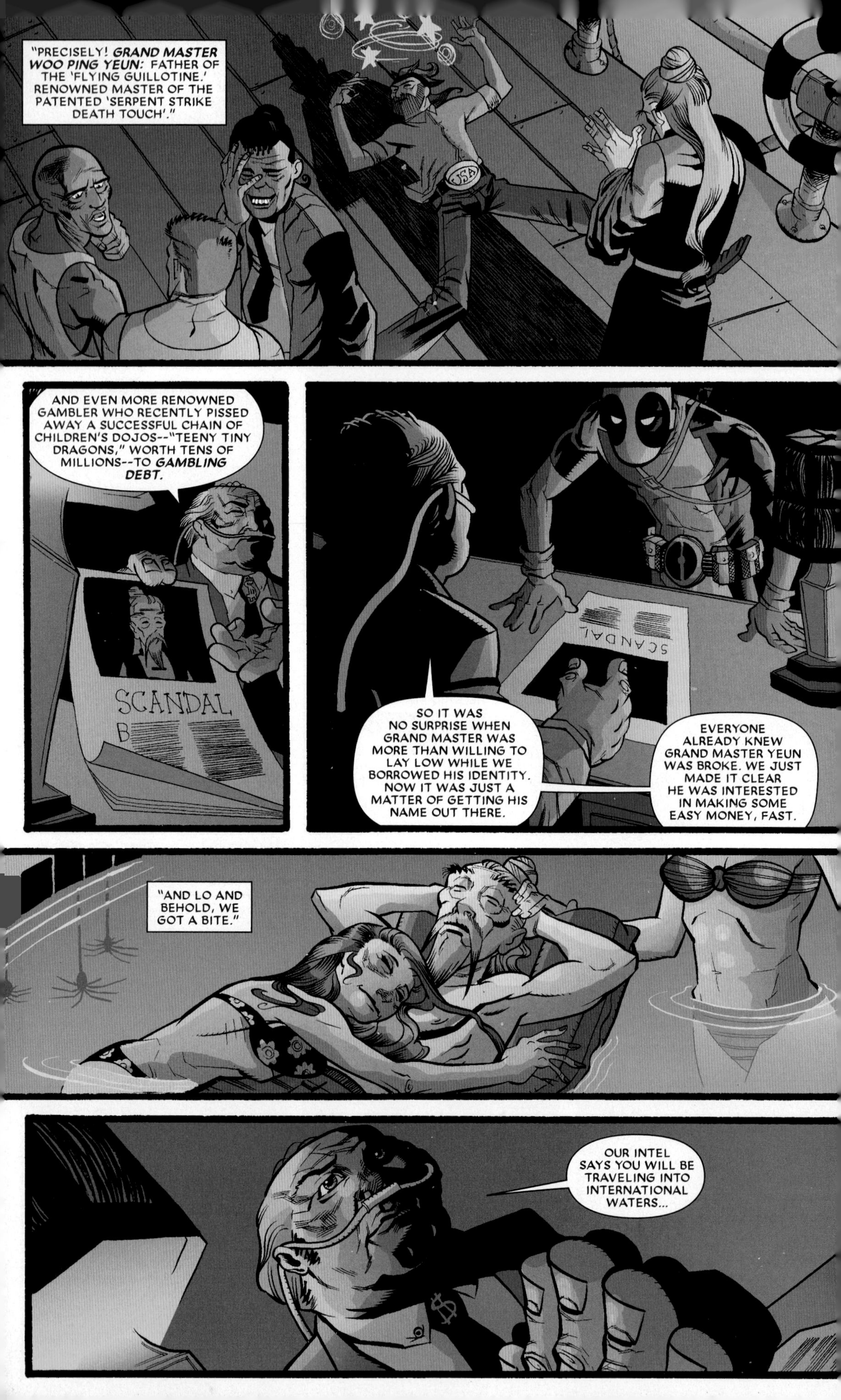
"PRECISELY! GRAND MASTER WOO PING YEUN: FATHER OF THE 'FLYING GUILLOTINE.' RENOWNED MASTER OF THE PATENTED 'SERPENT STRIKE DEATH TOUCH'."
AND EVEN MORE RENOWNED GAMBLER WHO RECENTLY PISSED AWAY A SUCCESSFUL CHAIN OF CHILDREN'S DOJOS--"TEENY TINY DRAGONS," WORTH TENS OF MILLIONS--TO GAMBLING DEBT.
SCANDAL
SCANDAL
SO IT WAS NO SURPRISE WHEN GRAND MASTER WAS MORE THAN WILLING TO LAY LOW WHILE WE BORROWED HIS IDENTITY. NOW IT WAS JUST A MATTER OF GETTING HIS NAME OUT THERE.
EVERYONE ALREADY KNEW GRAND MASTER YEUN WAS BROKE. WE JUST MADE IT CLEAR HE WAS INTERESTED IN MAKING SOME EASY MONEY, FAST.
"AND LO AND BEHOLD, WE GOT A BITE."
OUR INTEL SAYS YOU WILL BE TRAVELING INTO INTERNATIONAL WATERS...

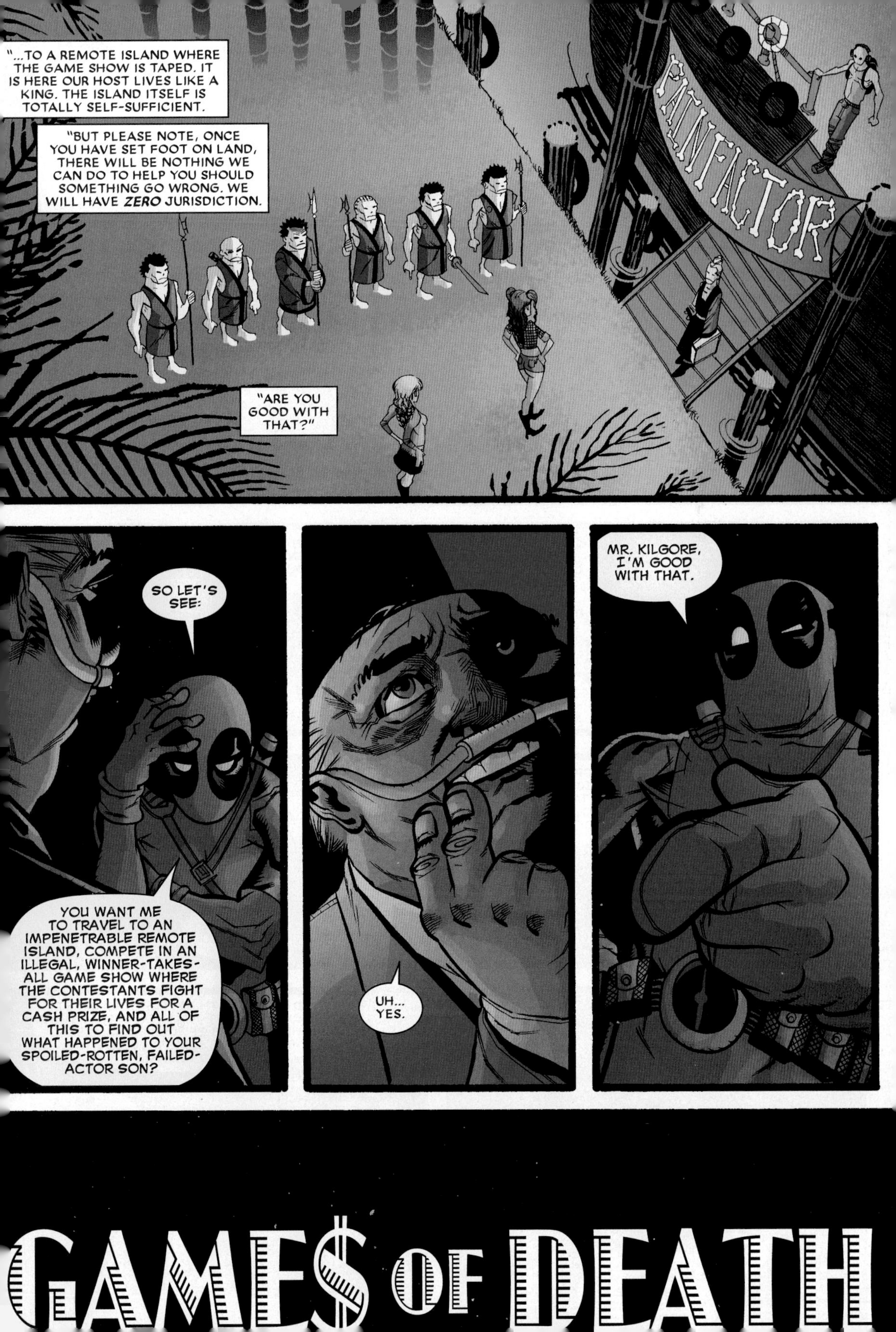
"...TO A REMOTE ISLAND WHERE THE GAME SHOW IS TAPED. IT IS HERE OUR HOST LIVES LIKE A KING. THE ISLAND ITSELF IS TOTALLY SELF-SUFFICIENT.
"BUT PLEASE NOTE, ONCE YOU HAVE SET FOOT ON LAND, THERE WILL BE NOTHING WE CAN DO TO HELP YOU SHOULD SOMETHING GO WRONG. WE WILL HAVE *ZERO* JURISDICTION.
PAIN FACTOR
"ARE YOU GOOD WITH THAT?"
SO LET'S SEE:
YOU WANT ME TO TRAVEL TO AN IMPENETRABLE REMOTE ISLAND, COMPETE IN AN ILLEGAL, WINNER-TAKES-ALL GAME SHOW WHERE THE CONTESTANTS FIGHT FOR THEIR LIVES FOR A CASH PRIZE, AND ALL OF THIS TO FIND OUT WHAT HAPPENED TO YOUR SPOILED-ROTTEN, FAILED-ACTOR SON?
UH... YES.
MR. KILGORE, I'M GOOD WITH THAT.

GAME$ OF DEATH

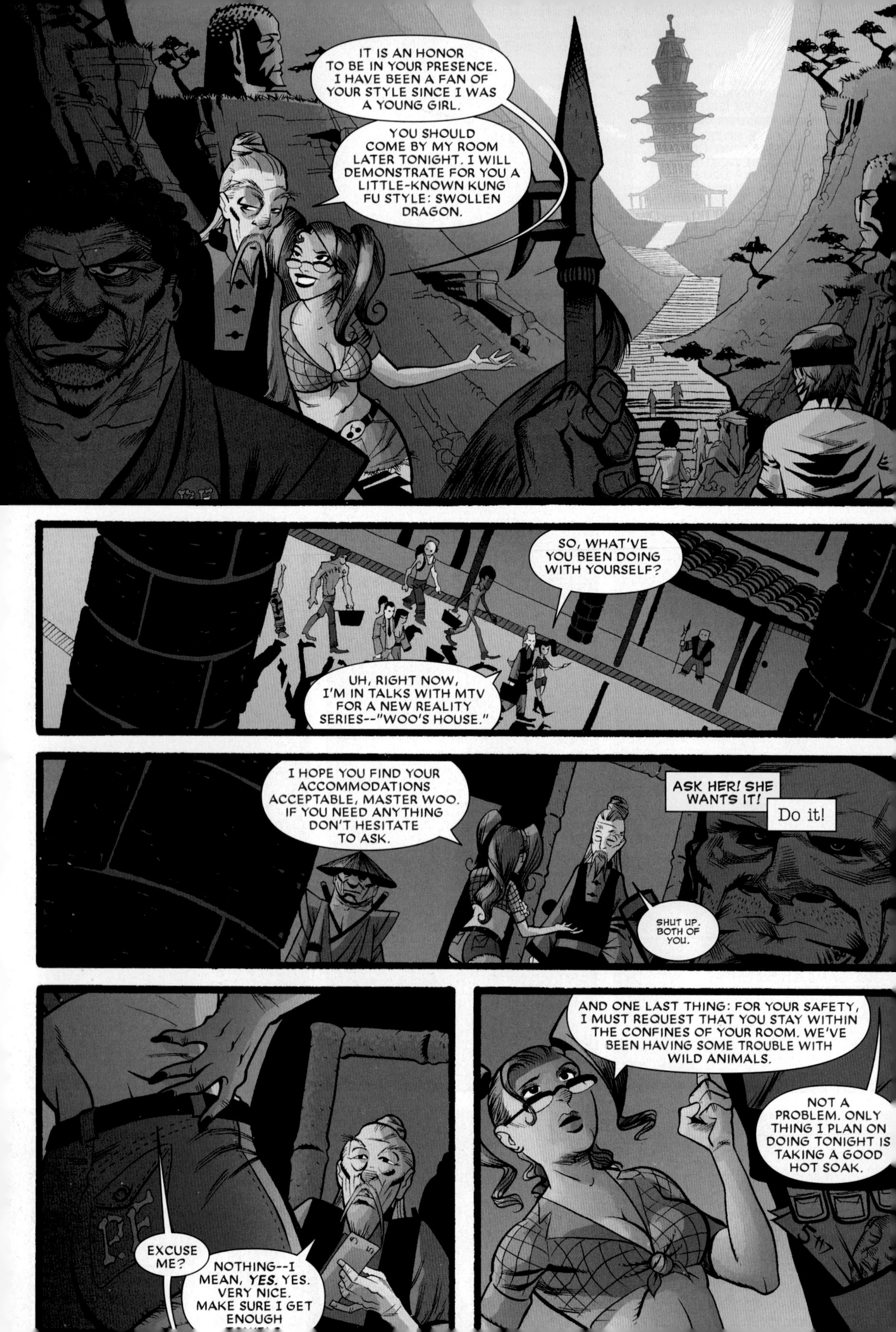

IT IS AN HONOR TO BE IN YOUR PRESENCE. I HAVE BEEN A FAN OF YOUR STYLE SINCE I WAS A YOUNG GIRL.
YOU SHOULD COME BY MY ROOM LATER TONIGHT. I WILL DEMONSTRATE FOR YOU A LITTLE-KNOWN KUNG FU STYLE: SWOLLEN DRAGON.
SO, WHAT'VE YOU BEEN DOING WITH YOURSELF?
UH, RIGHT NOW, I'M IN TALKS WITH MTV FOR A NEW REALITY SERIES--"WOO'S HOUSE."
I HOPE YOU FIND YOUR ACCOMMODATIONS ACCEPTABLE, MASTER WOO. IF YOU NEED ANYTHING DON'T HESITATE TO ASK.
ASK HER! SHE WANTS IT!
Do it!
SHUT UP. BOTH OF YOU.
EXCUSE ME?
NOTHING--I MEAN, YES. YES. VERY NICE. MAKE SURE I GET ENOUGH
AND ONE LAST THING: FOR YOUR SAFETY, I MUST REQUEST THAT YOU STAY WITHIN THE CONFINES OF YOUR ROOM. WE'VE BEEN HAVING SOME TROUBLE WITH WILD ANIMALS.
NOT A PROBLEM. ONLY THING I PLAN ON DOING TONIGHT IS TAKING A GOOD HOT SOAK.

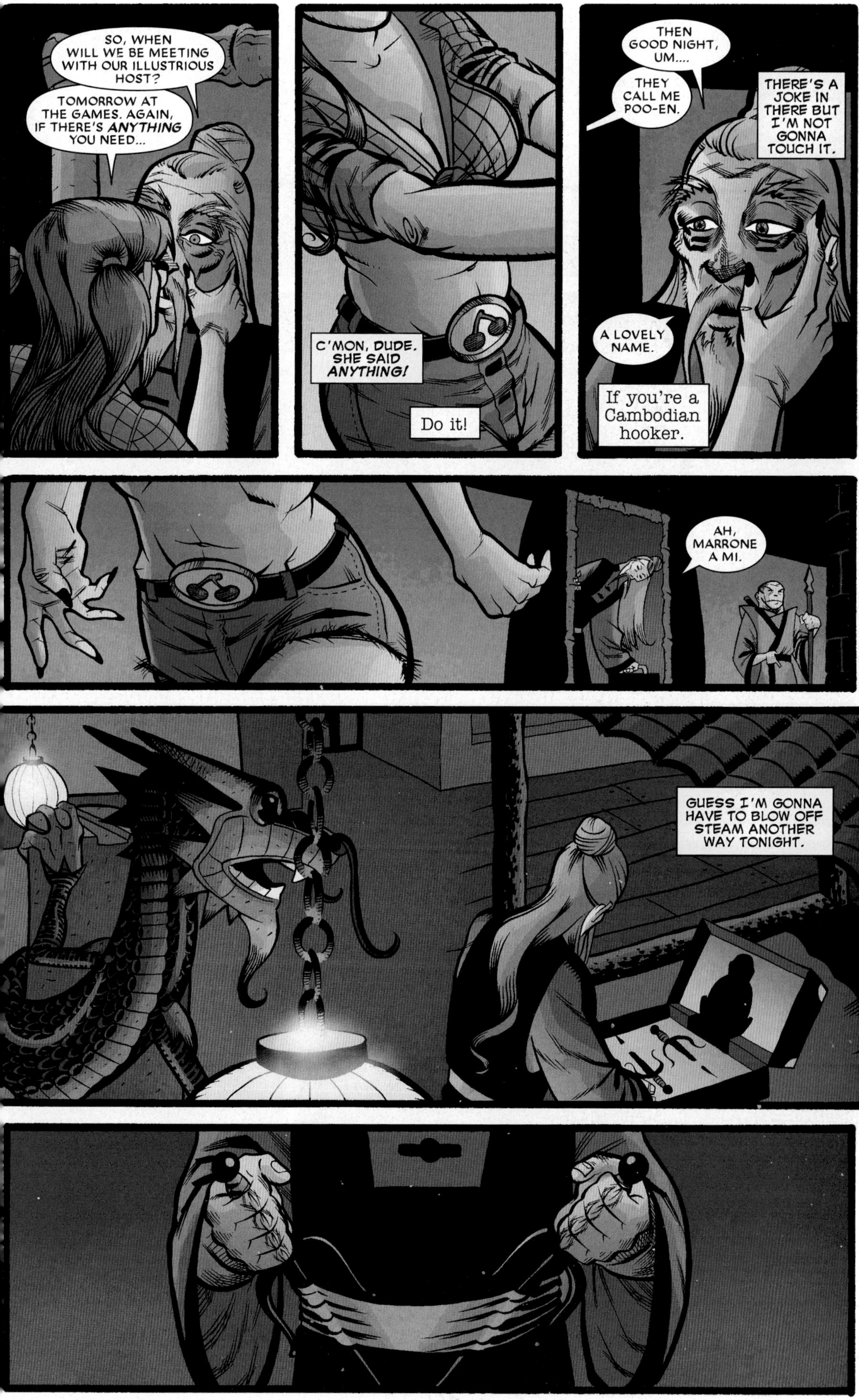
SO, WHEN WILL WE BE MEETING WITH OUR ILLUSTRIOUS HOST?
TOMORROW AT THE GAMES. AGAIN, IF THERE'S ANYTHING YOU NEED...
C'MON, DUDE. SHE SAID ANYTHING!
Do it!
THEN GOOD NIGHT, UM....
THEY CALL ME POO-EN.
THERE'S A JOKE IN THERE BUT I'M NOT GONNA TOUCH IT.
A LOVELY NAME.
If you're a Cambodian hooker.
AH, MARRONE A MI.
GUESS I'M GONNA HAVE TO BLOW OFF STEAM ANOTHER WAY TONIGHT.

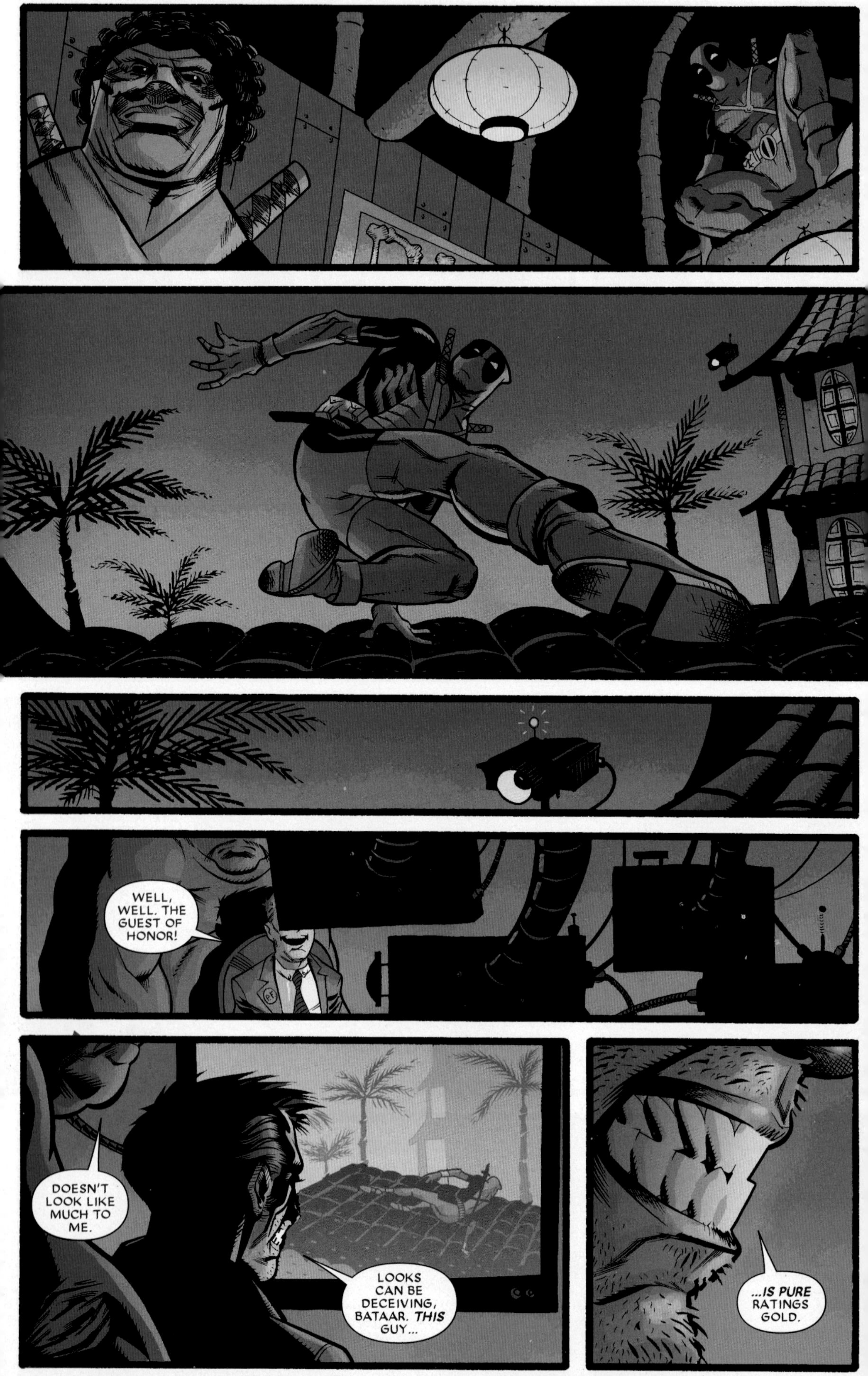
WELL, WELL. THE GUEST OF HONOR!
DOESN'T LOOK LIKE MUCH TO ME.
LOOKS CAN BE DECEIVING, BATAAR. *THIS* GUY...
...*IS PURE* RATINGS GOLD.

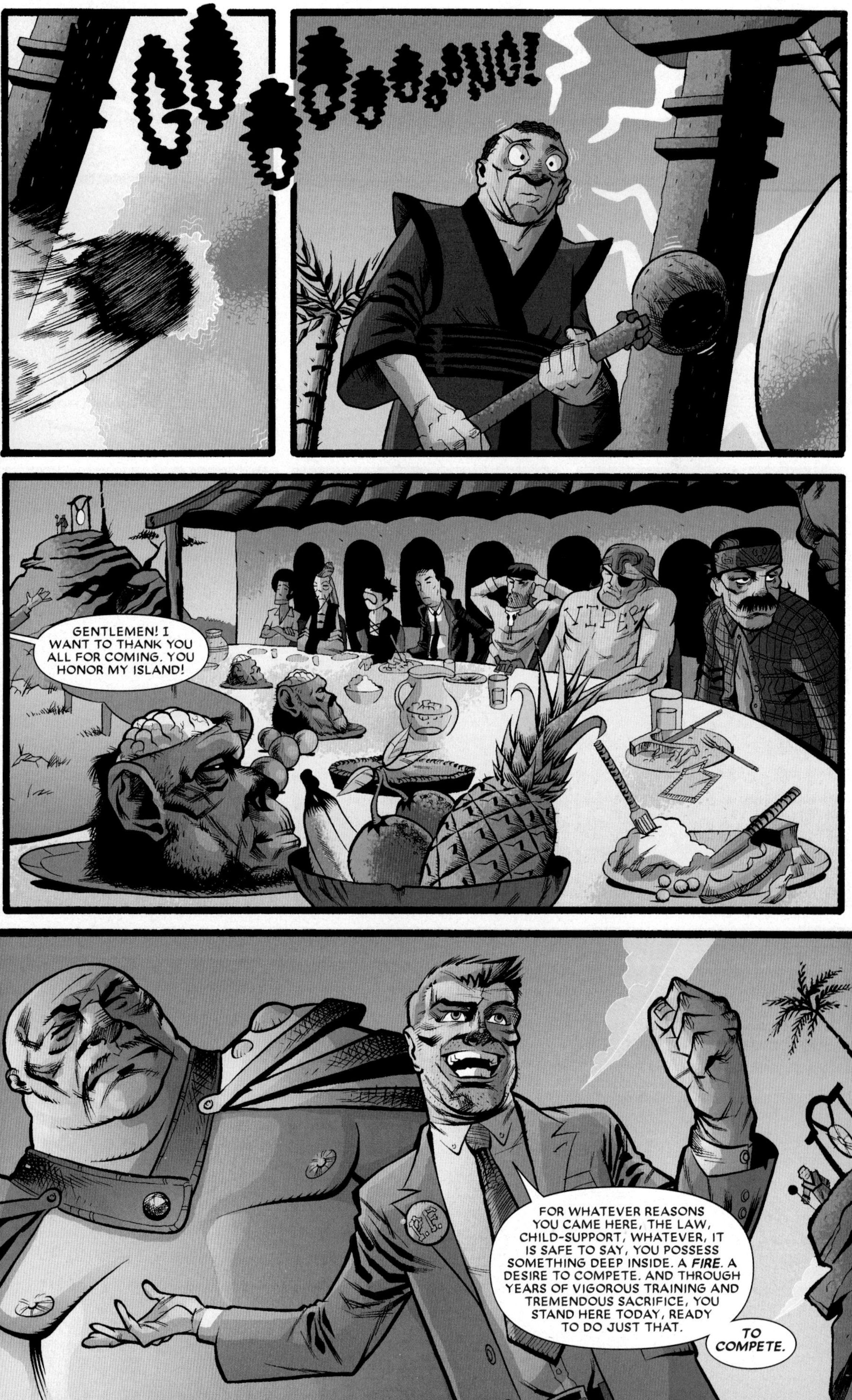
GENTLEMEN! I WANT TO THANK YOU ALL FOR COMING. YOU HONOR MY ISLAND!
FOR WHATEVER REASONS YOU CAME HERE, THE LAW, CHILD-SUPPORT, WHATEVER, IT IS SAFE TO SAY, YOU POSSESS SOMETHING DEEP INSIDE. A *FIRE*. A DESIRE TO COMPETE. AND THROUGH YEARS OF VIGOROUS TRAINING AND TREMENDOUS SACRIFICE, YOU STAND HERE TODAY, READY TO DO JUST THAT.
TO COMPETE.

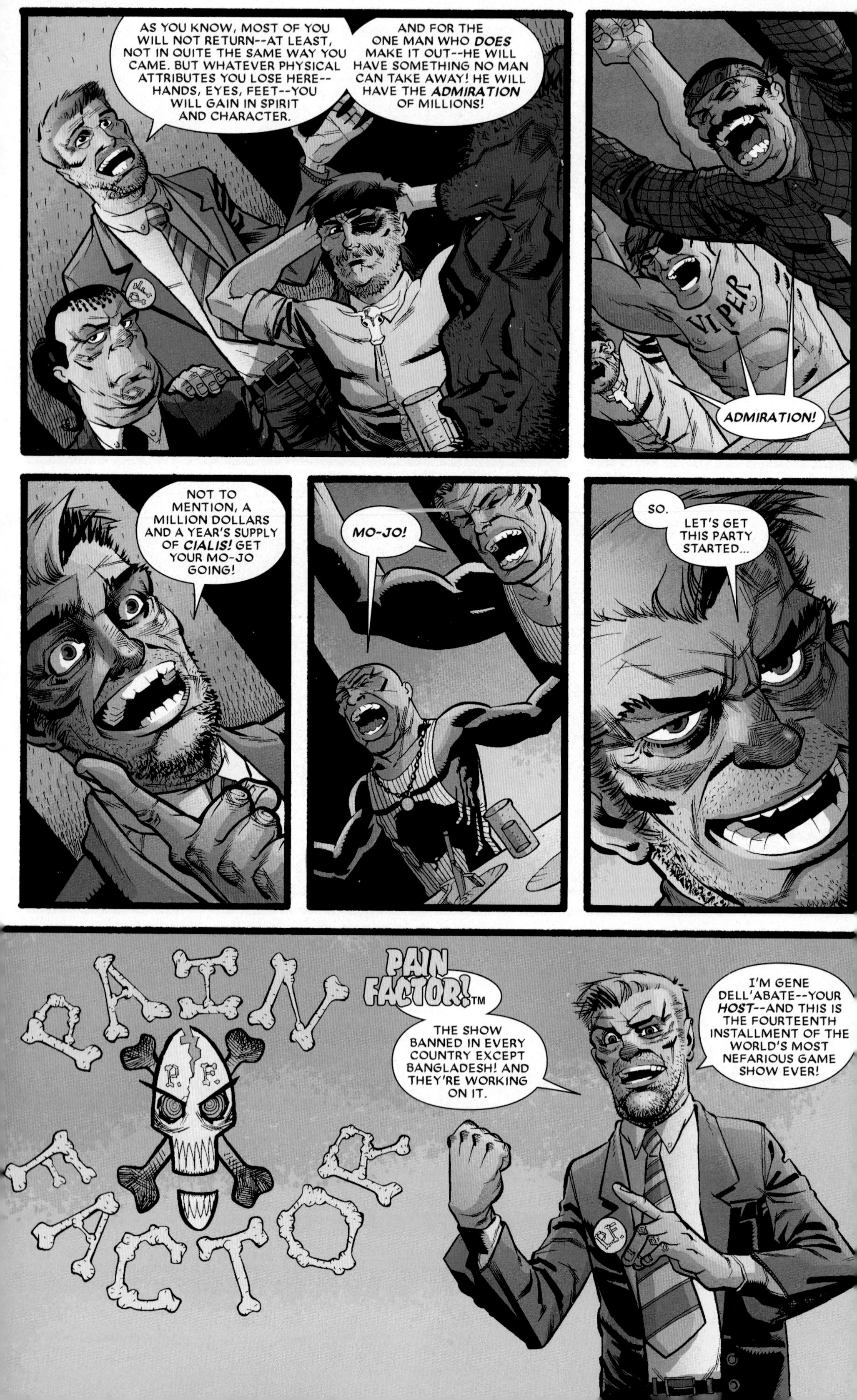
AS YOU KNOW, MOST OF YOU WILL NOT RETURN--AT LEAST, NOT IN QUITE THE SAME WAY YOU CAME. BUT WHATEVER PHYSICAL ATTRIBUTES YOU LOSE HERE--HANDS, EYES, FEET--YOU WILL GAIN IN SPIRIT AND CHARACTER.
AND FOR THE ONE MAN WHO DOES MAKE IT OUT--HE WILL HAVE SOMETHING NO MAN CAN TAKE AWAY! HE WILL HAVE THE ADMIRATION OF MILLIONS!
VIPER
ADMIRATION!
NOT TO MENTION, A MILLION DOLLARS AND A YEAR'S SUPPLY OF CIALIS! GET YOUR MO-JO GOING!
MO-JO!
SO.
LET'S GET THIS PARTY STARTED...
PAIN FACTOR
PAIN FACTOR!™
THE SHOW BANNED IN EVERY COUNTRY EXCEPT BANGLADESH! AND THEY'RE WORKING ON IT.
I'M GENE DELL'ABATE--YOUR HOST--AND THIS IS THE FOURTEENTH INSTALLMENT OF THE WORLD'S MOST NEFARIOUS GAME SHOW EVER!

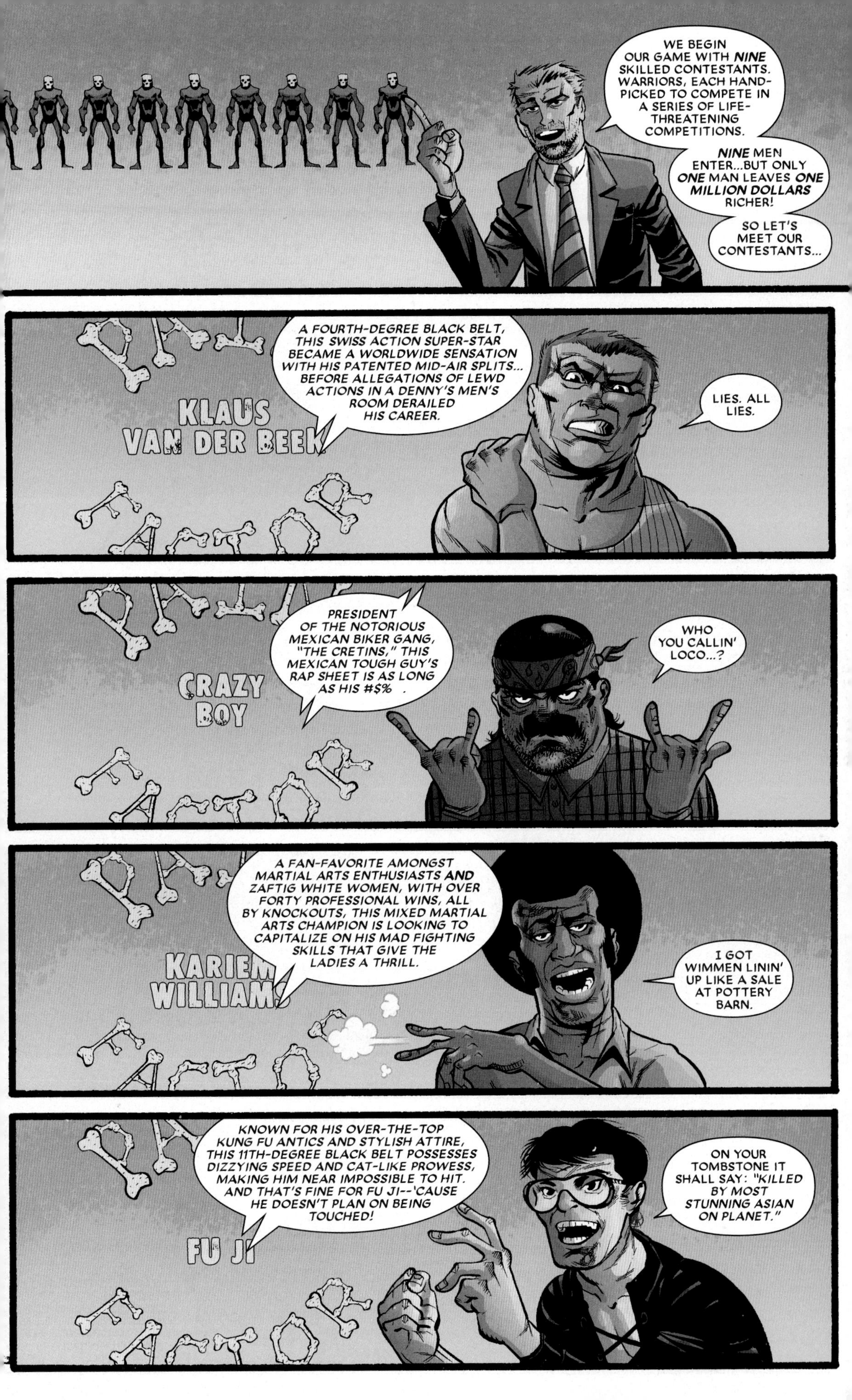
WE BEGIN OUR GAME WITH NINE SKILLED CONTESTANTS. WARRIORS, EACH HAND-PICKED TO COMPETE IN A SERIES OF LIFE-THREATENING COMPETITIONS.
NINE MEN ENTER...BUT ONLY ONE MAN LEAVES ONE MILLION DOLLARS RICHER!
SO LET'S MEET OUR CONTESTANTS...
KLAUS VAN DER BEEK
A FOURTH-DEGREE BLACK BELT, THIS SWISS ACTION SUPER-STAR BECAME A WORLDWIDE SENSATION WITH HIS PATENTED MID-AIR SPLITS... BEFORE ALLEGATIONS OF LEWD ACTIONS IN A DENNY'S MEN'S ROOM DERAILED HIS CAREER.
LIES. ALL LIES.
CRAZY BOY
PRESIDENT OF THE NOTORIOUS MEXICAN BIKER GANG, "THE CRETINS," THIS MEXICAN TOUGH GUY'S RAP SHEET IS AS LONG AS HIS #$% .
WHO YOU CALLIN' LOCO...?
KARIEM WILLIAMS
A FAN-FAVORITE AMONGST MARTIAL ARTS ENTHUSIASTS AND ZAFTIG WHITE WOMEN, WITH OVER FORTY PROFESSIONAL WINS, ALL BY KNOCKOUTS, THIS MIXED MARTIAL ARTS CHAMPION IS LOOKING TO CAPITALIZE ON HIS MAD FIGHTING SKILLS THAT GIVE THE LADIES A THRILL.
I GOT WIMMEN LININ' UP LIKE A SALE AT POTTERY BARN.
FU JI
KNOWN FOR HIS OVER-THE-TOP KUNG FU ANTICS AND STYLISH ATTIRE, THIS 11TH-DEGREE BLACK BELT POSSESSES DIZZYING SPEED AND CAT-LIKE PROWESS, MAKING HIM NEAR IMPOSSIBLE TO HIT. AND THAT'S FINE FOR FU JI--'CAUSE HE DOESN'T PLAN ON BEING TOUCHED!
ON YOUR TOMBSTONE IT SHALL SAY: "KILLED BY MOST STUNNING ASIAN ON PLANET."

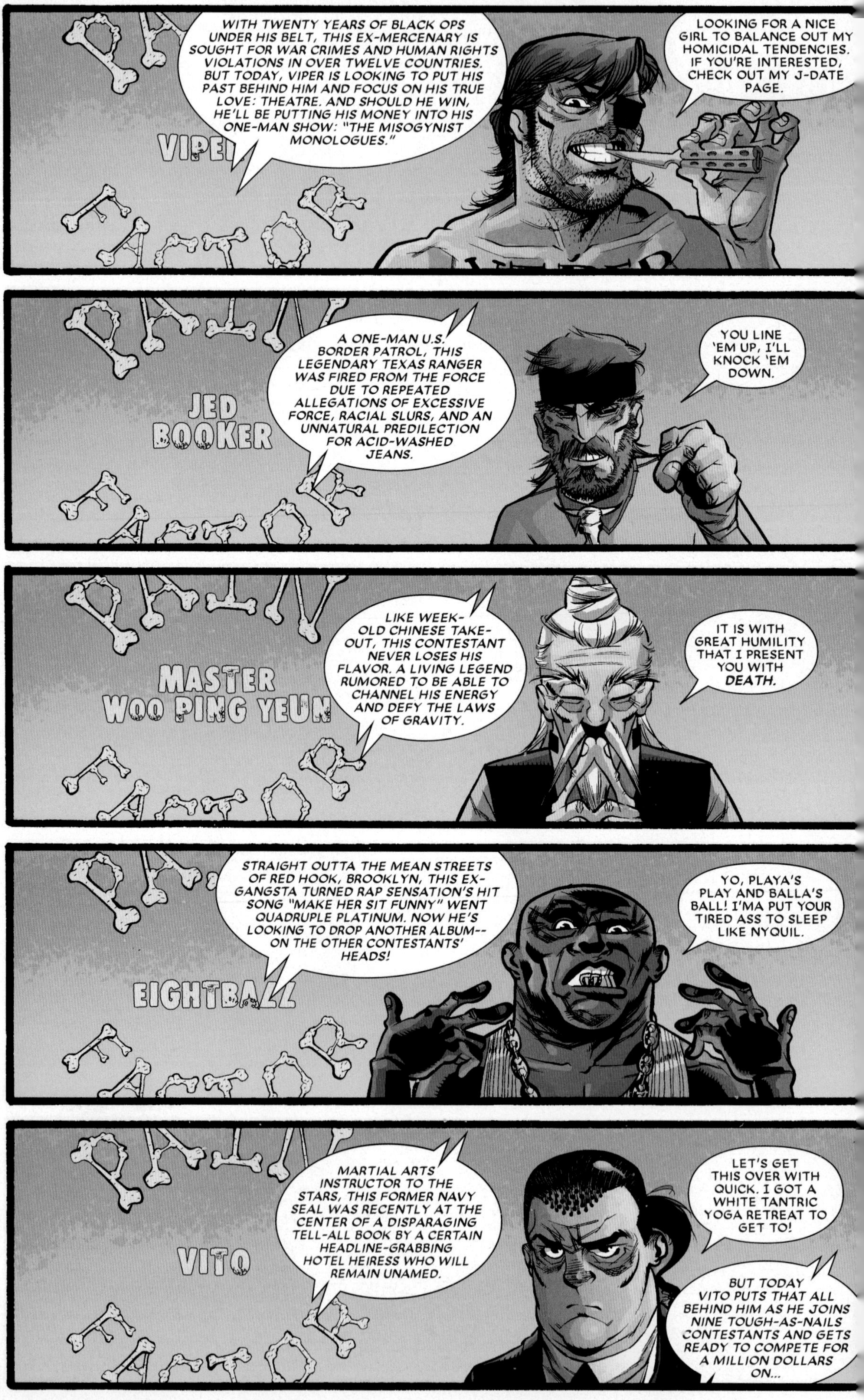
WITH TWENTY YEARS OF BLACK OPS UNDER HIS BELT, THIS EX-MERCENARY IS SOUGHT FOR WAR CRIMES AND HUMAN RIGHTS VIOLATIONS IN OVER TWELVE COUNTRIES. BUT TODAY, VIPER IS LOOKING TO PUT HIS PAST BEHIND HIM AND FOCUS ON HIS TRUE LOVE: THEATRE. AND SHOULD HE WIN, HE'LL BE PUTTING HIS MONEY INTO HIS ONE-MAN SHOW: "THE MISOGYNIST MONOLOGUES."
LOOKING FOR A NICE GIRL TO BALANCE OUT MY HOMICIDAL TENDENCIES. IF YOU'RE INTERESTED, CHECK OUT MY J-DATE PAGE.
JED BOOKER
A ONE-MAN U.S. BORDER PATROL, THIS LEGENDARY TEXAS RANGER WAS FIRED FROM THE FORCE DUE TO REPEATED ALLEGATIONS OF EXCESSIVE FORCE, RACIAL SLURS, AND AN UNNATURAL PREDILECTION FOR ACID-WASHED JEANS.
YOU LINE 'EM UP, I'LL KNOCK 'EM DOWN.
MASTER WOO PING YEUN
LIKE WEEK-OLD CHINESE TAKE-OUT, THIS CONTESTANT NEVER LOSES HIS FLAVOR. A LIVING LEGEND RUMORED TO BE ABLE TO CHANNEL HIS ENERGY AND DEFY THE LAWS OF GRAVITY.
IT IS WITH GREAT HUMILITY THAT I PRESENT YOU WITH *DEATH.*
STRAIGHT OUTTA THE MEAN STREETS OF RED HOOK, BROOKLYN, THIS EX-GANGSTA TURNED RAP SENSATION'S HIT SONG "MAKE HER SIT FUNNY" WENT QUADRUPLE PLATINUM. NOW HE'S LOOKING TO DROP ANOTHER ALBUM-- ON THE OTHER CONTESTANTS' HEADS!
YO, PLAYA'S PLAY AND BALLA'S BALL! I'MA PUT YOUR TIRED ASS TO SLEEP LIKE NYQUIL.
EIGHTBALL
MARTIAL ARTS INSTRUCTOR TO THE STARS, THIS FORMER NAVY SEAL WAS RECENTLY AT THE CENTER OF A DISPARAGING TELL-ALL BOOK BY A CERTAIN HEADLINE-GRABBING HOTEL HEIRESS WHO WILL REMAIN UNAMED.
LET'S GET THIS OVER WITH QUICK. I GOT A WHITE TANTRIC YOGA RETREAT TO GET TO!
VITO
BUT TODAY VITO PUTS THAT ALL BEHIND HIM AS HE JOINS NINE TOUGH-AS-NAILS CONTESTANTS AND GETS READY TO COMPETE FOR A MILLION DOLLARS ON...

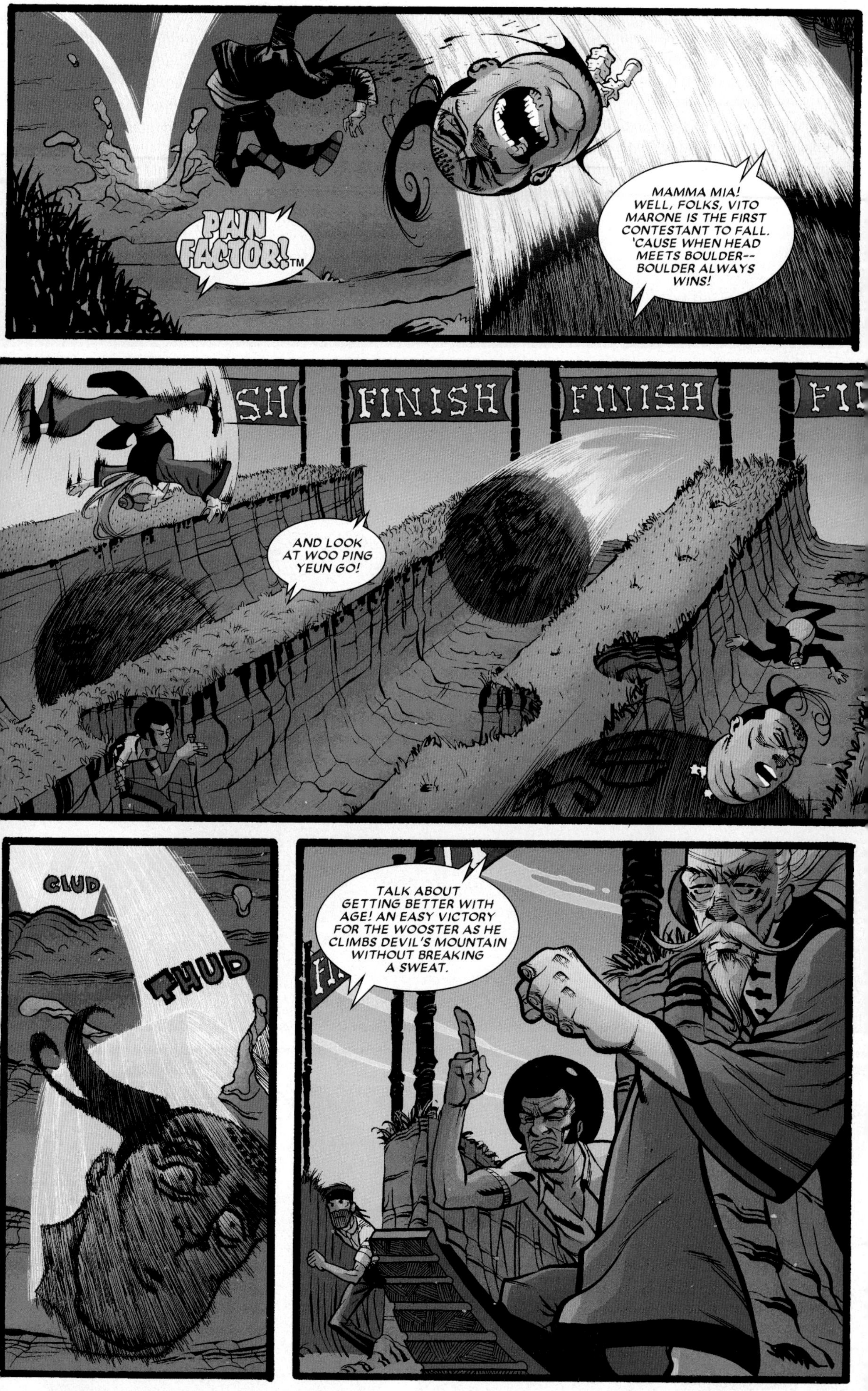
PAIN FACTOR!™
MAMMA MIA! WELL, FOLKS, VITO MARONE IS THE FIRST CONTESTANT TO FALL. 'CAUSE WHEN HEAD MEETS BOULDER-- BOULDER ALWAYS WINS!
SH FINISH FINISH FI
AND LOOK AT WOO PING YEUN GO!
CLUD
THUD
TALK ABOUT GETTING BETTER WITH AGE! AN EASY VICTORY FOR THE WOOSTER AS HE CLIMBS DEVIL'S MOUNTAIN WITHOUT BREAKING A SWEAT.

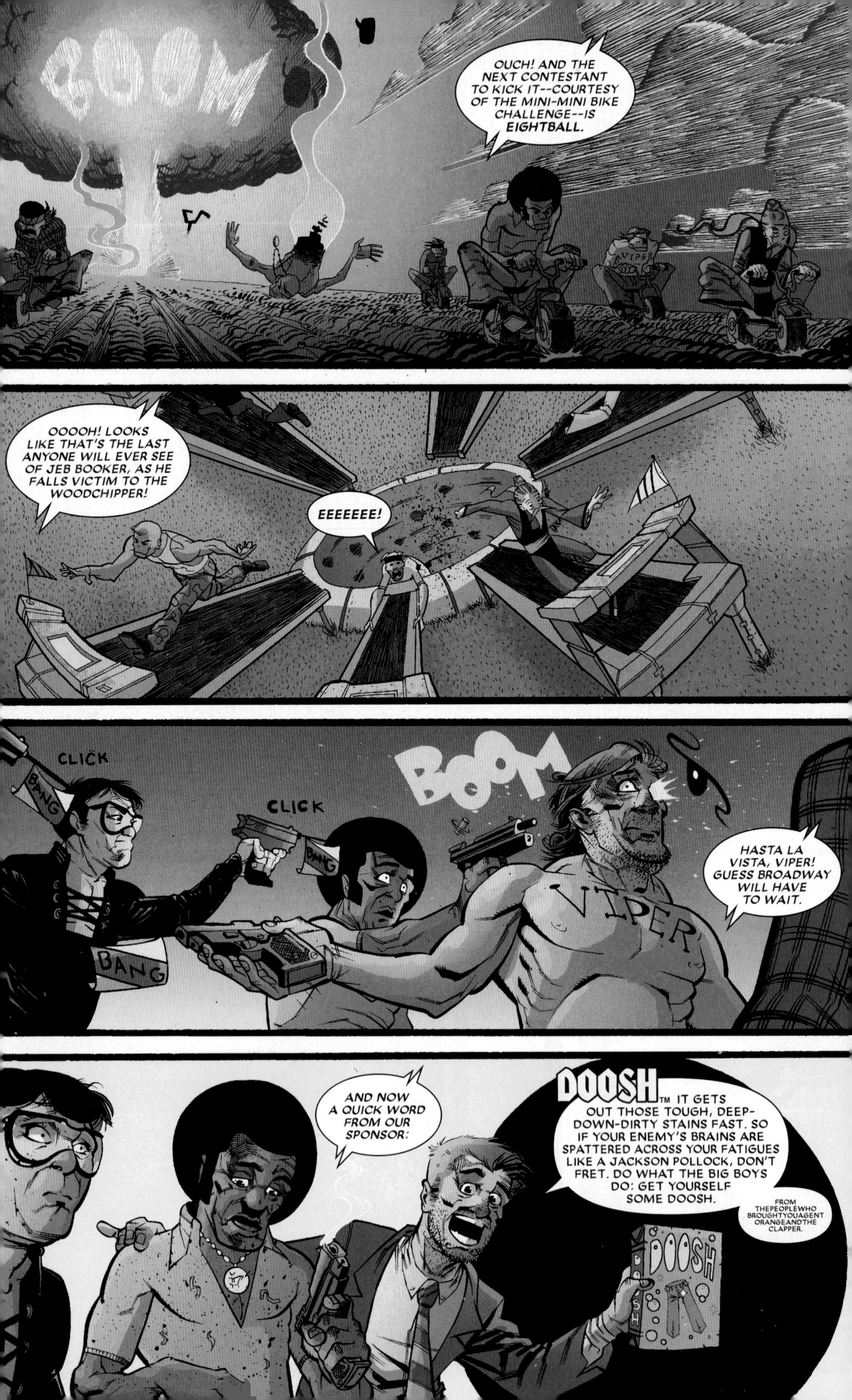
BOOM
OUCH! AND THE NEXT CONTESTANT TO KICK IT--COURTESY OF THE MINI-MINI BIKE CHALLENGE--IS EIGHTBALL.
OOOOH! LOOKS LIKE THAT'S THE LAST ANYONE WILL EVER SEE OF JEB BOOKER, AS HE FALLS VICTIM TO THE WOODCHIPPER!
EEEEEEE!
CLICK
BANG
CLICK
BANG
BANG
BOOM
VIPER
HASTA LA VISTA, VIPER! GUESS BROADWAY WILL HAVE TO WAIT.
AND NOW A QUICK WORD FROM OUR SPONSOR:
DOOSH™ IT GETS OUT THOSE TOUGH, DEEP-DOWN-DIRTY STAINS FAST. SO IF YOUR ENEMY'S BRAINS ARE SPATTERED ACROSS YOUR FATIGUES LIKE A JACKSON POLLOCK, DON'T FRET. DO WHAT THE BIG BOYS DO: GET YOURSELF SOME DOOSH.
FROM THEPEOPLEWHO BROUGHTYOUAGENT ORANGEANDTHE CLAPPER.
DOOSH

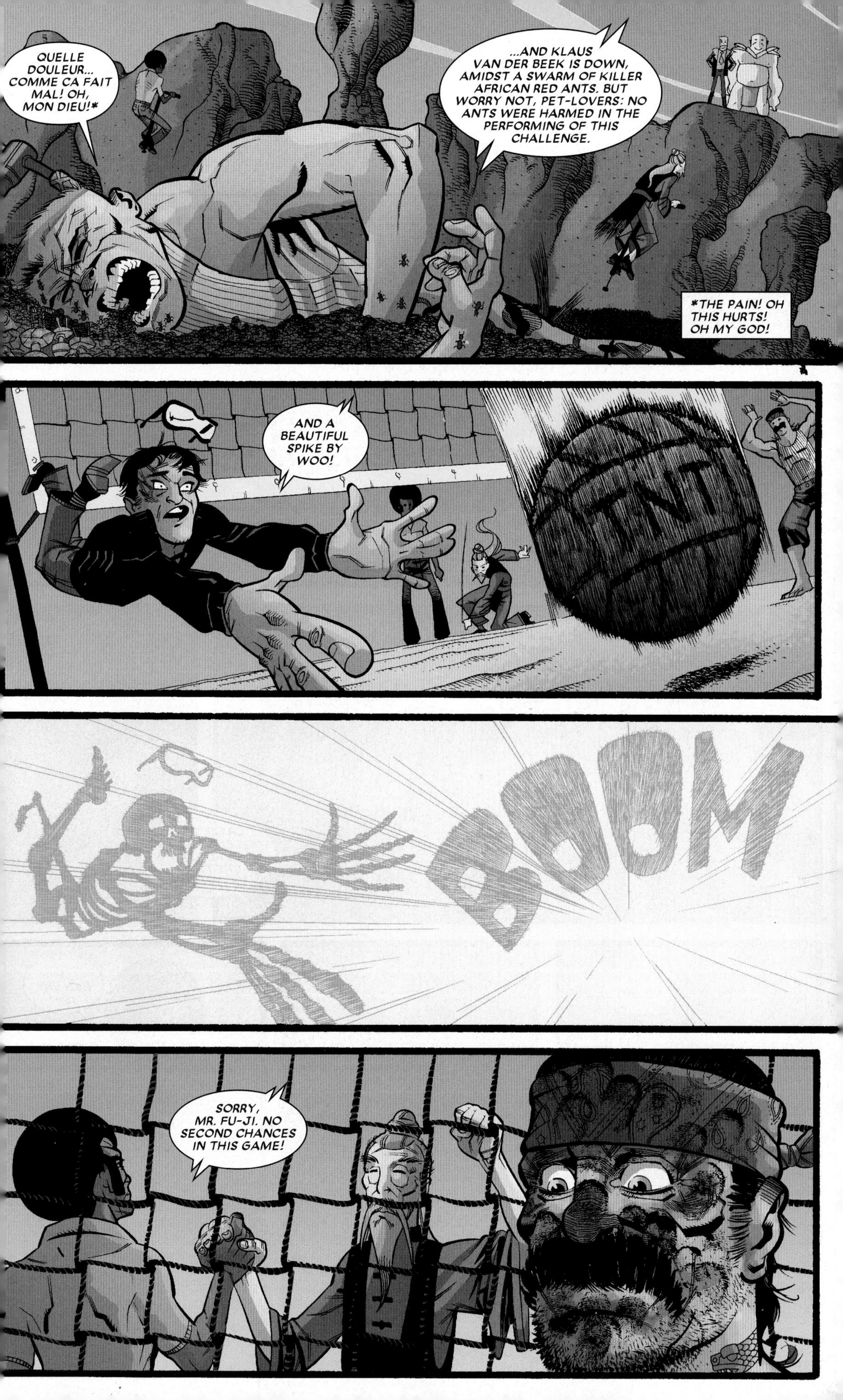
QUELLE DOULEUR... COMME CA FAIT MAL! OH, MON DIEU!*
...AND KLAUS VAN DER BEEK IS DOWN, AMIDST A SWARM OF KILLER AFRICAN RED ANTS. BUT WORRY NOT, PET-LOVERS: NO ANTS WERE HARMED IN THE PERFORMING OF THIS CHALLENGE.
*THE PAIN! OH THIS HURTS! OH MY GOD!
AND A BEAUTIFUL SPIKE BY WOO!
TNT
BOOM
SORRY, MR. FU-JI. NO SECOND CHANCES IN THIS GAME!

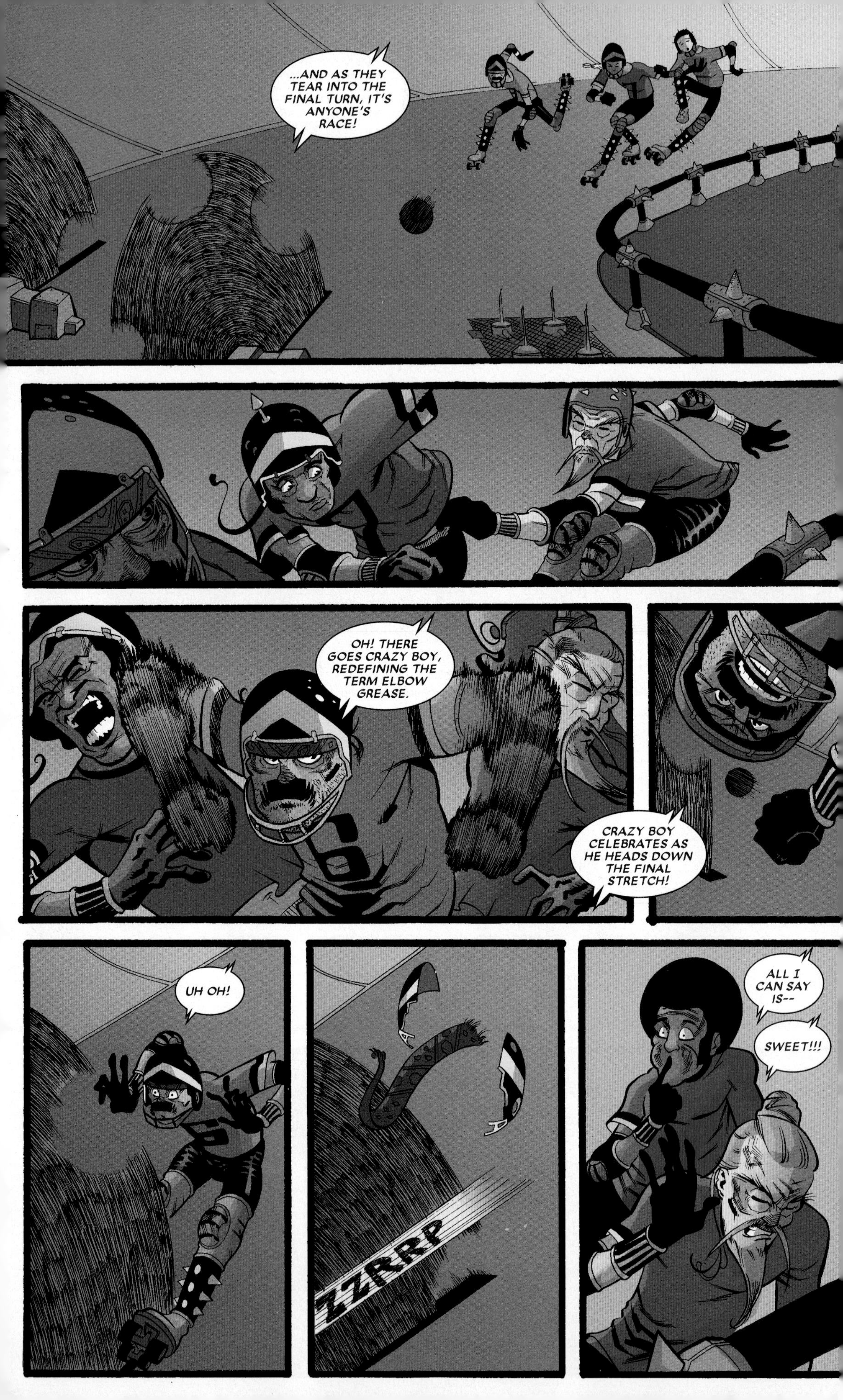
...AND AS THEY TEAR INTO THE FINAL TURN, IT'S ANYONE'S RACE!
OH! THERE GOES CRAZY BOY, REDEFINING THE TERM ELBOW GREASE.
CRAZY BOY CELEBRATES AS HE HEADS DOWN THE FINAL STRETCH!
UH OH!
ZZRRP
ALL I CAN SAY IS--
SWEET!!!

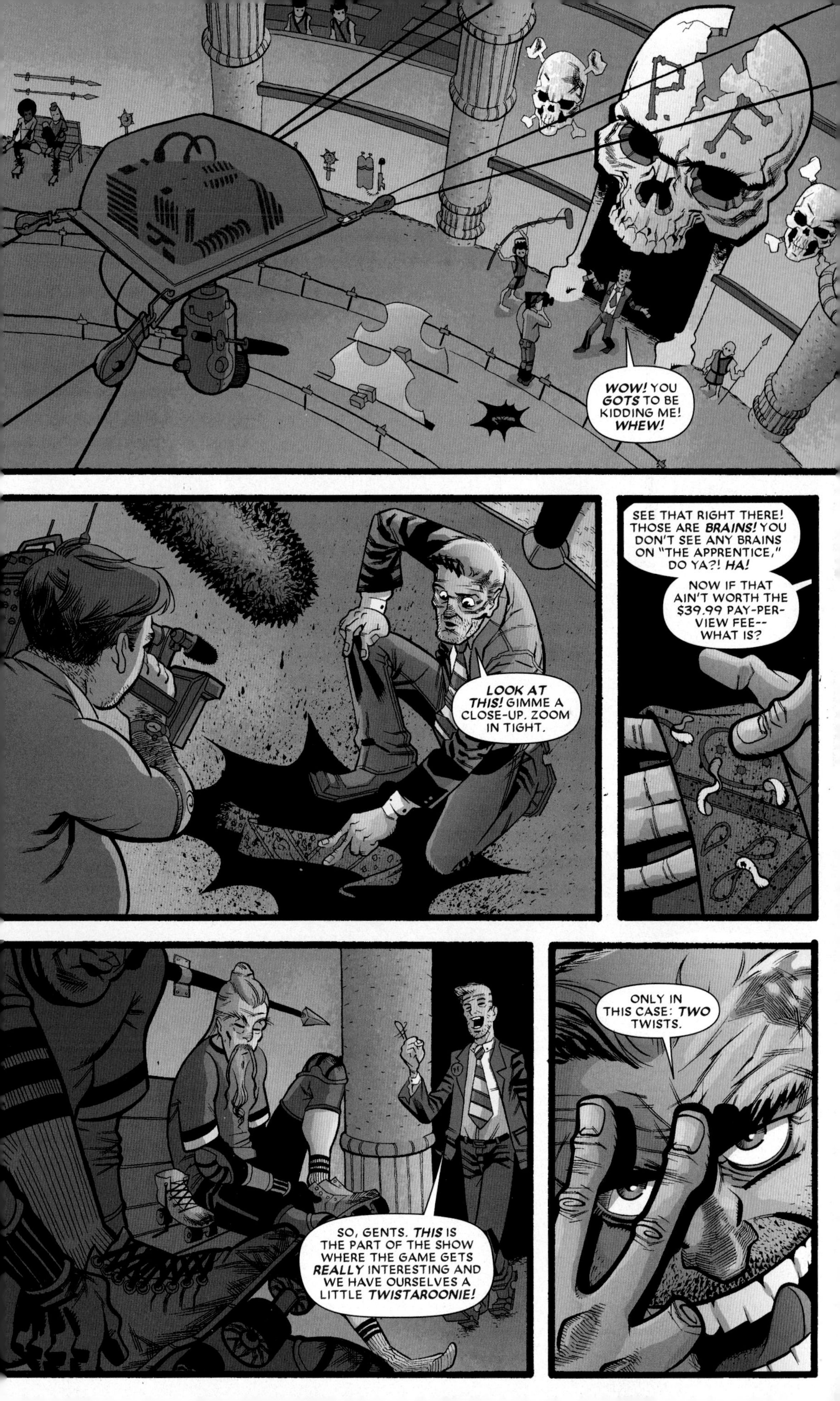
WOW! YOU GOTS TO BE KIDDING ME! WHEW!
LOOK AT THIS! GIMME A CLOSE-UP. ZOOM IN TIGHT.
SEE THAT RIGHT THERE! THOSE ARE BRAINS! YOU DON'T SEE ANY BRAINS ON "THE APPRENTICE," DO YA?! HA!
NOW IF THAT AIN'T WORTH THE $39.99 PAY-PER-VIEW FEE-- WHAT IS?
SO, GENTS. THIS IS THE PART OF THE SHOW WHERE THE GAME GETS REALLY INTERESTING AND WE HAVE OURSELVES A LITTLE TWISTAROONIE!
ONLY IN THIS CASE: TWO TWISTS.

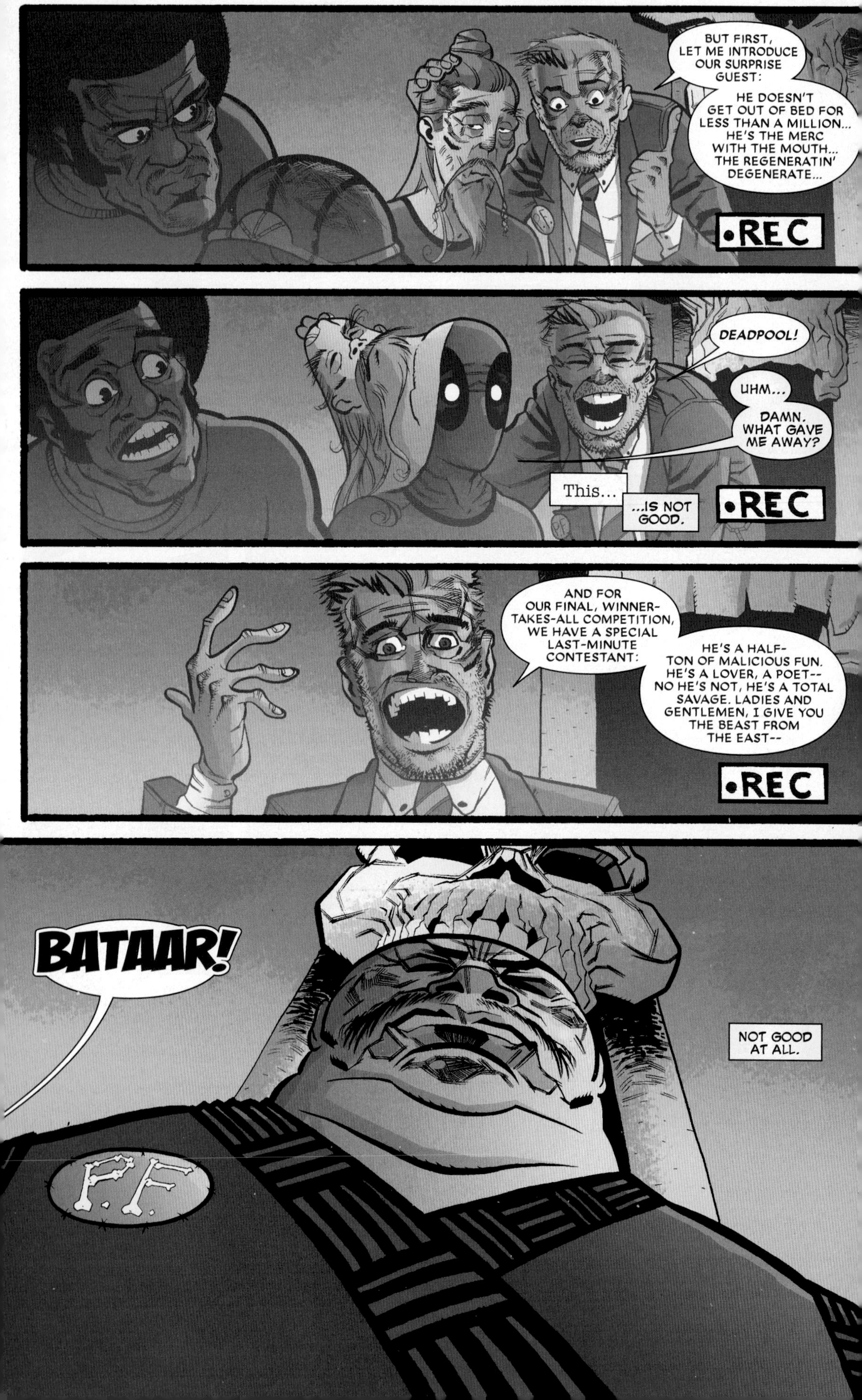
BUT FIRST, LET ME INTRODUCE OUR SURPRISE GUEST:
HE DOESN'T GET OUT OF BED FOR LESS THAN A MILLION... HE'S THE MERC WITH THE MOUTH... THE REGENERATIN' DEGENERATE...
•REC
DEADPOOL!
UHM...
DAMN. WHAT GAVE ME AWAY?
This...
...IS NOT GOOD.
•REC
AND FOR OUR FINAL, WINNER-TAKES-ALL COMPETITION, WE HAVE A SPECIAL LAST-MINUTE CONTESTANT:
HE'S A HALF-TON OF MALICIOUS FUN. HE'S A LOVER, A POET--NO HE'S NOT, HE'S A TOTAL SAVAGE. LADIES AND GENTLEMEN, I GIVE YOU THE BEAST FROM THE EAST--
•REC
BATAAR!
NOT GOOD AT ALL.
P.F.

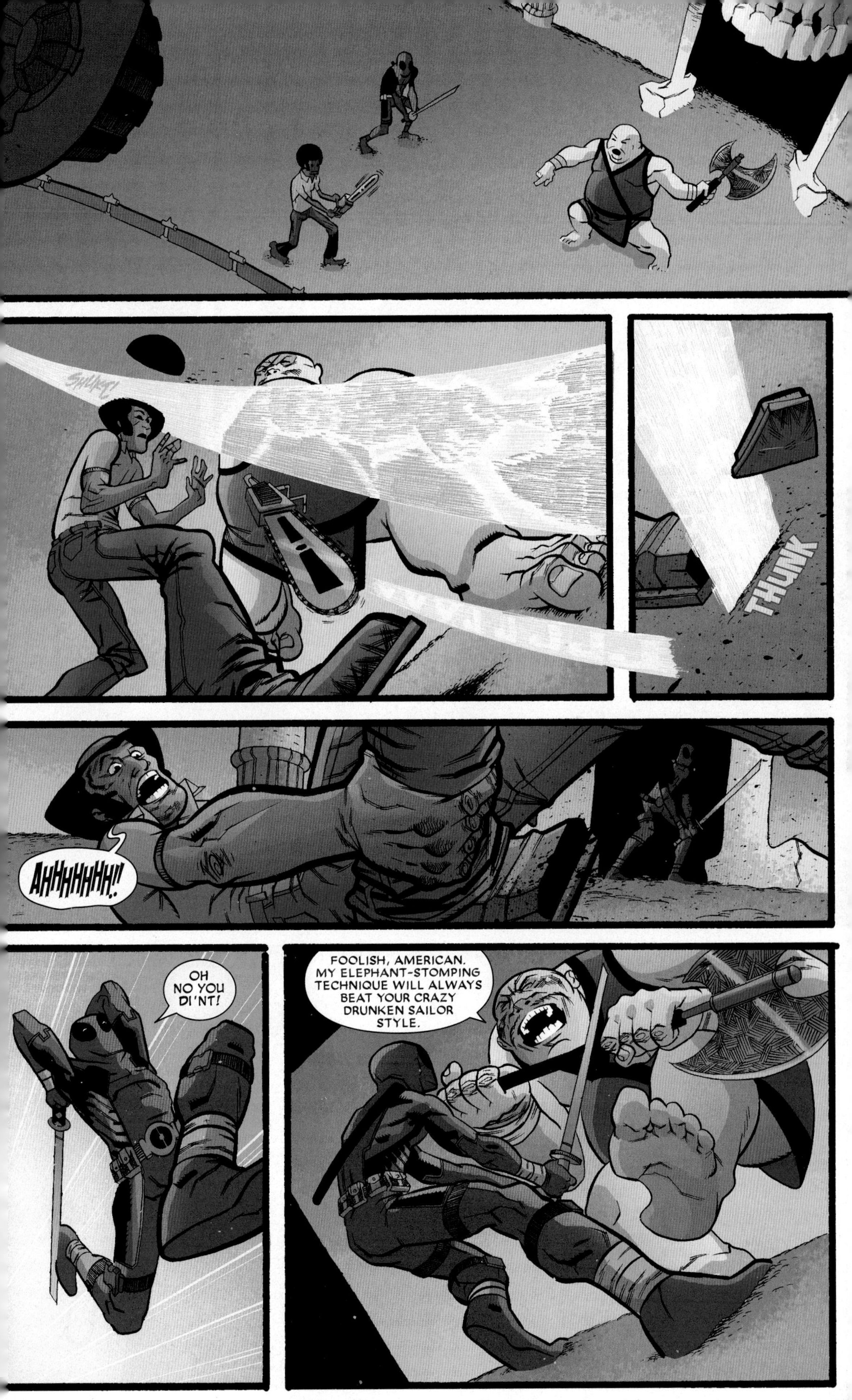

SHUKK!
THUNK
AHHHHHHH!!
OH NO YOU DI'NT!
FOOLISH, AMERICAN. MY ELEPHANT-STOMPING TECHNIQUE WILL ALWAYS BEAT YOUR CRAZY DRUNKEN SAILOR STYLE.

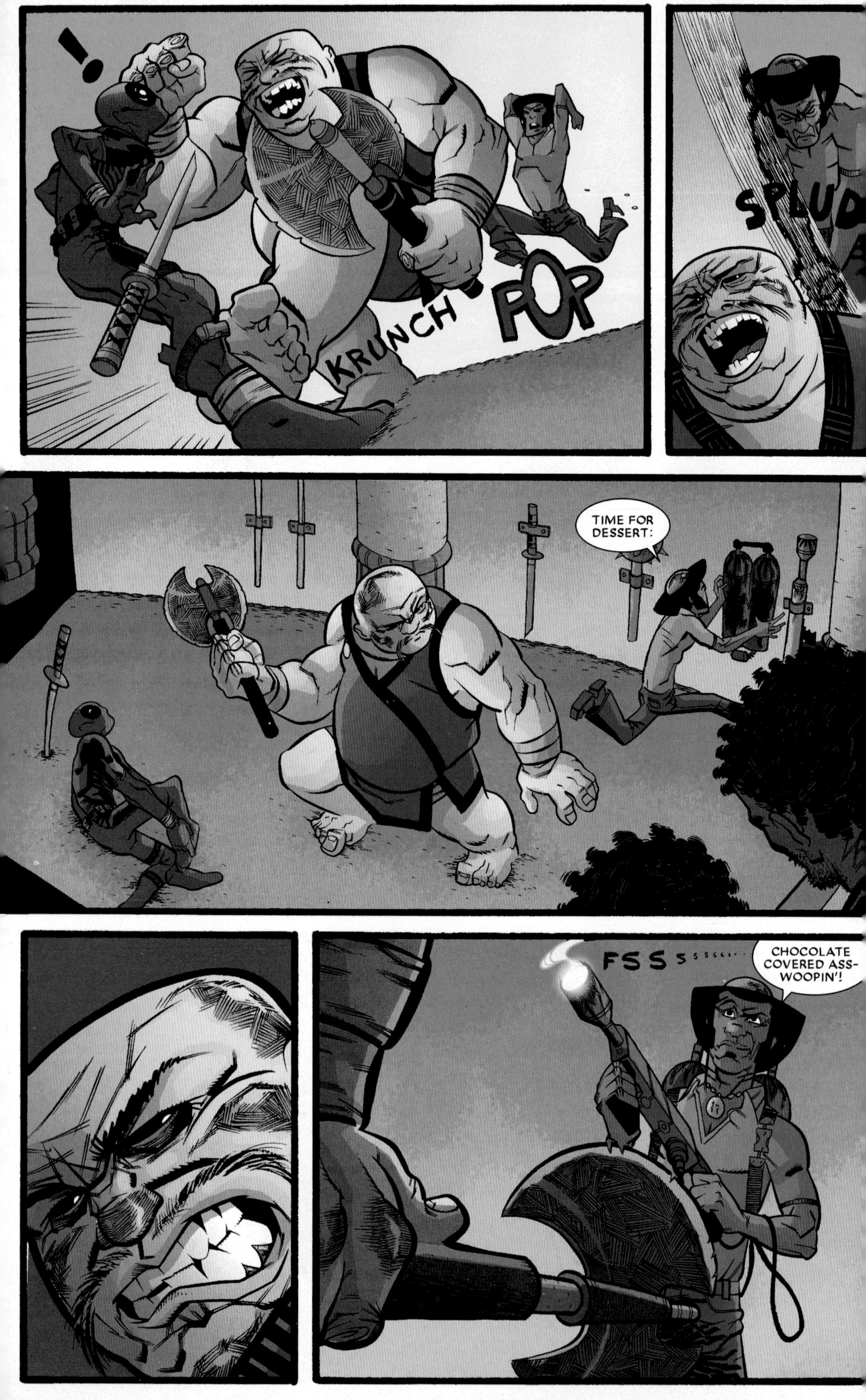
!
KRUNCH
POP
SPLUD
TIME FOR DESSERT:
FSS sssss...
CHOCOLATE COVERED ASS-WOOPIN'!

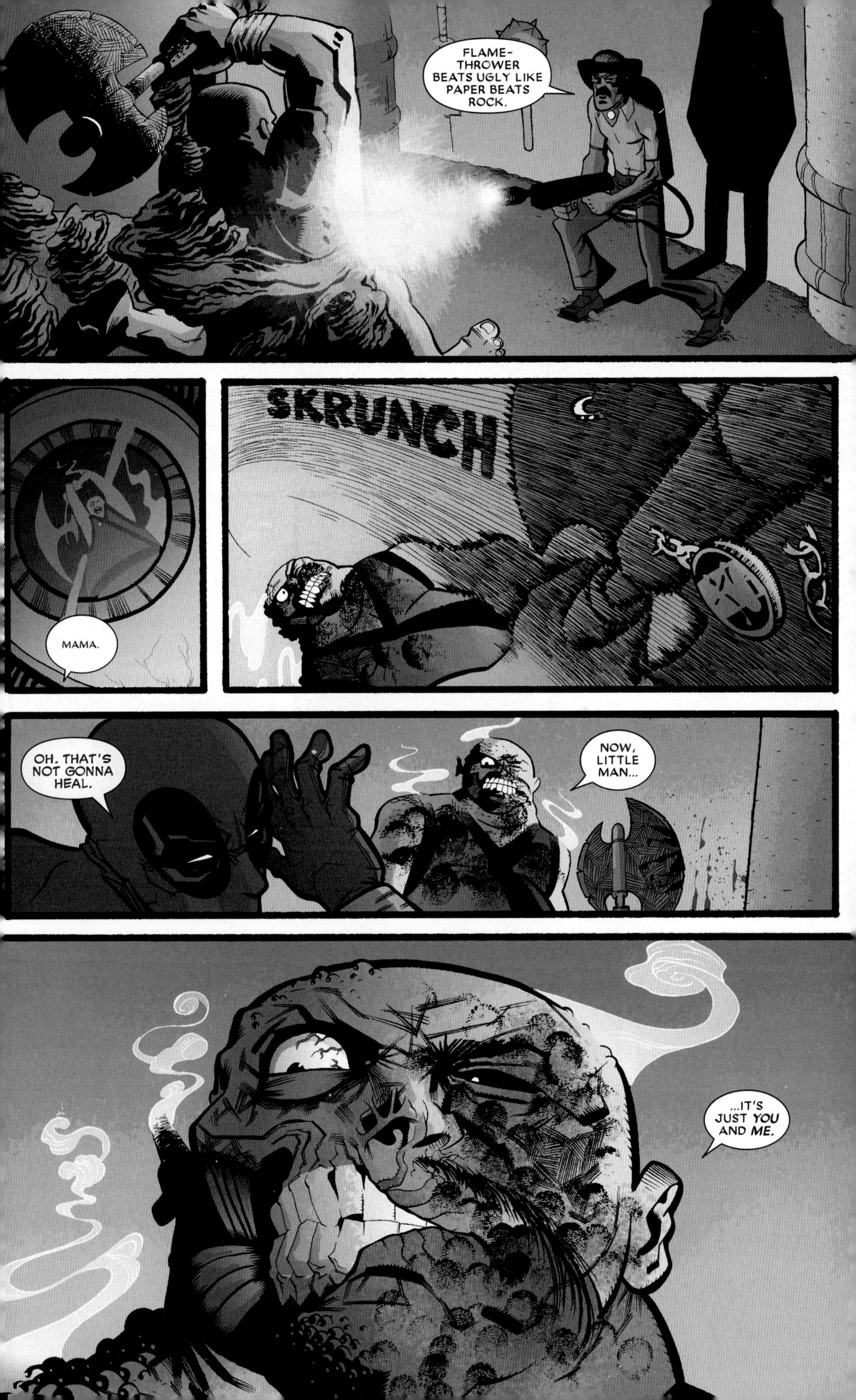
FLAME-THROWER BEATS UGLY LIKE PAPER BEATS ROCK.
MAMA.
SKRUNCH
OH. THAT'S NOT GONNA HEAL.
NOW, LITTLE MAN...
...IT'S JUST *YOU* AND *ME.*

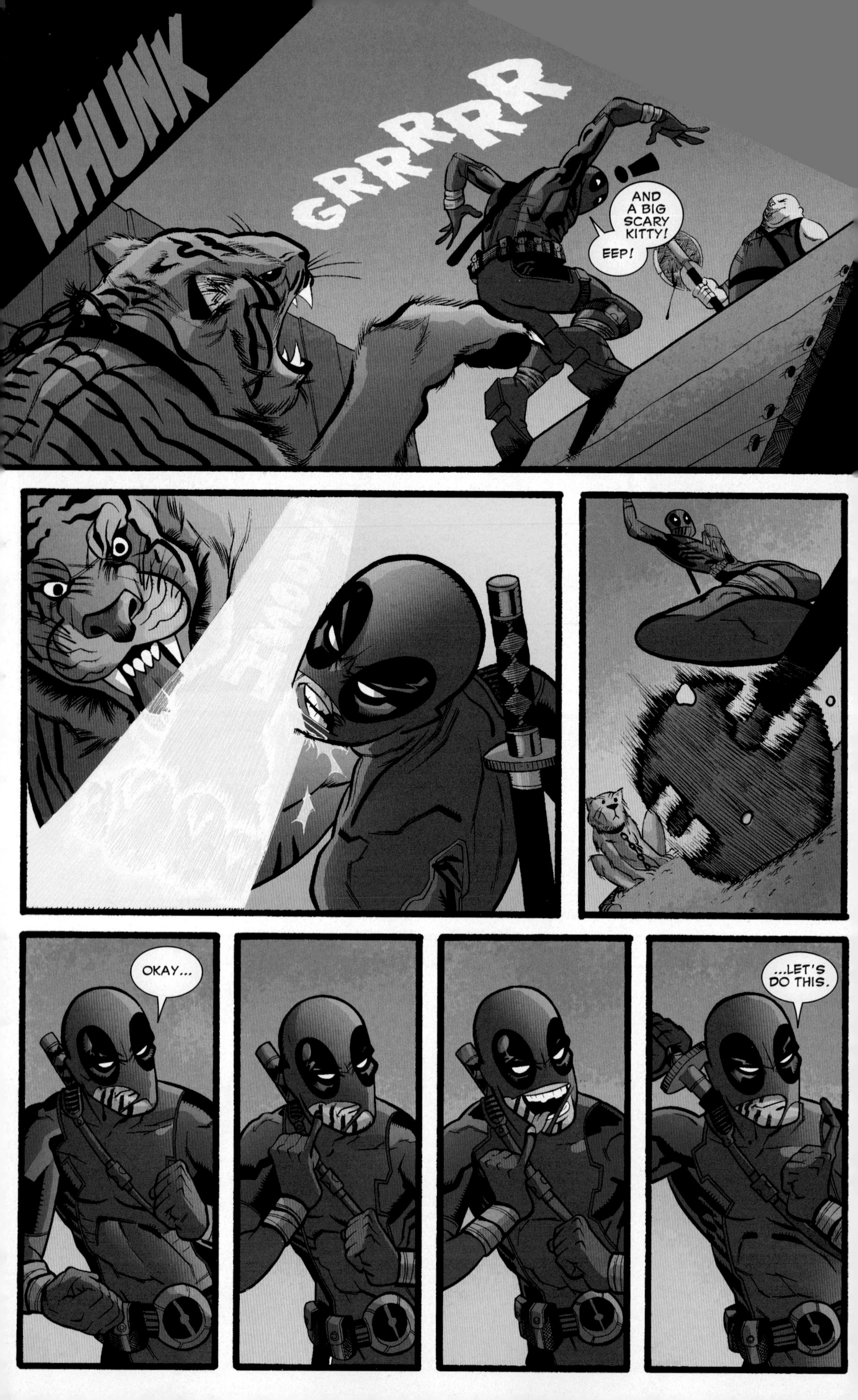
WHUNK
GRRRRR
!
AND A BIG SCARY KITTY!
EEP!
OKAY...
...LET'S DO THIS.

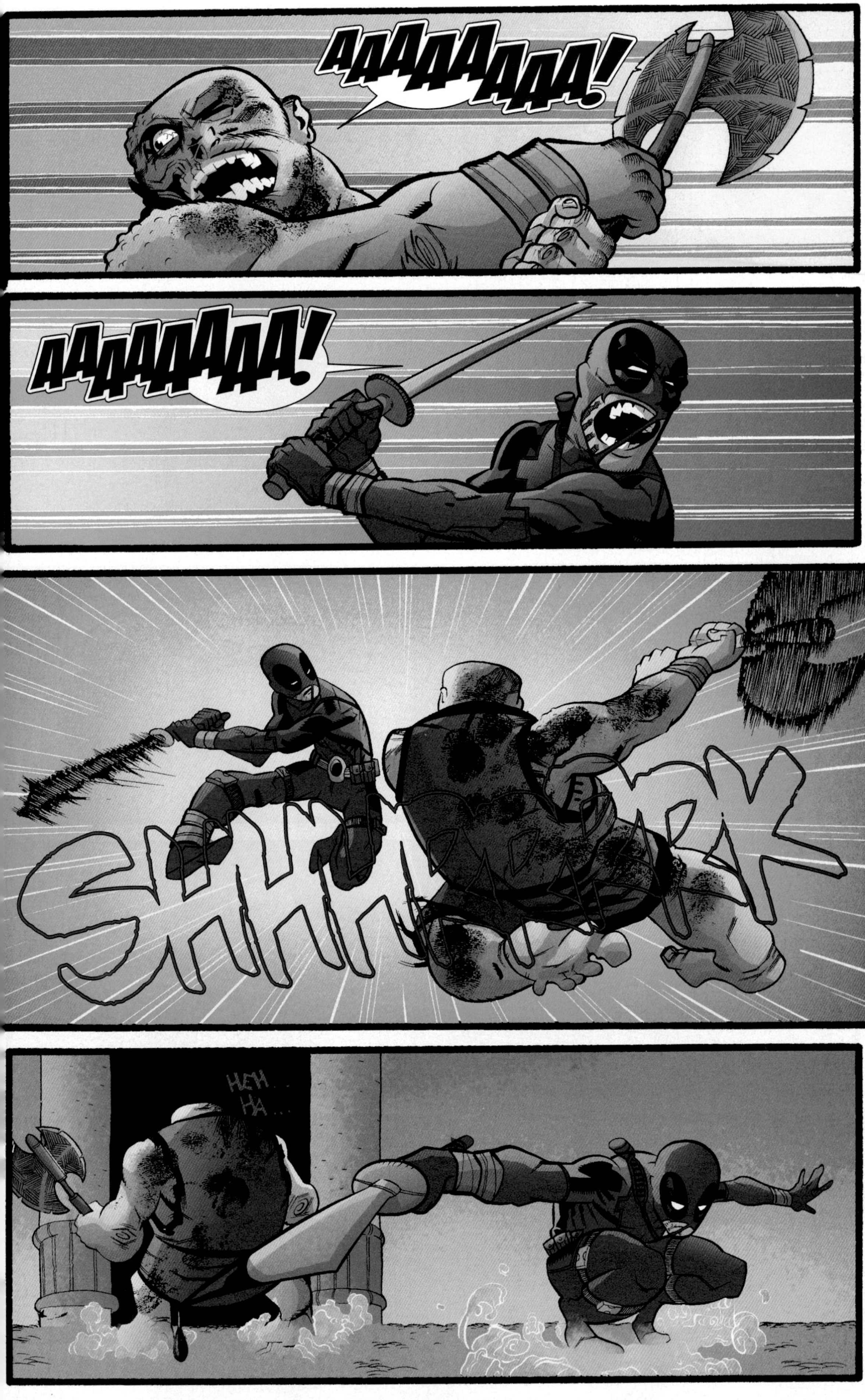
AAAAAAAAA!
AAAAAAAA!
HEH...
HA...

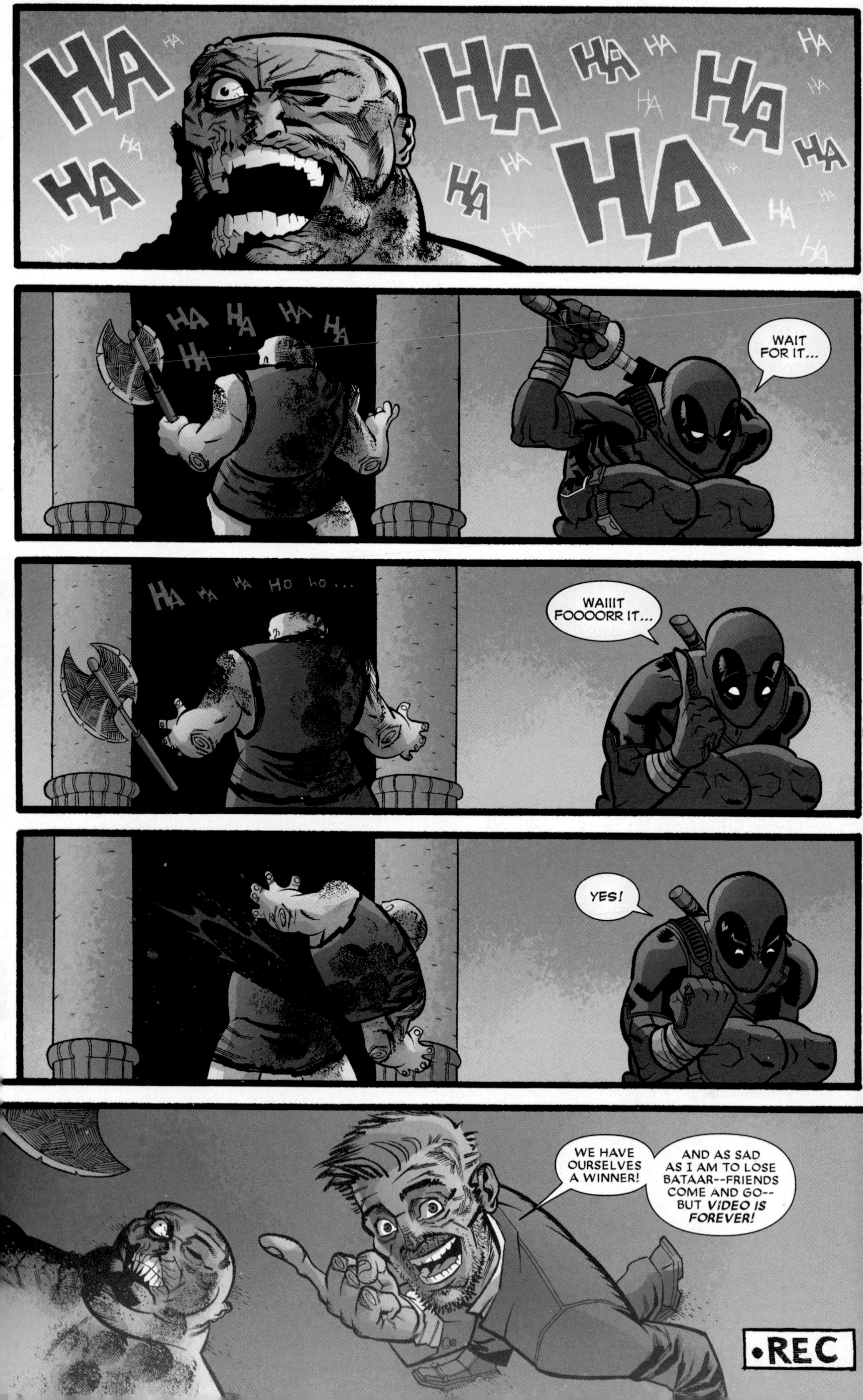
HA HA HA HA HA HA HA HA HA HA HA HA HA HA HA HA HA HA HA HA
HA HA HA HA HA
WAIT FOR IT...
HA HA HA HO ho...
WAIIIT FOOOORR IT...
YES!
WE HAVE OURSELVES A WINNER!
AND AS SAD AS I AM TO LOSE BATAAR--FRIENDS COME AND GO-- BUT *VIDEO IS FOREVER!*
•REC

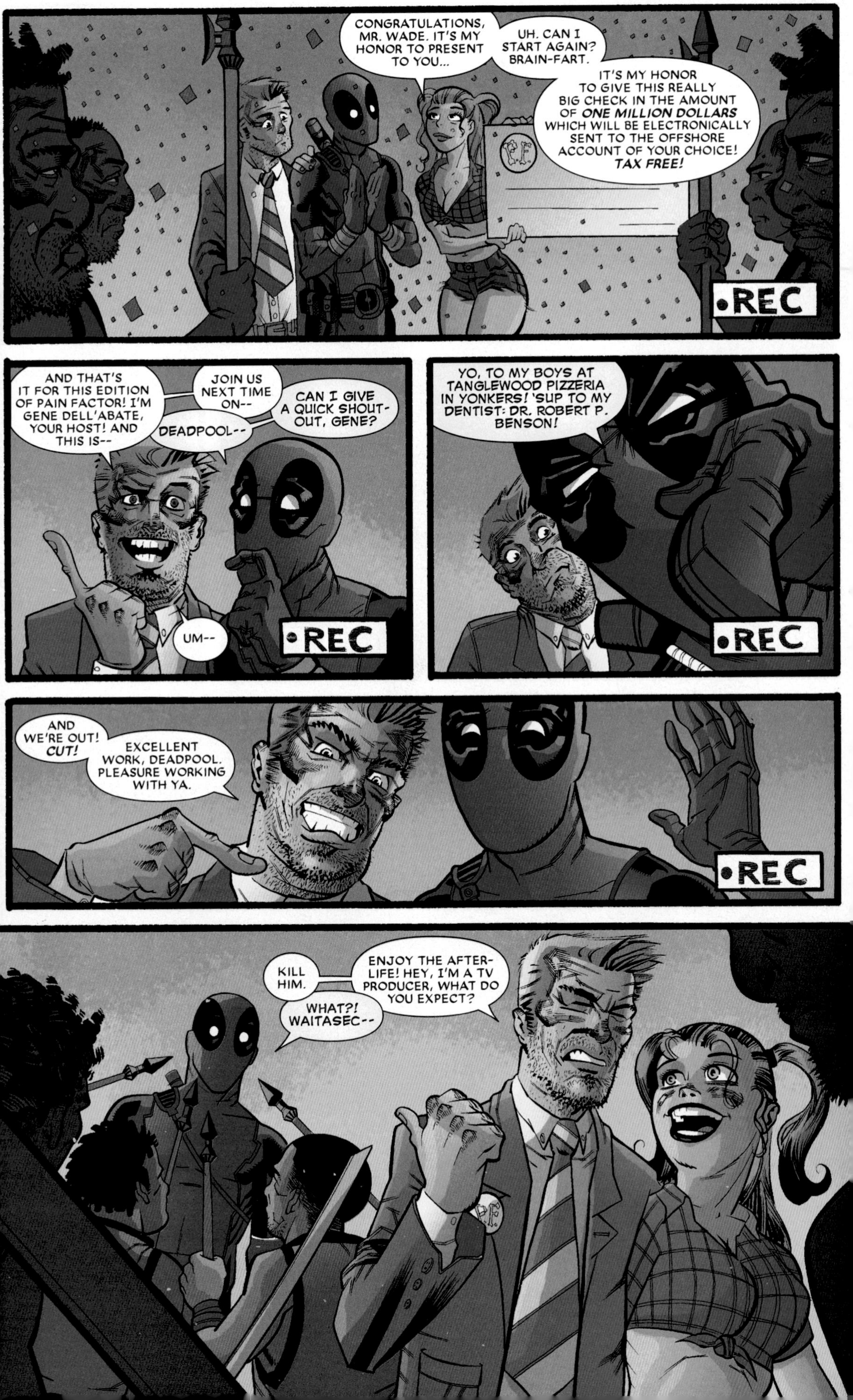

CONGRATULATIONS, MR. WADE. IT'S MY HONOR TO PRESENT TO YOU...
UH. CAN I START AGAIN? BRAIN-FART.
IT'S MY HONOR TO GIVE THIS REALLY BIG CHECK IN THE AMOUNT OF ONE MILLION DOLLARS WHICH WILL BE ELECTRONICALLY SENT TO THE OFFSHORE ACCOUNT OF YOUR CHOICE! TAX FREE!
•REC
AND THAT'S IT FOR THIS EDITION OF PAIN FACTOR! I'M GENE DELL'ABATE, YOUR HOST! AND THIS IS--
JOIN US NEXT TIME ON--
DEADPOOL--
CAN I GIVE A QUICK SHOUT-OUT, GENE?
UM--
•REC
YO, TO MY BOYS AT TANGLEWOOD PIZZERIA IN YONKERS! 'SUP TO MY DENTIST: DR. ROBERT P. BENSON!
•REC
AND WE'RE OUT! CUT!
EXCELLENT WORK, DEADPOOL. PLEASURE WORKING WITH YA.
•REC
KILL HIM.
ENJOY THE AFTER-LIFE! HEY, I'M A TV PRODUCER, WHAT DO YOU EXPECT?
WHAT?! WAITASEC--

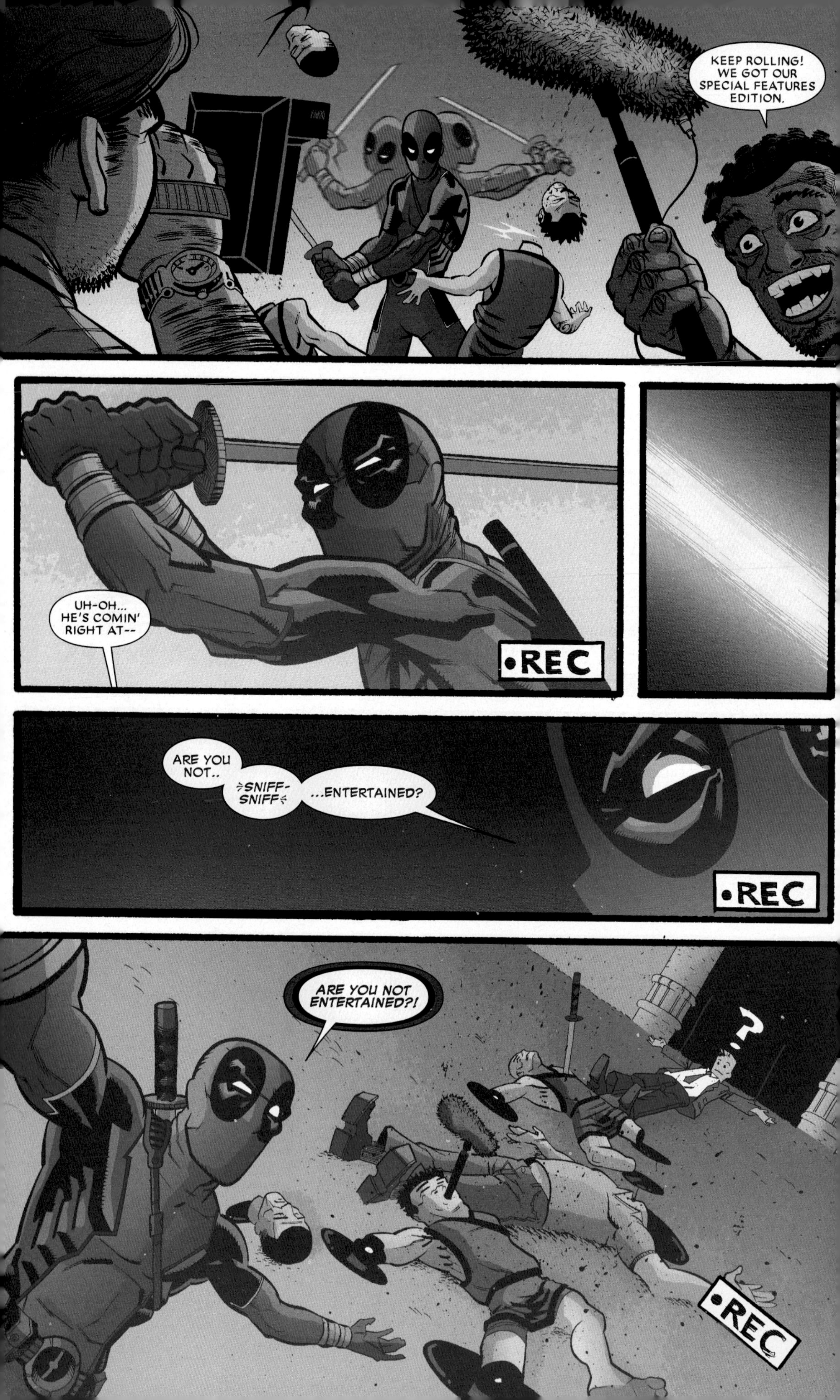
KEEP ROLLING! WE GOT OUR SPECIAL FEATURES EDITION.
UH-OH... HE'S COMIN' RIGHT AT--
•REC
ARE YOU NOT..
SNIFF-SNIFF
...ENTERTAINED?
•REC
ARE YOU NOT ENTERTAINED?!
?
•REC

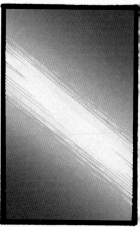

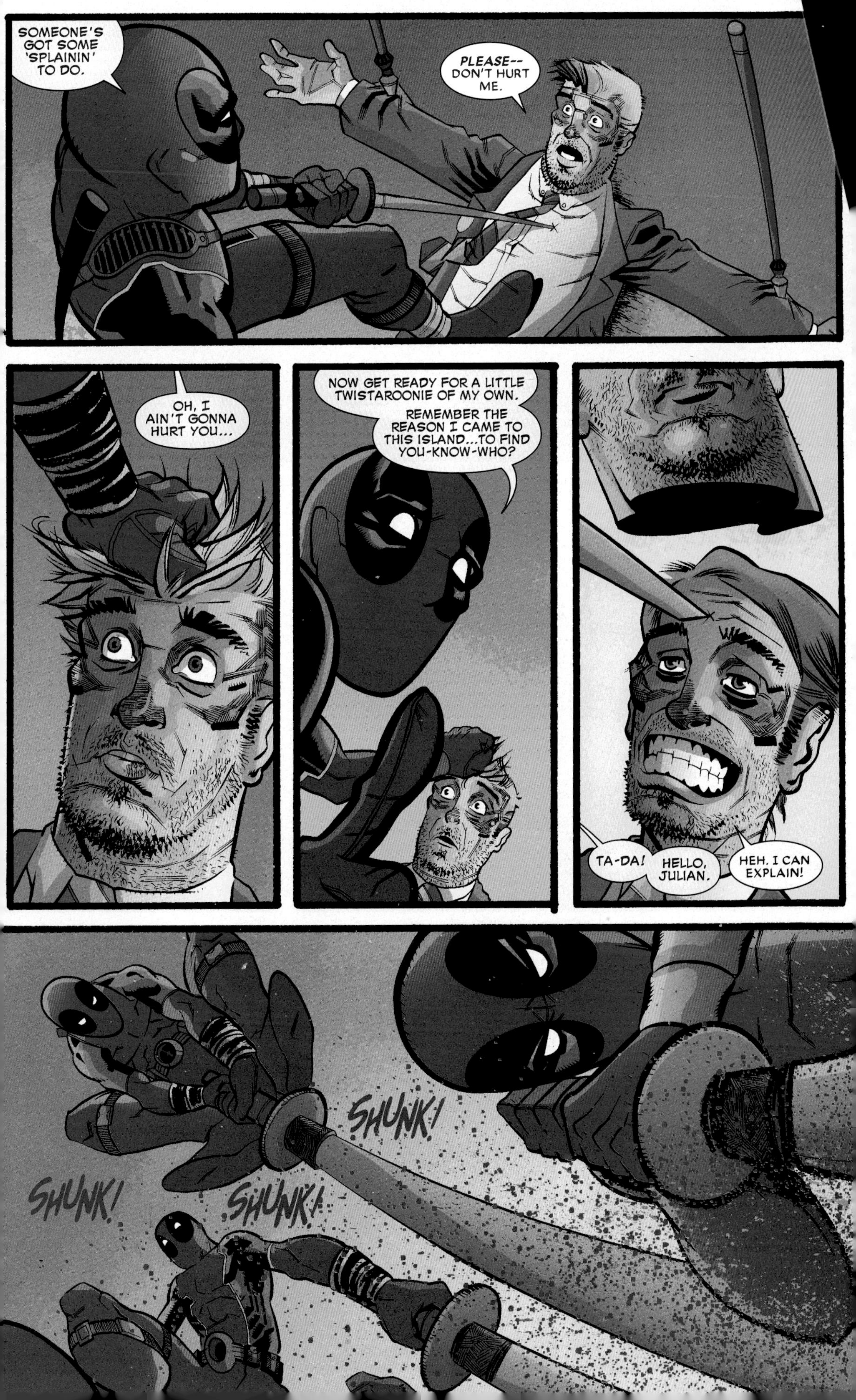
SOMEONE'S GOT SOME 'SPLAININ' TO DO.
PLEASE-- DON'T HURT ME.
OH, I AIN'T GONNA HURT YOU...
NOW GET READY FOR A LITTLE TWISTAROONIE OF MY OWN.
REMEMBER THE REASON I CAME TO THIS ISLAND...TO FIND YOU-KNOW-WHO?
TA-DA!
HELLO, JULIAN.
HEH. I CAN EXPLAIN!
SHUNK!
SHUNK!
SHUNK!

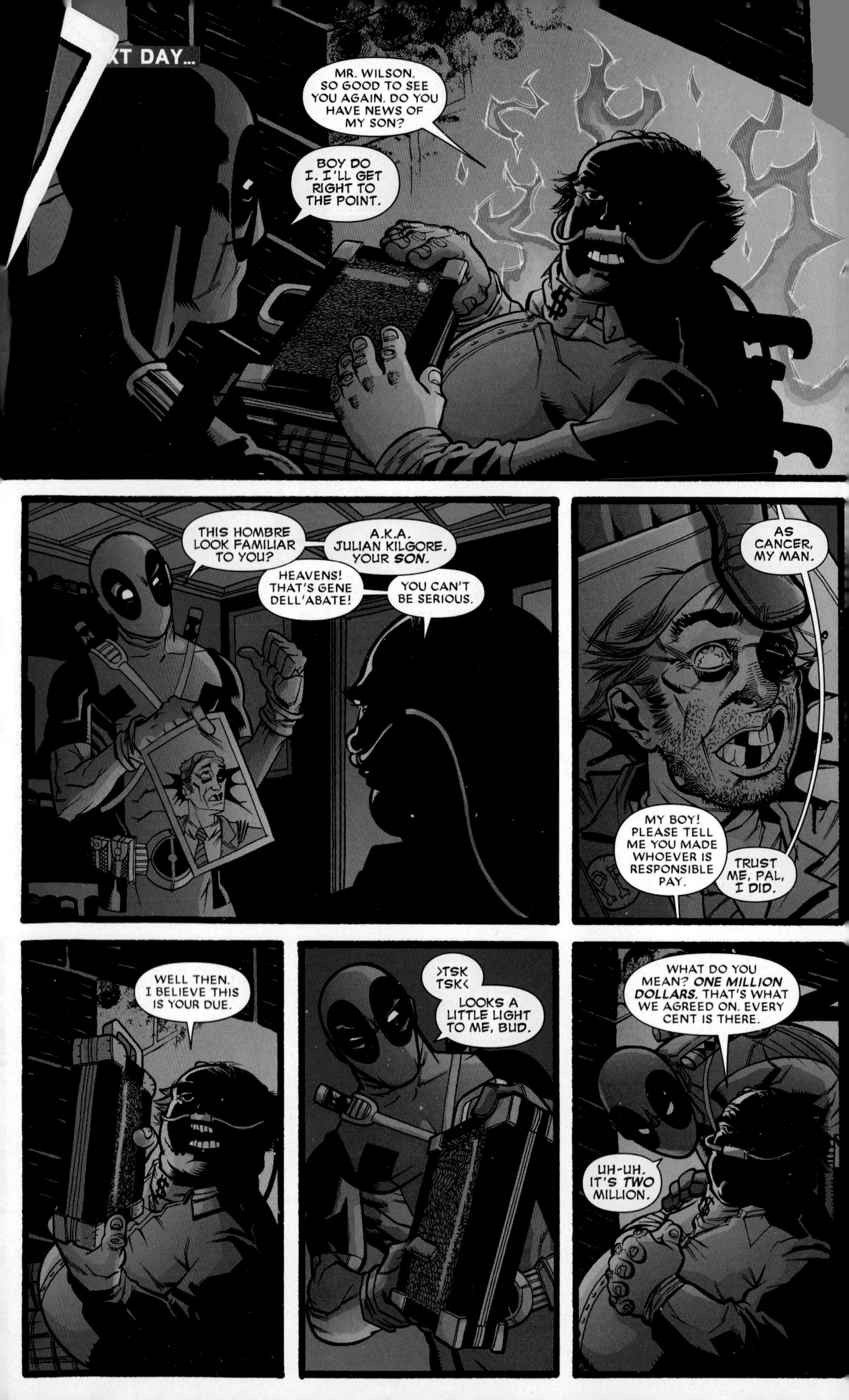
XT DAY...
MR. WILSON. SO GOOD TO SEE YOU AGAIN. DO YOU HAVE NEWS OF MY SON?
BOY DO I. I'LL GET RIGHT TO THE POINT.
THIS HOMBRE LOOK FAMILIAR TO YOU?
A.K.A. JULIAN KILGORE. YOUR SON.
HEAVENS! THAT'S GENE DELL'ABATE!
YOU CAN'T BE SERIOUS.
AS CANCER, MY MAN.
MY BOY! PLEASE TELL ME YOU MADE WHOEVER IS RESPONSIBLE PAY.
TRUST ME, PAL, I DID.
WELL THEN. I BELIEVE THIS IS YOUR DUE.
>TSK TSK<
LOOKS A LITTLE LIGHT TO ME, BUD.
WHAT DO YOU MEAN? ONE MILLION DOLLARS. THAT'S WHAT WE AGREED ON. EVERY CENT IS THERE.
UH-UH. IT'S TWO MILLION.

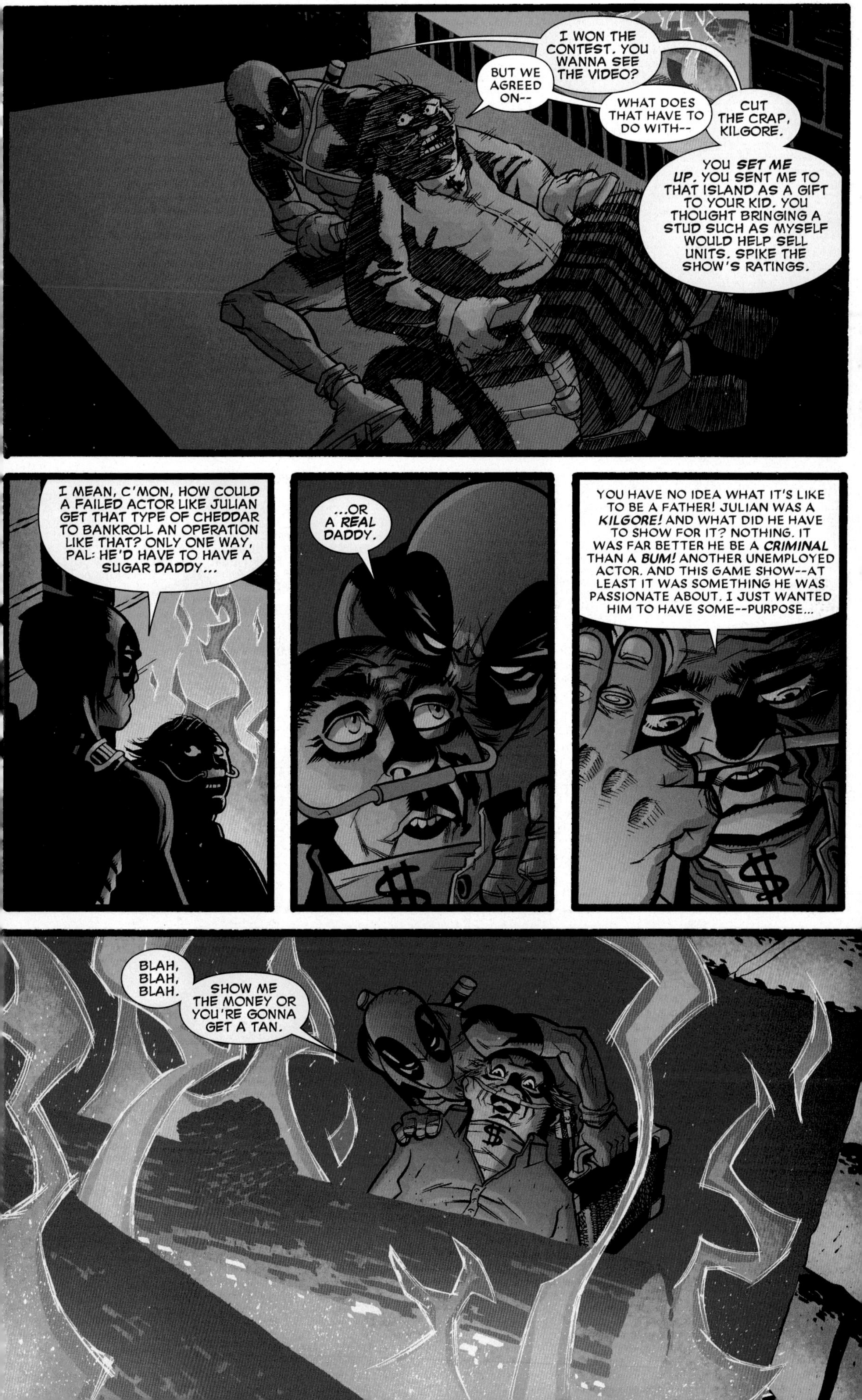
I WON THE CONTEST. YOU WANNA SEE THE VIDEO?
BUT WE AGREED ON--
WHAT DOES THAT HAVE TO DO WITH--
CUT THE CRAP, KILGORE.
YOU SET ME UP. YOU SENT ME TO THAT ISLAND AS A GIFT TO YOUR KID. YOU THOUGHT BRINGING A STUD SUCH AS MYSELF WOULD HELP SELL UNITS. SPIKE THE SHOW'S RATINGS.
I MEAN, C'MON, HOW COULD A FAILED ACTOR LIKE JULIAN GET THAT TYPE OF CHEDDAR TO BANKROLL AN OPERATION LIKE THAT? ONLY ONE WAY, PAL: HE'D HAVE TO HAVE A SUGAR DADDY...
...OR A REAL DADDY.
YOU HAVE NO IDEA WHAT IT'S LIKE TO BE A FATHER! JULIAN WAS A KILGORE! AND WHAT DID HE HAVE TO SHOW FOR IT? NOTHING. IT WAS FAR BETTER HE BE A CRIMINAL THAN A BUM! ANOTHER UNEMPLOYED ACTOR. AND THIS GAME SHOW--AT LEAST IT WAS SOMETHING HE WAS PASSIONATE ABOUT. I JUST WANTED HIM TO HAVE SOME--PURPOSE...
BLAH, BLAH, BLAH.
SHOW ME THE MONEY OR YOU'RE GONNA GET A TAN.

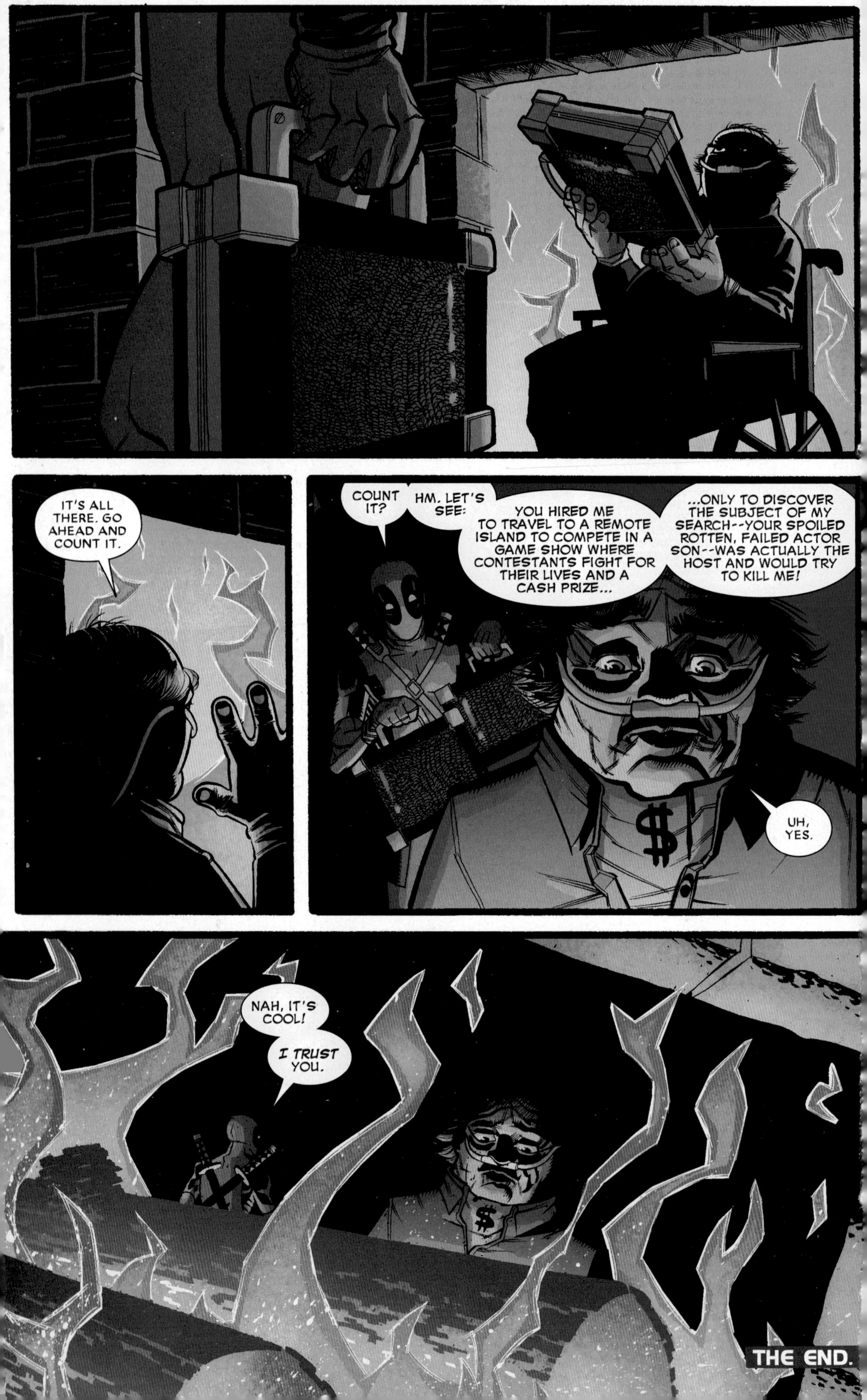
IT'S ALL THERE. GO AHEAD AND COUNT IT.
COUNT IT?
HM. LET'S SEE:
YOU HIRED ME TO TRAVEL TO A REMOTE ISLAND TO COMPETE IN A GAME SHOW WHERE CONTESTANTS FIGHT FOR THEIR LIVES AND A CASH PRIZE...
...ONLY TO DISCOVER THE SUBJECT OF MY SEARCH--YOUR SPOILED ROTTEN, FAILED ACTOR SON--WAS ACTUALLY THE HOST AND WOULD TRY TO KILL ME!
UH, YES.
NAH, IT'S COOL!
I TRUST YOU.
THE END.